VIZ GRAPHIC NOVEL

THE ALL-NEW
TENCHI MUYŌ!

ALIEN NATION

STORY AND ART BY
HITOSHI OKUDA

This volume contains the first five issues of
THE ALL-NEW TENCHI MUYÔ! monthly comic series.

STORY AND ART BY HITOSHI OKUDA

English Adaptation/Fred Burke
Translation/Lillian Olsen
Touch-up & Lettering/Dan Nakrosis
Cover Design/Hidemi Sahara
Graphic Design/Carolina Ugalde
Editor/Jason Thompson
Graphic Novel Editor/Eric Searleman

Managing Editor/Annette Roman
Editor-in-Chief/William Flanagan
VP of Sales & Marketing/Rick Bauer
Sr. VP of Editorial/Hyoe Narita
Publisher/Seiji Horibuchi

©2001 HITOSHI OKUDA ©2001 AIC/PIONEER LDC, INC. Originally published in
Japan in 2001 by KADOKAWA SHOTEN PUBLISHING CO., LTD., Tokyo. English
translation rights arranged with KADOKAWA SHOTEN PUBLISHING CO.,
LTD., Tokyo. Original artwork reversed for this edition.

New and adapted artwork and text © 2003 VIZ, LLC.
All rights reserved.

Printed in Canada.

Published by VIZ, LLC
P.O. Box 77010
San Francisco, CA 94107

10 9 8 7 6 5 4 3 2
First printing, March 2003
Second Printing, May 2003

For advertising rates or media kit,
e-mail advertising@viz.com

www.viz.com   store.viz.com
www.animerica-mag.com

CONTENTS

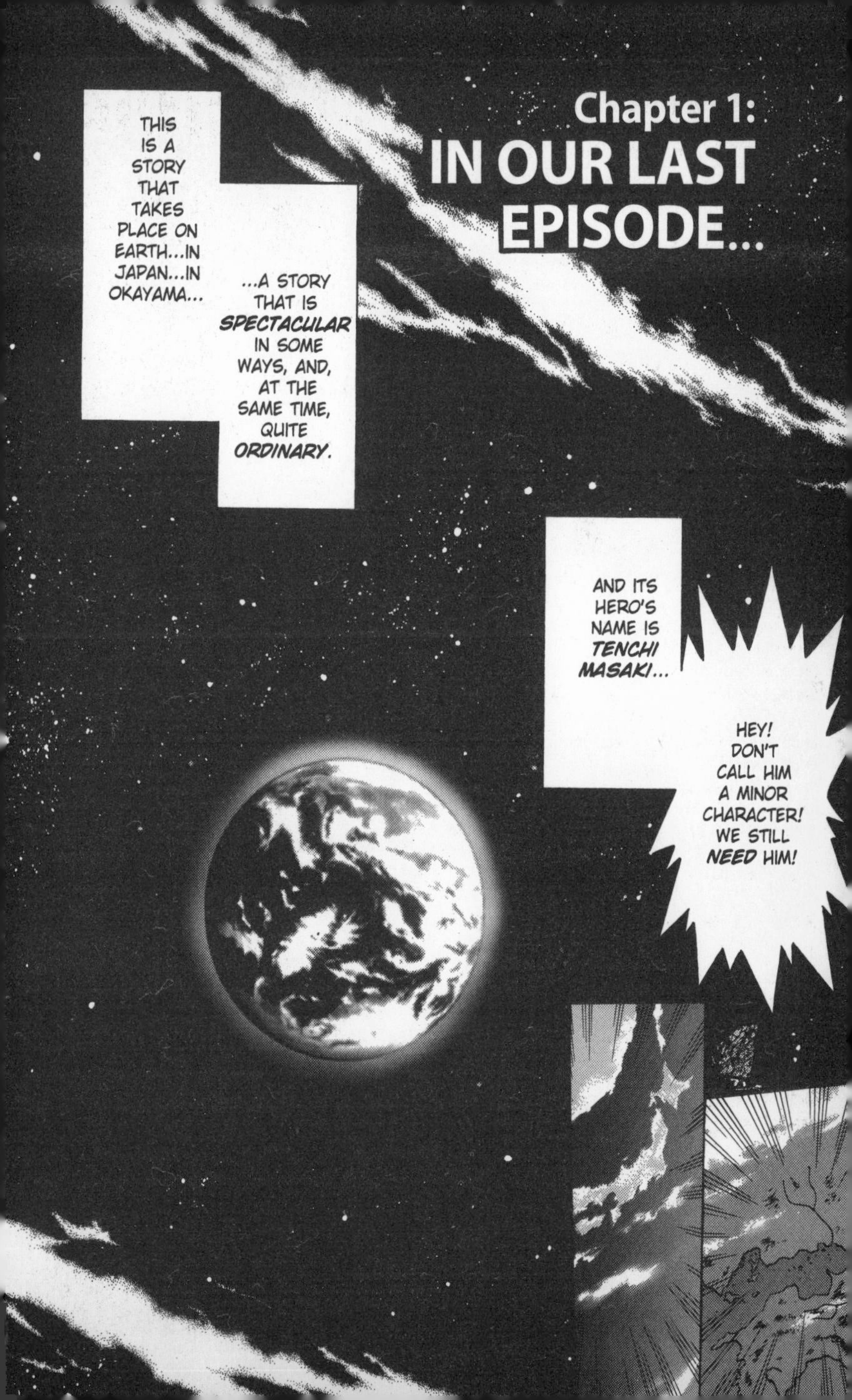
Chapter 1:
IN OUR LAST EPISODE...
THIS IS A STORY THAT TAKES PLACE ON EARTH...IN JAPAN...IN OKAYAMA...
...A STORY THAT IS SPECTACULAR IN SOME WAYS, AND, AT THE SAME TIME, QUITE ORDINARY.
AND ITS HERO'S NAME IS TENCHI MASAKI...
HEY! DON'T CALL HIM A MINOR CHARACTER! WE STILL NEED HIM!

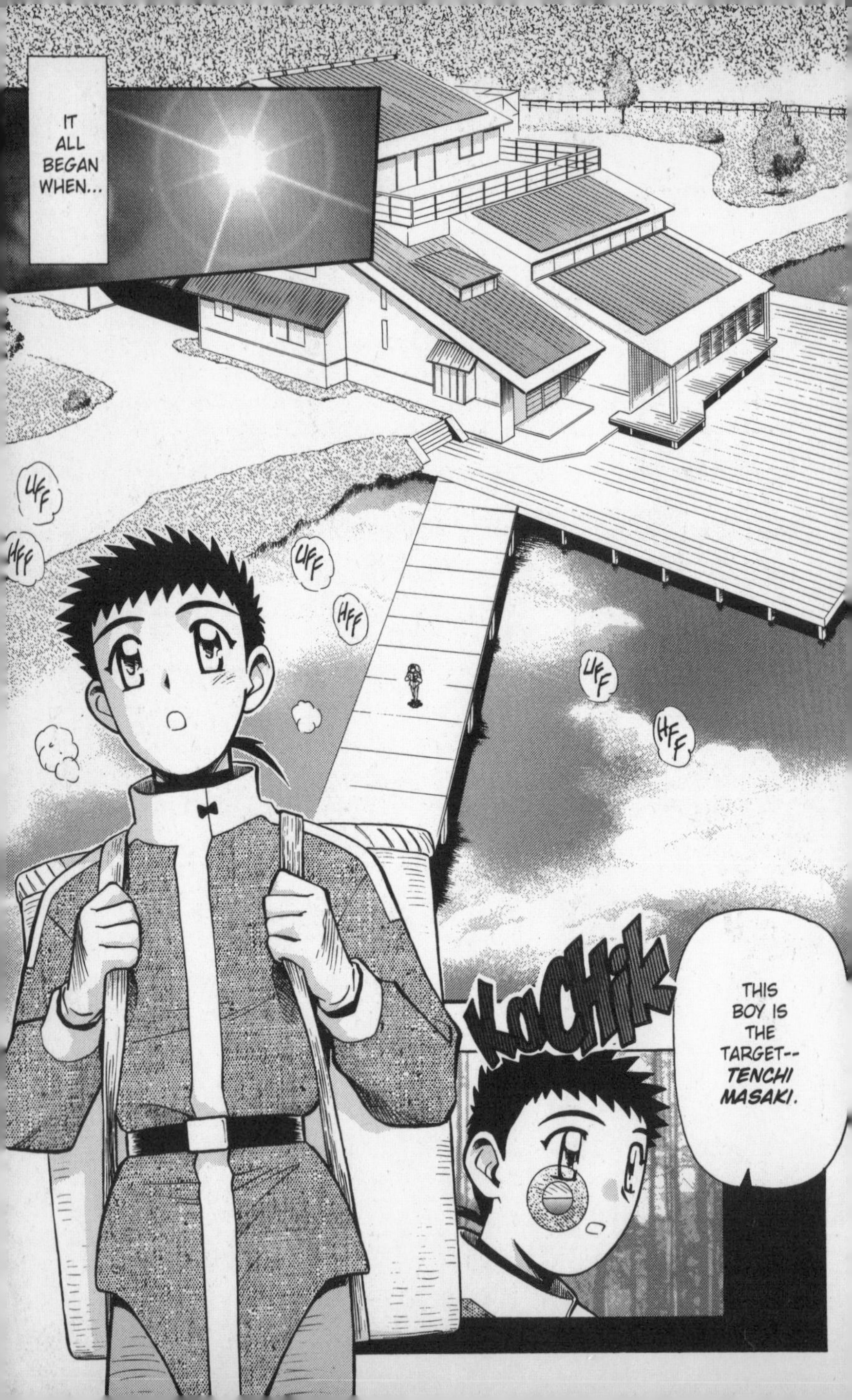
IT ALL BEGAN WHEN...
UFF
HFF
UFF
HFF
UFF
HFF
KACHIK
THIS BOY IS THE TARGET-- *TENCHI MASAKI.*

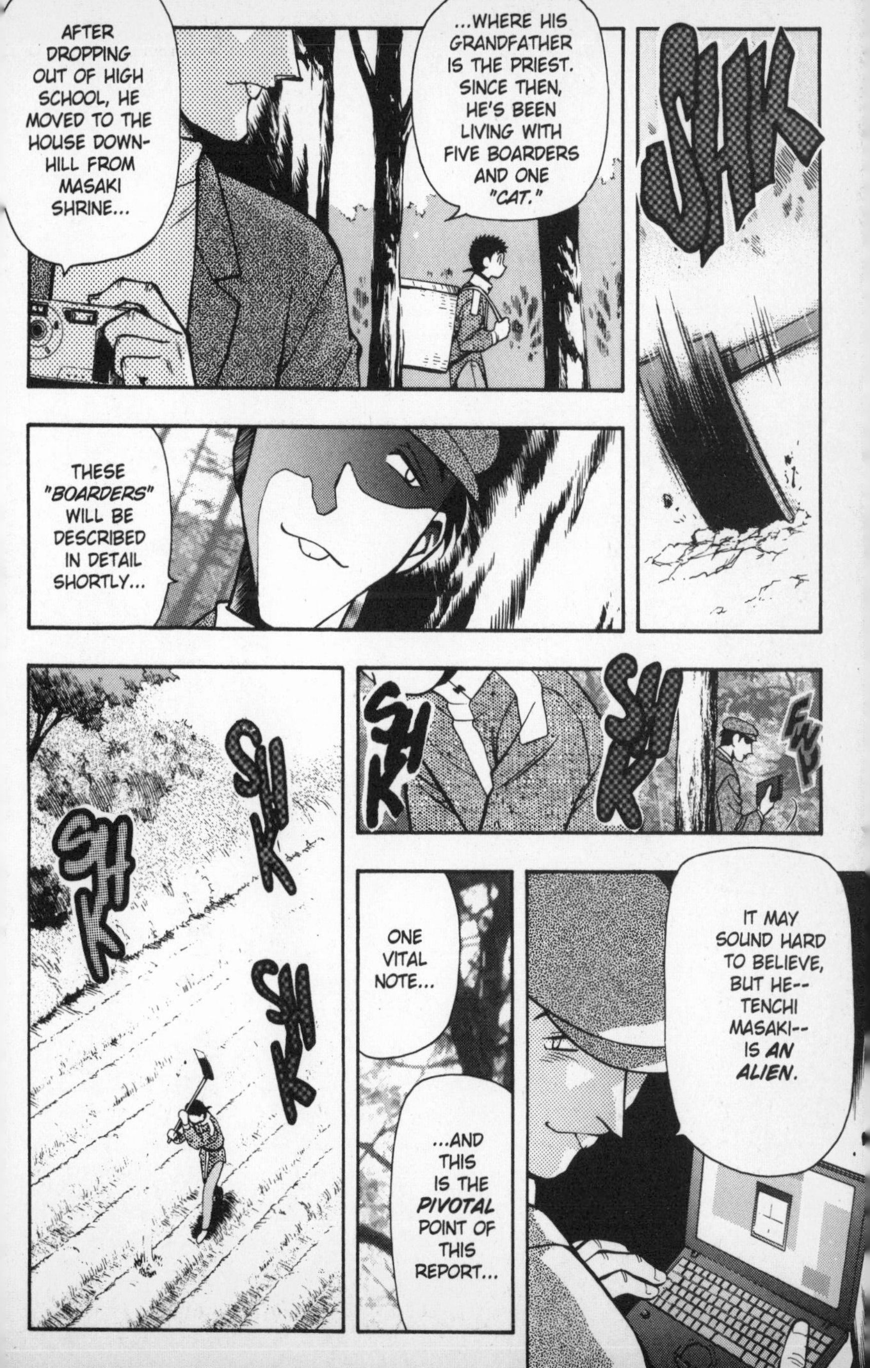
AFTER DROPPING OUT OF HIGH SCHOOL, HE MOVED TO THE HOUSE DOWN-HILL FROM MASAKI SHRINE...
...WHERE HIS GRANDFATHER IS THE PRIEST. SINCE THEN, HE'S BEEN LIVING WITH FIVE BOARDERS AND ONE "CAT."
SHK
THESE "BOARDERS" WILL BE DESCRIBED IN DETAIL SHORTLY...
SHK
SHK
SHK
SHK
SHK
FWP
ONE VITAL NOTE...
...AND THIS IS THE PIVOTAL POINT OF THIS REPORT...
IT MAY SOUND HARD TO BELIEVE, BUT HE--TENCHI MASAKI--IS AN ALIEN.

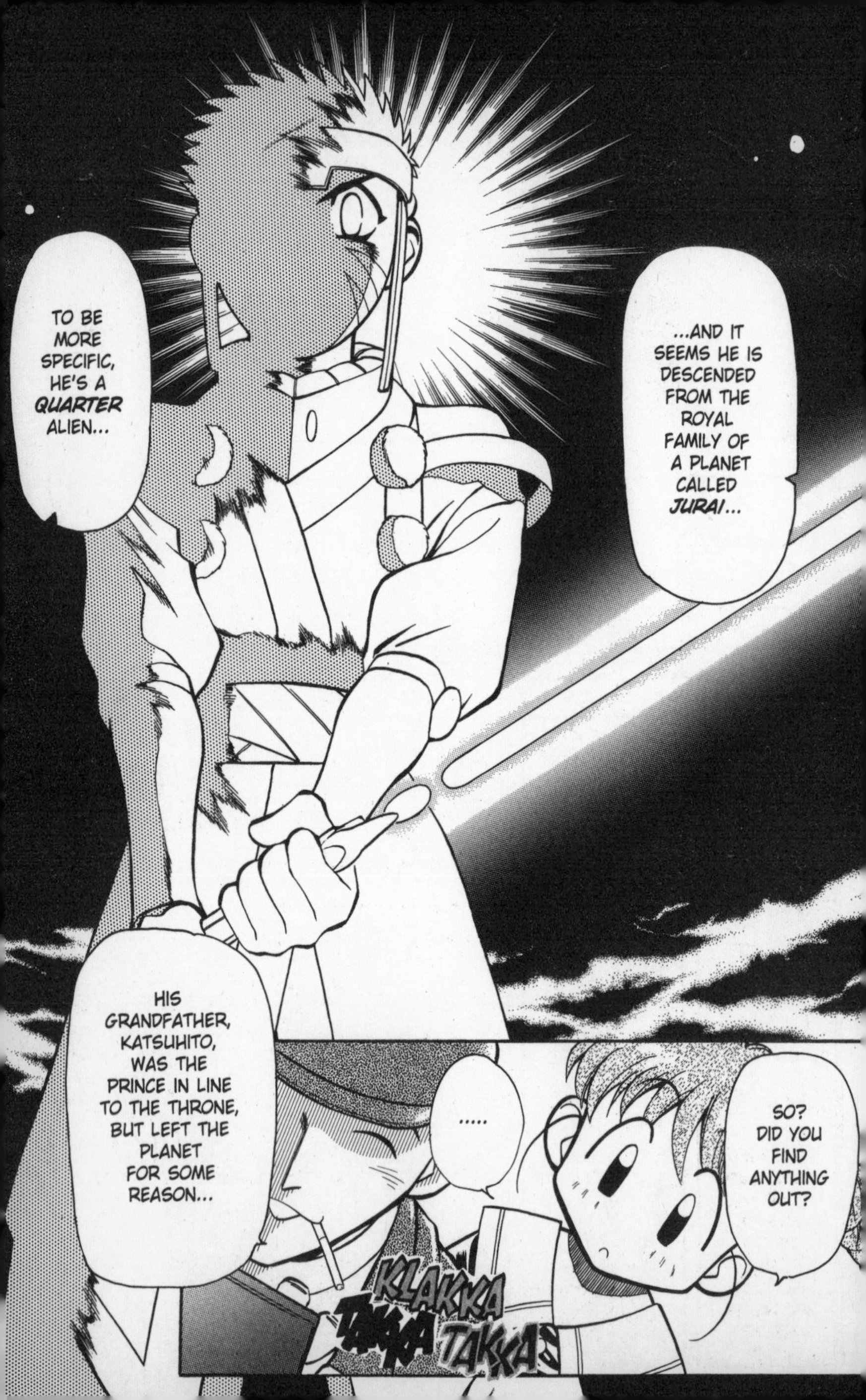
TO BE MORE SPECIFIC, HE'S A QUARTER ALIEN...
...AND IT SEEMS HE IS DESCENDED FROM THE ROYAL FAMILY OF A PLANET CALLED JURAI...
HIS GRANDFATHER, KATSUHITO, WAS THE PRINCE IN LINE TO THE THRONE, BUT LEFT THE PLANET FOR SOME REASON...
.....
SO? DID YOU FIND ANYTHING OUT?
KLAKKA TAKKA TAKKA

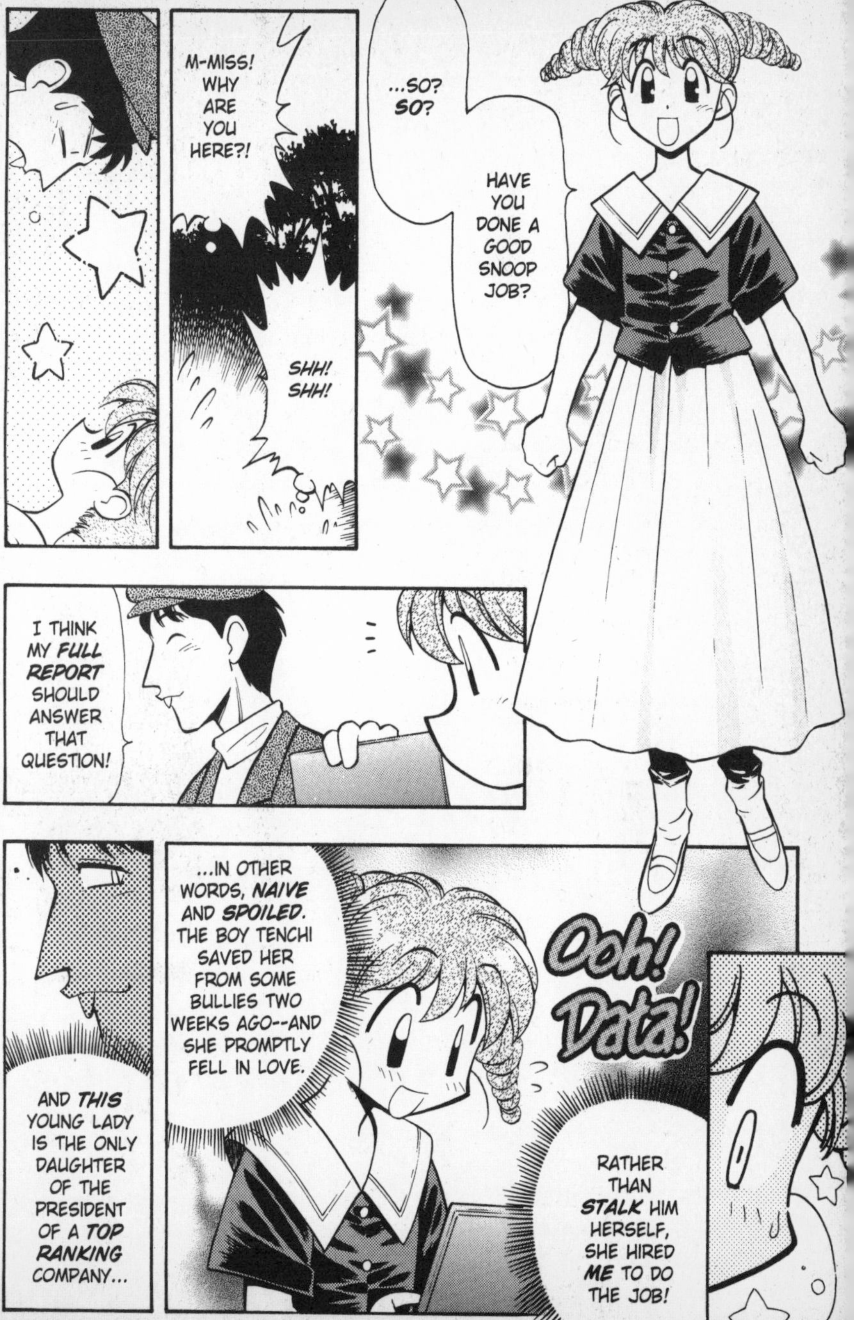
M-MISS! WHY ARE YOU HERE?!
SHH! SHH!
I THINK MY FULL REPORT SHOULD ANSWER THAT QUESTION!
...SO? SO?
HAVE YOU DONE A GOOD SNOOP JOB?
AND THIS YOUNG LADY IS THE ONLY DAUGHTER OF THE PRESIDENT OF A TOP RANKING COMPANY...
...IN OTHER WORDS, NAIVE AND SPOILED. THE BOY TENCHI SAVED HER FROM SOME BULLIES TWO WEEKS AGO--AND SHE PROMPTLY FELL IN LOVE.
Ooh! Data!
RATHER THAN STALK HIM HERSELF, SHE HIRED ME TO DO THE JOB!

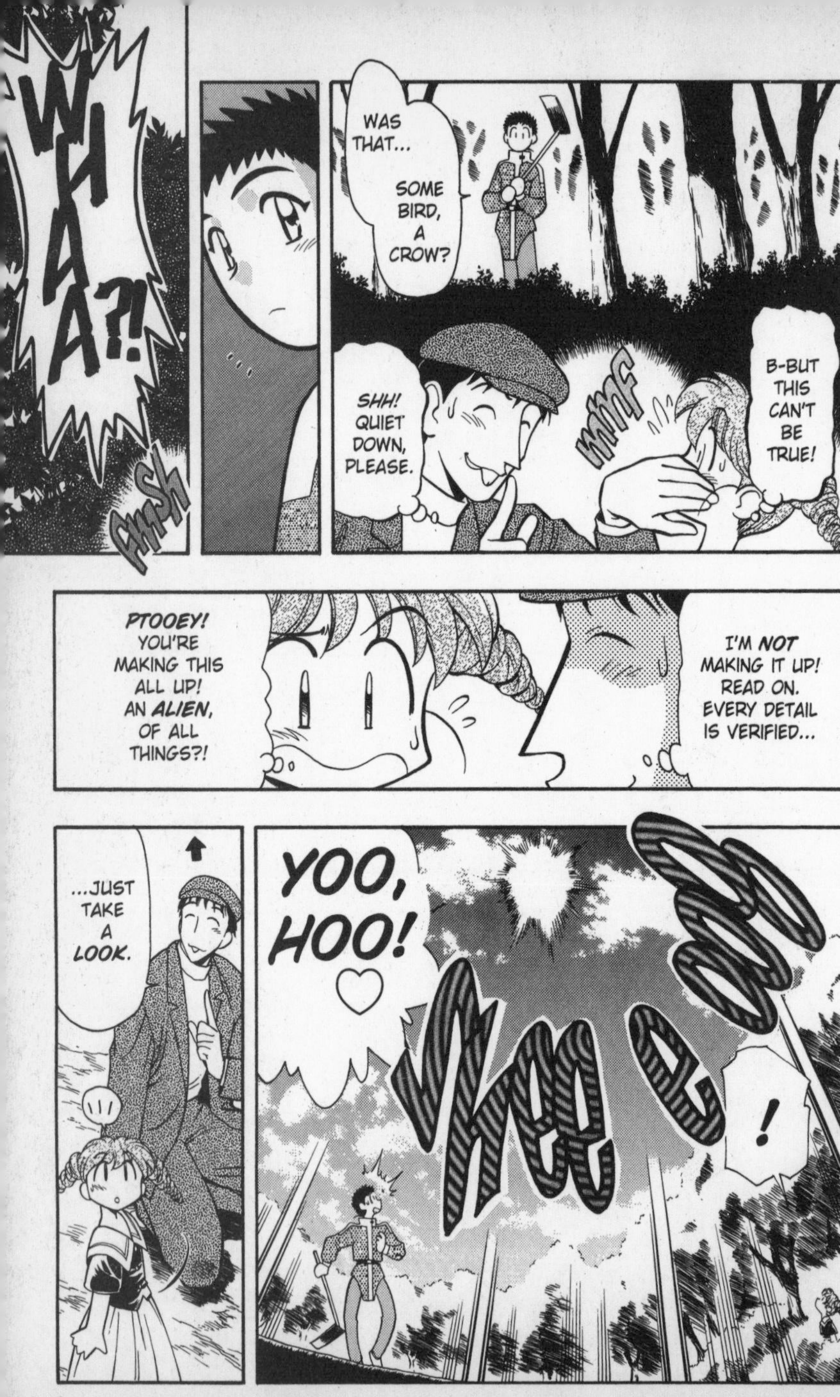
WHAA?!
WAS THAT...
SOME BIRD, A CROW?
SHH! QUIET DOWN, PLEASE.
B-BUT THIS CAN'T BE TRUE!
PTOOEY! YOU'RE MAKING THIS ALL UP! AN ALIEN, OF ALL THINGS?!
I'M NOT MAKING IT UP! READ ON. EVERY DETAIL IS VERIFIED...
...JUST TAKE A LOOK.
YOO, HOO! ♥
!

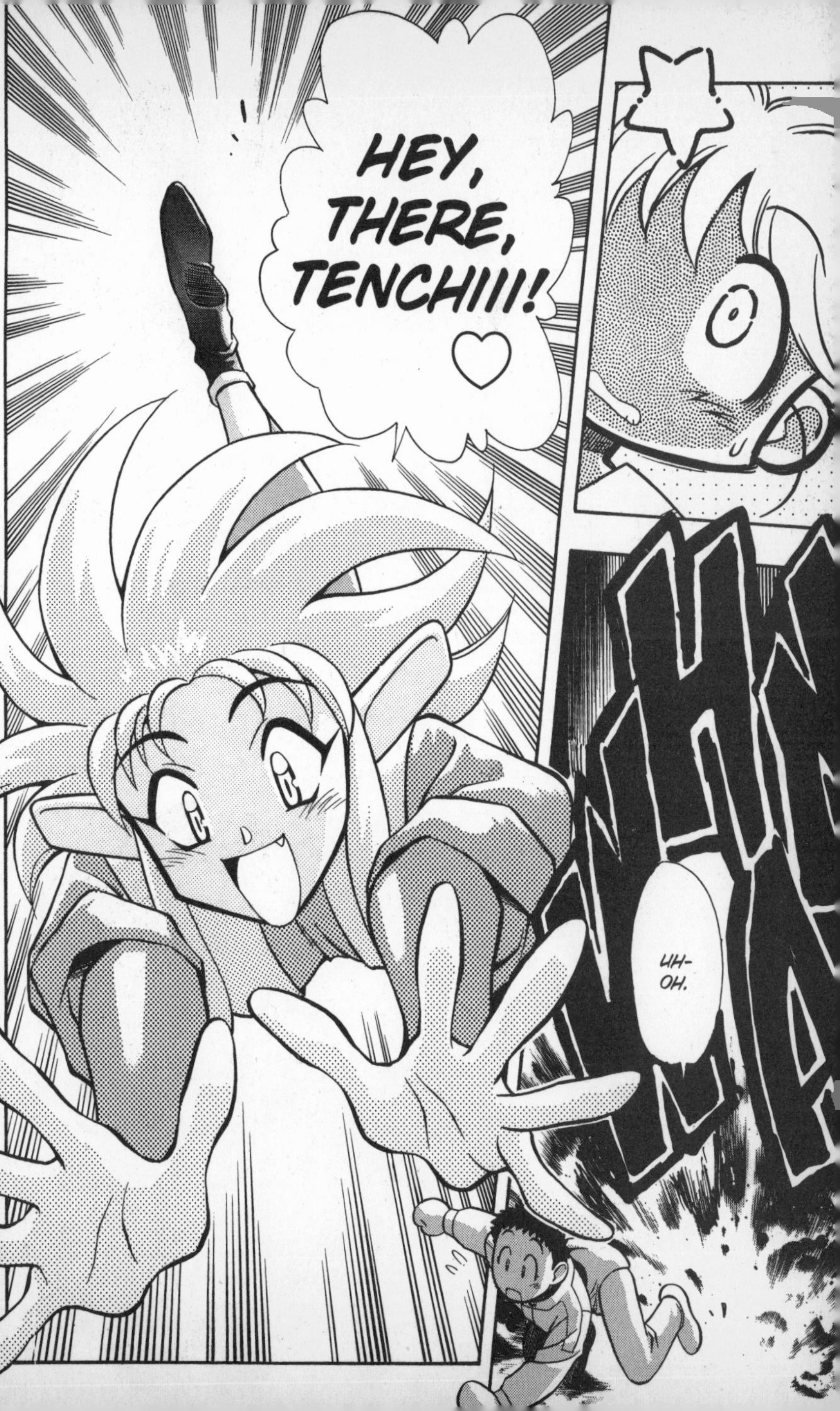
HEY, THERE, TENCHIII!
UH-OH.

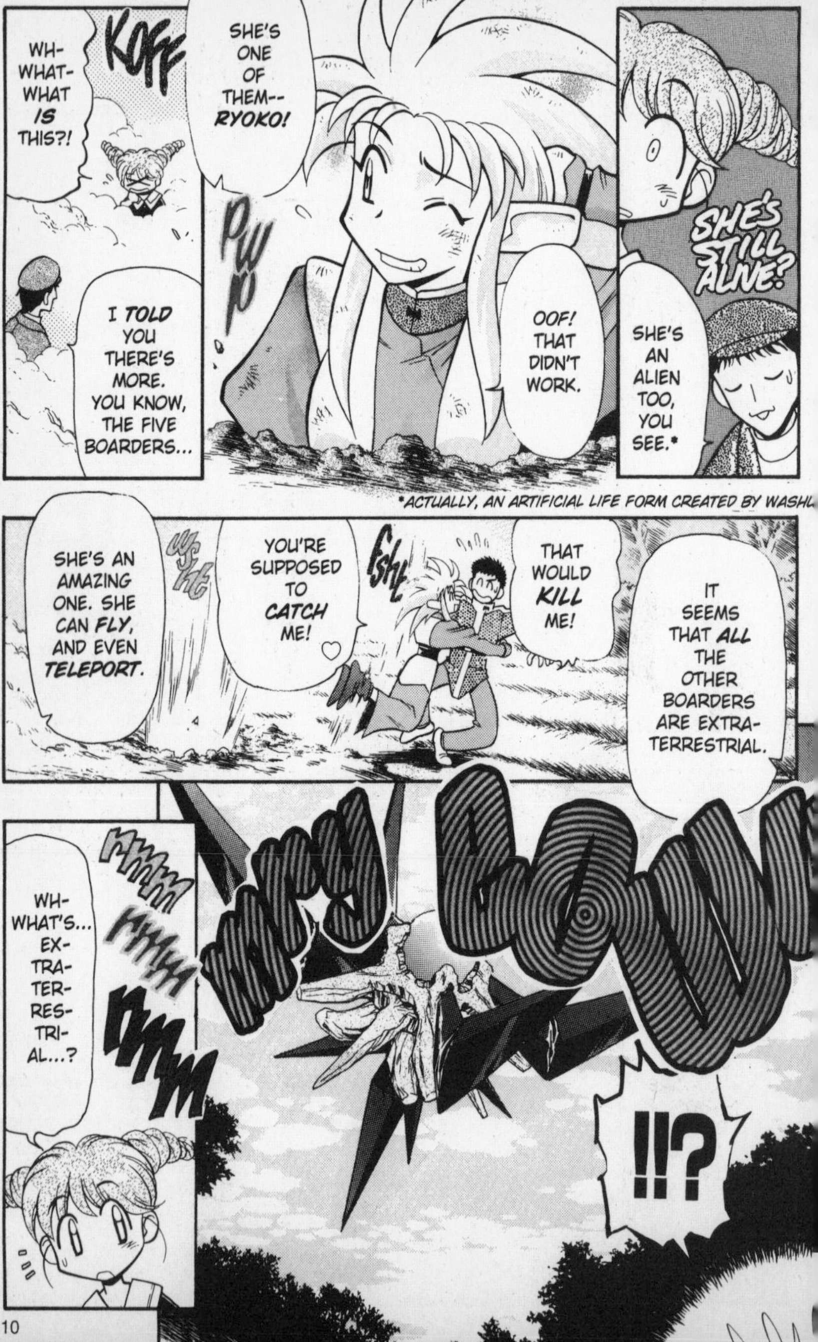
WH-WHAT-WHAT IS THIS?!
KOFF
I TOLD YOU THERE'S MORE. YOU KNOW, THE FIVE BOARDERS...
SHE'S ONE OF THEM--RYOKO!
OOF! THAT DIDN'T WORK.
SHE'S STILL ALIVE?
SHE'S AN ALIEN TOO, YOU SEE.*
*ACTUALLY, AN ARTIFICIAL LIFE FORM CREATED BY WASHU
SHE'S AN AMAZING ONE. SHE CAN FLY, AND EVEN TELEPORT.
YOU'RE SUPPOSED TO CATCH ME!
THAT WOULD KILL ME!
IT SEEMS THAT ALL THE OTHER BOARDERS ARE EXTRA-TERRESTRIAL.
WH-WHAT'S... EX-TRA-TER-RES-TRI-AL...?
!!?

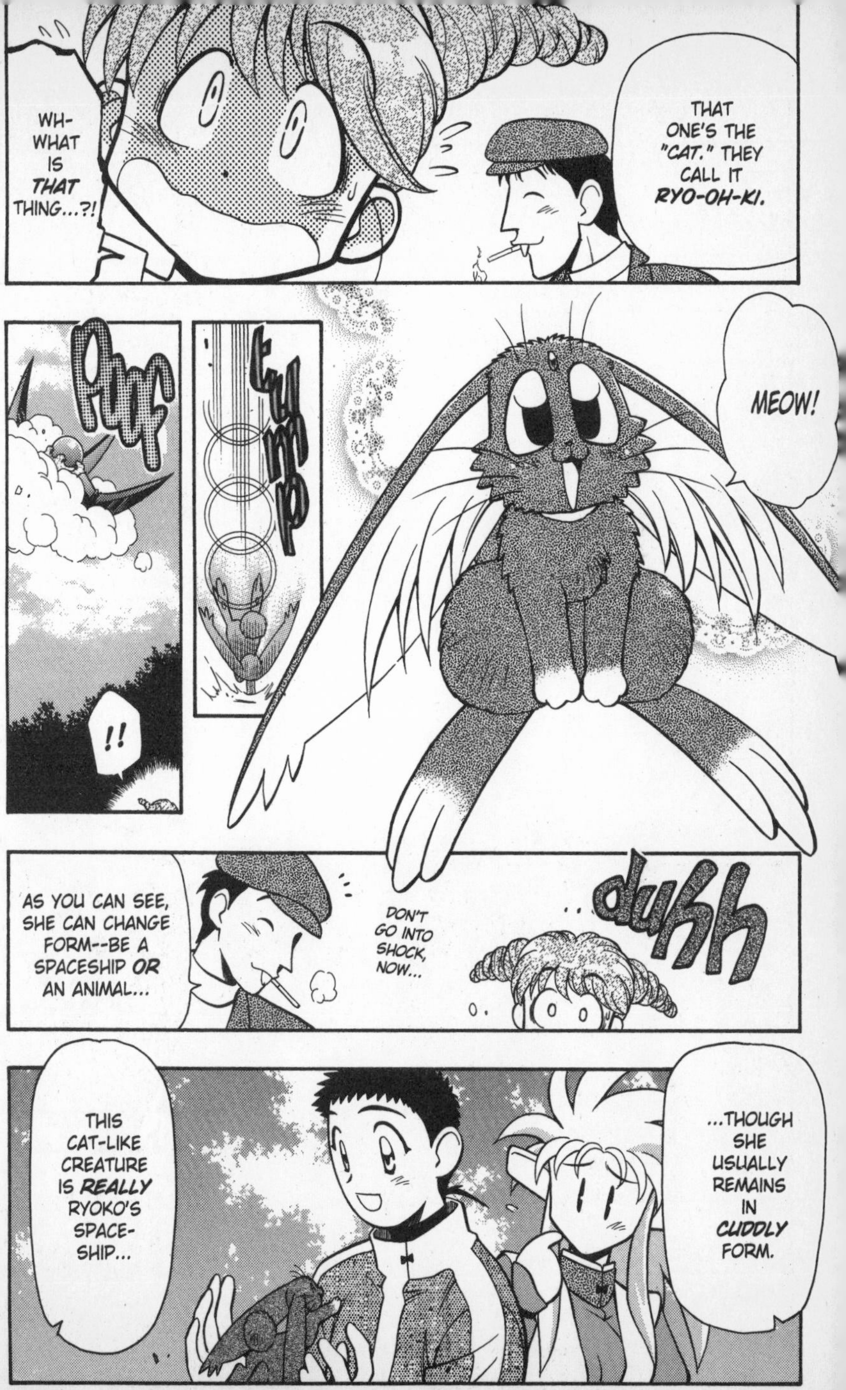

WH- WHAT IS THAT THING...?!
THAT ONE'S THE "CAT." THEY CALL IT RYO-OH-KI.
Puf
trump
!!
MEOW!
AS YOU CAN SEE, SHE CAN CHANGE FORM--BE A SPACESHIP OR AN ANIMAL...
DON'T GO INTO SHOCK, NOW...
duhh
THIS CAT-LIKE CREATURE IS REALLY RYOKO'S SPACE- SHIP...
...THOUGH SHE USUALLY REMAINS IN CUDDLY FORM.

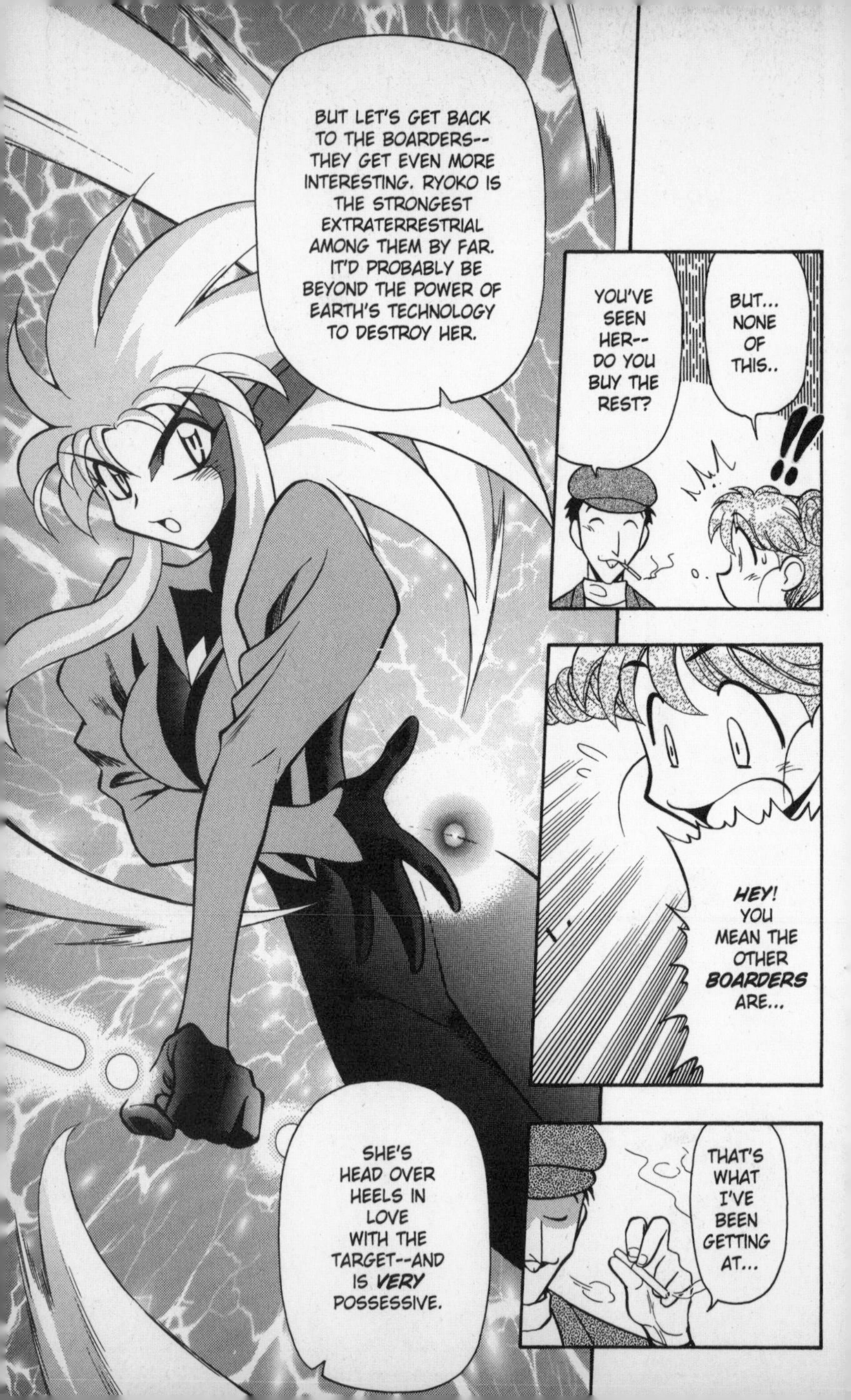
BUT LET'S GET BACK TO THE BOARDERS-- THEY GET EVEN MORE INTERESTING. RYOKO IS THE STRONGEST EXTRATERRESTRIAL AMONG THEM BY FAR. IT'D PROBABLY BE BEYOND THE POWER OF EARTH'S TECHNOLOGY TO DESTROY HER.
SHE'S HEAD OVER HEELS IN LOVE WITH THE TARGET--AND IS VERY POSSESSIVE.
YOU'VE SEEN HER-- DO YOU BUY THE REST?
BUT... NONE OF THIS..
!!
HEY! YOU MEAN THE OTHER BOARDERS ARE...
THAT'S WHAT I'VE BEEN GETTING AT...

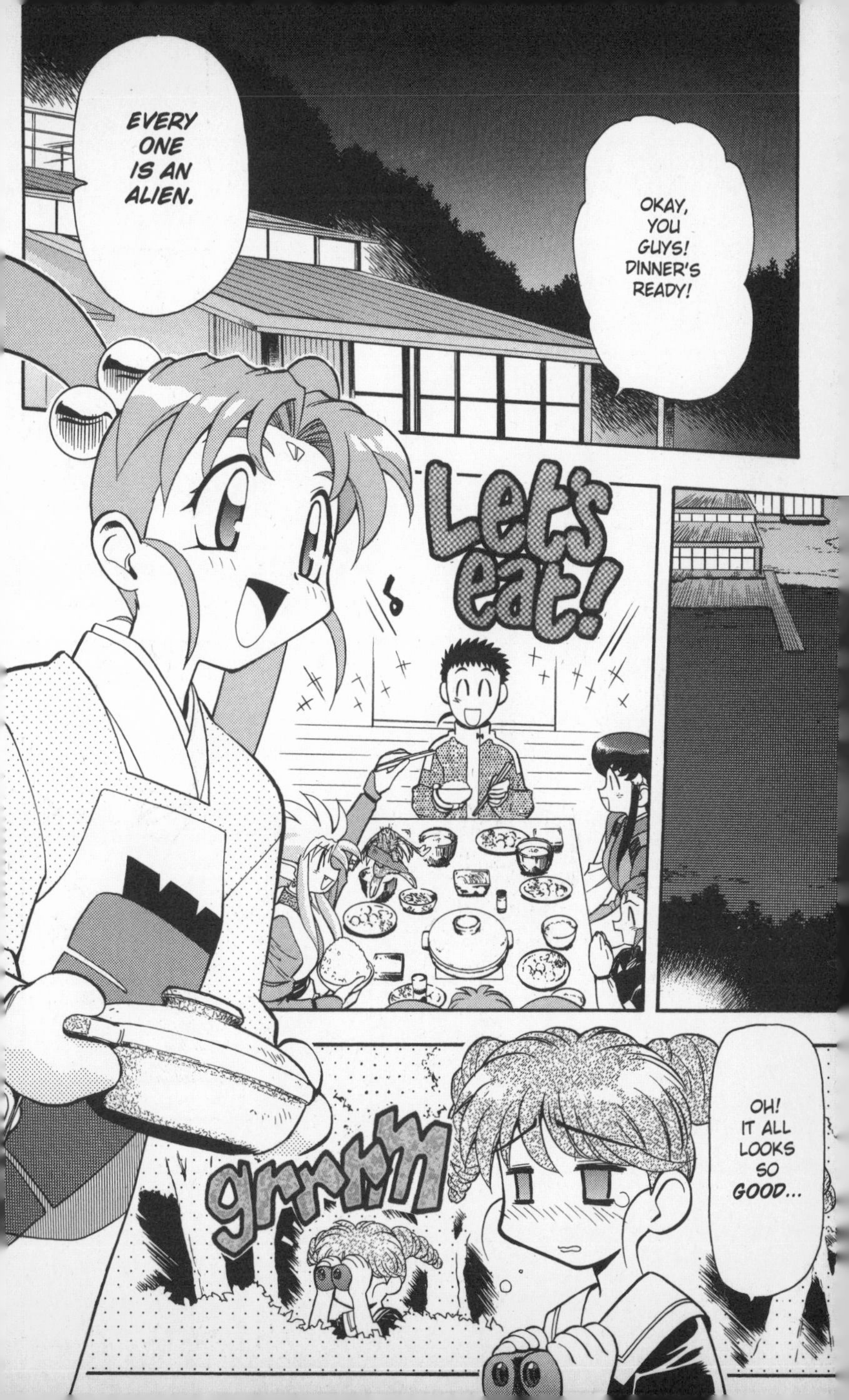
EVERY ONE IS AN ALIEN.
OKAY, YOU GUYS! DINNER'S READY!
Let's eat!
grrrrrn
OH! IT ALL LOOKS SO GOOD...

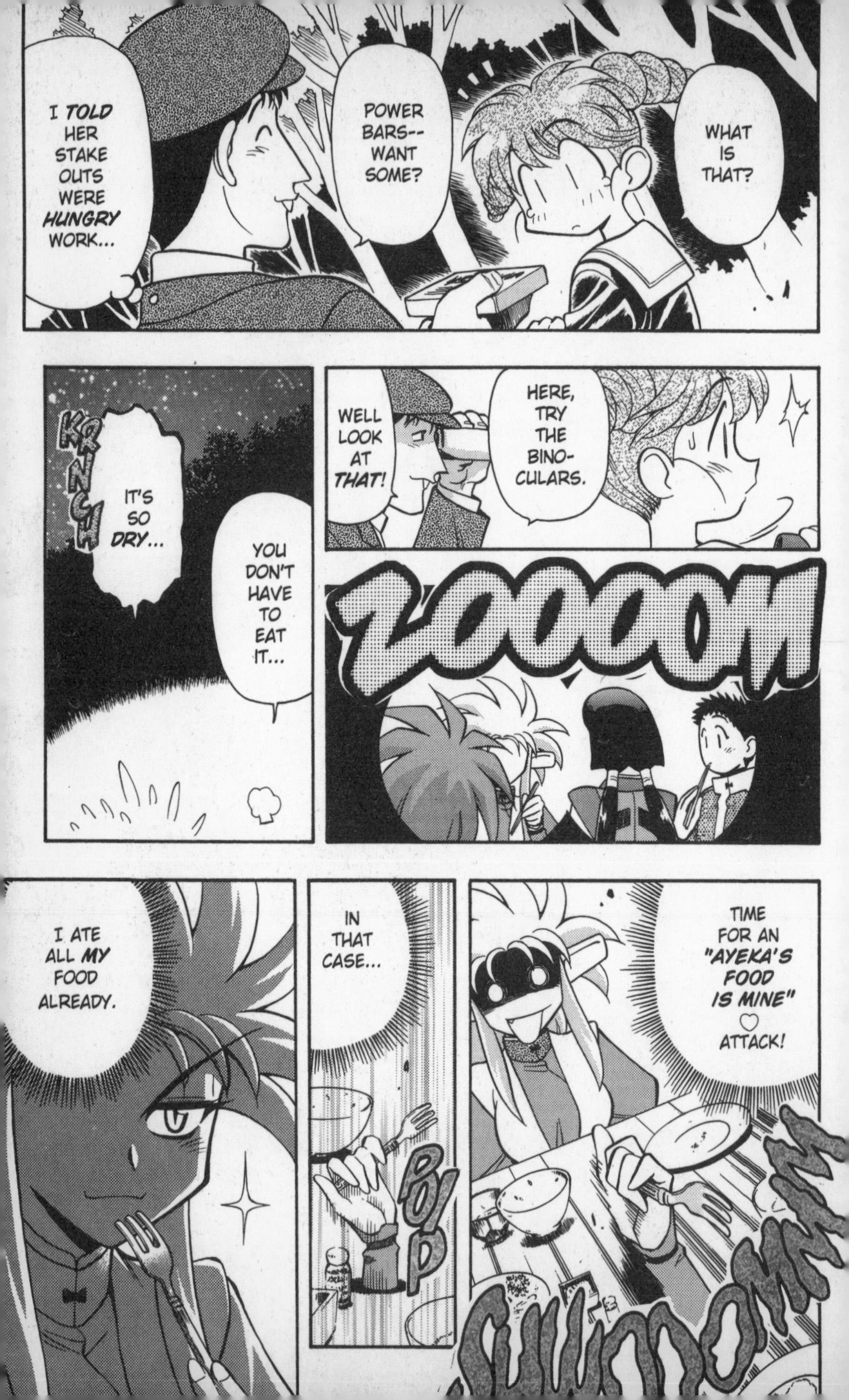
I TOLD HER STAKE OUTS WERE HUNGRY WORK...
POWER BARS--WANT SOME?
WHAT IS THAT?
KRNCH
IT'S SO DRY...
YOU DON'T HAVE TO EAT IT...
WELL LOOK AT THAT!
HERE, TRY THE BINOCULARS.
ZOOOOM
I ATE ALL MY FOOD ALREADY.
IN THAT CASE...
POP
TIME FOR AN "AYEKA'S FOOD IS MINE" ♡ ATTACK!

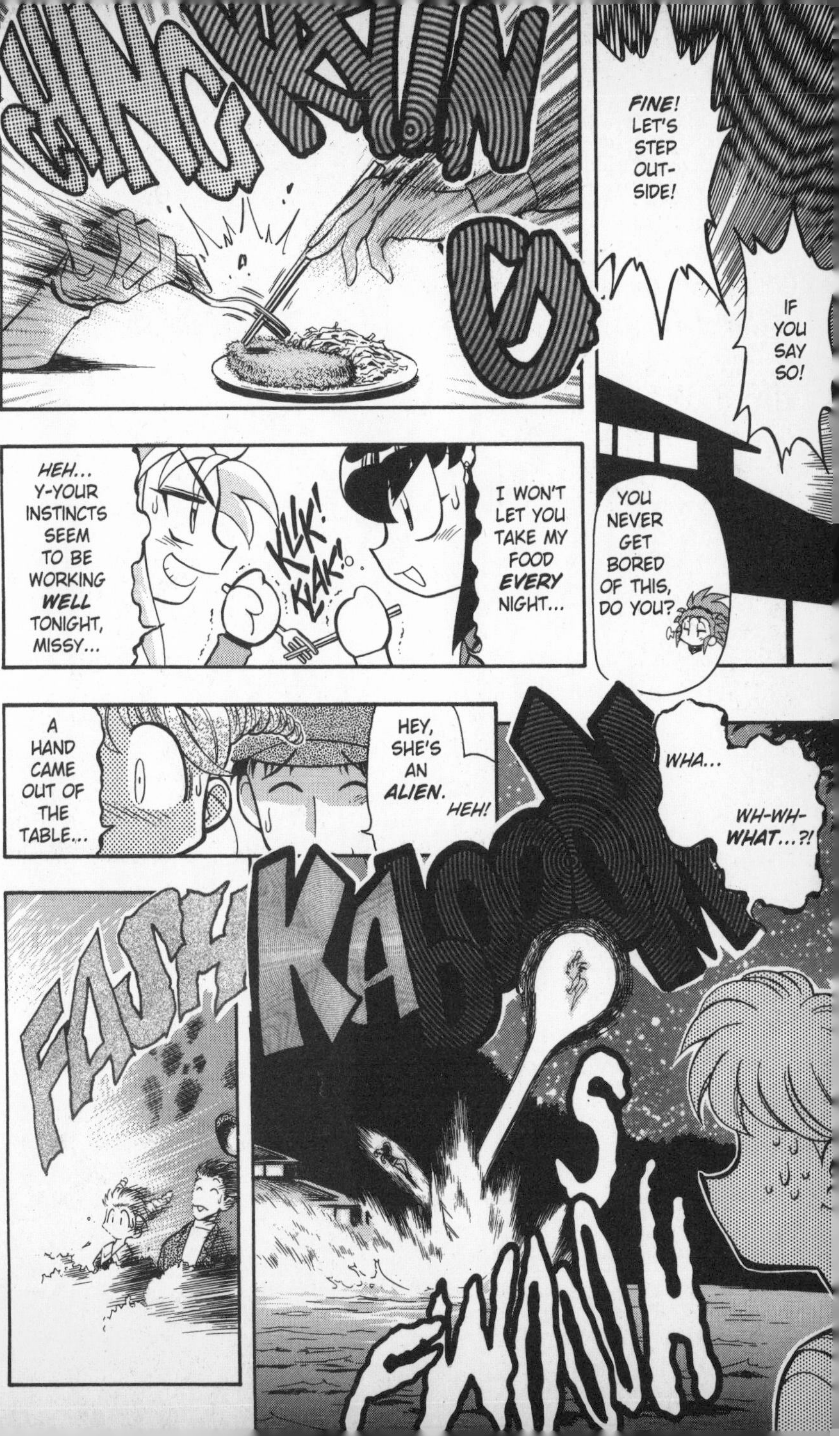
HEH... Y-YOUR INSTINCTS SEEM TO BE WORKING WELL TONIGHT, MISSY...
KLIK! KLAK!
I WON'T LET YOU TAKE MY FOOD EVERY NIGHT...
FINE! LET'S STEP OUT-SIDE!
IF YOU SAY SO!
YOU NEVER GET BORED OF THIS, DO YOU?
A HAND CAME OUT OF THE TABLE...
HEY, SHE'S AN ALIEN.
HEH!
WHA...
WH-WH-WHAT...?!

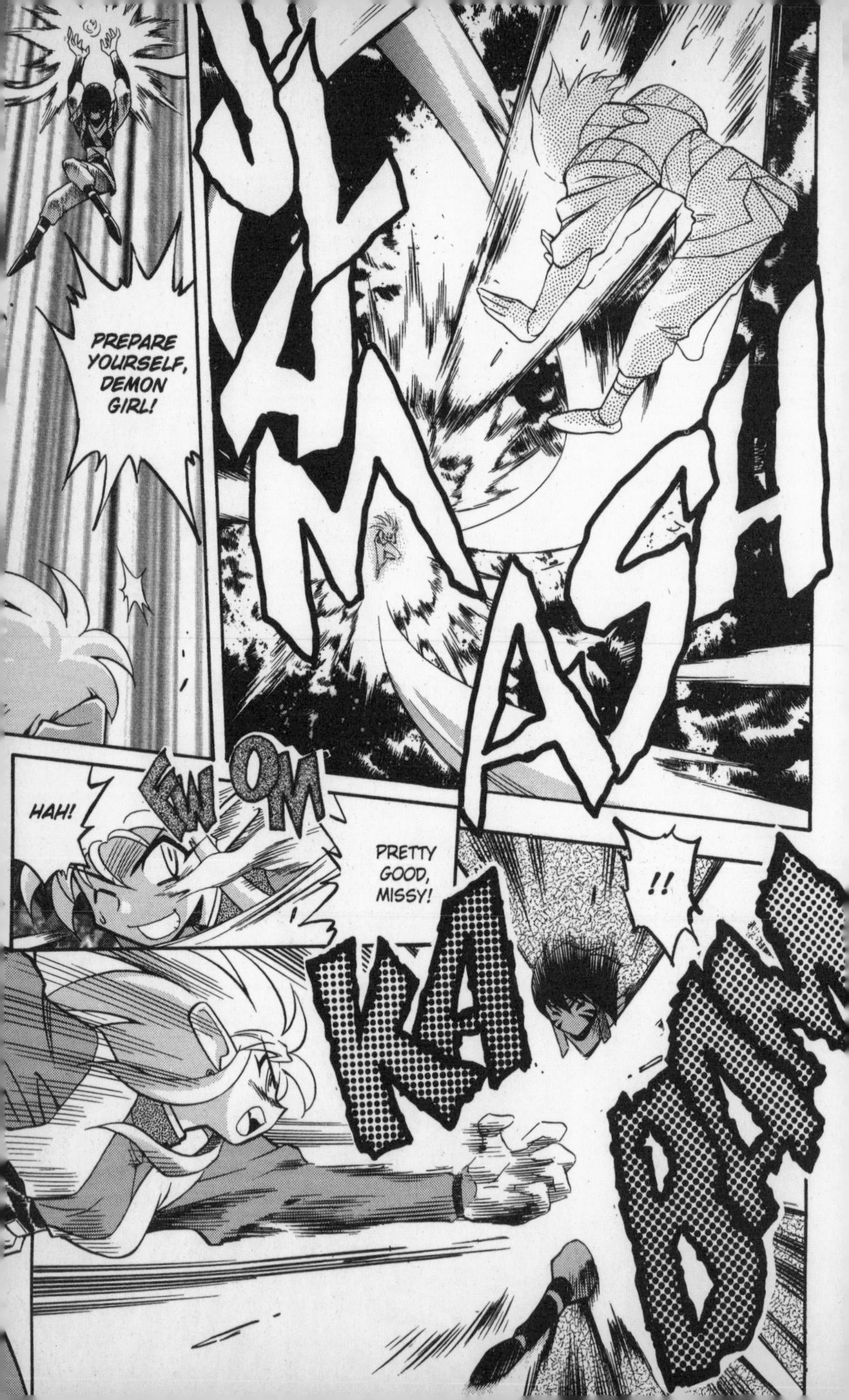
PREPARE YOURSELF, DEMON GIRL!
HAH!
PRETTY GOOD, MISSY!
!!

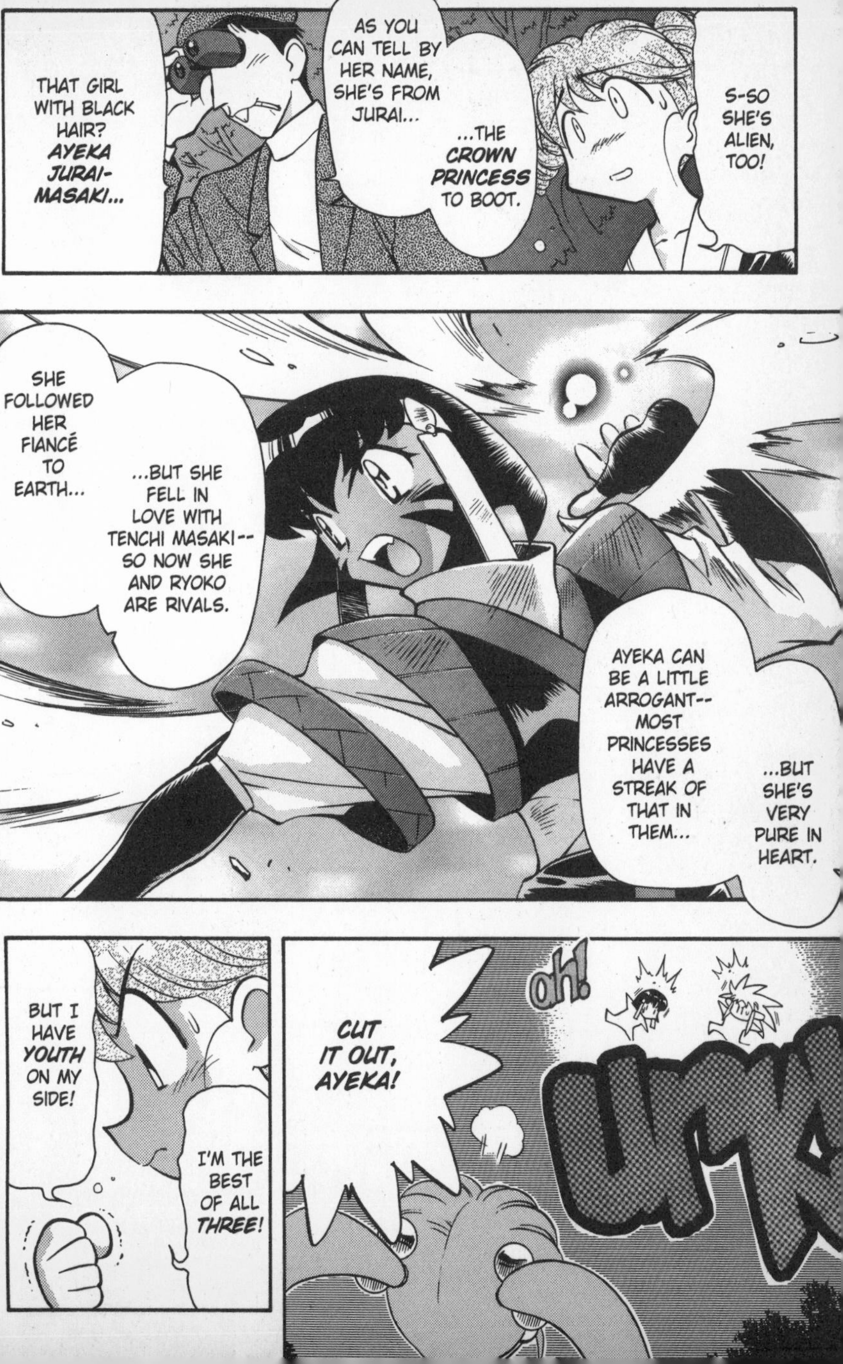
THAT GIRL WITH BLACK HAIR? *AYEKA JURAI-MASAKI...*
AS YOU CAN TELL BY HER NAME, SHE'S FROM JURAI...
...THE *CROWN PRINCESS* TO BOOT.
S-SO SHE'S ALIEN, TOO!
SHE FOLLOWED HER FIANCÉ TO EARTH...
...BUT SHE FELL IN LOVE WITH TENCHI MASAKI-- SO NOW SHE AND RYOKO ARE RIVALS.
AYEKA CAN BE A LITTLE ARROGANT-- MOST PRINCESSES HAVE A STREAK OF THAT IN THEM...
...BUT SHE'S VERY PURE IN HEART.
BUT I HAVE *YOUTH* ON MY SIDE!
I'M THE BEST OF ALL *THREE*!
CUT IT OUT, AYEKA!
oh!

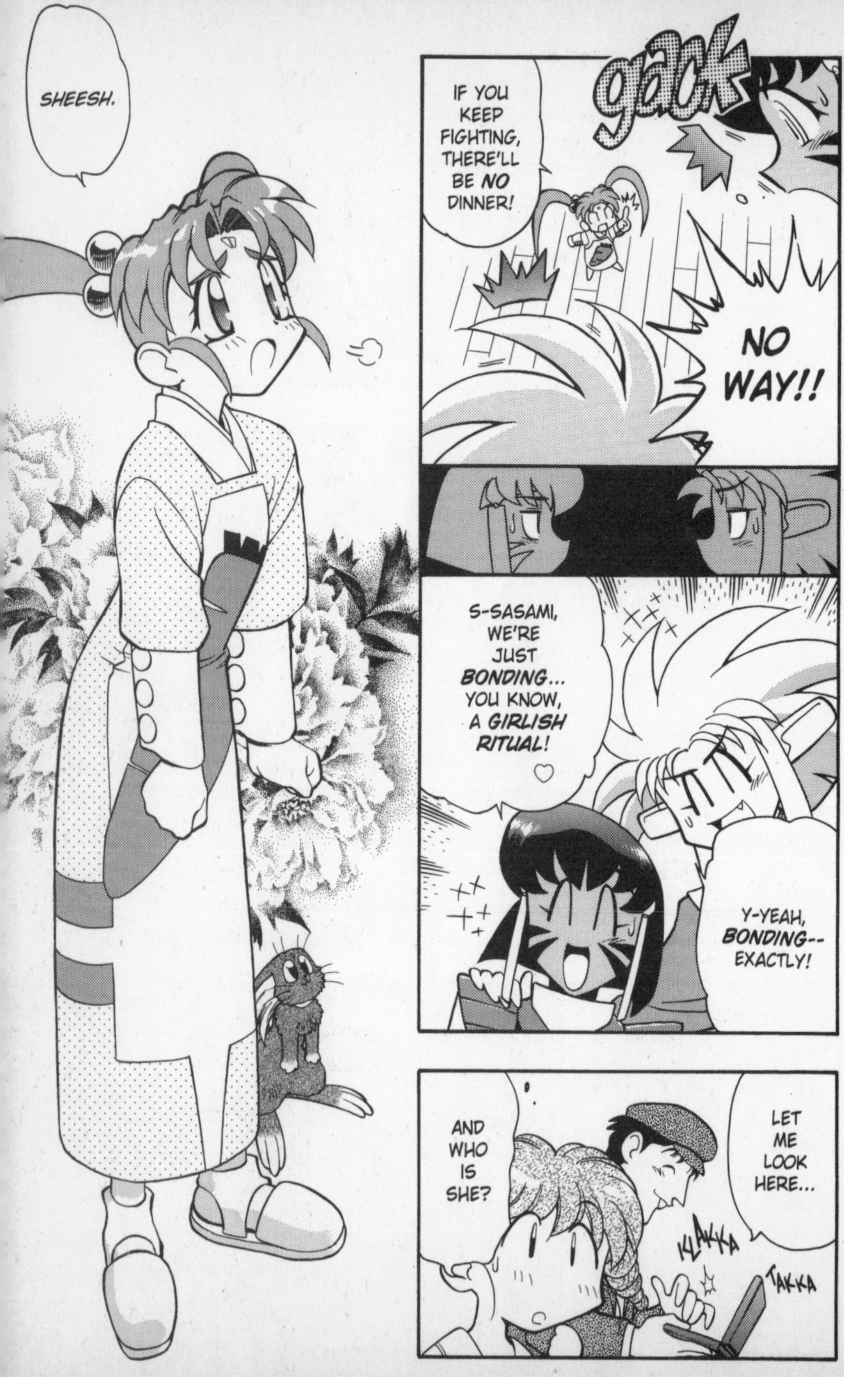
SHEESH.
IF YOU KEEP FIGHTING, THERE'LL BE NO DINNER!
gack
NO WAY!!
S-SASAMI, WE'RE JUST BONDING... YOU KNOW, A GIRLISH RITUAL!
Y-YEAH, BONDING-- EXACTLY!
AND WHO IS SHE?
LET ME LOOK HERE...
KLAKKA
TAKKA

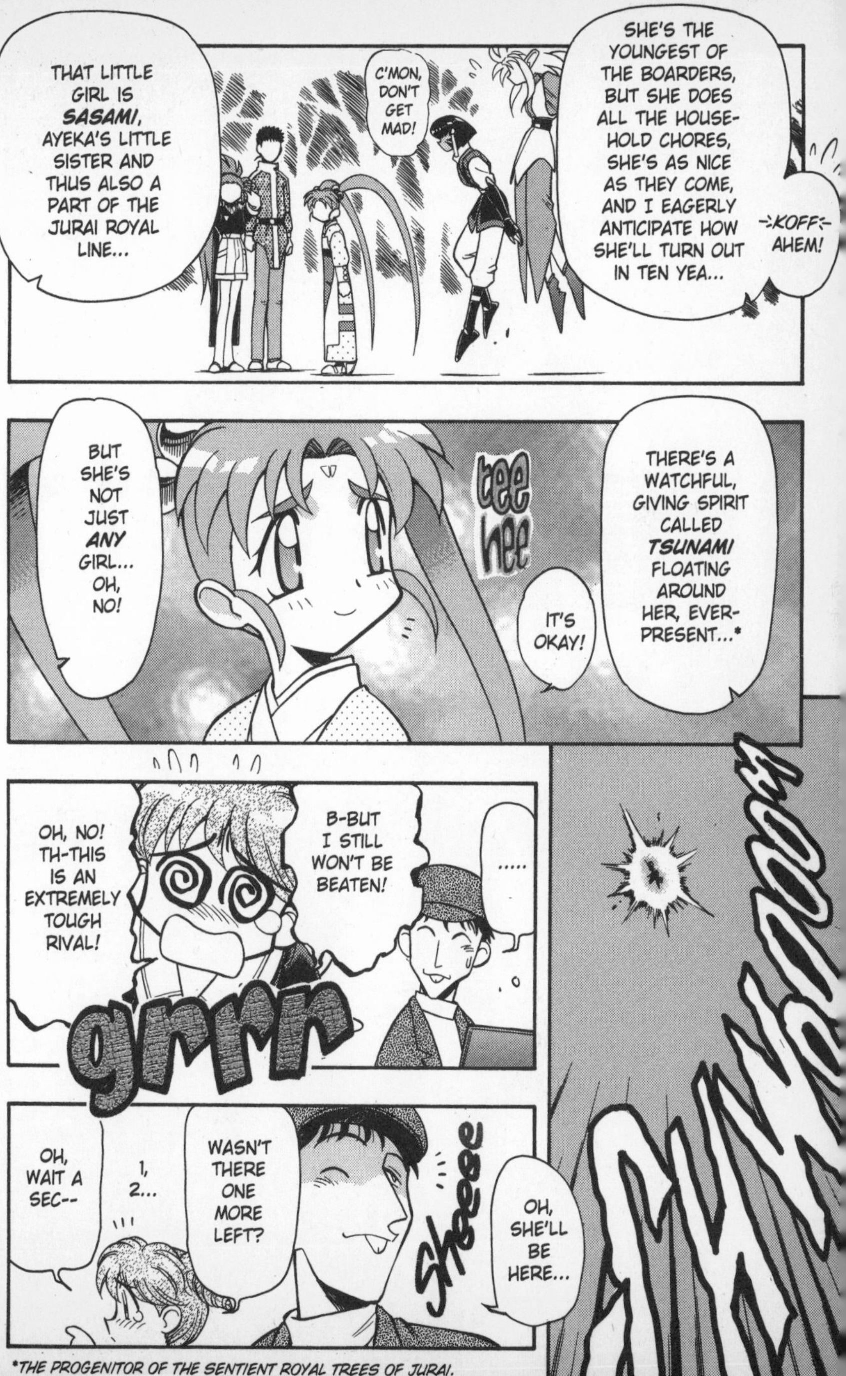
THAT LITTLE GIRL IS SASAMI, AYEKA'S LITTLE SISTER AND THUS ALSO A PART OF THE JURAI ROYAL LINE...
C'MON, DON'T GET MAD!
SHE'S THE YOUNGEST OF THE BOARDERS, BUT SHE DOES ALL THE HOUSEHOLD CHORES, SHE'S AS NICE AS THEY COME, AND I EAGERLY ANTICIPATE HOW SHE'LL TURN OUT IN TEN YEA...
-KOFF- AHEM!
BUT SHE'S NOT JUST ANY GIRL... OH, NO!
tee hee
IT'S OKAY!
THERE'S A WATCHFUL, GIVING SPIRIT CALLED TSUNAMI FLOATING AROUND HER, EVER-PRESENT...*
OH, NO! TH-THIS IS AN EXTREMELY TOUGH RIVAL!
B-BUT I STILL WON'T BE BEATEN!
.....
grrr
OH, WAIT A SEC--
1, 2...
WASN'T THERE ONE MORE LEFT?
OH, SHE'LL BE HERE...

*THE PROGENITOR OF THE SENTIENT ROYAL TREES OF JURAI.

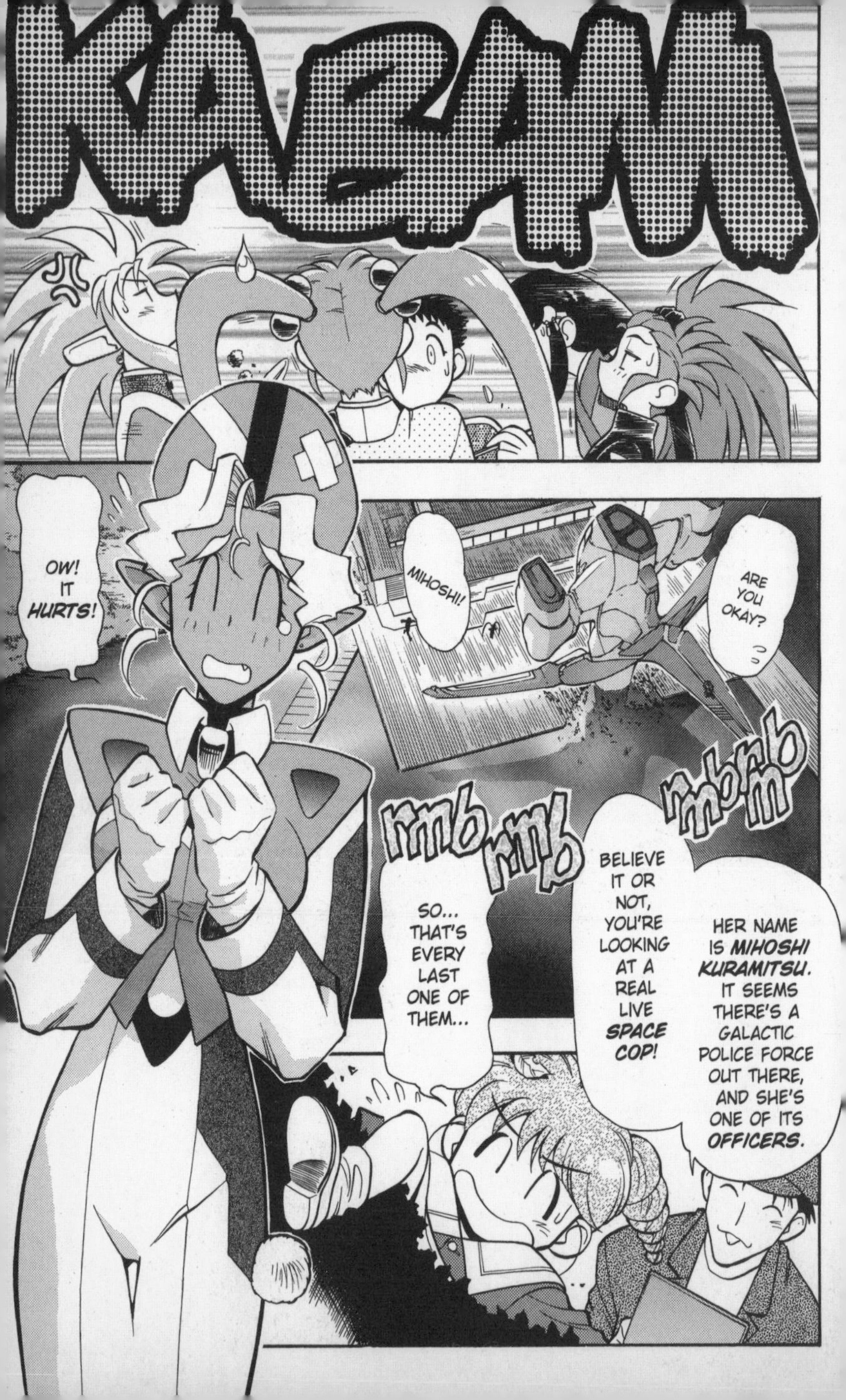
KAZAM
OW! IT HURTS!
MIHOSHI!
ARE YOU OKAY?
rmb rmb
rmb rmb
SO... THAT'S EVERY LAST ONE OF THEM...
BELIEVE IT OR NOT, YOU'RE LOOKING AT A REAL LIVE SPACE COP!
HER NAME IS MIHOSHI KURAMITSU. IT SEEMS THERE'S A GALACTIC POLICE FORCE OUT THERE, AND SHE'S ONE OF ITS OFFICERS.

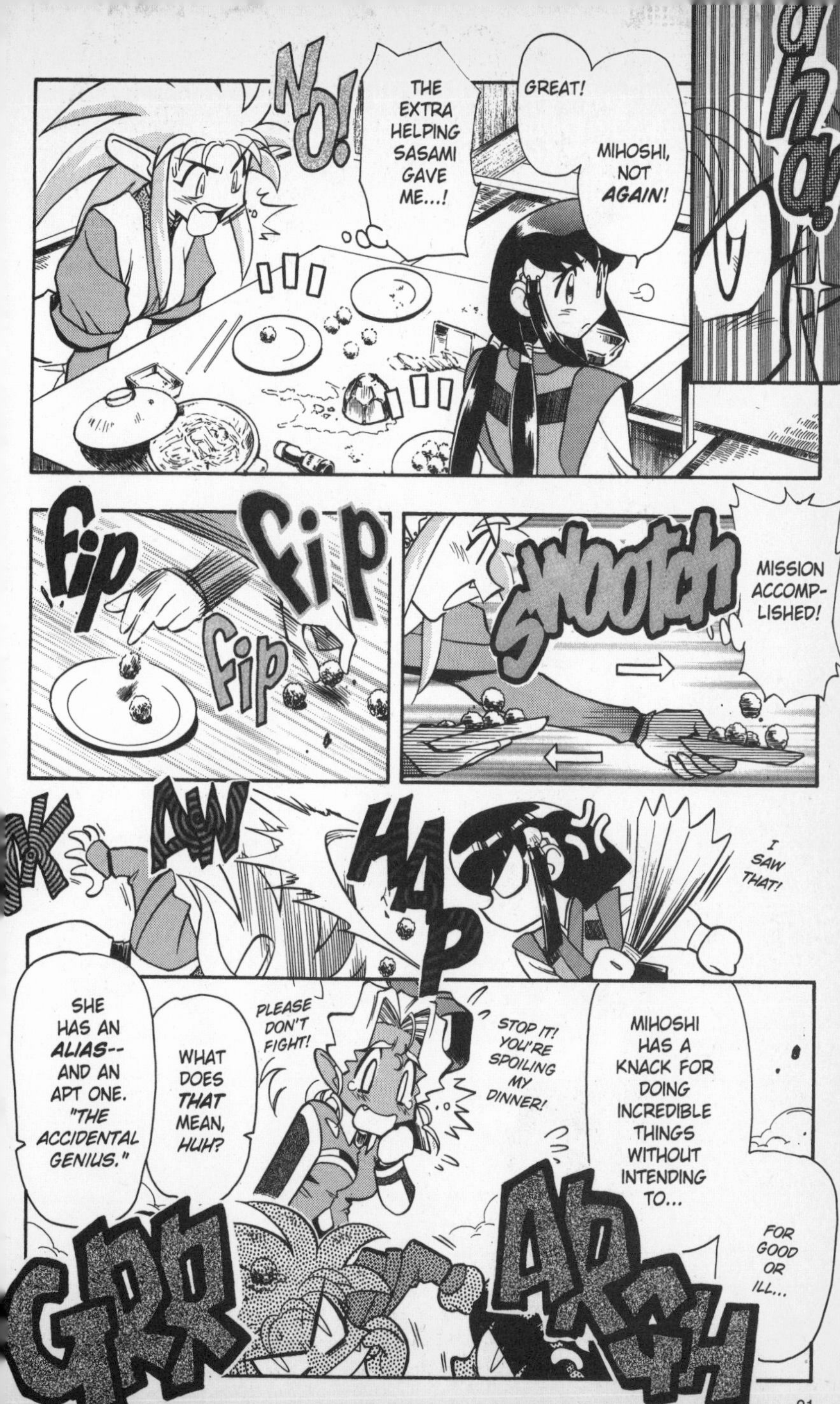
NO!
THE EXTRA HELPING SASAMI GAVE ME...!
GREAT!
MIHOSHI, NOT AGAIN!
gha!
fip
fip
fip
swootch
MISSION ACCOMPLISHED!
HAP
I SAW THAT!
SHE HAS AN ALIAS-- AND AN APT ONE. "THE ACCIDENTAL GENIUS."
WHAT DOES THAT MEAN, HUH?
PLEASE DON'T FIGHT!
STOP IT! YOU'RE SPOILING MY DINNER!
MIHOSHI HAS A KNACK FOR DOING INCREDIBLE THINGS WITHOUT INTENDING TO...
FOR GOOD OR ILL...
GRR
ARGH

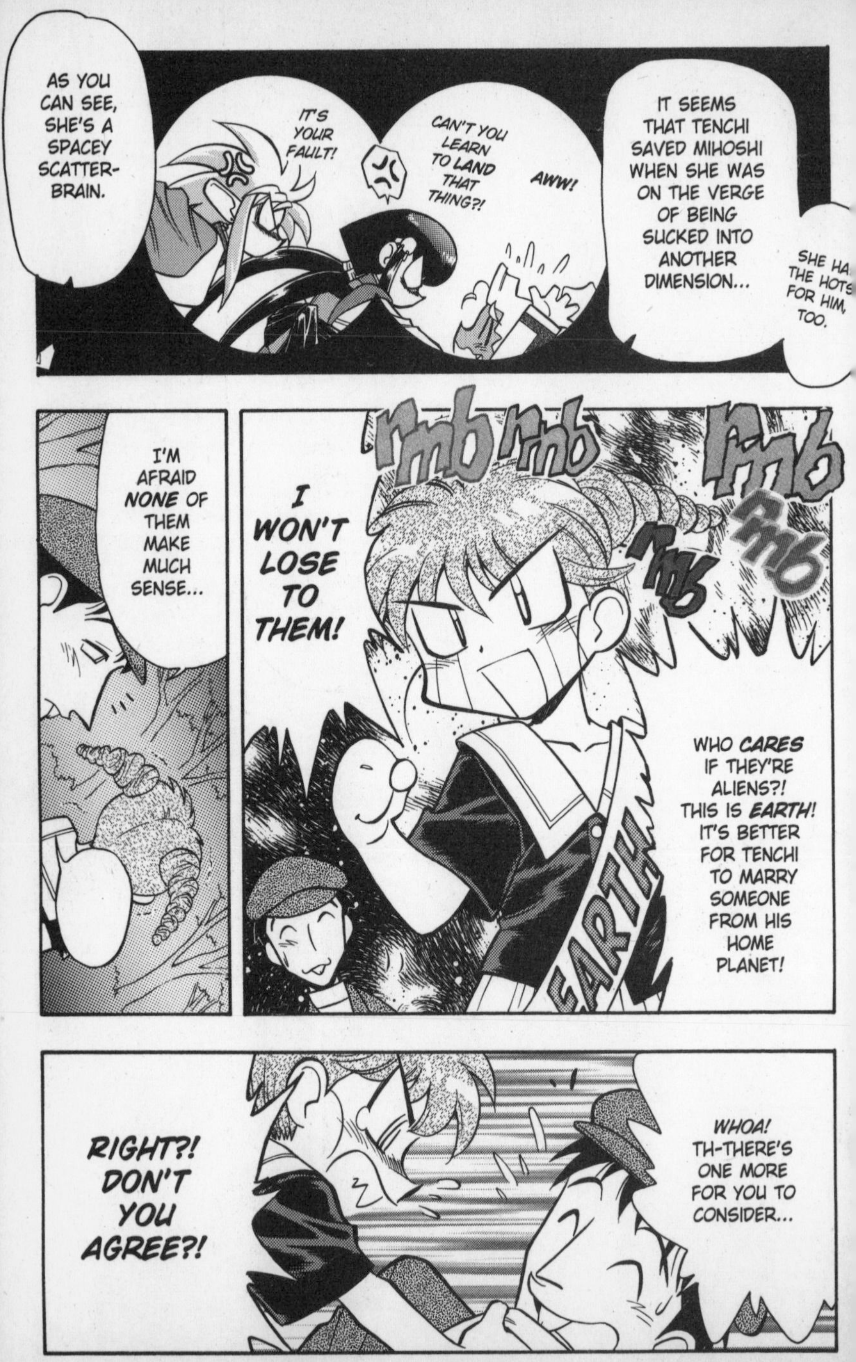
AS YOU CAN SEE, SHE'S A SPACEY SCATTER-BRAIN.
IT'S YOUR FAULT!
CAN'T YOU LEARN TO LAND THAT THING?!
AWW!
IT SEEMS THAT TENCHI SAVED MIHOSHI WHEN SHE WAS ON THE VERGE OF BEING SUCKED INTO ANOTHER DIMENSION...
SHE HA THE HOTS FOR HIM, TOO.
I'M AFRAID NONE OF THEM MAKE MUCH SENSE...
rmb rmb rmb rmb rmb
I WON'T LOSE TO THEM!
EARTH
WHO CARES IF THEY'RE ALIENS?! THIS IS EARTH! IT'S BETTER FOR TENCHI TO MARRY SOMEONE FROM HIS HOME PLANET!
RIGHT?! DON'T YOU AGREE?!
WHOA! TH-THERE'S ONE MORE FOR YOU TO CONSIDER...

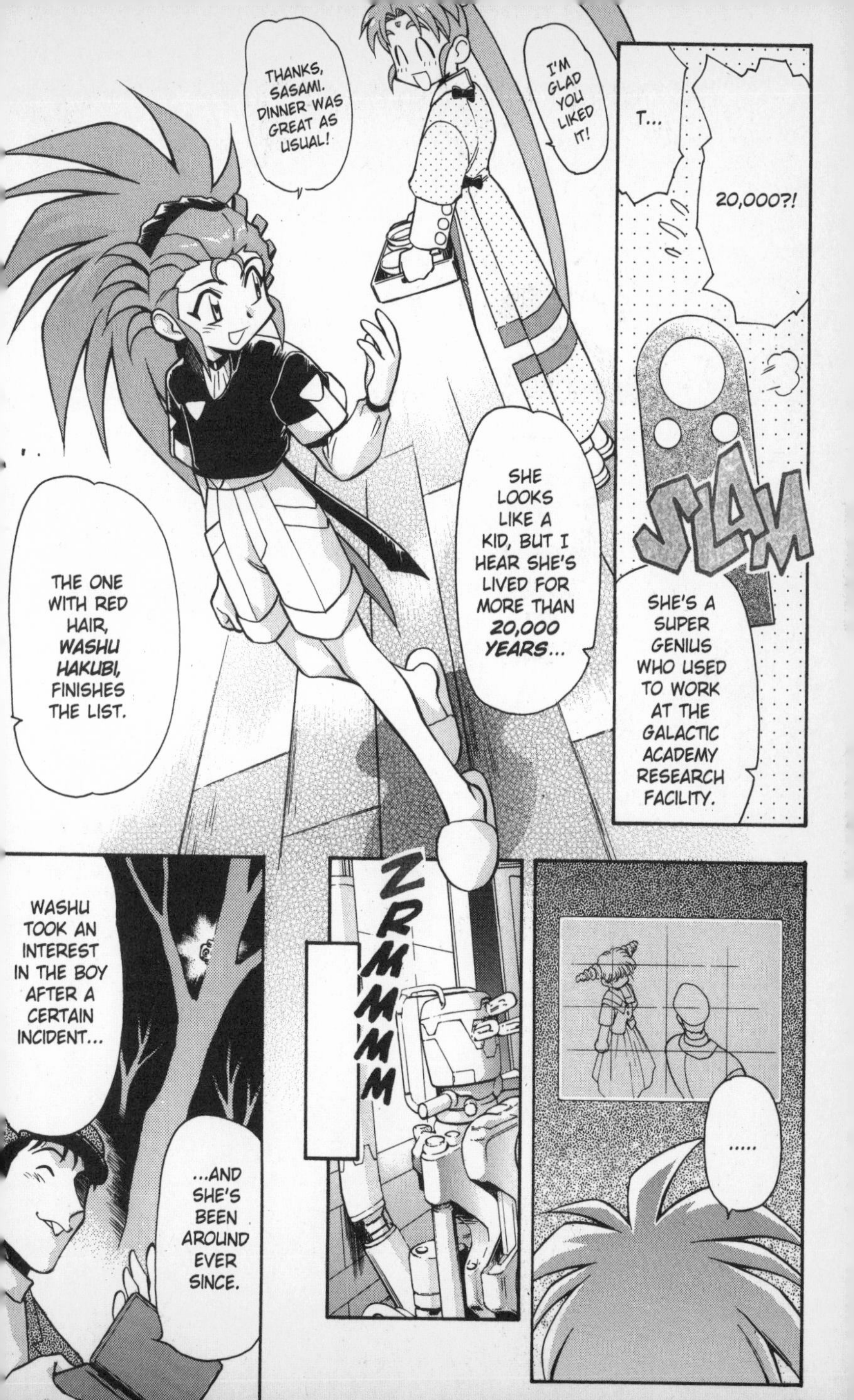
THANKS, SASAMI. DINNER WAS GREAT AS USUAL!
I'M GLAD YOU LIKED IT!
THE ONE WITH RED HAIR, WASHU HAKUBI, FINISHES THE LIST.
SHE LOOKS LIKE A KID, BUT I HEAR SHE'S LIVED FOR MORE THAN 20,000 YEARS...
T...
20,000?!
SLAM
SHE'S A SUPER GENIUS WHO USED TO WORK AT THE GALACTIC ACADEMY RESEARCH FACILITY.
WASHU TOOK AN INTEREST IN THE BOY AFTER A CERTAIN INCIDENT...
...AND SHE'S BEEN AROUND EVER SINCE.
ZRMMMMM
.....

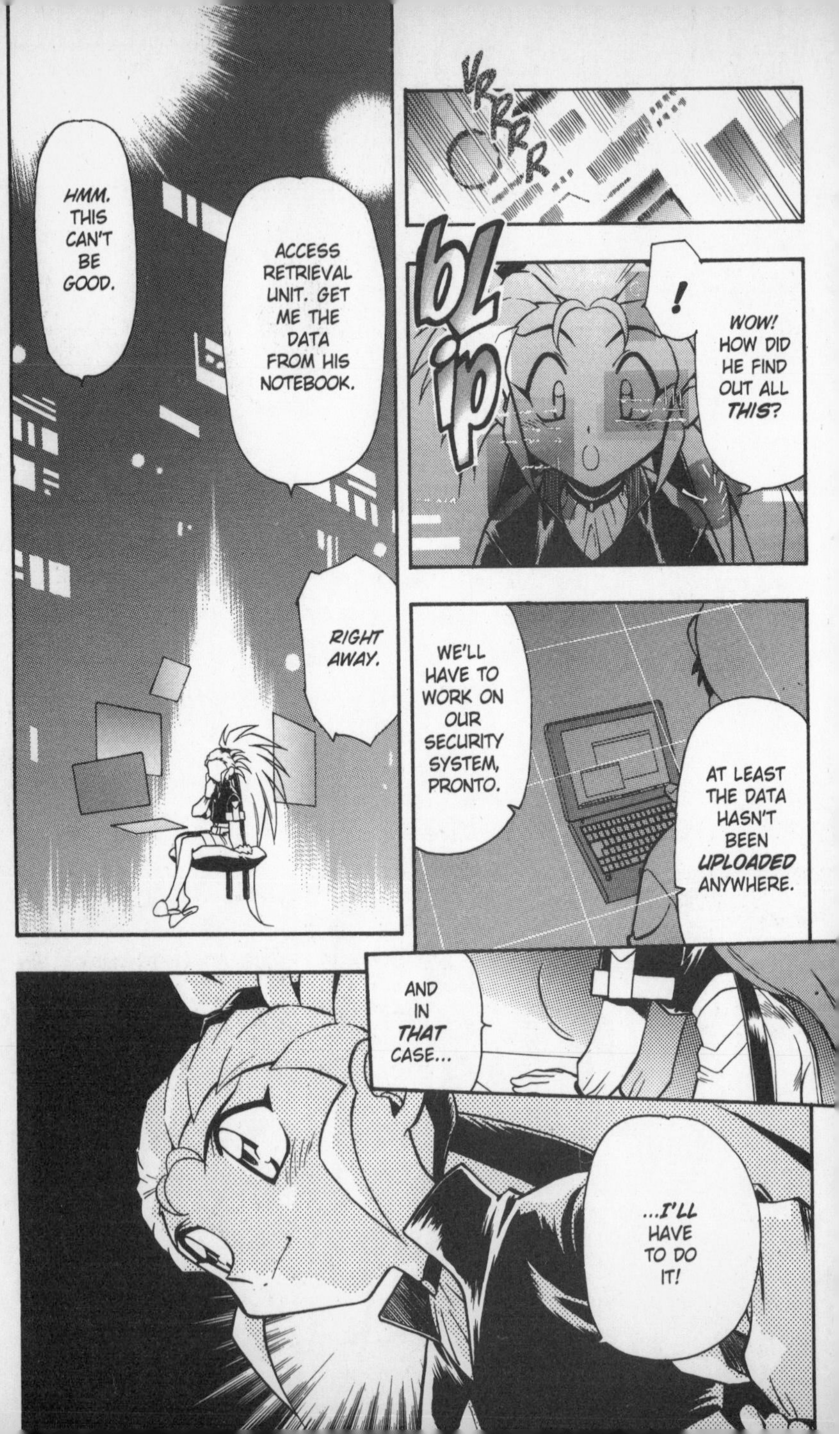
HMM. THIS CAN'T BE GOOD.
ACCESS RETRIEVAL UNIT. GET ME THE DATA FROM HIS NOTEBOOK.
RIGHT AWAY.
VRRRR
bLip
!
WOW! HOW DID HE FIND OUT ALL THIS?
WE'LL HAVE TO WORK ON OUR SECURITY SYSTEM, PRONTO.
AT LEAST THE DATA HASN'T BEEN UPLOADED ANYWHERE.
AND IN THAT CASE...
...I'LL HAVE TO DO IT!

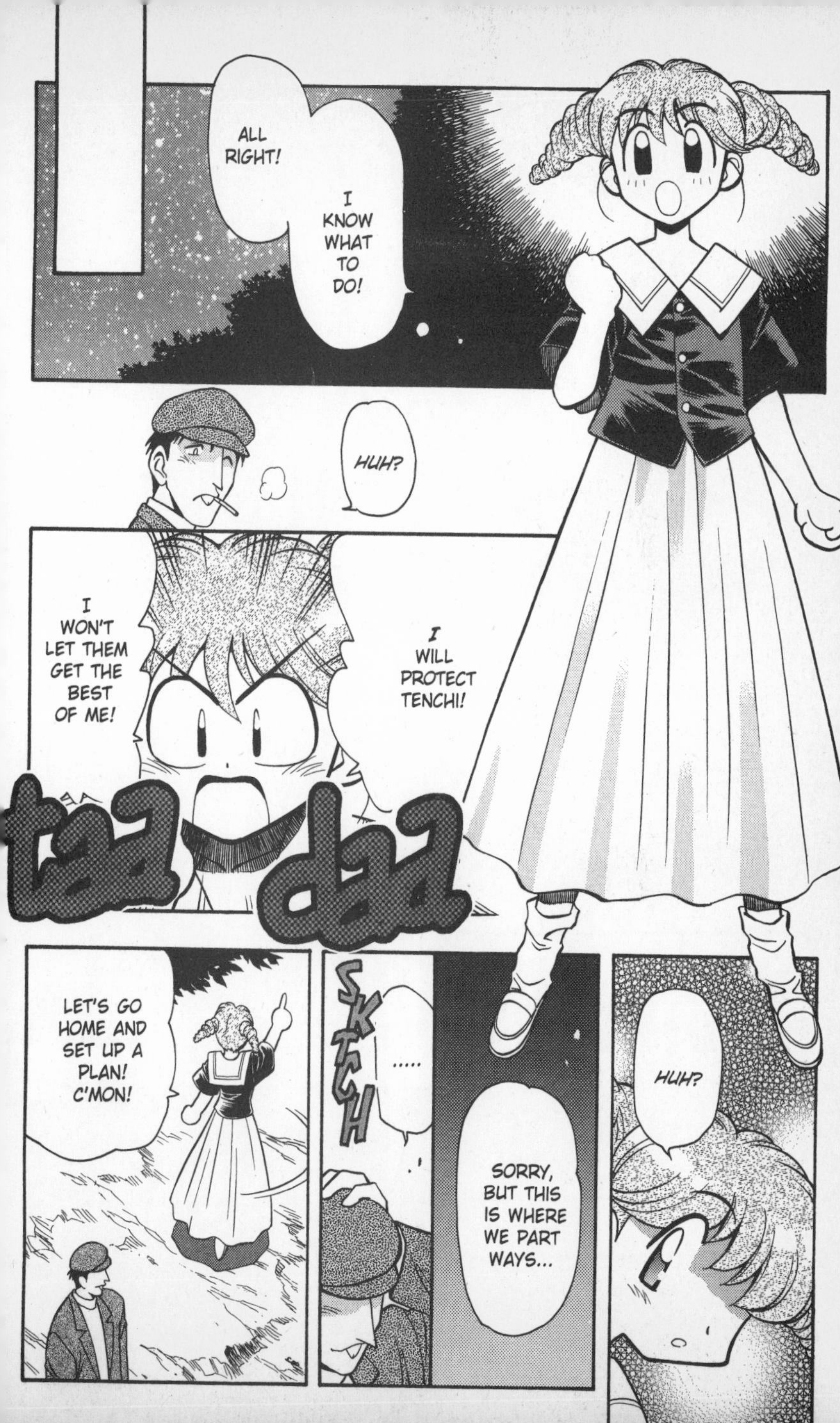
ALL RIGHT!
I KNOW WHAT TO DO!
HUH?
I WON'T LET THEM GET THE BEST OF ME!
I WILL PROTECT TENCHI!
ta da
LET'S GO HOME AND SET UP A PLAN! C'MON!
SKTCH
.....
SORRY, BUT THIS IS WHERE WE PART WAYS...
HUH?

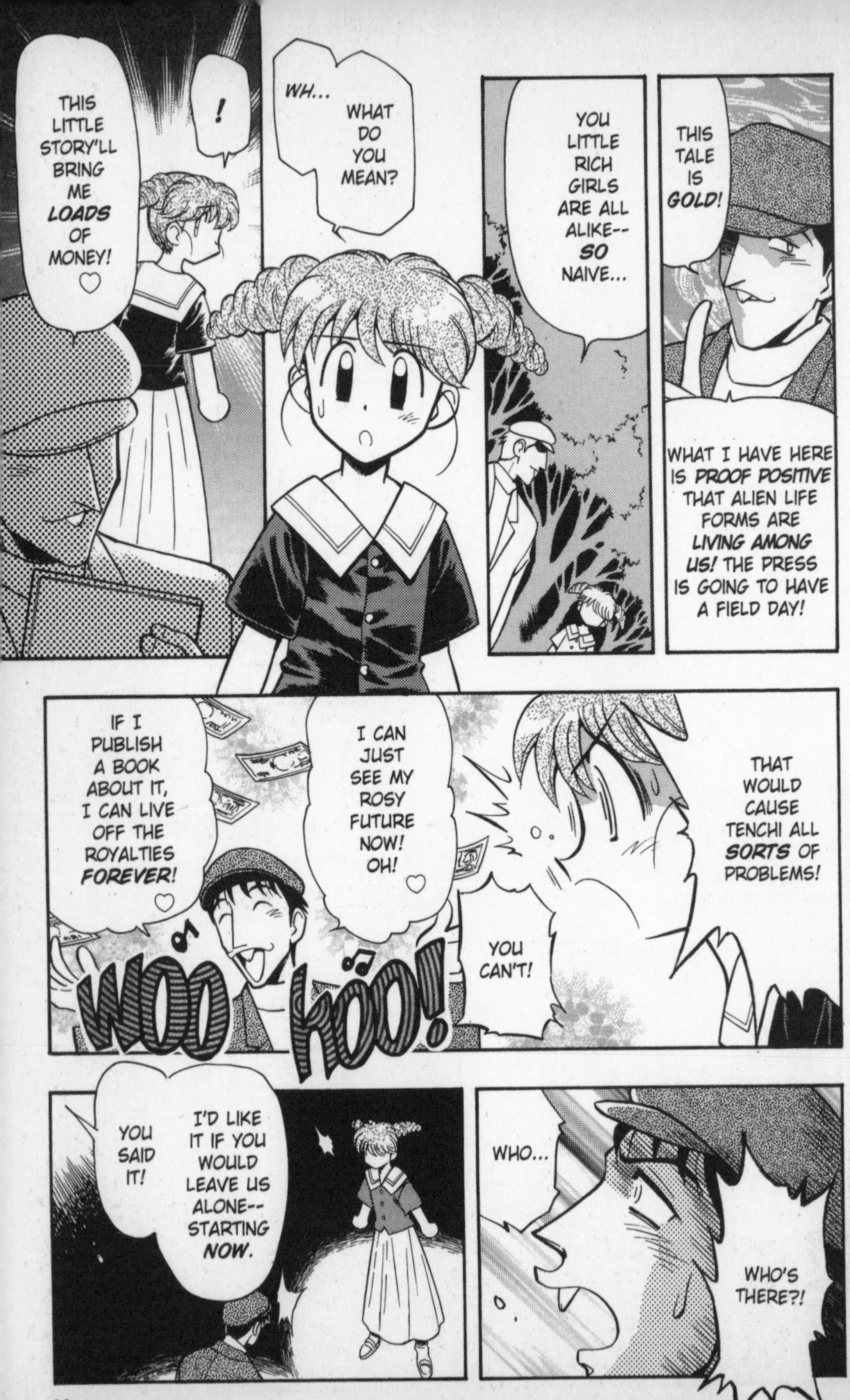
THIS LITTLE STORY'LL BRING ME LOADS OF MONEY! ♡
!
WH... WHAT DO YOU MEAN?
YOU LITTLE RICH GIRLS ARE ALL ALIKE-- SO NAIVE...
THIS TALE IS GOLD!
WHAT I HAVE HERE IS PROOF POSITIVE THAT ALIEN LIFE FORMS ARE LIVING AMONG US! THE PRESS IS GOING TO HAVE A FIELD DAY!
IF I PUBLISH A BOOK ABOUT IT, I CAN LIVE OFF THE ROYALTIES FOREVER! ♡
I CAN JUST SEE MY ROSY FUTURE NOW! OH! ♡
WOO HOO!
YOU CAN'T!
THAT WOULD CAUSE TENCHI ALL SORTS OF PROBLEMS!
YOU SAID IT!
I'D LIKE IT IF YOU WOULD LEAVE US ALONE-- STARTING NOW.
WHO...
WHO'S THERE?!

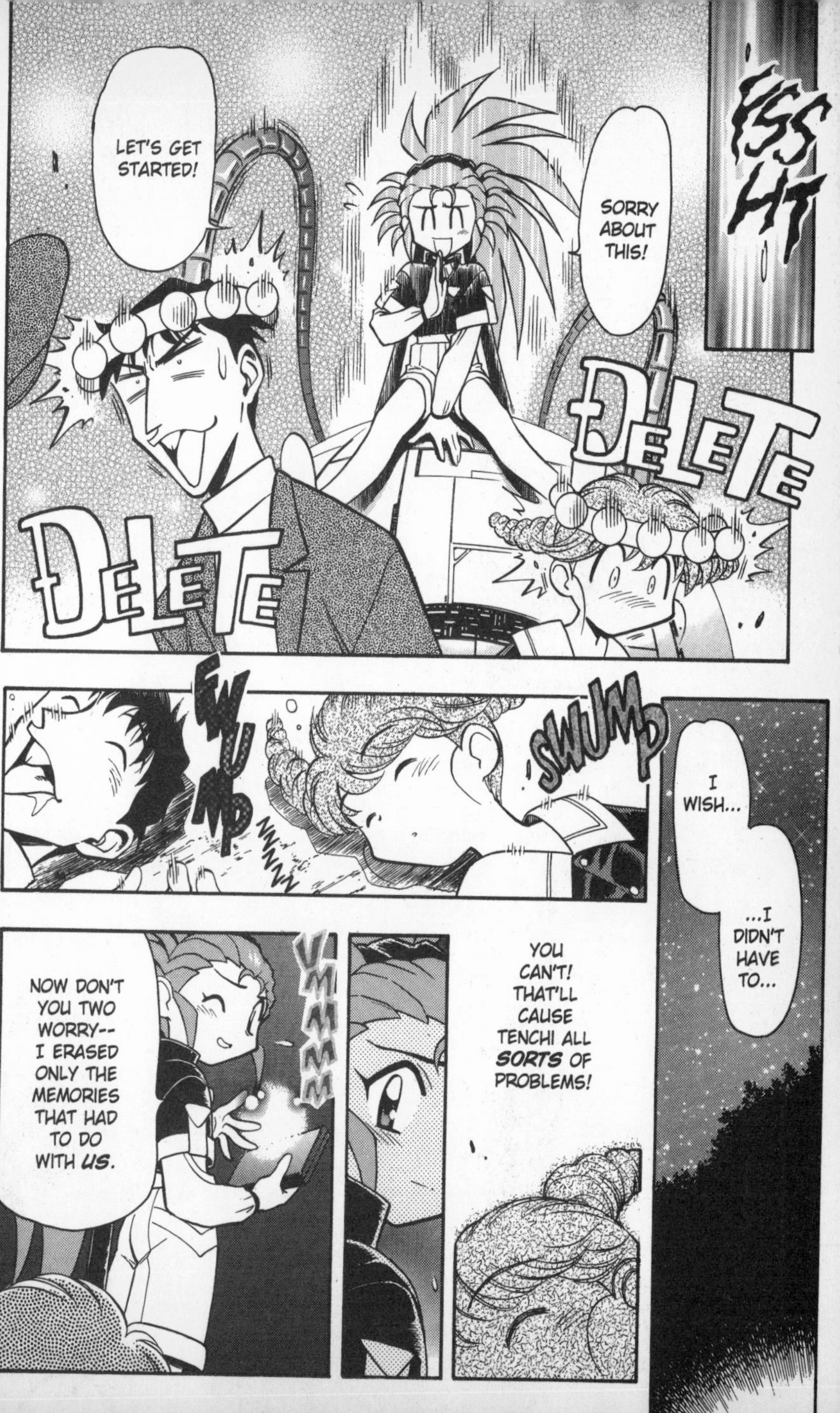
LET'S GET STARTED!
SORRY ABOUT THIS!
DELETE
DELETE
FISS HT
FWUMP
NNNNN
SWUMP
NOW DON'T YOU TWO WORRY-- I ERASED ONLY THE MEMORIES THAT HAD TO DO WITH *US*.
VMMMM
YOU CAN'T! THAT'LL CAUSE TENCHI ALL *SORTS* OF PROBLEMS!
I WISH...
...I DIDN'T HAVE TO...

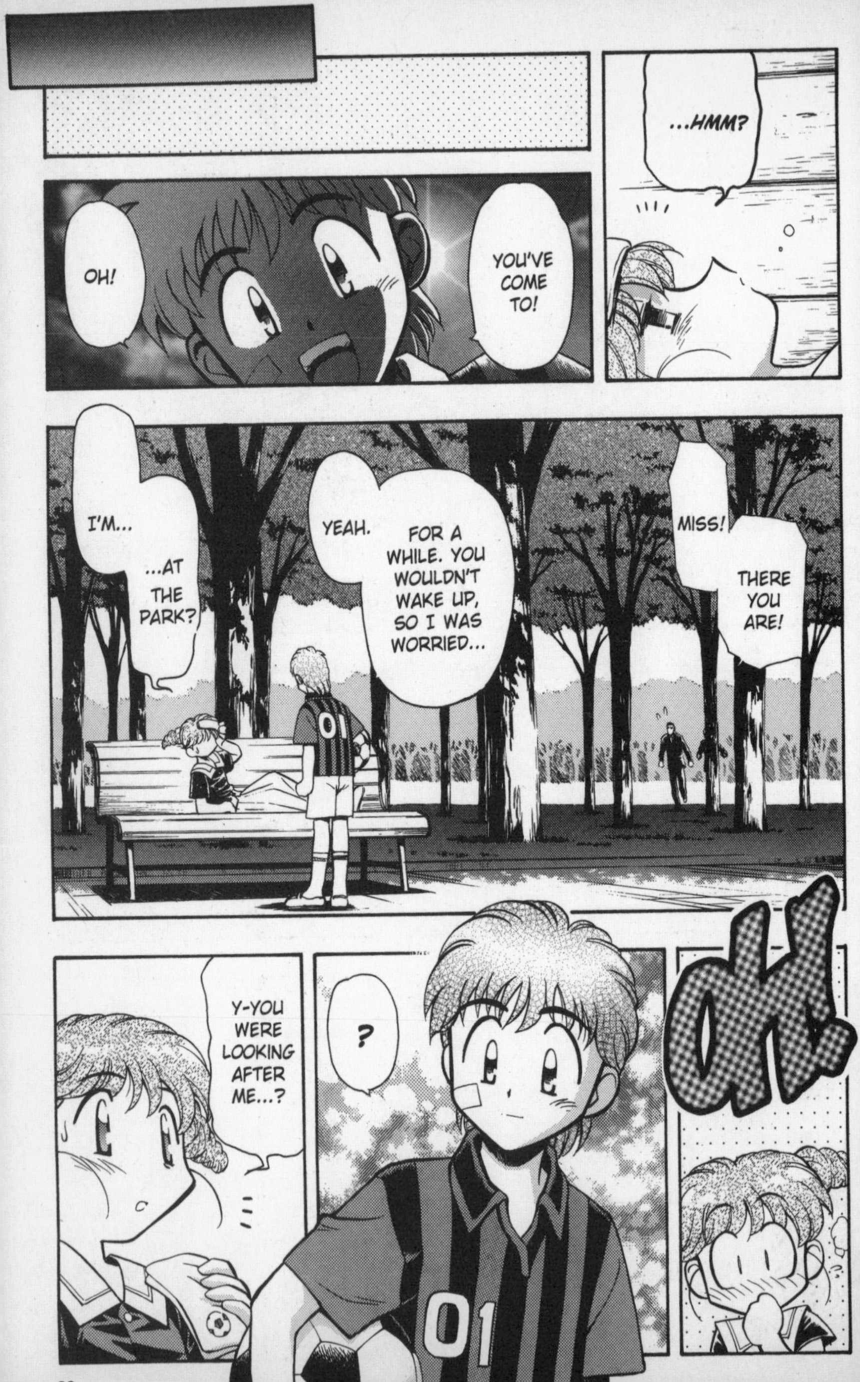
OH!
YOU'VE COME TO!
...HMM?
I'M...
...AT THE PARK?
YEAH.
FOR A WHILE. YOU WOULDN'T WAKE UP, SO I WAS WORRIED...
MISS!
THERE YOU ARE!
Y-YOU WERE LOOKING AFTER ME...?
?
OH!

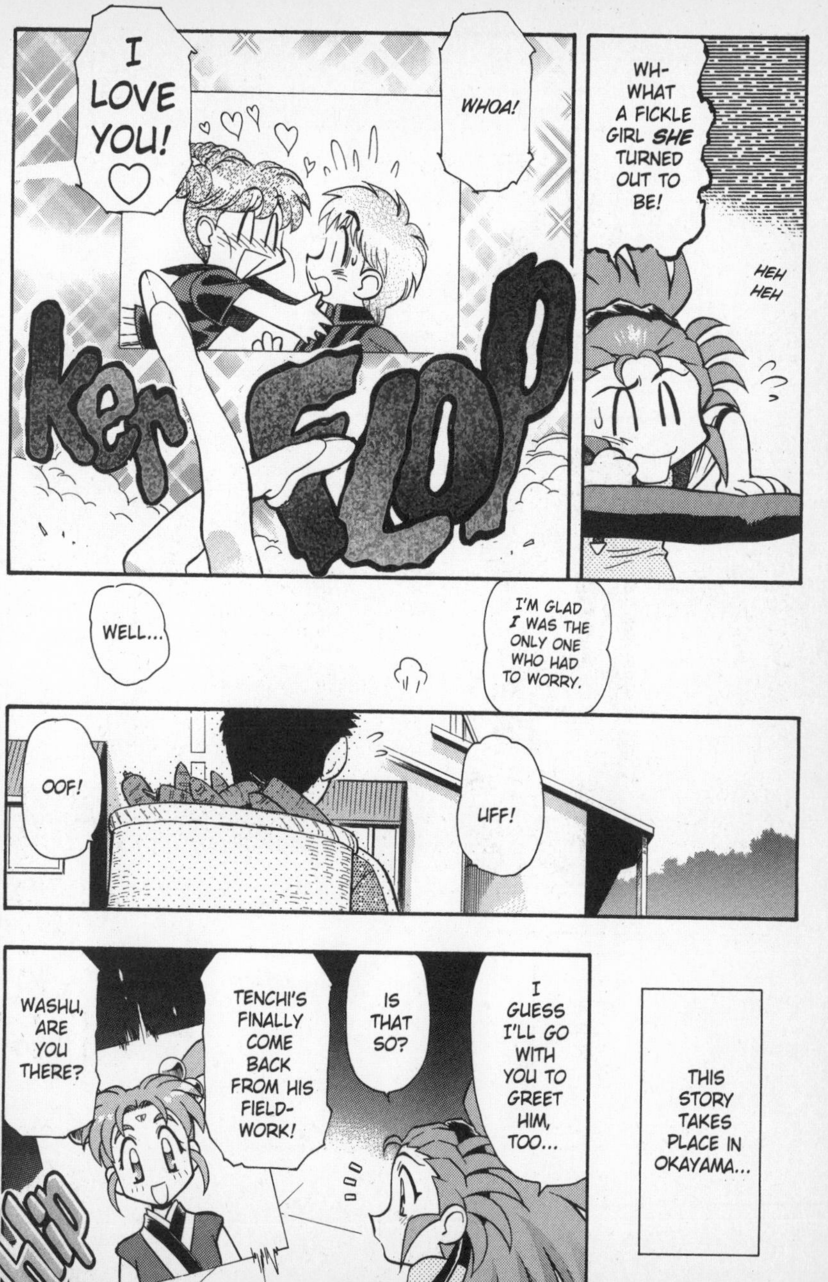

I LOVE YOU! ♡
WHOA!
kerFLOP
WH- WHAT A FICKLE GIRL SHE TURNED OUT TO BE!
HEH HEH
WELL...
I'M GLAD I WAS THE ONLY ONE WHO HAD TO WORRY.
OOF!
UFF!
WASHU, ARE YOU THERE?
TENCHI'S FINALLY COME BACK FROM HIS FIELD-WORK!
IS THAT SO?
I GUESS I'LL GO WITH YOU TO GREET HIM, TOO...
blip
THIS STORY TAKES PLACE IN OKAYAMA...

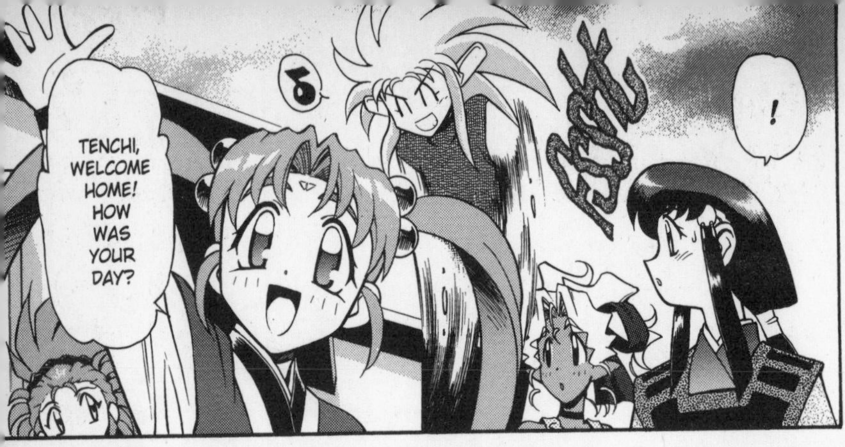
TENCHI, WELCOME HOME! HOW WAS YOUR DAY?

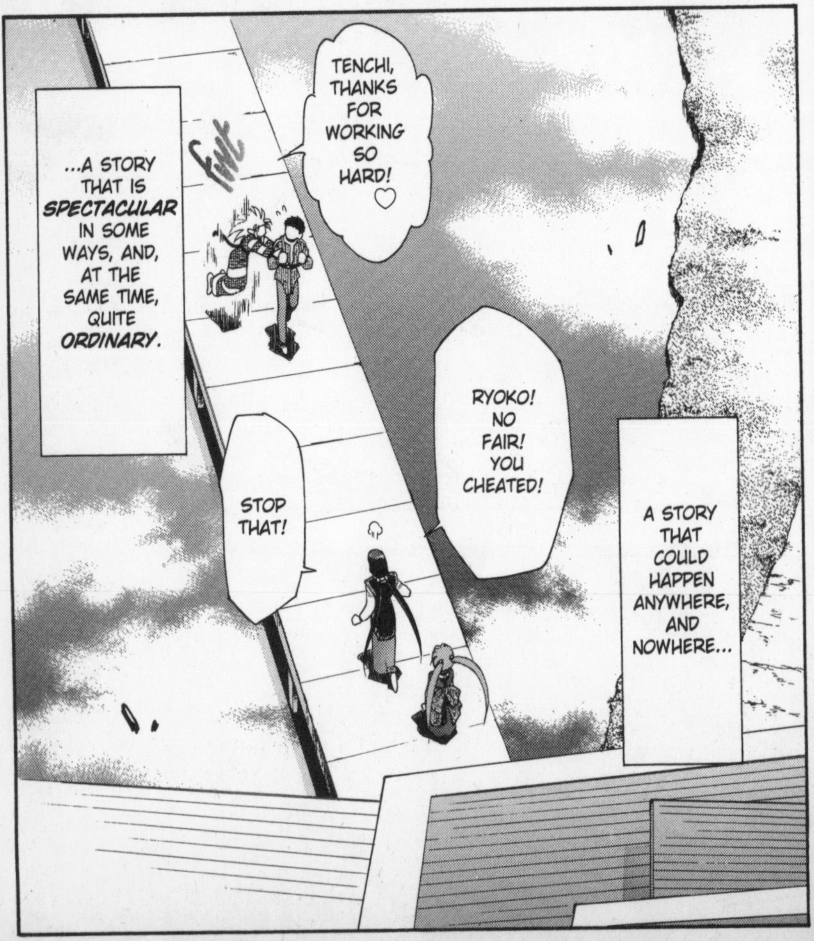
...A STORY THAT IS SPECTACULAR IN SOME WAYS, AND, AT THE SAME TIME, QUITE ORDINARY.
TENCHI, THANKS FOR WORKING SO HARD! ♡
RYOKO! NO FAIR! YOU CHEATED!
STOP THAT!
A STORY THAT COULD HAPPEN ANYWHERE, AND NOWHERE...

Chapter 2:
IDLE HANDS

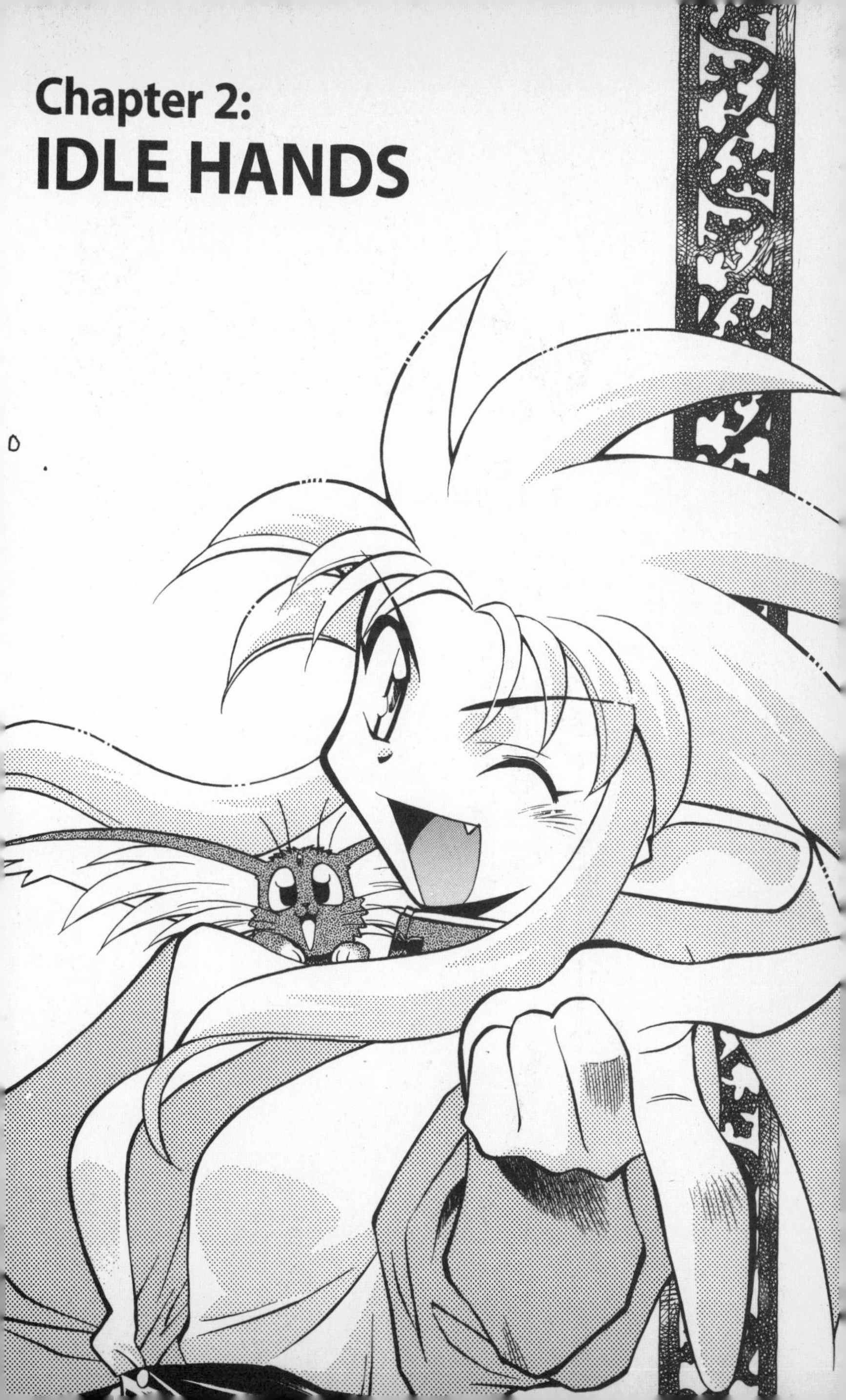

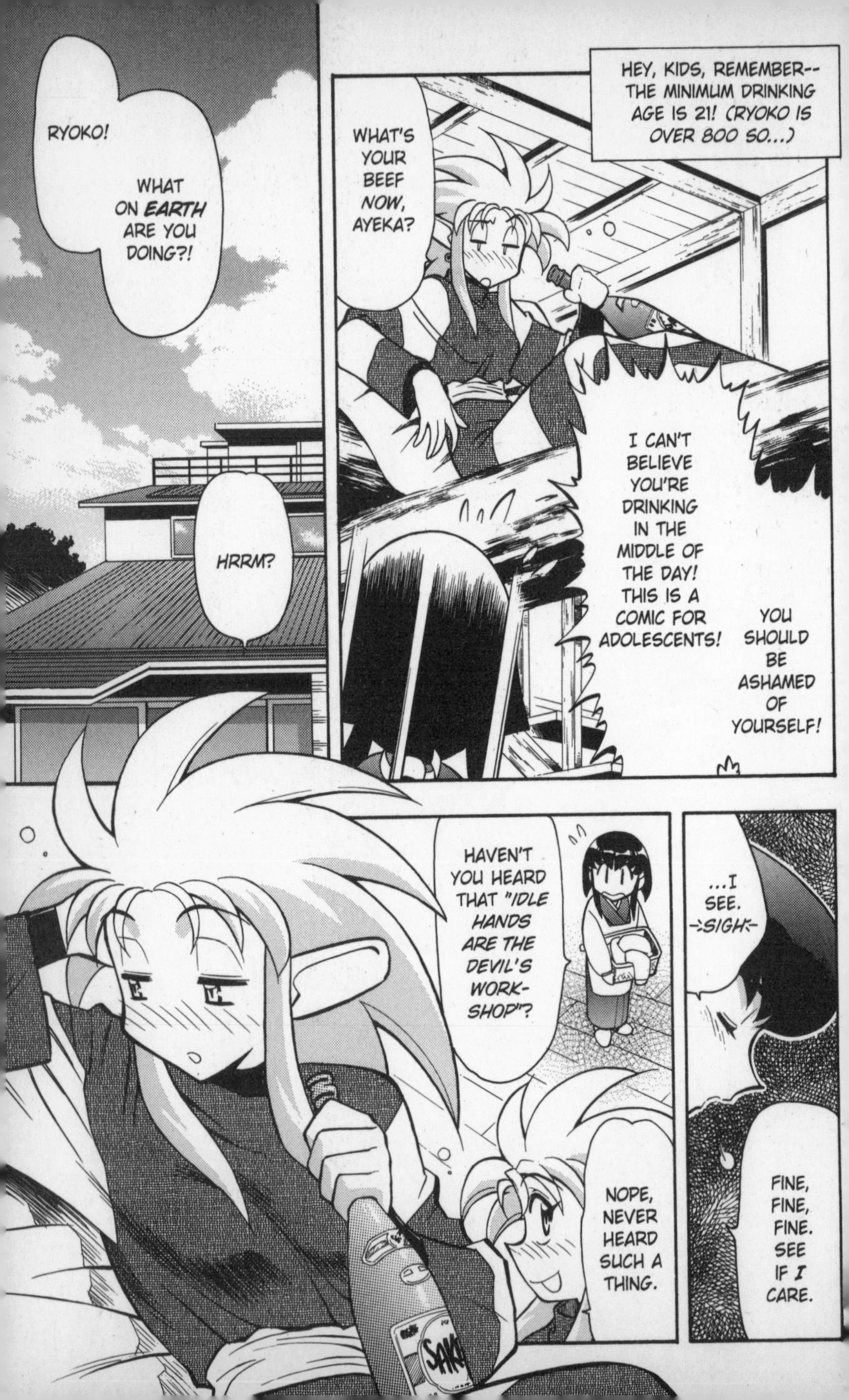
RYOKO!
WHAT ON EARTH ARE YOU DOING?!
HRRM?
HEY, KIDS, REMEMBER-- THE MINIMUM DRINKING AGE IS 21! (RYOKO IS OVER 800 SO...)
WHAT'S YOUR BEEF NOW, AYEKA?
I CAN'T BELIEVE YOU'RE DRINKING IN THE MIDDLE OF THE DAY! THIS IS A COMIC FOR ADOLESCENTS!
YOU SHOULD BE ASHAMED OF YOURSELF!
HAVEN'T YOU HEARD THAT "IDLE HANDS ARE THE DEVIL'S WORK-SHOP"?
NOPE, NEVER HEARD SUCH A THING.
...I SEE.
SIGH
FINE, FINE, FINE. SEE IF I CARE.
SAKE

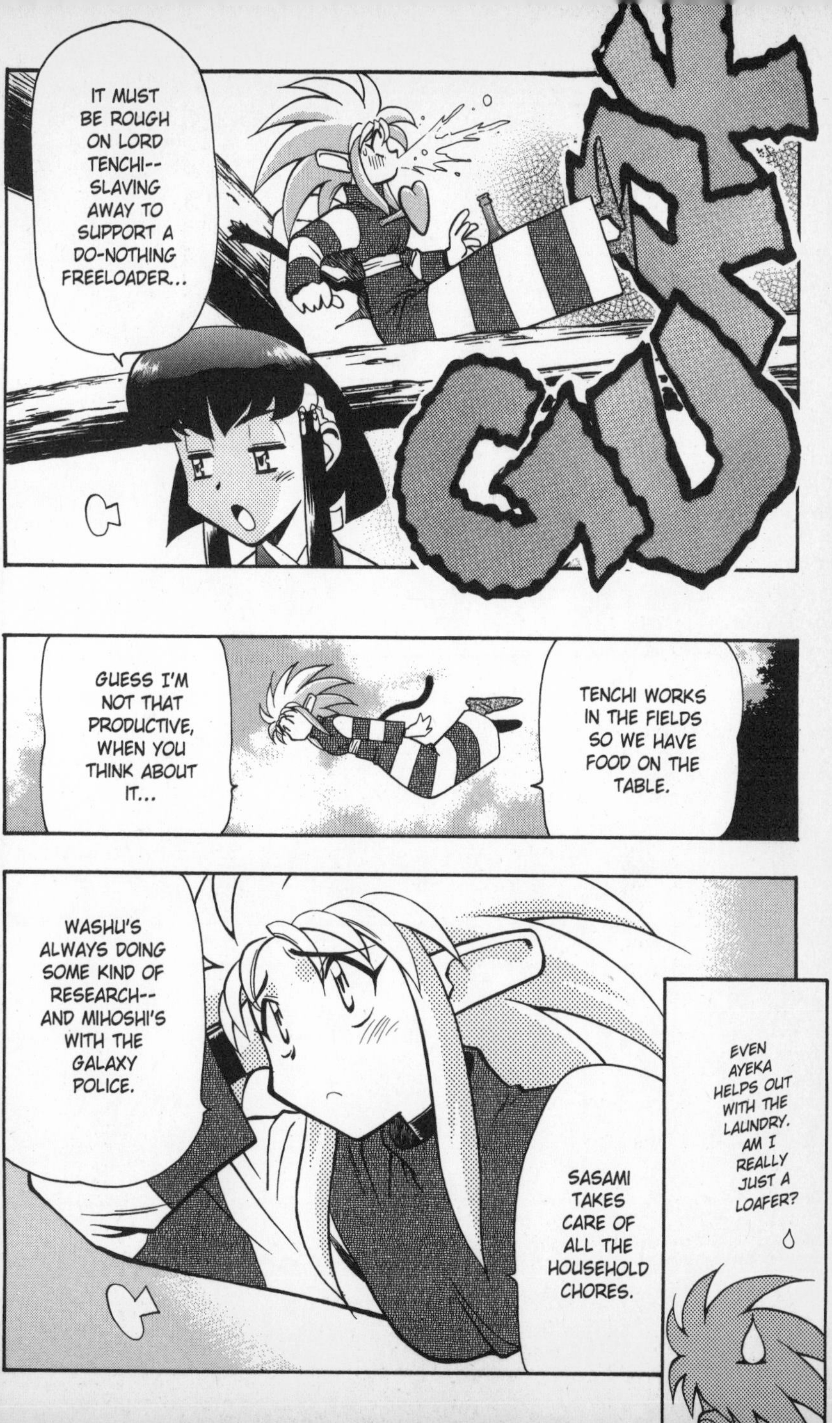
IT MUST BE ROUGH ON LORD TENCHI-- SLAVING AWAY TO SUPPORT A DO-NOTHING FREELOADER...
GU
GUESS I'M NOT THAT PRODUCTIVE, WHEN YOU THINK ABOUT IT...
TENCHI WORKS IN THE FIELDS SO WE HAVE FOOD ON THE TABLE.
WASHU'S ALWAYS DOING SOME KIND OF RESEARCH-- AND MIHOSHI'S WITH THE GALAXY POLICE.
SASAMI TAKES CARE OF ALL THE HOUSEHOLD CHORES.
EVEN AYEKA HELPS OUT WITH THE LAUNDRY. AM I REALLY JUST A LOAFER?

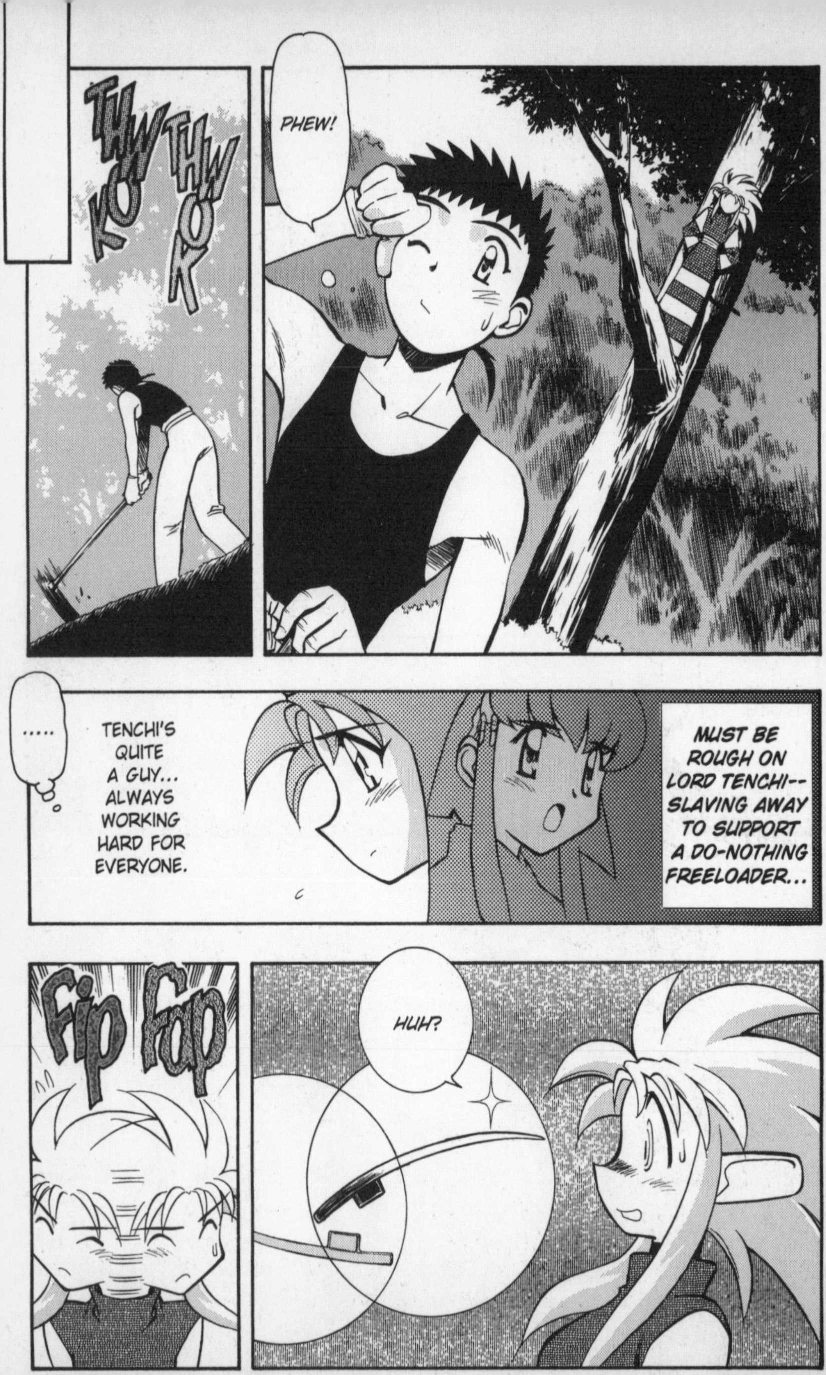
THWKO THWKOR
PHEW!
.....
TENCHI'S QUITE A GUY... ALWAYS WORKING HARD FOR EVERYONE.
MUST BE ROUGH ON LORD TENCHI-- SLAVING AWAY TO SUPPORT A DO-NOTHING FREELOADER...
Fip Fap
HUH?

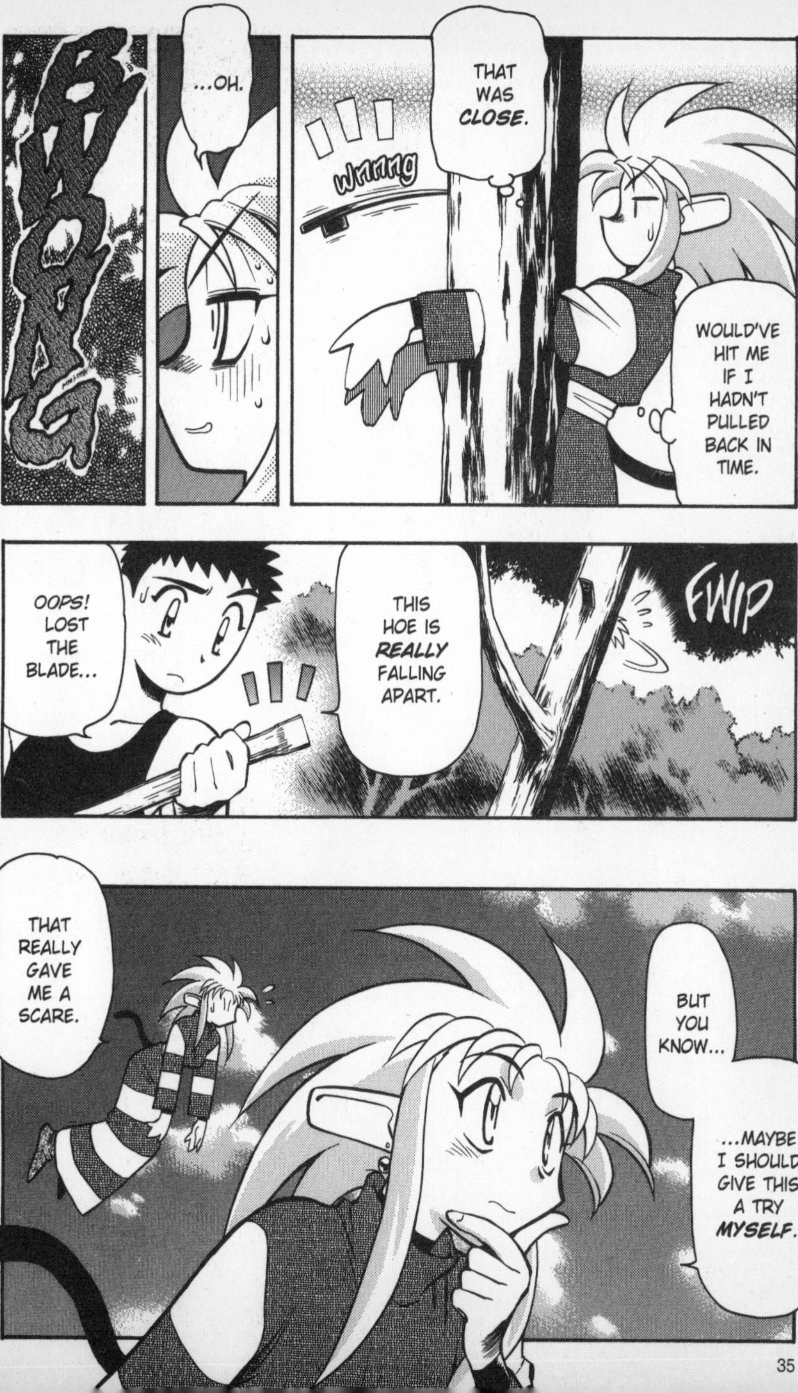
...OH.
THAT WAS CLOSE.
wnnng
WOULD'VE HIT ME IF I HADN'T PULLED BACK IN TIME.
OOPS! LOST THE BLADE...
THIS HOE IS REALLY FALLING APART.
FWIP
THAT REALLY GAVE ME A SCARE.
BUT YOU KNOW...
...MAYBE I SHOULD GIVE THIS A TRY MYSELF.

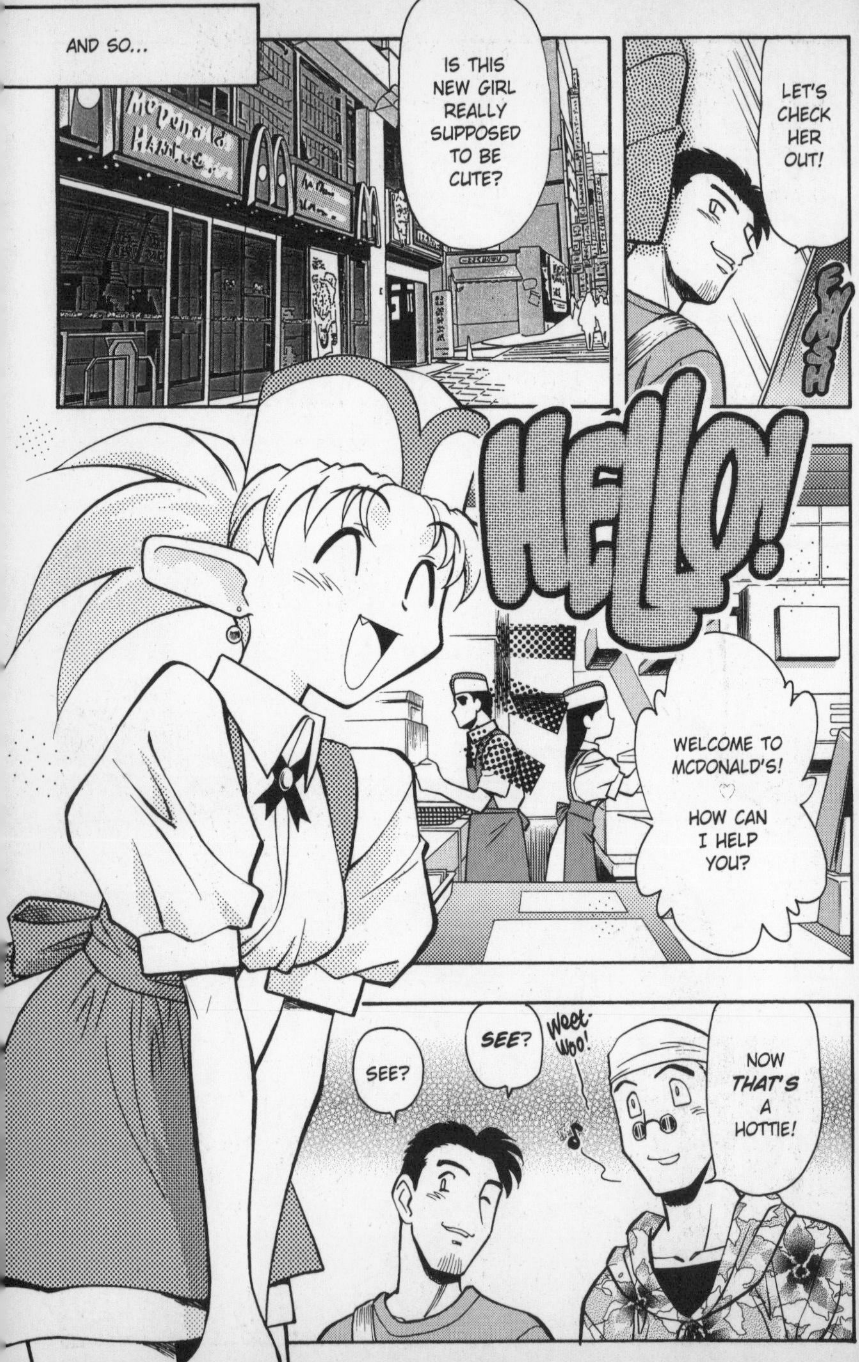
AND SO...
IS THIS NEW GIRL REALLY SUPPOSED TO BE CUTE?
LET'S CHECK HER OUT!
HELLO!
WELCOME TO MCDONALD'S! ♡ HOW CAN I HELP YOU?
SEE?
SEE?
Weet-Woo!
NOW *THAT'S* A HOTTIE!

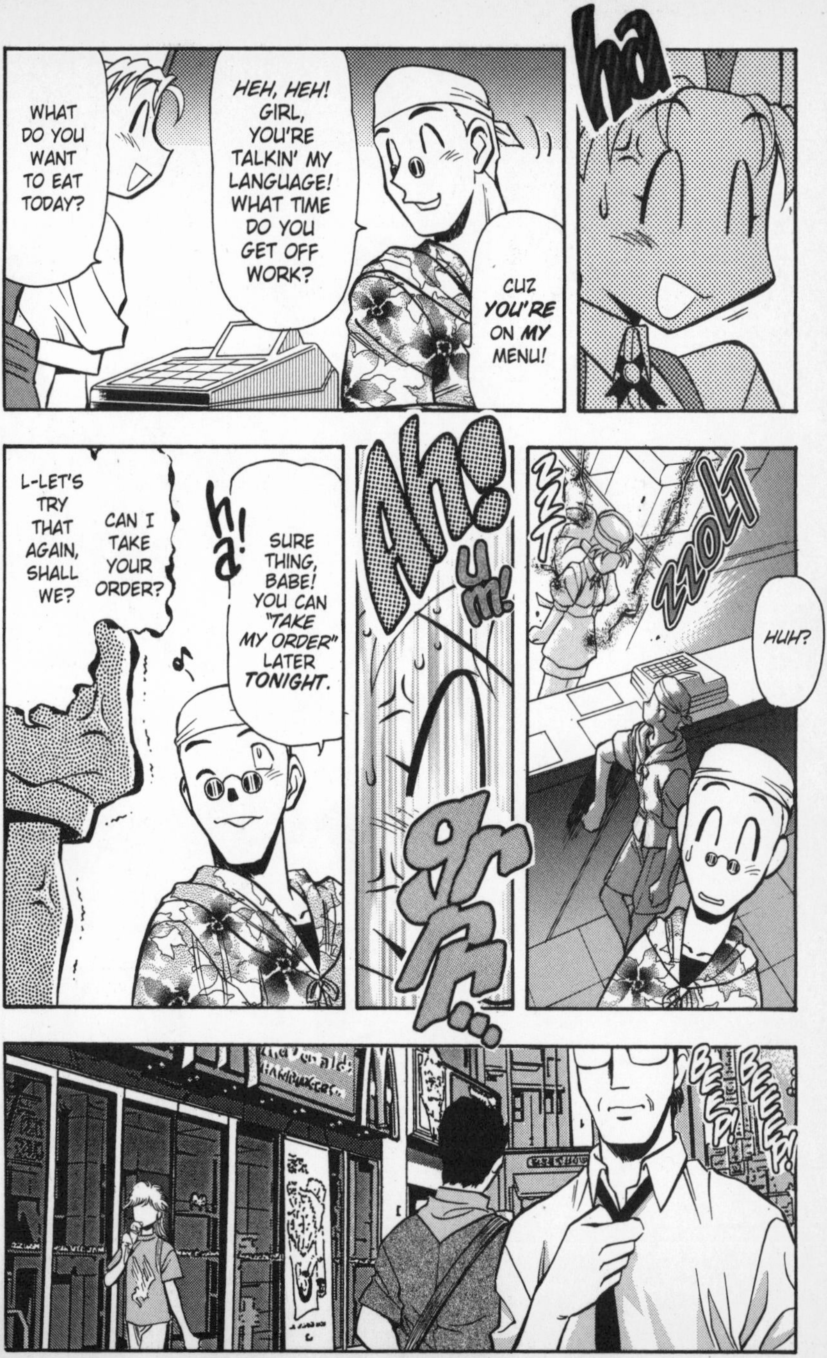
WHAT DO YOU WANT TO EAT TODAY?
HEH, HEH! GIRL, YOU'RE TALKIN' MY LANGUAGE! WHAT TIME DO YOU GET OFF WORK?
CUZ YOU'RE ON MY MENU!
ha
L-LET'S TRY THAT AGAIN, SHALL WE?
CAN I TAKE YOUR ORDER?
ha!
SURE THING, BABE! YOU CAN "TAKE MY ORDER" LATER TONIGHT.
Ah!
um!
grr...
ZZZT
ZZOLT
HUH?
BEEP!
BEEEP!

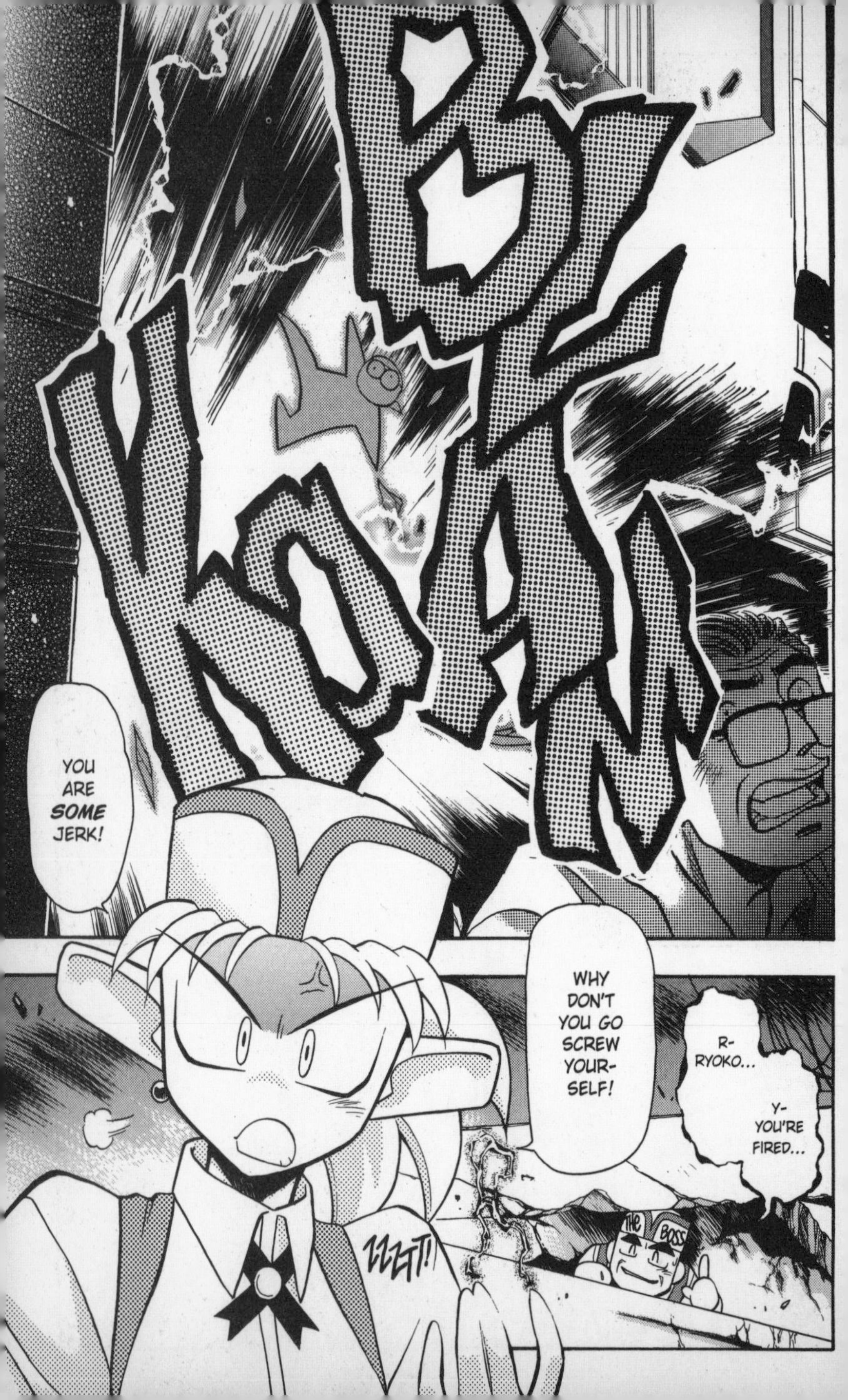
YOU ARE *SOME* JERK!
WHY DON'T YOU GO SCREW YOUR-SELF!
R-RYOKO...
Y-YOU'RE FIRED...
ZZZZT!
THE BOSS

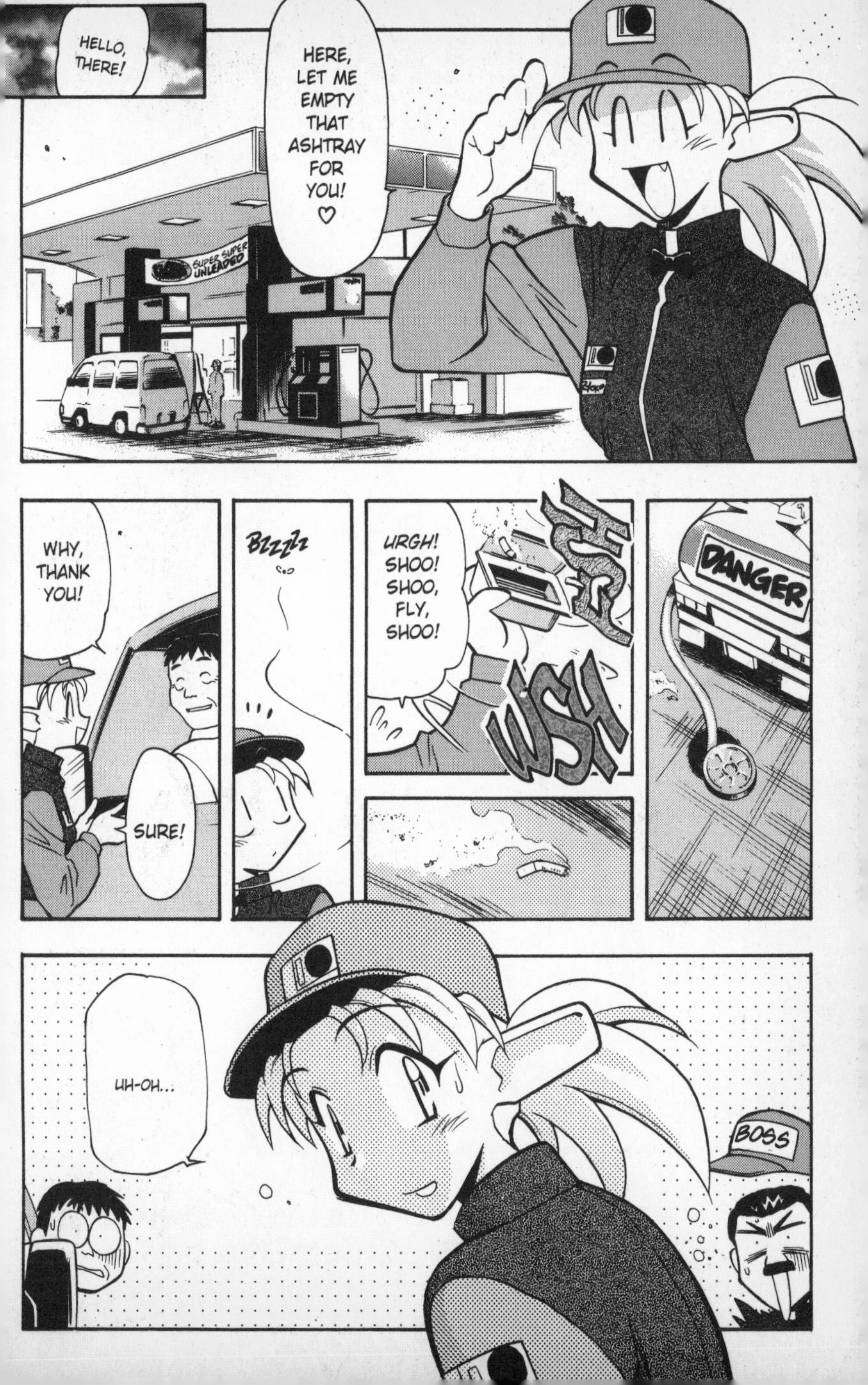
HELLO, THERE!
HERE, LET ME EMPTY THAT ASHTRAY FOR YOU! ♡
SUPER SUPER UNLEADED
WHY, THANK YOU!
SURE!
BZZZZZ
URGH! SHOO! SHOO, FLY, SHOO!
WSH
DANGER
UH-OH...
BOSS

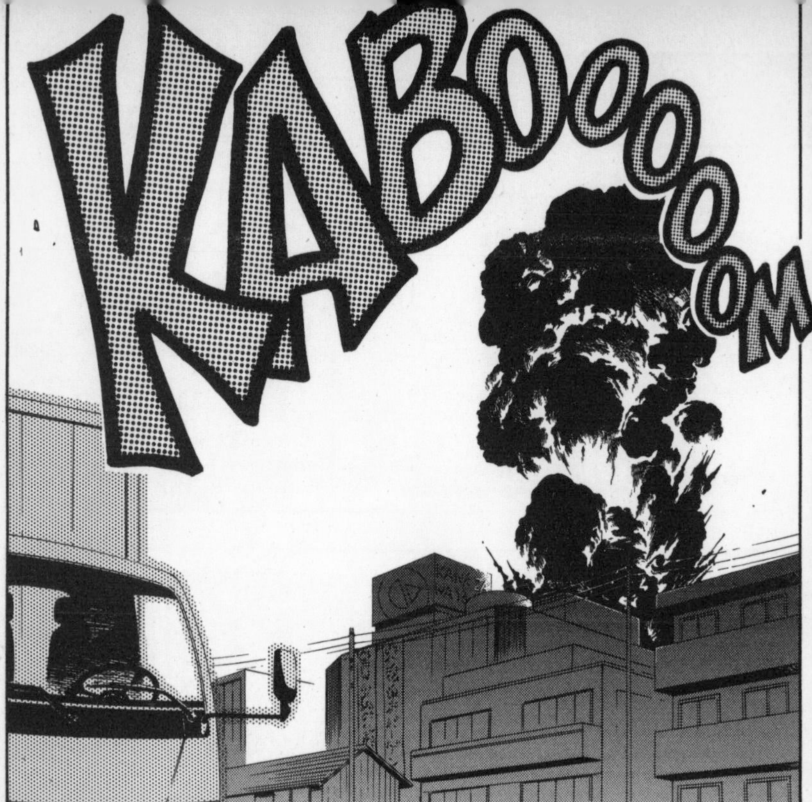
KABOOOOOOM

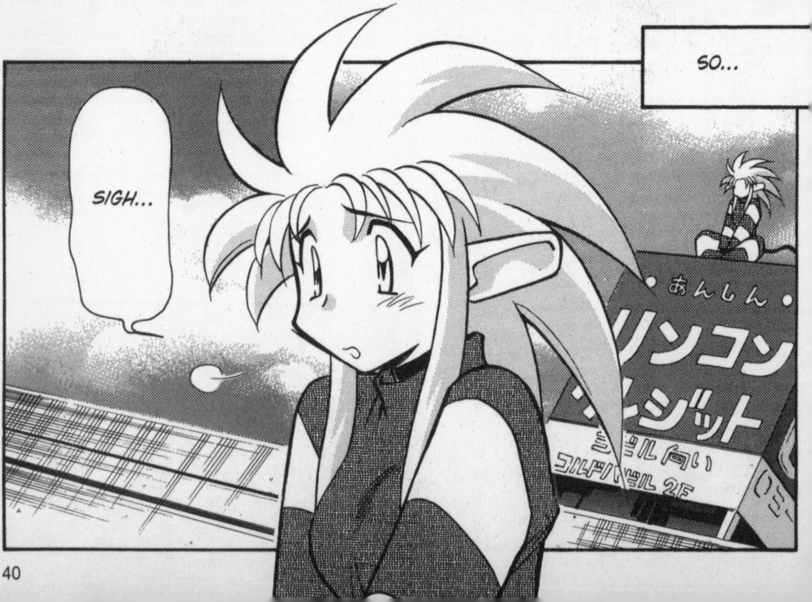
SO...
SIGH...
あんしん
リンコン

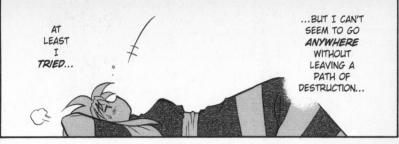

AT LEAST I *TRIED...*

...BUT I CAN'T SEEM TO GO *ANYWHERE* WITHOUT LEAVING A PATH OF DESTRUCTION...

KAN! THIS IS *RECKLESS!* DON'T DO IT!

I'M FINE! DON'T MIND ME!

NO WAY! YOU HAVE A 102° FEVER!

WINDOW WASHING A HIGH-RISE IS DANGEROUS BUSINESS!

IF I TAKE A DAY OFF, I'LL GET FIRED.

MY GRAND KID...

I MADE A PRO-MISE!

KOFF

KOFF

JUST LET ME GO!

swing

HUH...?

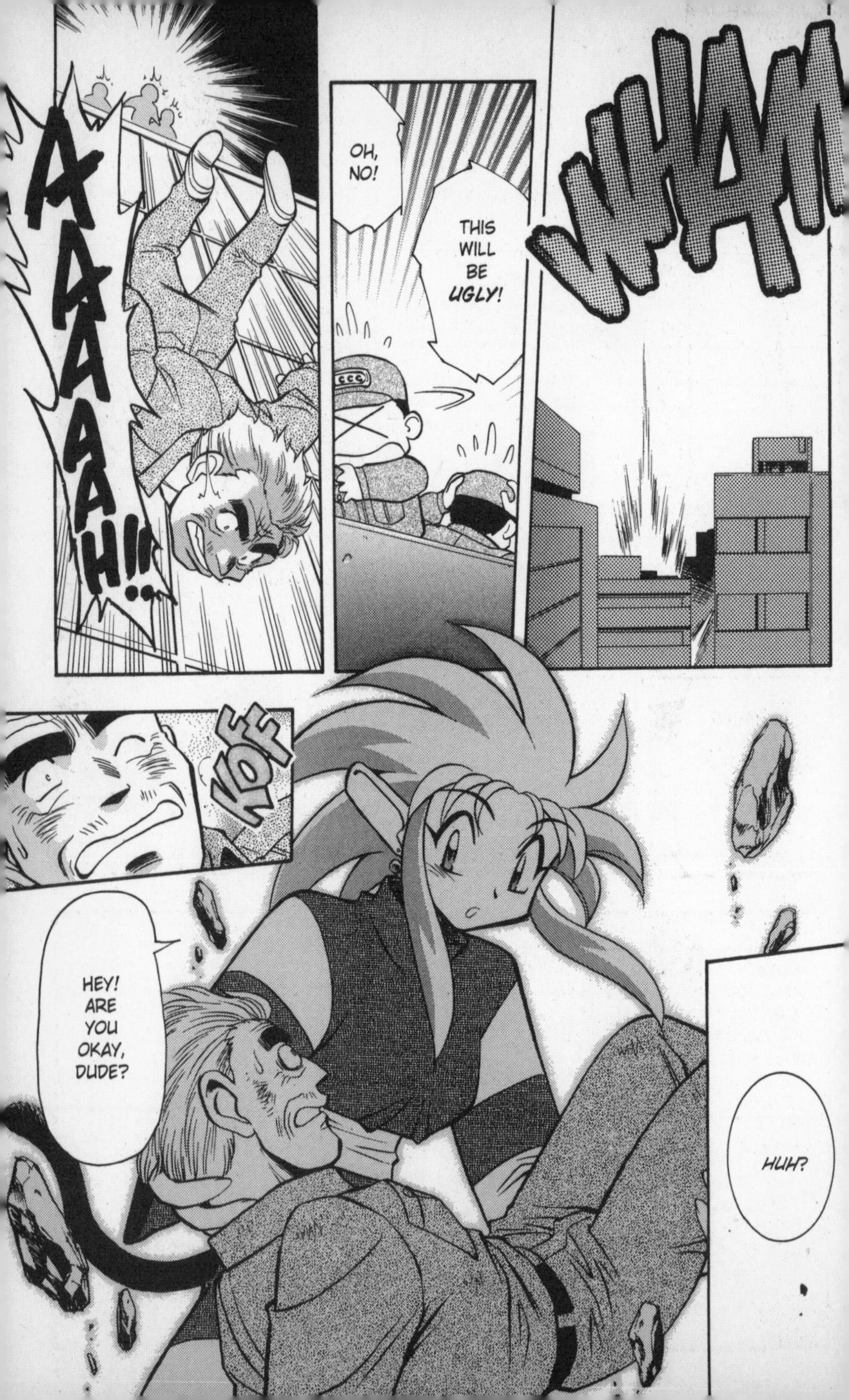
AAAAAH!!
OH, NO!
THIS WILL BE *UGLY*!
WHAM
KOF
HEY! ARE YOU OKAY, DUDE?
HUH?

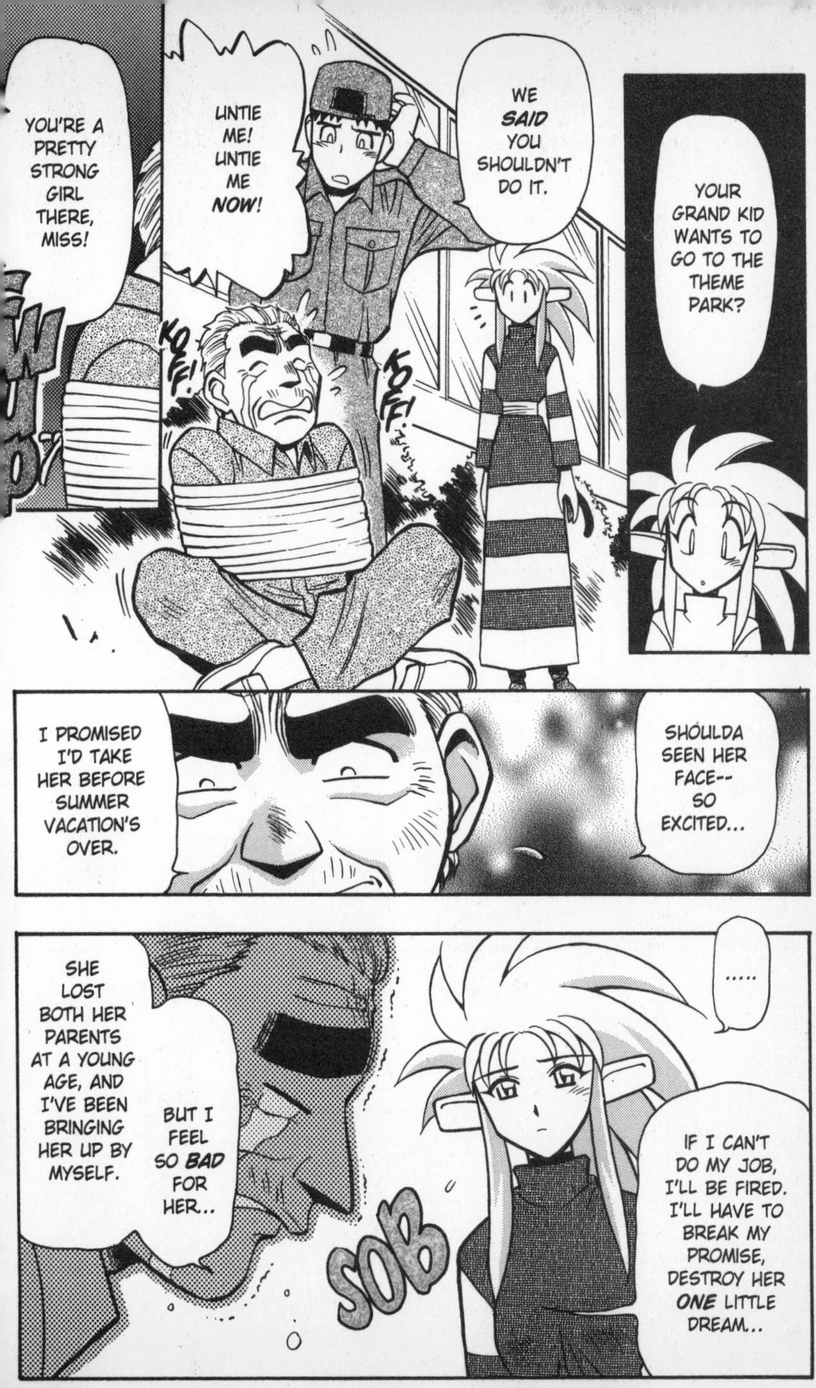
YOU'RE A PRETTY STRONG GIRL THERE, MISS!
UNTIE ME! UNTIE ME NOW!
WE SAID YOU SHOULDN'T DO IT.
KOFF!
KOFF!
YOUR GRAND KID WANTS TO GO TO THE THEME PARK?
I PROMISED I'D TAKE HER BEFORE SUMMER VACATION'S OVER.
SHOULDA SEEN HER FACE-- SO EXCITED...
SHE LOST BOTH HER PARENTS AT A YOUNG AGE, AND I'VE BEEN BRINGING HER UP BY MYSELF.
BUT I FEEL SO BAD FOR HER...
SOB
.....
IF I CAN'T DO MY JOB, I'LL BE FIRED. I'LL HAVE TO BREAK MY PROMISE, DESTROY HER ONE LITTLE DREAM...

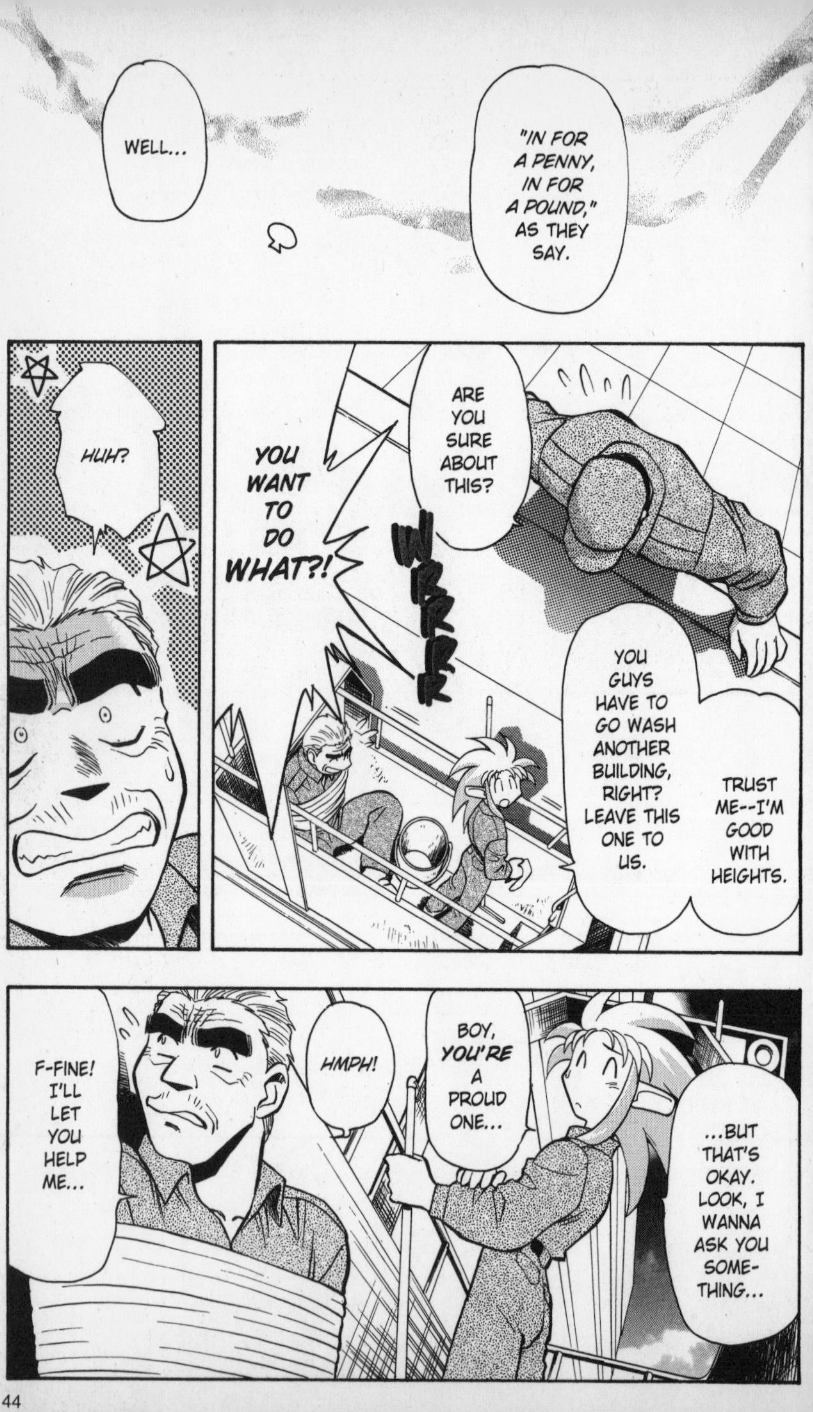
WELL...
"IN FOR A PENNY, IN FOR A POUND," AS THEY SAY.
HUH?
YOU WANT TO DO WHAT?!
ARE YOU SURE ABOUT THIS?
YOU GUYS HAVE TO GO WASH ANOTHER BUILDING, RIGHT? LEAVE THIS ONE TO US.
TRUST ME--I'M GOOD WITH HEIGHTS.
F-FINE! I'LL LET YOU HELP ME...
HMPH!
BOY, YOU'RE A PROUD ONE...
...BUT THAT'S OKAY. LOOK, I WANNA ASK YOU SOME-THING...

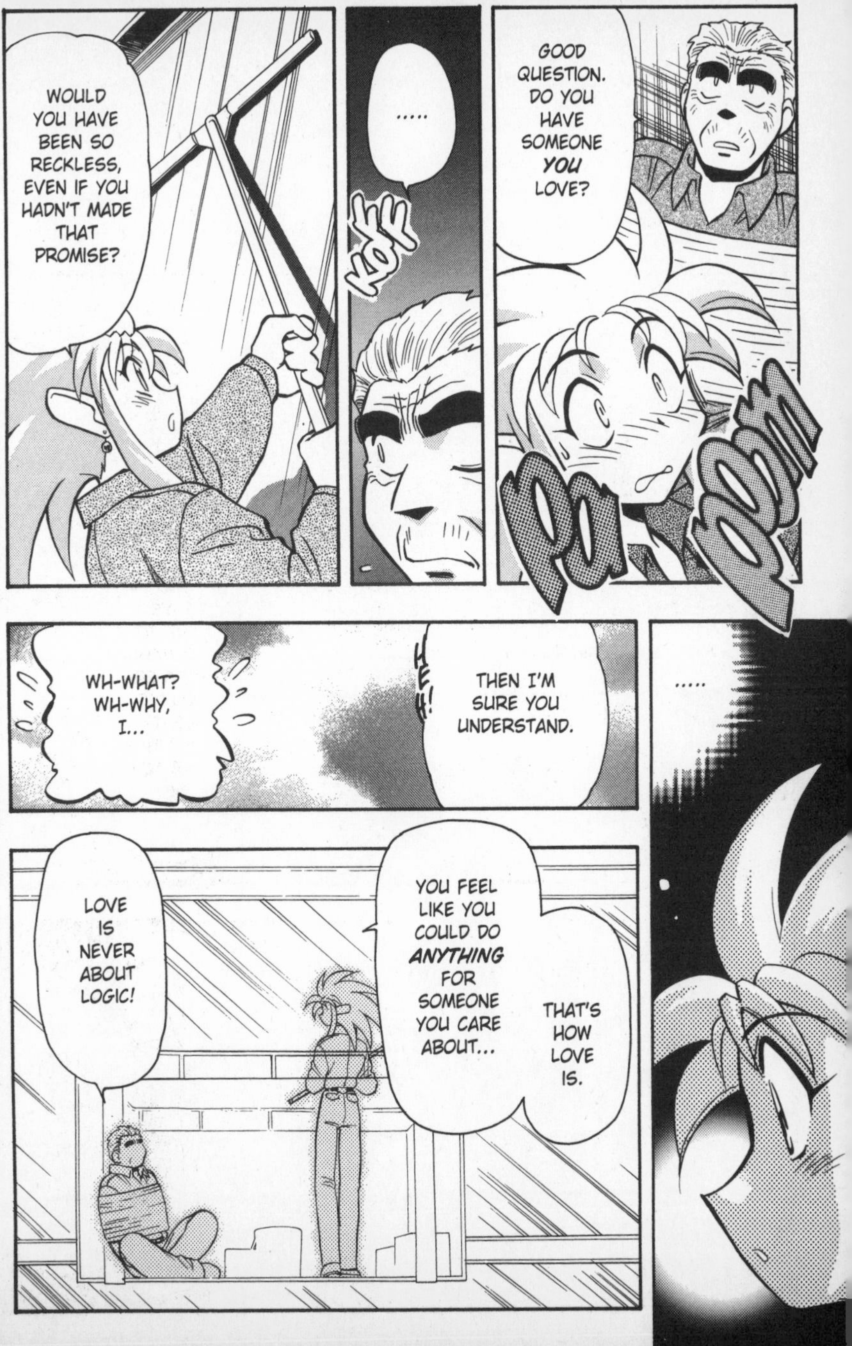
WOULD YOU HAVE BEEN SO RECKLESS, EVEN IF YOU HADN'T MADE THAT PROMISE?
.....
KOFF
GOOD QUESTION. DO YOU HAVE SOMEONE YOU LOVE?
PA-BOOM
WH-WHAT? WH-WHY, I...
HEH!
THEN I'M SURE YOU UNDERSTAND.
LOVE IS NEVER ABOUT LOGIC!
YOU FEEL LIKE YOU COULD DO ANYTHING FOR SOMEONE YOU CARE ABOUT...
THAT'S HOW LOVE IS.
.....

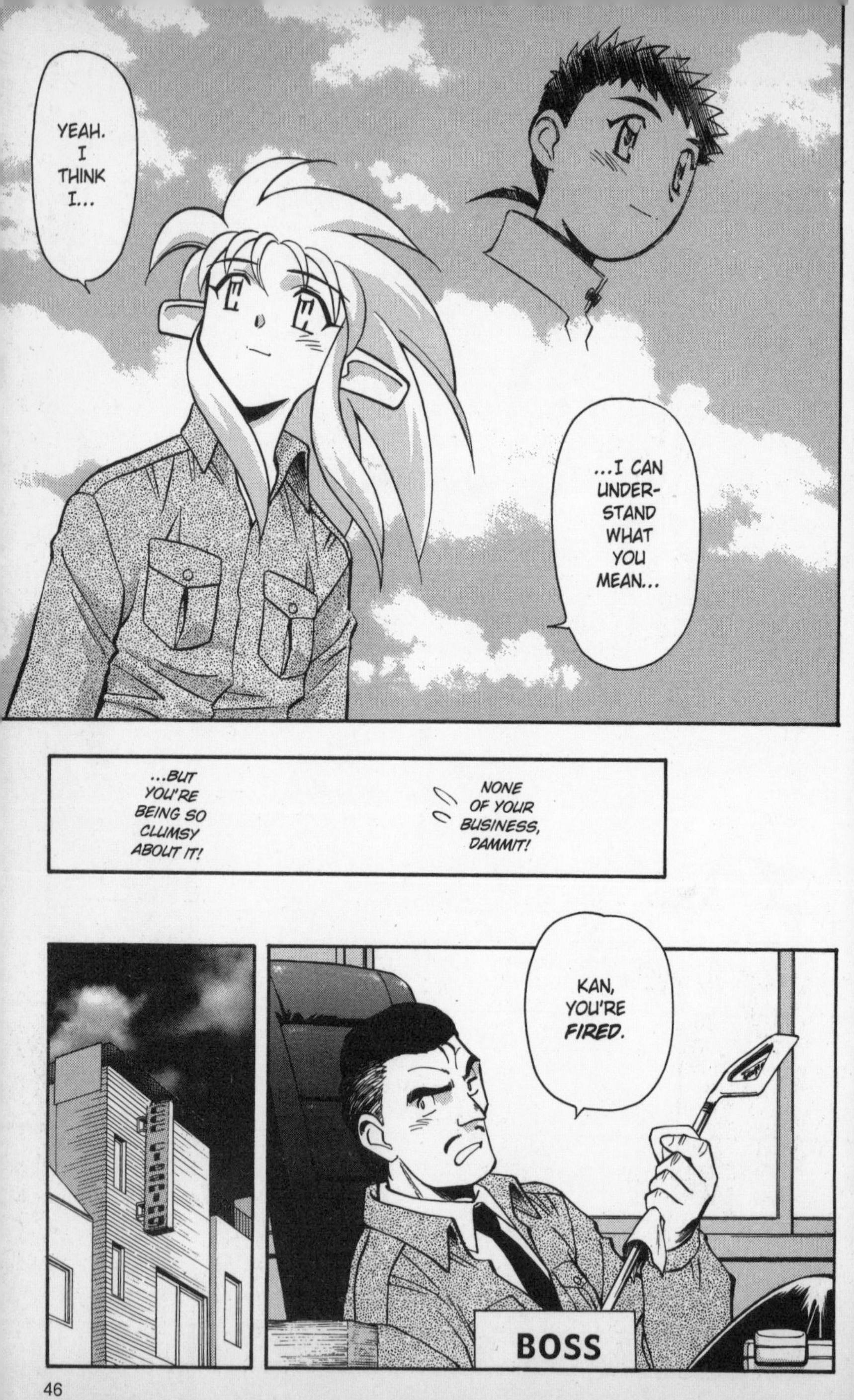
YEAH. I THINK I...
...I CAN UNDERSTAND WHAT YOU MEAN...
...BUT YOU'RE BEING SO CLUMSY ABOUT IT!
NONE OF YOUR BUSINESS, DAMMIT!
KAN, YOU'RE *FIRED*.
BOSS

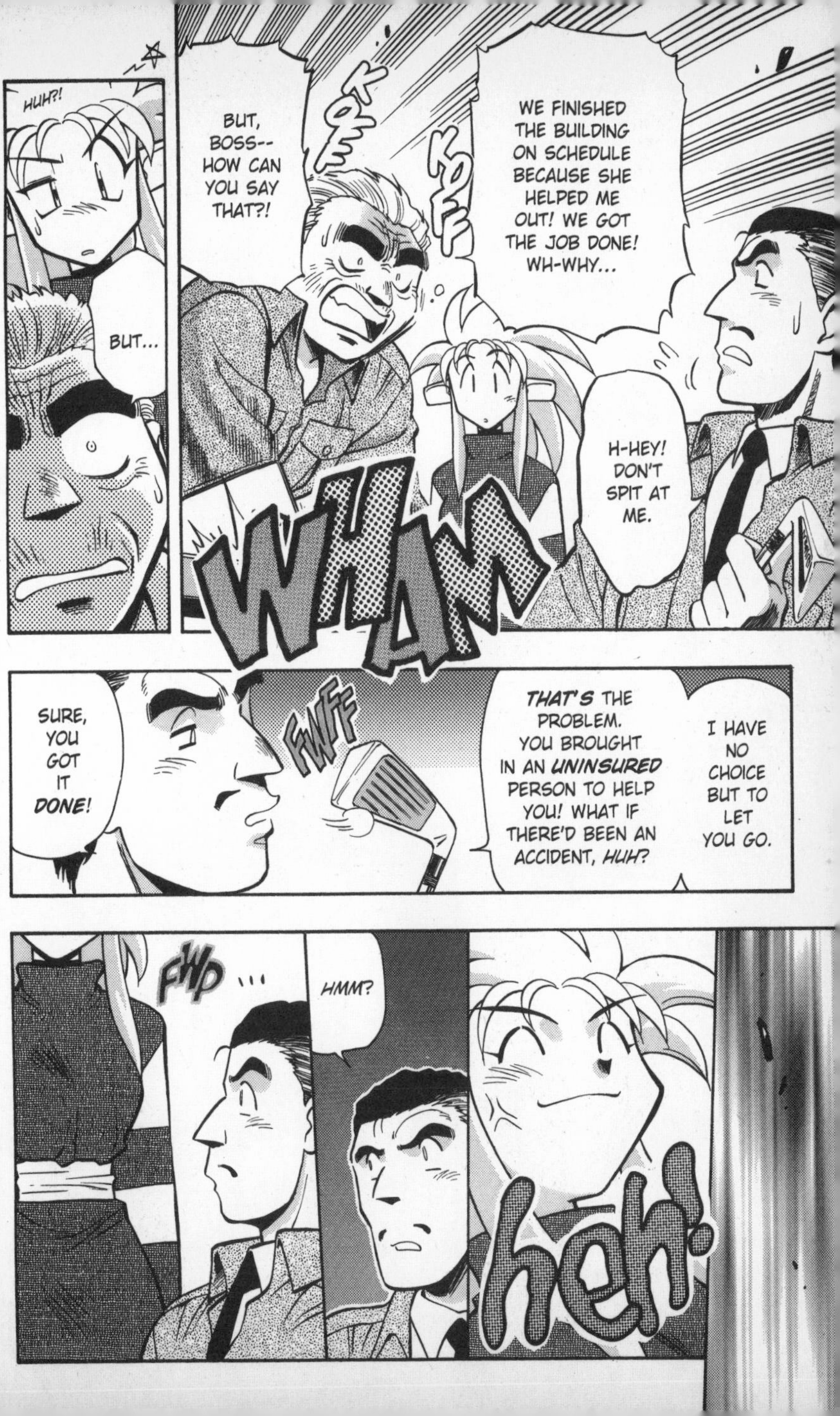
HUH?!
BUT...
BUT, BOSS-- HOW CAN YOU SAY THAT?!
KOF
KOF
WE FINISHED THE BUILDING ON SCHEDULE BECAUSE SHE HELPED ME OUT! WE GOT THE JOB DONE! WH-WHY...
H-HEY! DON'T SPIT AT ME.
WHAM
SURE, YOU GOT IT DONE!
FWFF
THAT'S THE PROBLEM. YOU BROUGHT IN AN UNINSURED PERSON TO HELP YOU! WHAT IF THERE'D BEEN AN ACCIDENT, HUH?
I HAVE NO CHOICE BUT TO LET YOU GO.
FWP ...
HMM?
heh!

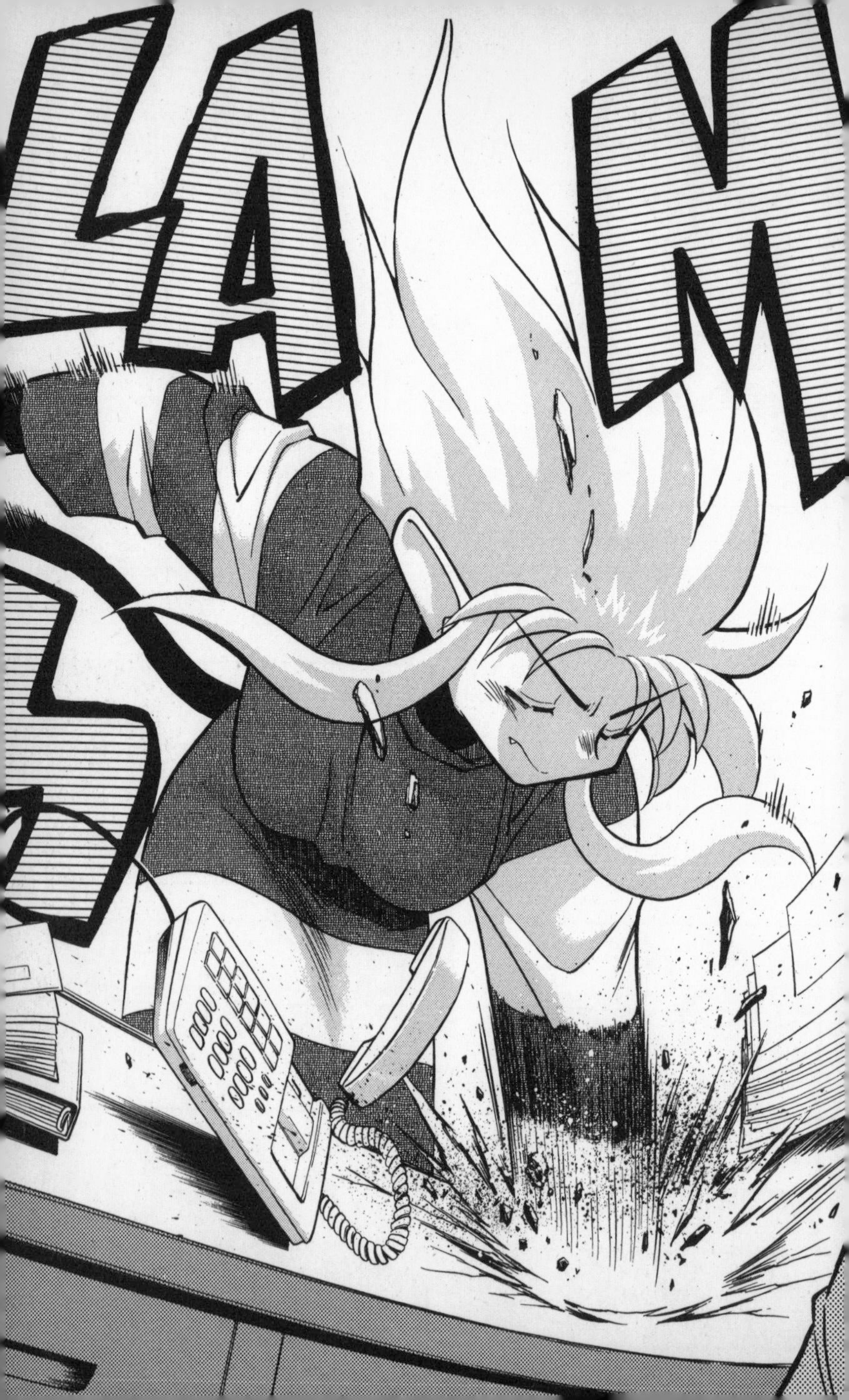
SLAM

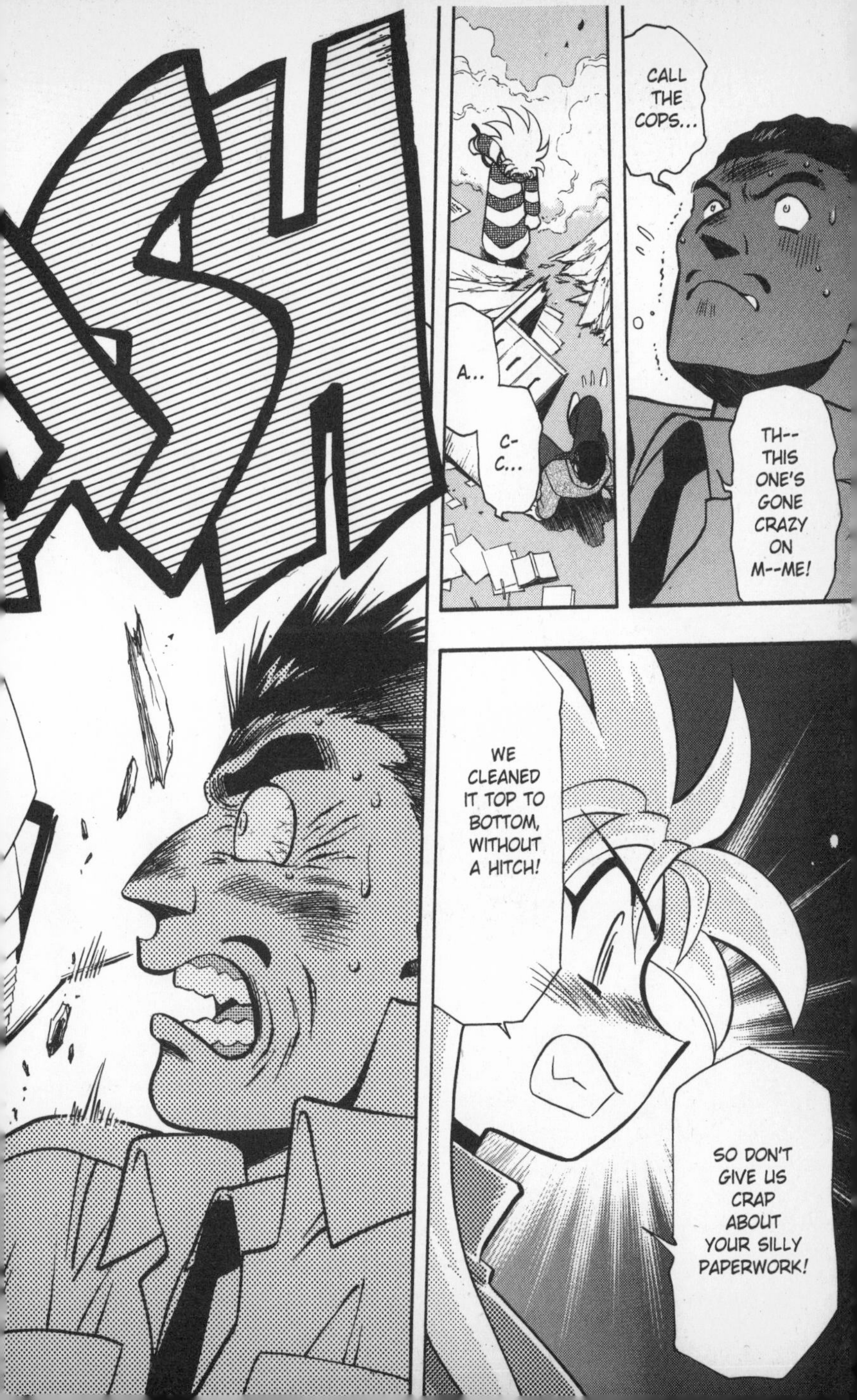
A...
C- C...
CALL THE COPS...
TH--THIS ONE'S GONE CRAZY ON M--ME!
WE CLEANED IT TOP TO BOTTOM, WITHOUT A HITCH!
SO DON'T GIVE US CRAP ABOUT YOUR SILLY PAPERWORK!

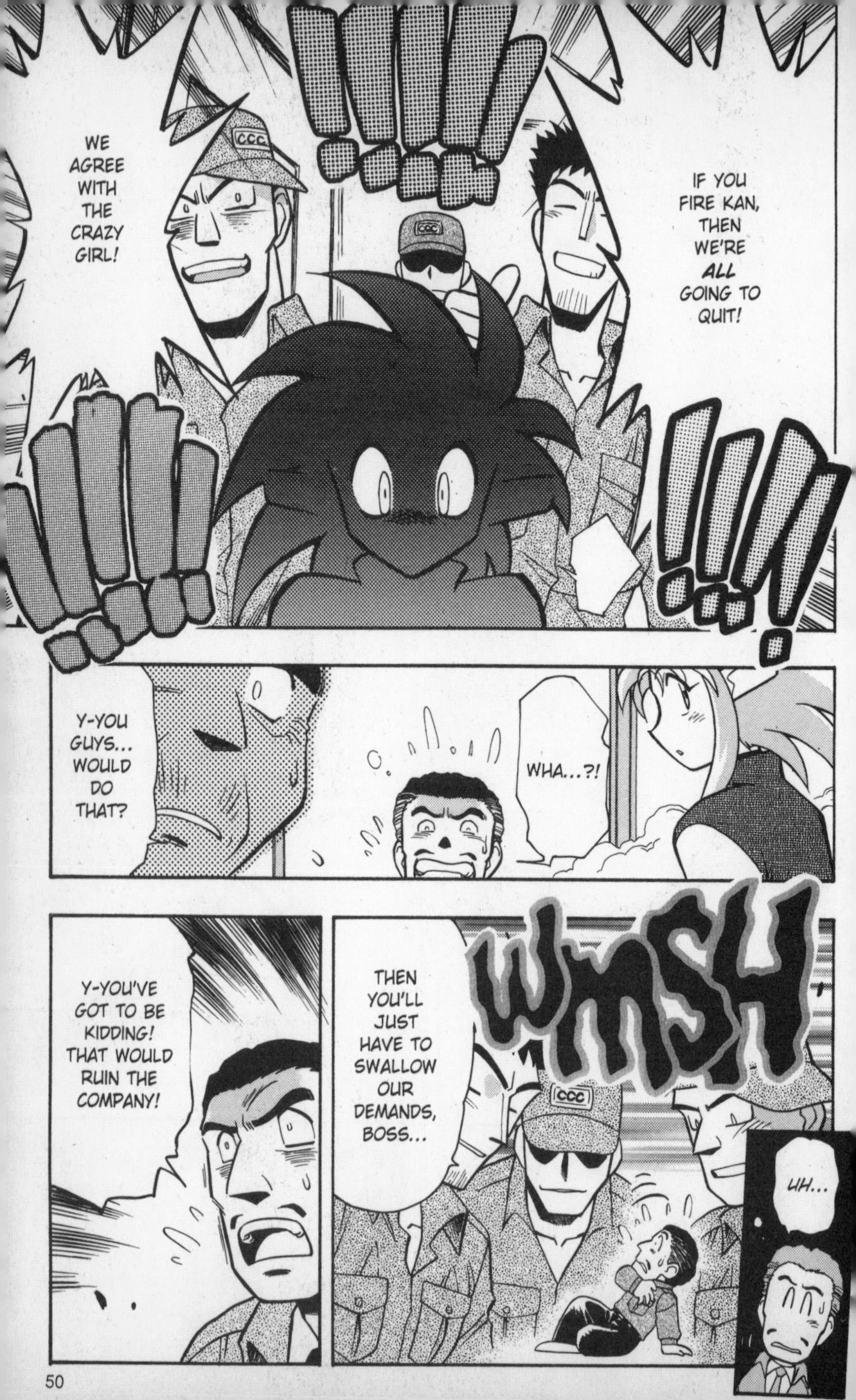
WE AGREE WITH THE CRAZY GIRL!
IF YOU FIRE KAN, THEN WE'RE ALL GOING TO QUIT!
Y-YOU GUYS... WOULD DO THAT?
WHA...?!
Y-YOU'VE GOT TO BE KIDDING! THAT WOULD RUIN THE COMPANY!
THEN YOU'LL JUST HAVE TO SWALLOW OUR DEMANDS, BOSS...
WHSH
UH...

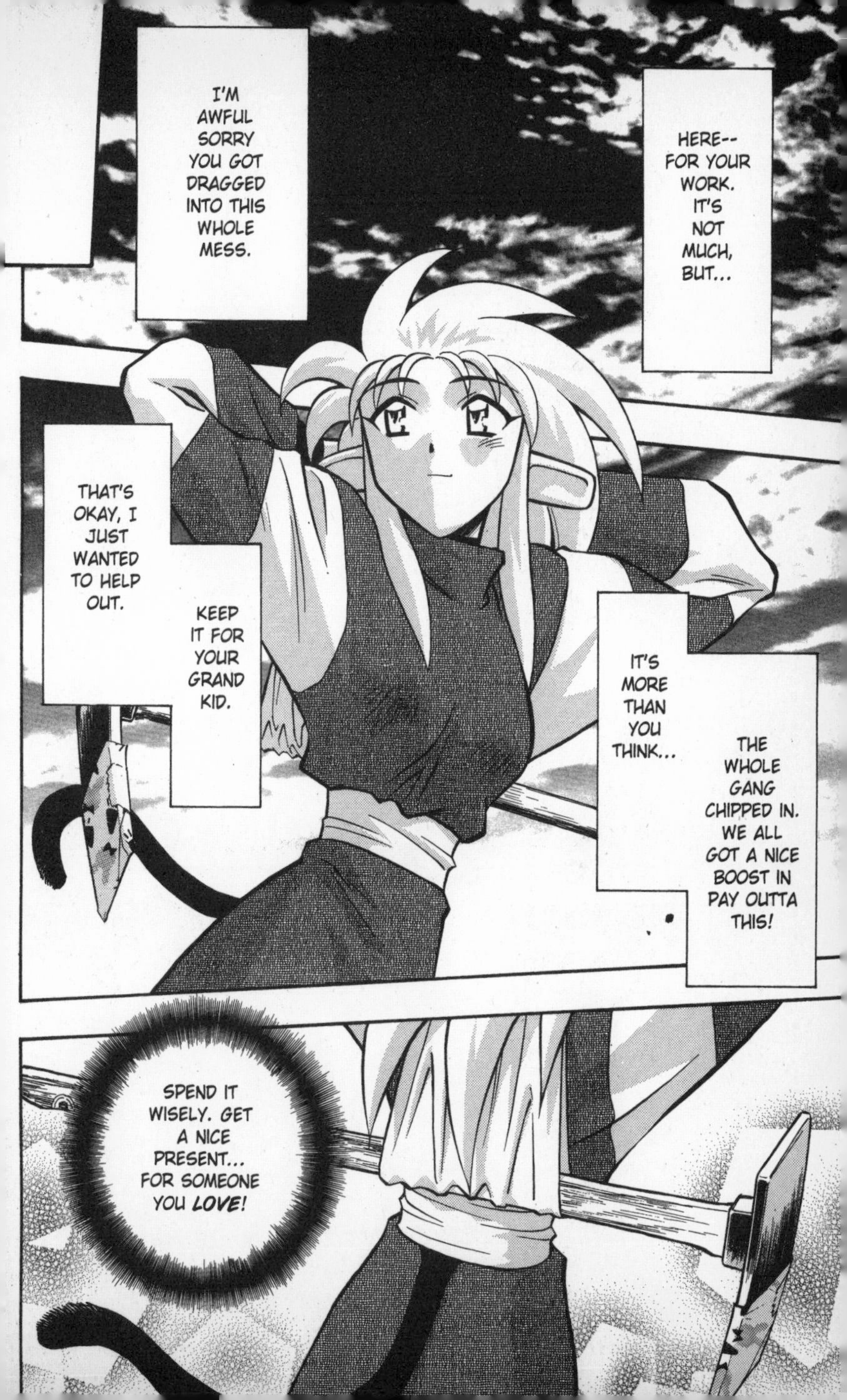
I'M AWFUL SORRY YOU GOT DRAGGED INTO THIS WHOLE MESS.
HERE-- FOR YOUR WORK. IT'S NOT MUCH, BUT...
THAT'S OKAY, I JUST WANTED TO HELP OUT.
KEEP IT FOR YOUR GRAND KID.
IT'S MORE THAN YOU THINK...
THE WHOLE GANG CHIPPED IN. WE ALL GOT A NICE BOOST IN PAY OUTTA THIS!
SPEND IT WISELY. GET A NICE PRESENT... FOR SOMEONE YOU *LOVE*!

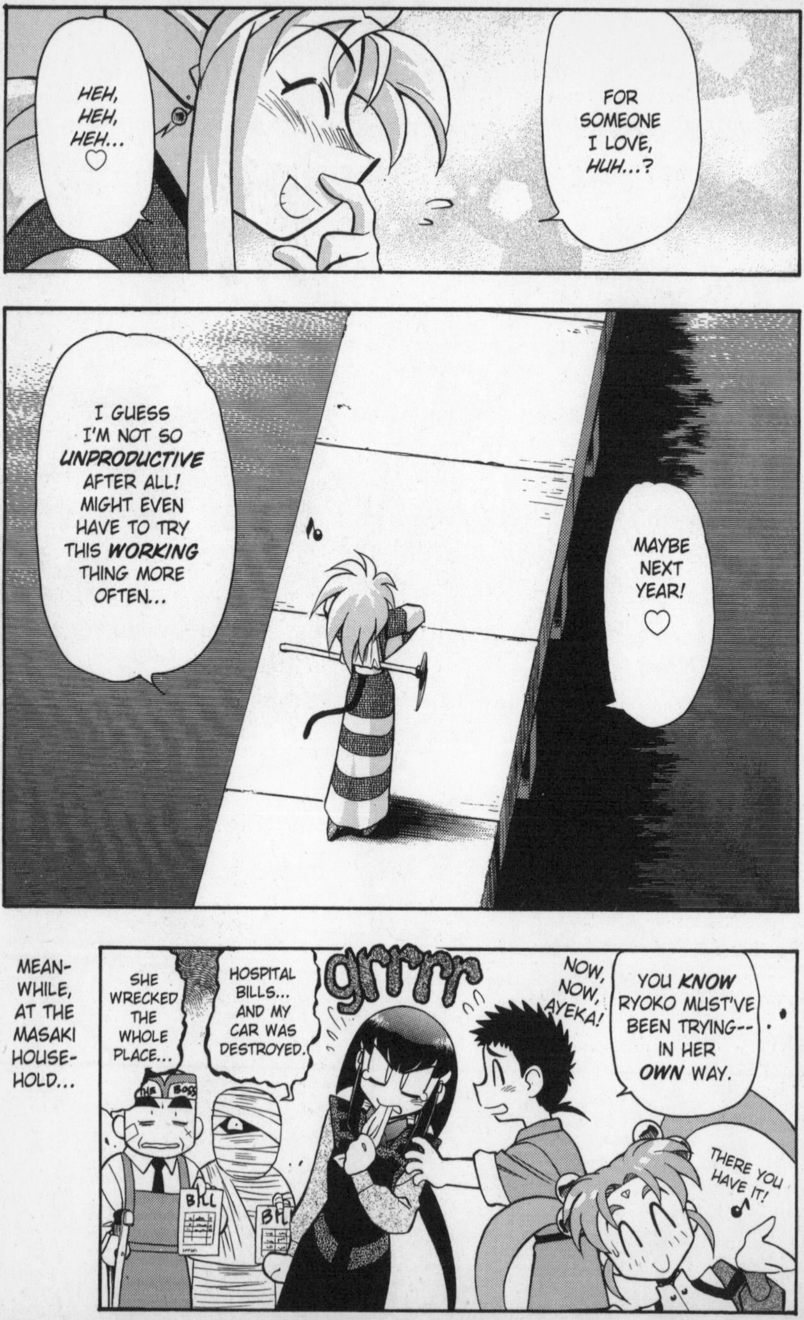
HEH, HEH, HEH... ♡
FOR SOMEONE I LOVE, HUH...?
I GUESS I'M NOT SO UNPRODUCTIVE AFTER ALL! MIGHT EVEN HAVE TO TRY THIS WORKING THING MORE OFTEN...
MAYBE NEXT YEAR! ♡
MEAN-WHILE, AT THE MASAKI HOUSE-HOLD...
SHE WRECKED THE WHOLE PLACE...
HOSPITAL BILLS... AND MY CAR WAS DESTROYED.
grrrr
NOW, NOW, AYEKA!
YOU KNOW RYOKO MUST'VE BEEN TRYING-- IN HER OWN WAY.
THE BOSS
BILL
BILL
THERE YOU HAVE IT!

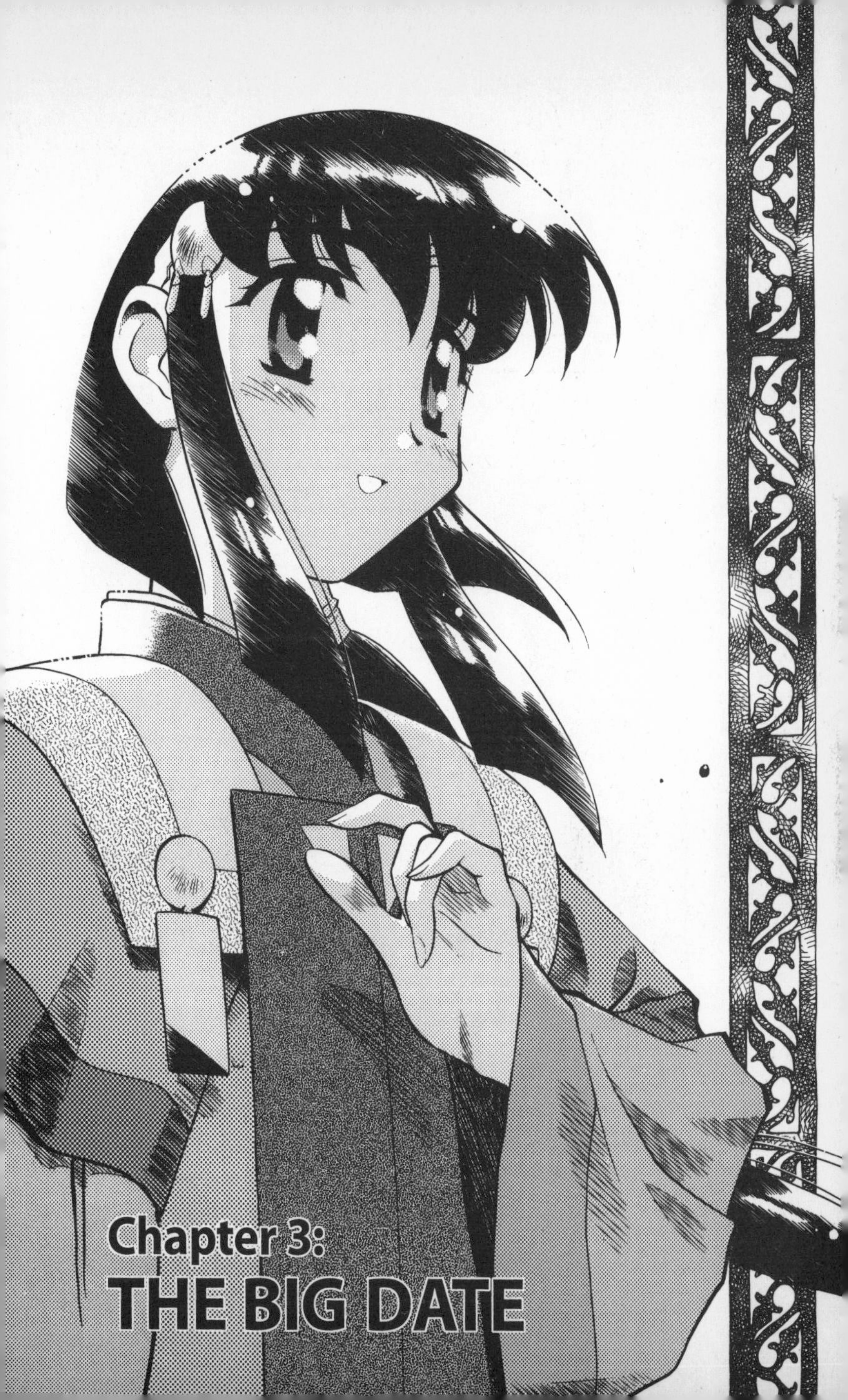

Chapter 3:
THE BIG DATE

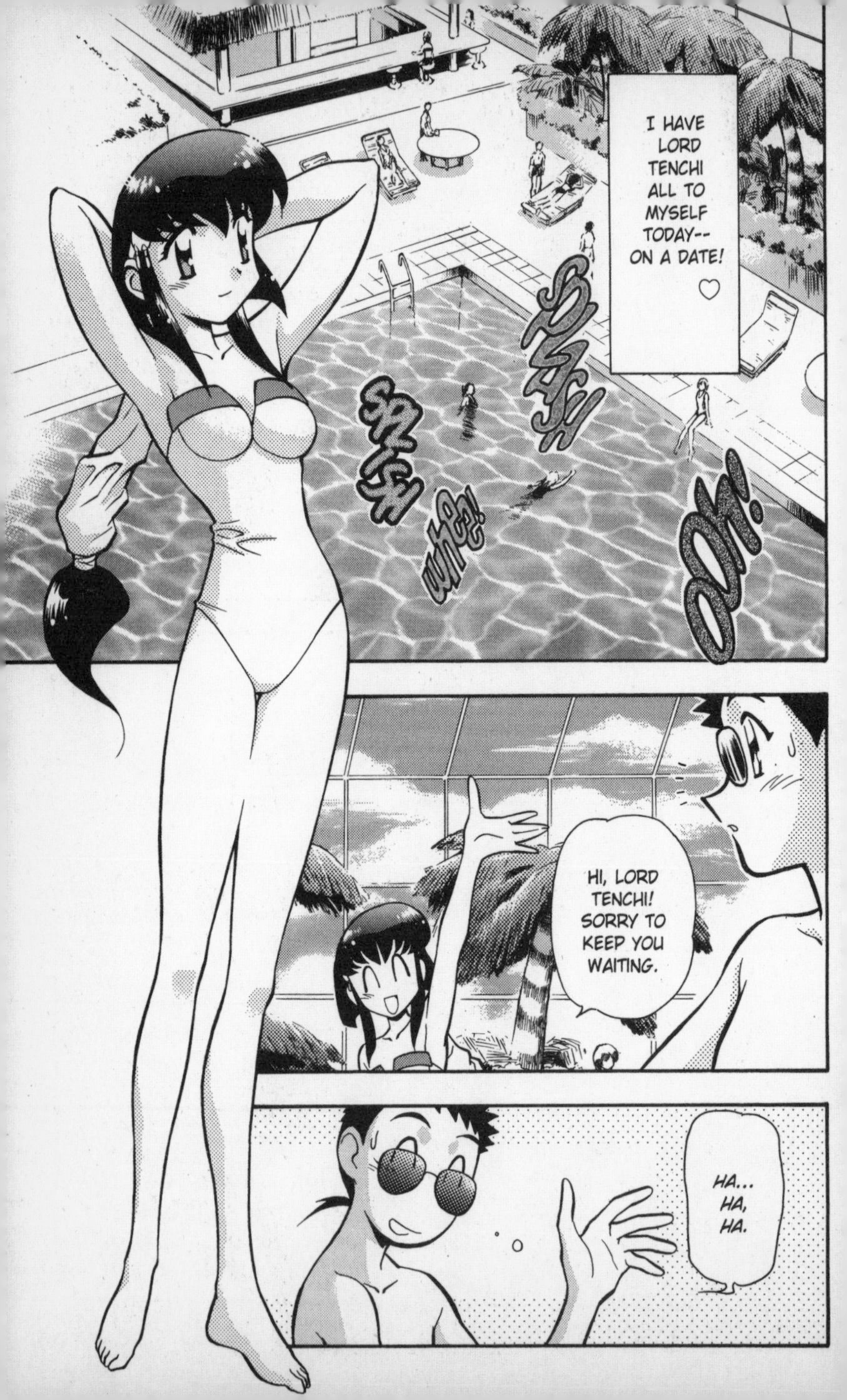
I HAVE LORD TENCHI ALL TO MYSELF TODAY-- ON A DATE! ♡
SPLASH!!
SPLASH
WHEE!
OOH!
HI, LORD TENCHI! SORRY TO KEEP YOU WAITING.
HA... HA, HA.

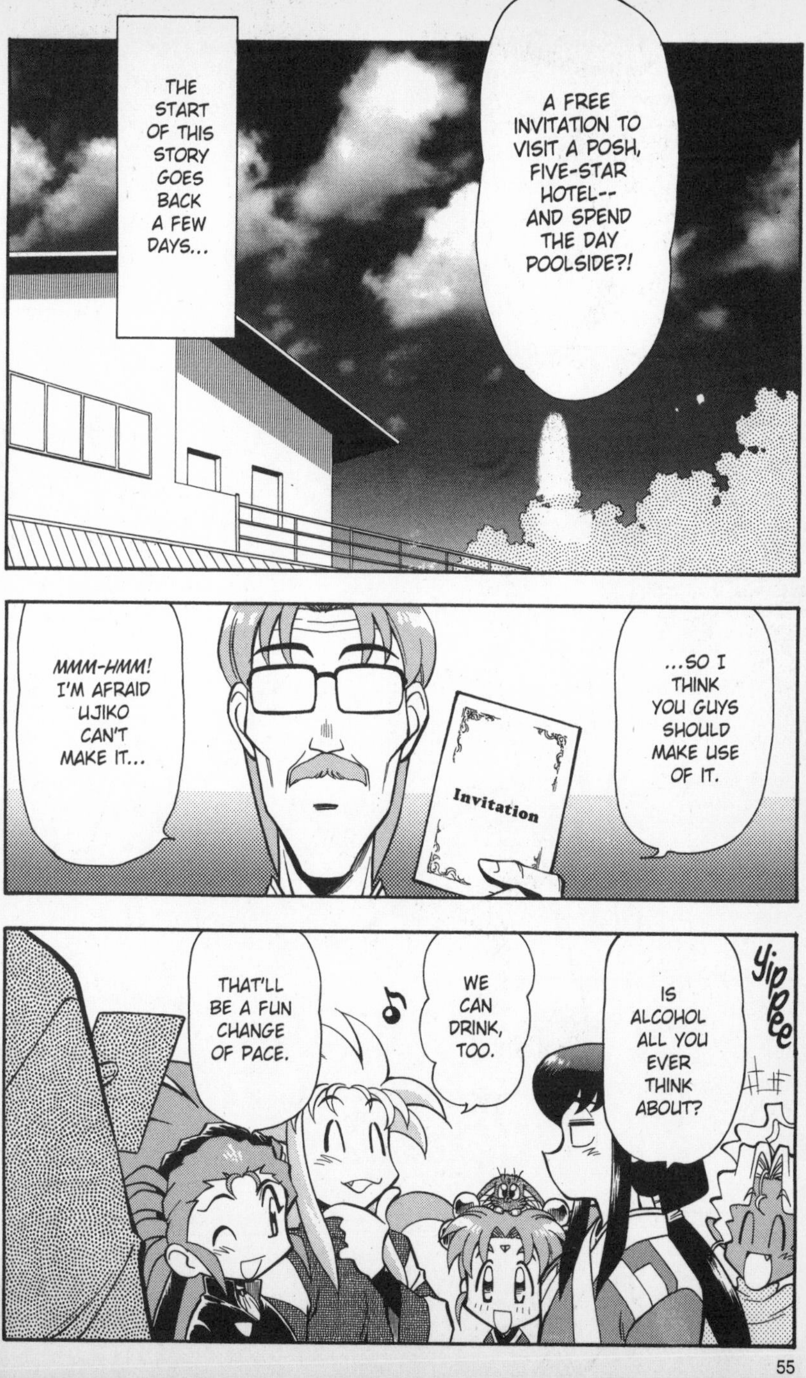
THE START OF THIS STORY GOES BACK A FEW DAYS...
A FREE INVITATION TO VISIT A POSH, FIVE-STAR HOTEL-- AND SPEND THE DAY POOLSIDE?!
MMM-HMM! I'M AFRAID UJIKO CAN'T MAKE IT...
Invitation
...SO I THINK YOU GUYS SHOULD MAKE USE OF IT.
THAT'LL BE A FUN CHANGE OF PACE.
WE CAN DRINK, TOO.
IS ALCOHOL ALL YOU EVER THINK ABOUT?
Yippee

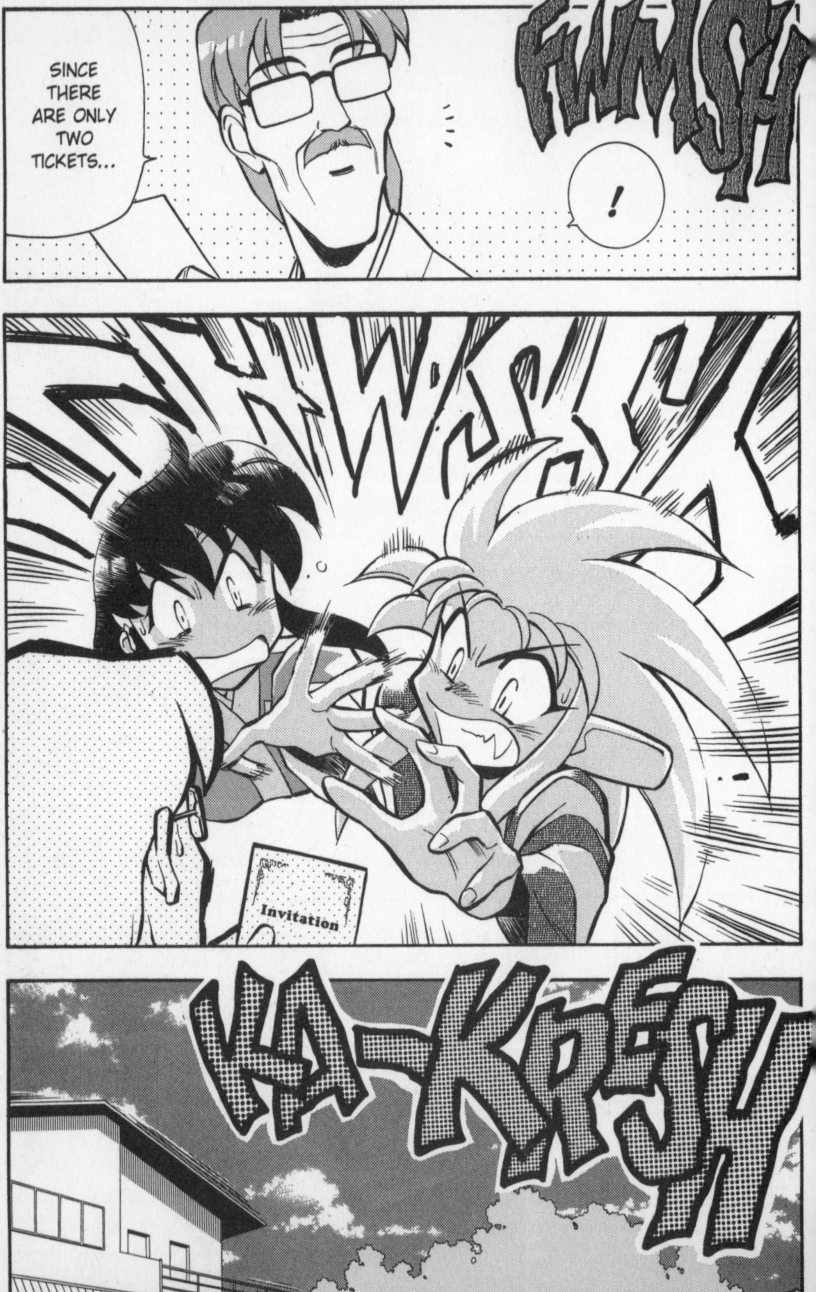
FWMSH
SINCE THERE ARE ONLY TWO TICKETS...
!
WHASH
Invitation
KA-KRESH

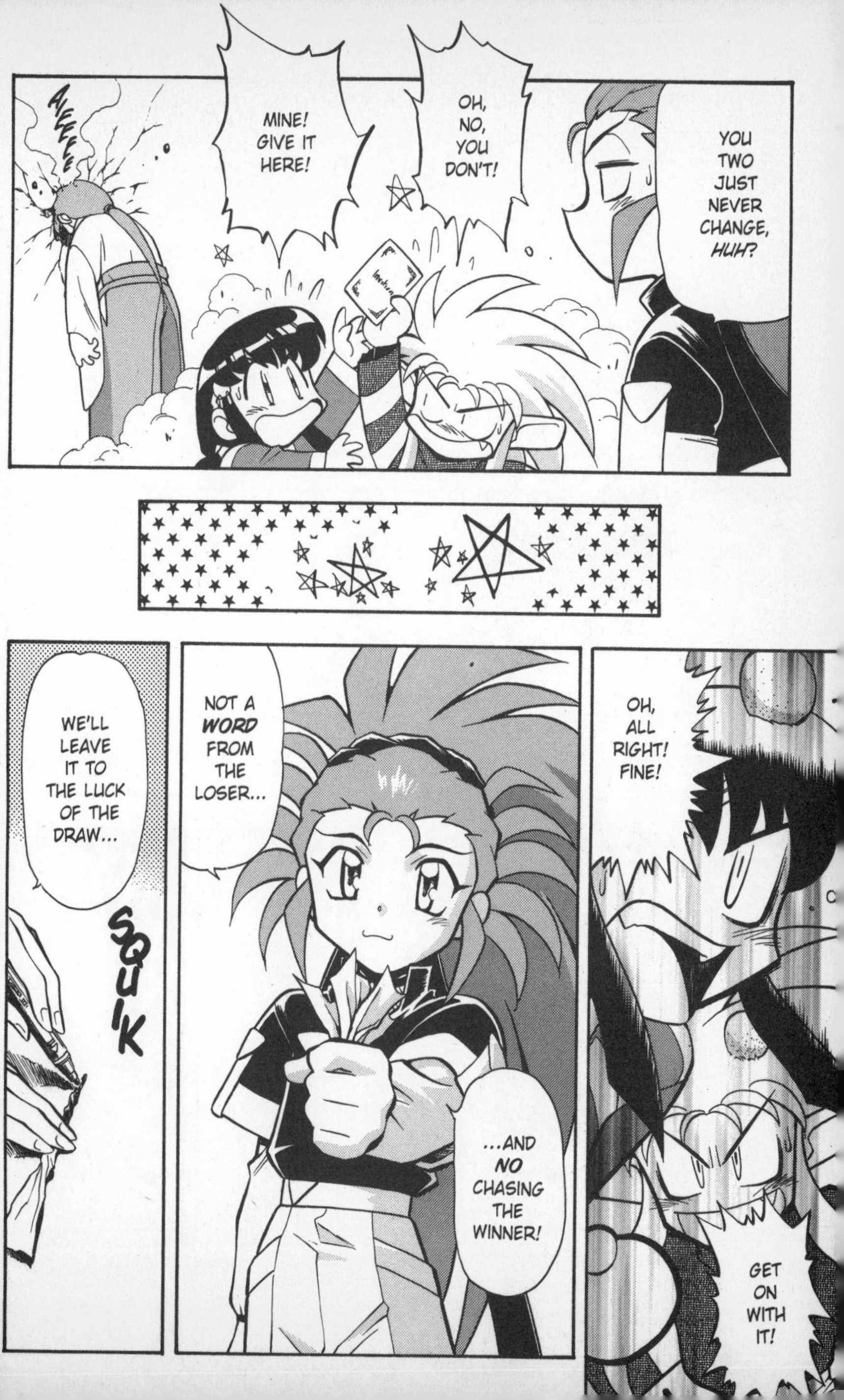
AIEEEE
MINE! GIVE IT HERE!
OH, NO, YOU DON'T!
YOU TWO JUST NEVER CHANGE, *HUH?*
WE'LL LEAVE IT TO THE LUCK OF THE DRAW...
SQUIK
NOT A ***WORD*** FROM THE LOSER...
...AND ***NO*** CHASING THE WINNER!
OH, ALL RIGHT! FINE!
GET ON WITH IT!

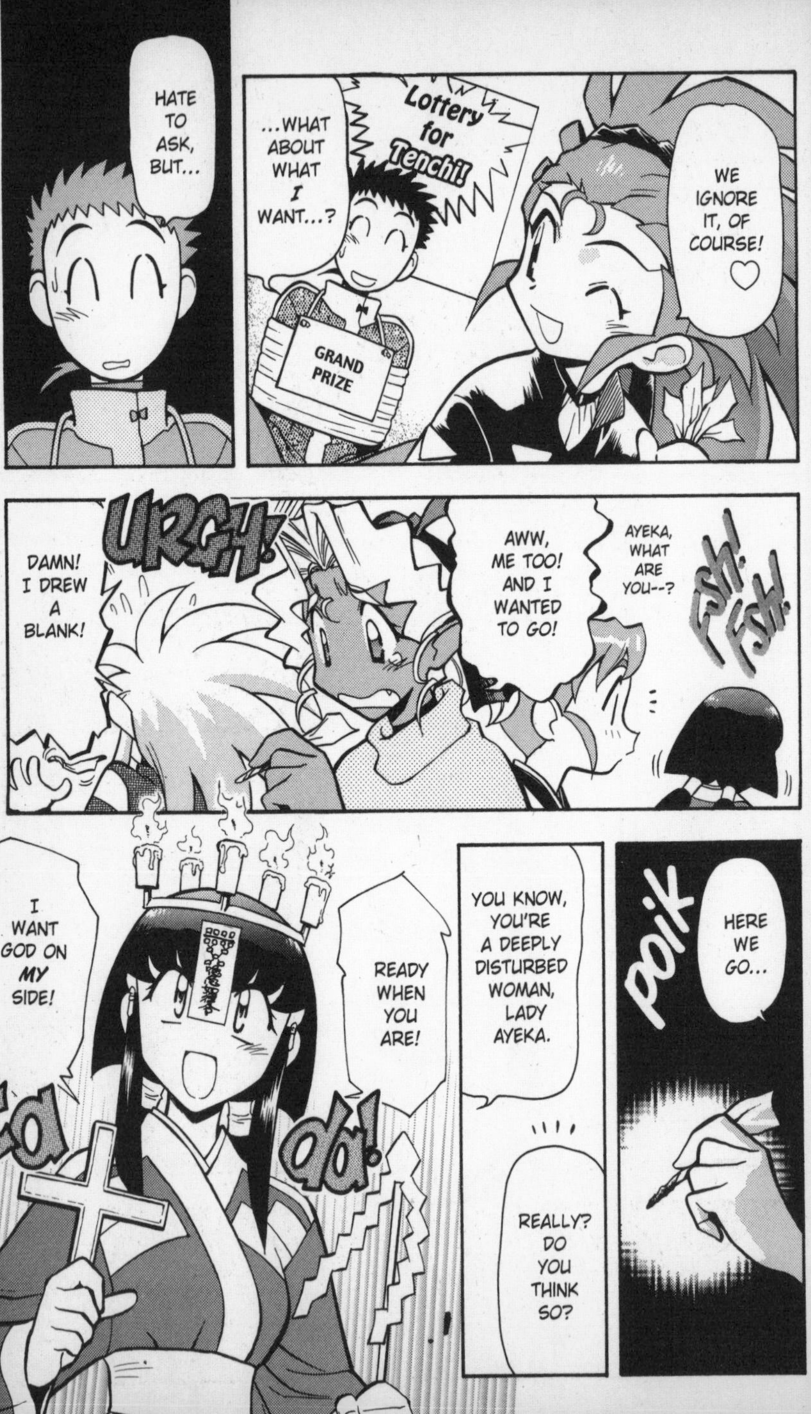
HATE TO ASK, BUT...
...WHAT ABOUT WHAT I WANT...?
Lottery for Tenchi!
GRAND PRIZE
WE IGNORE IT, OF COURSE! ♡
URGH!
DAMN! I DREW A BLANK!
AWW, ME TOO! AND I WANTED TO GO!
AYEKA, WHAT ARE YOU--?
FSH! FSH!
I WANT GOD ON MY SIDE!
READY WHEN YOU ARE!
ta da!
YOU KNOW, YOU'RE A DEEPLY DISTURBED WOMAN, LADY AYEKA.
REALLY? DO YOU THINK SO?
poik
HERE WE GO...

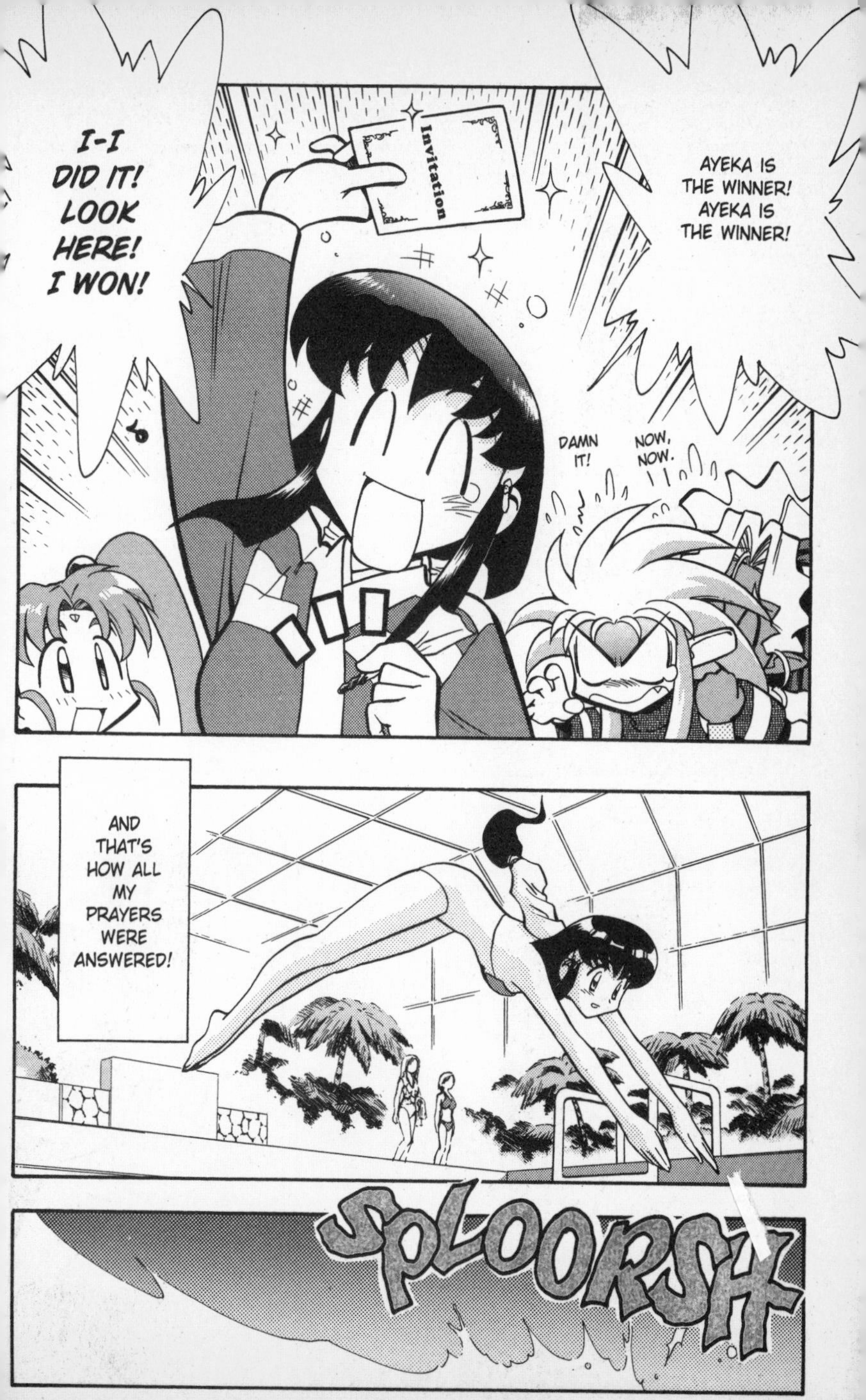
I-I DID IT! LOOK HERE! I WON!
Invitation
AYEKA IS THE WINNER! AYEKA IS THE WINNER!
DAMN IT!
NOW, NOW.
AND THAT'S HOW ALL MY PRAYERS WERE ANSWERED!
SPLOORSH

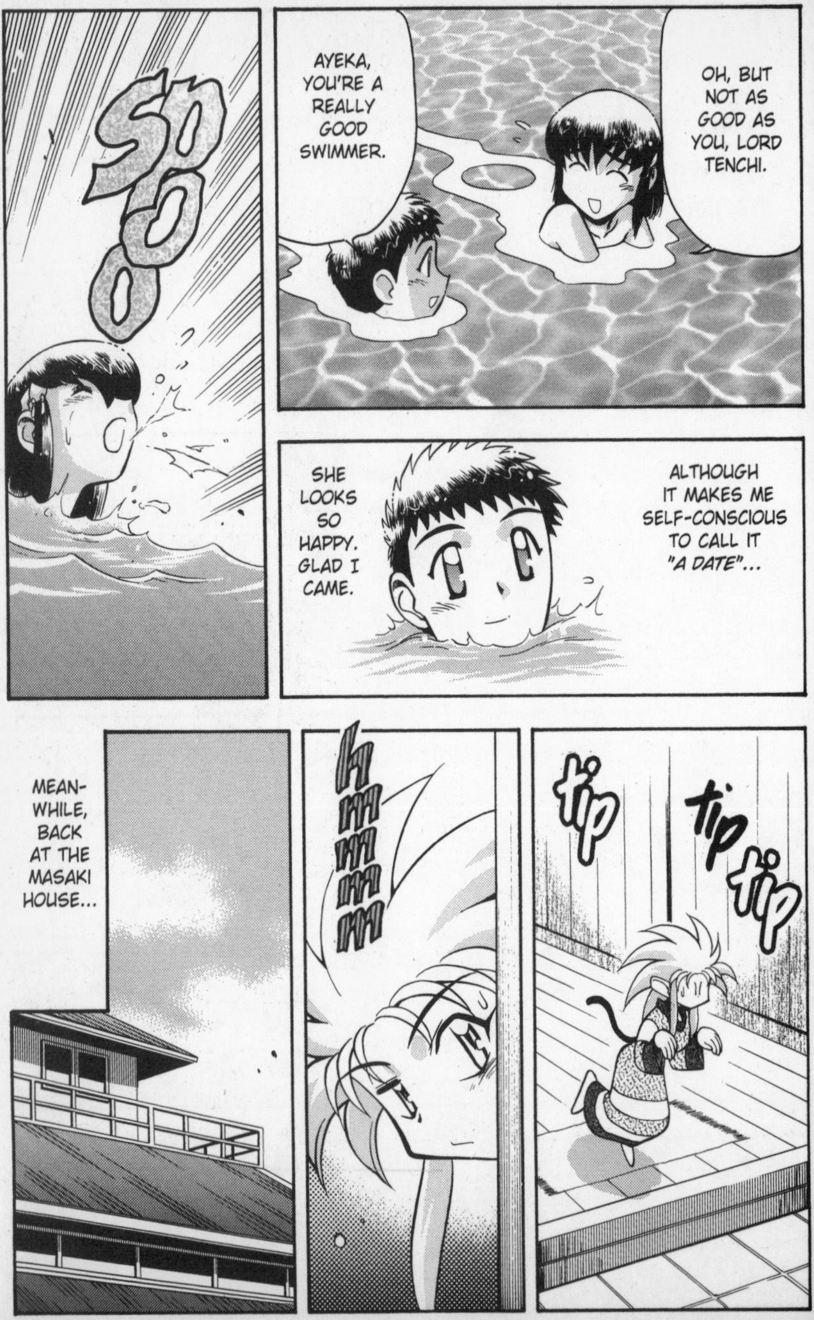
SPOO
AYEKA, YOU'RE A REALLY GOOD SWIMMER.
OH, BUT NOT AS GOOD AS YOU, LORD TENCHI.
SHE LOOKS SO HAPPY. GLAD I CAME.
ALTHOUGH IT MAKES ME SELF-CONSCIOUS TO CALL IT "A DATE"...
MEAN-WHILE, BACK AT THE MASAKI HOUSE...
hmmmmmm
tip tip tip

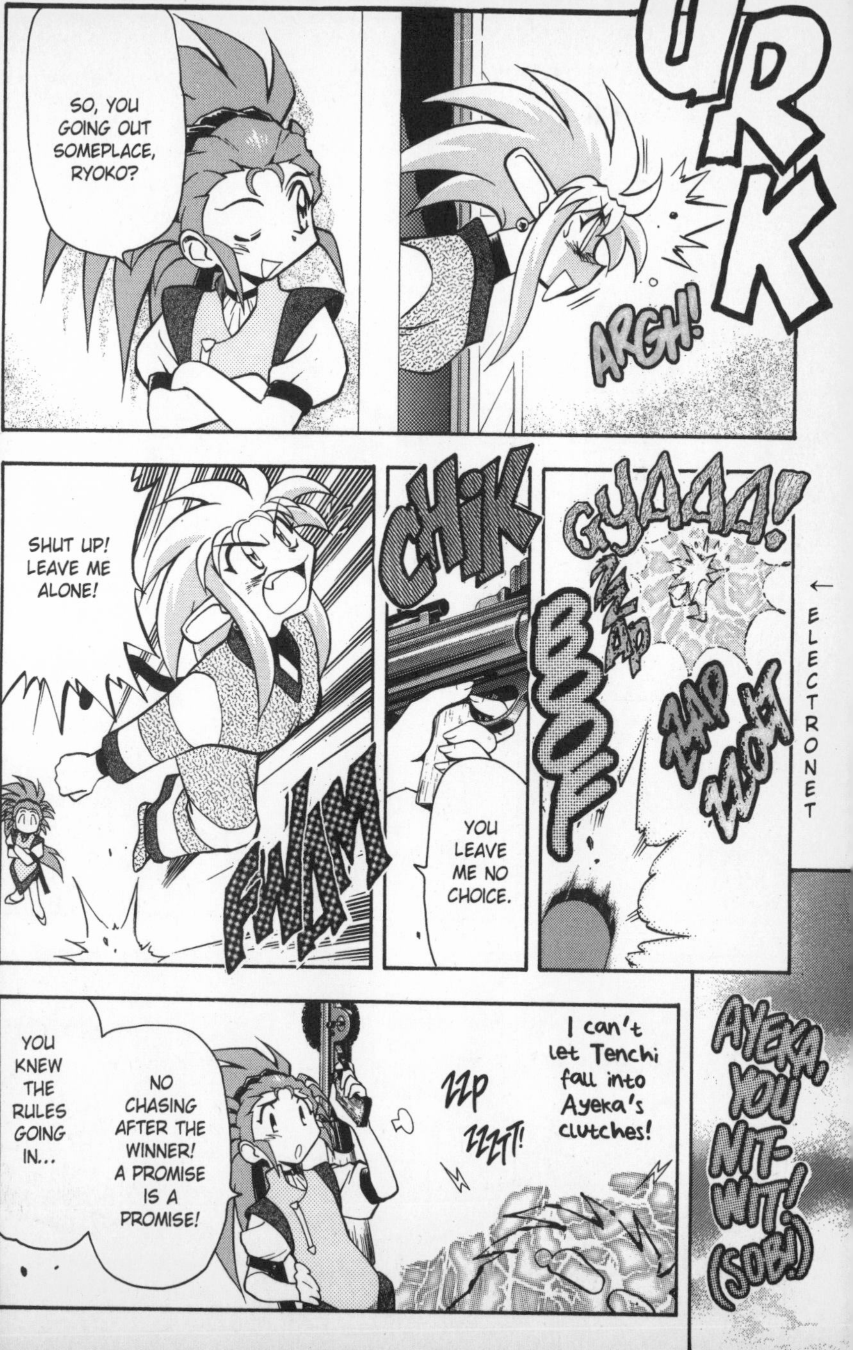
SO, YOU GOING OUT SOMEPLACE, RYOKO?
URK
ARGH!
SHUT UP! LEAVE ME ALONE!
FWMM
CHIK
YOU LEAVE ME NO CHOICE.
GYAAAA!
ZAP
ZAP ZZOT
← ELECTRONET
YOU KNEW THE RULES GOING IN...
NO CHASING AFTER THE WINNER! A PROMISE IS A PROMISE!
ZZP
ZZZZT!
I can't let Tenchi fall into Ayeka's clutches!
AYEKA, YOU NIT-WIT! (SOB!)

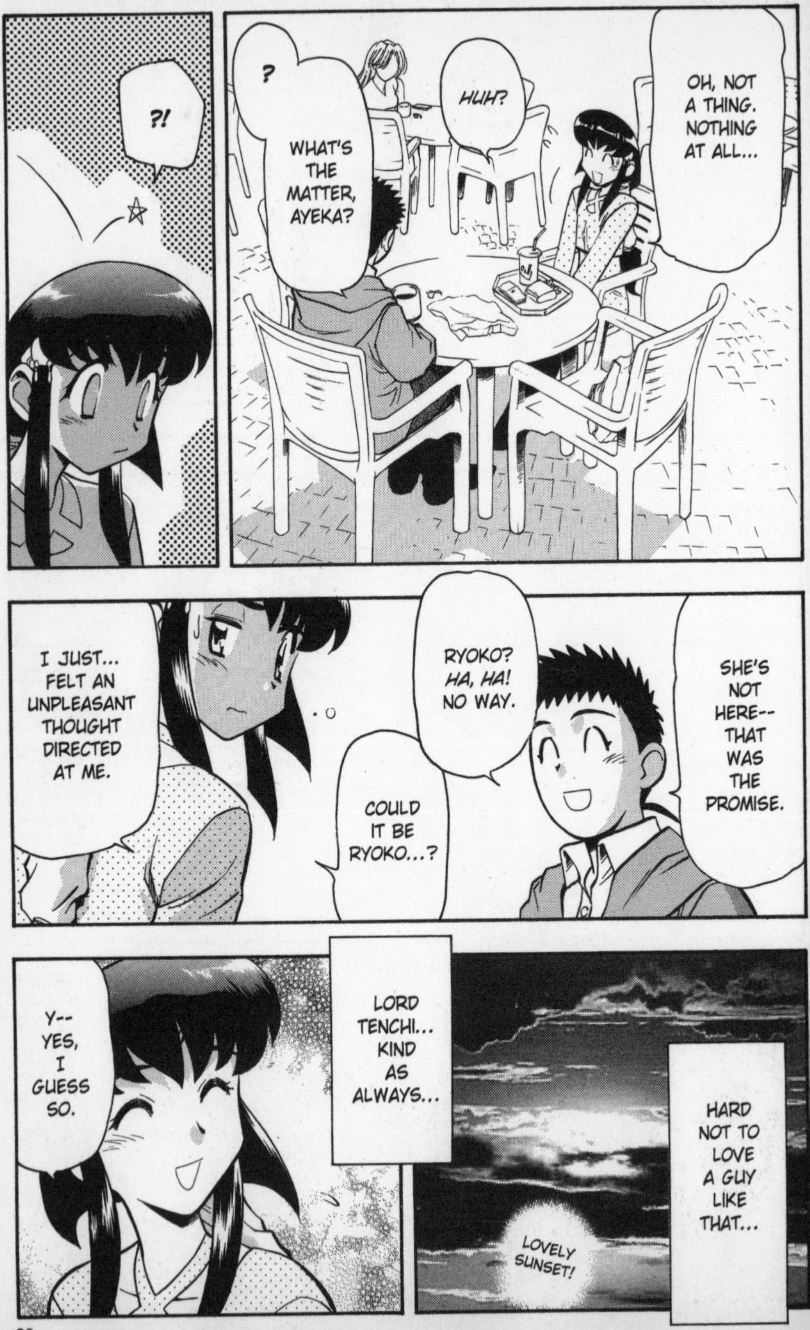
?!
?
WHAT'S THE MATTER, AYEKA?
HUH?
OH, NOT A THING. NOTHING AT ALL...
I JUST... FELT AN UNPLEASANT THOUGHT DIRECTED AT ME.
COULD IT BE RYOKO...?
RYOKO? HA, HA! NO WAY.
SHE'S NOT HERE--THAT WAS THE PROMISE.
Y--YES, I GUESS SO.
LORD TENCHI... KIND AS ALWAYS...
HARD NOT TO LOVE A GUY LIKE THAT...
LOVELY SUNSET!

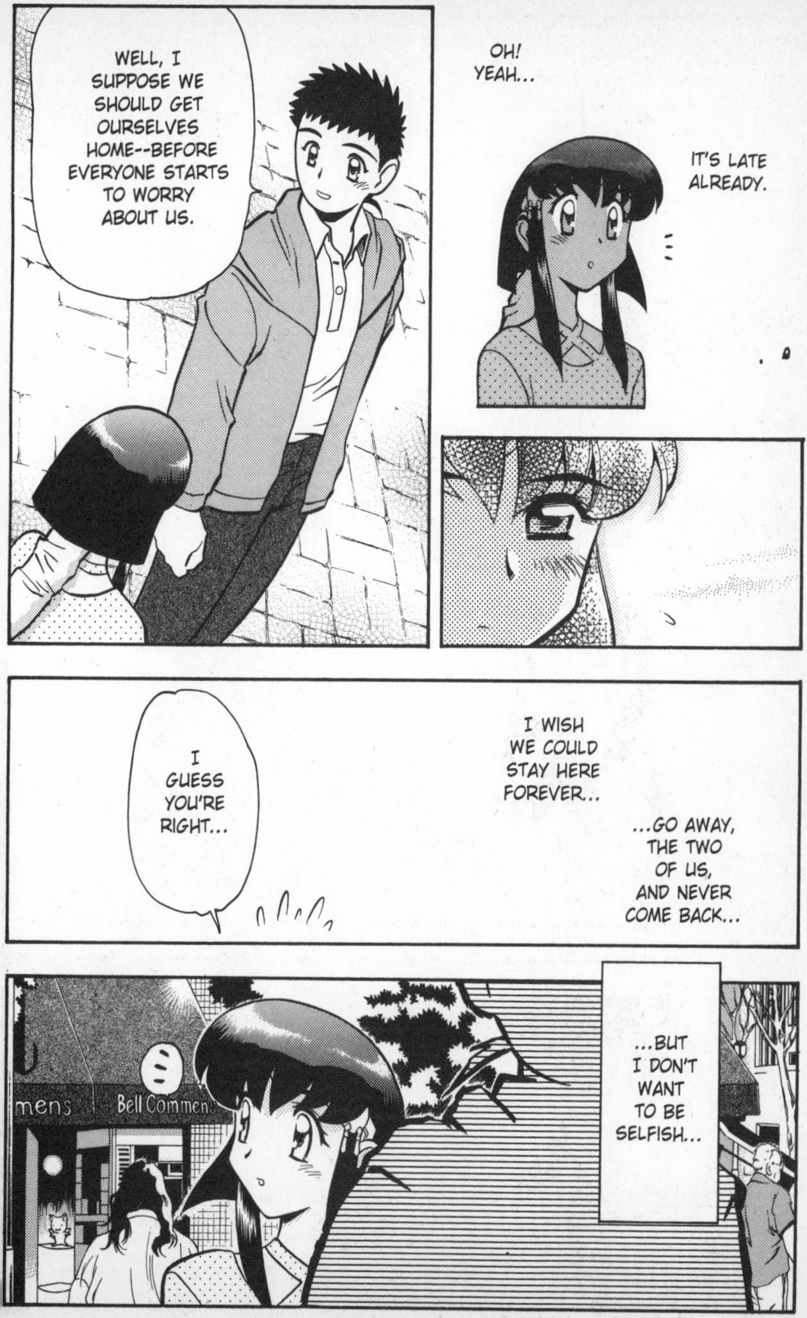
WELL, I SUPPOSE WE SHOULD GET OURSELVES HOME--BEFORE EVERYONE STARTS TO WORRY ABOUT US.
OH! YEAH...
IT'S LATE ALREADY.
I GUESS YOU'RE RIGHT...
I WISH WE COULD STAY HERE FOREVER...
...GO AWAY, THE TWO OF US, AND NEVER COME BACK...
mens
Bell Commen
...BUT I DON'T WANT TO BE SELFISH...

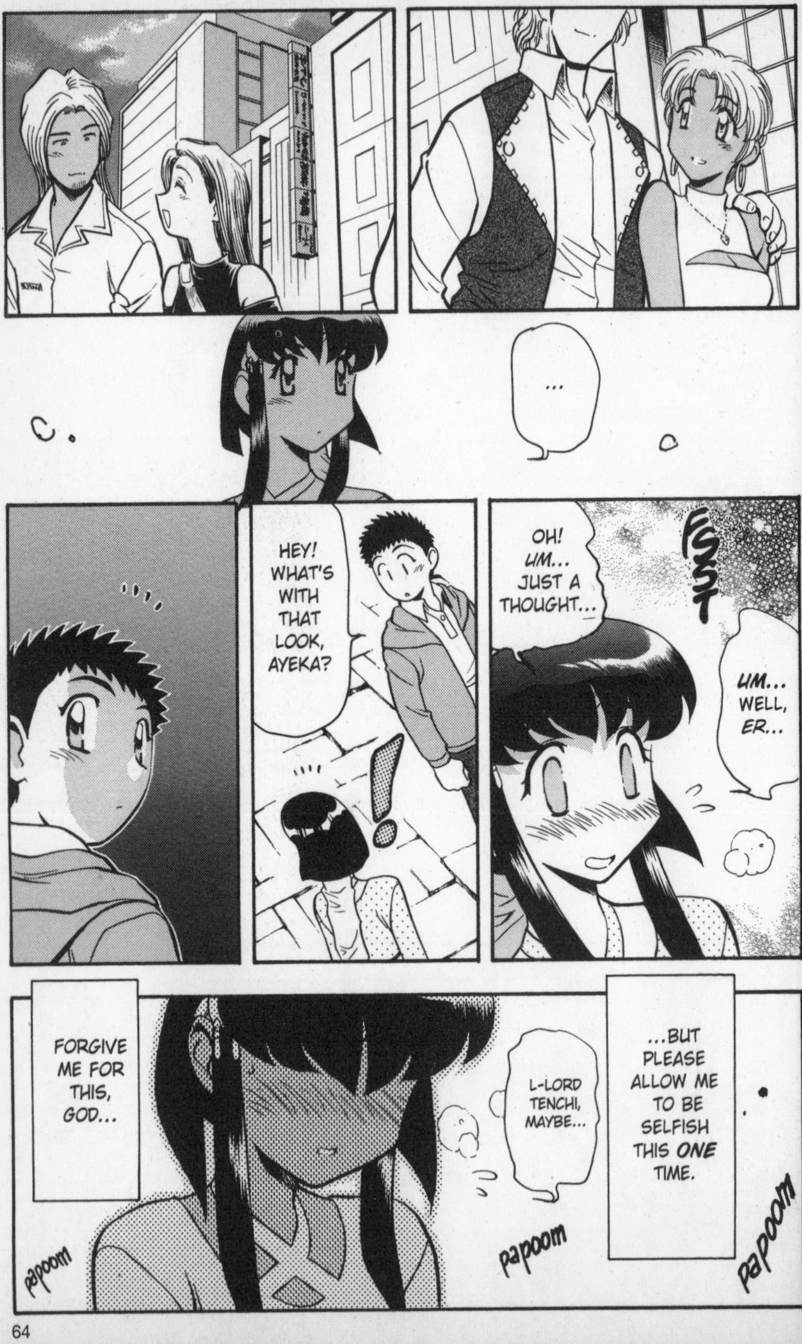
...
HEY! WHAT'S WITH THAT LOOK, AYEKA?
OH! UM... JUST A THOUGHT...
FSST
UM... WELL, ER...
FORGIVE ME FOR THIS, GOD...
L-LORD TENCHI, MAYBE...
...BUT PLEASE ALLOW ME TO BE SELFISH THIS ONE TIME.
papoom
papoom
papoom

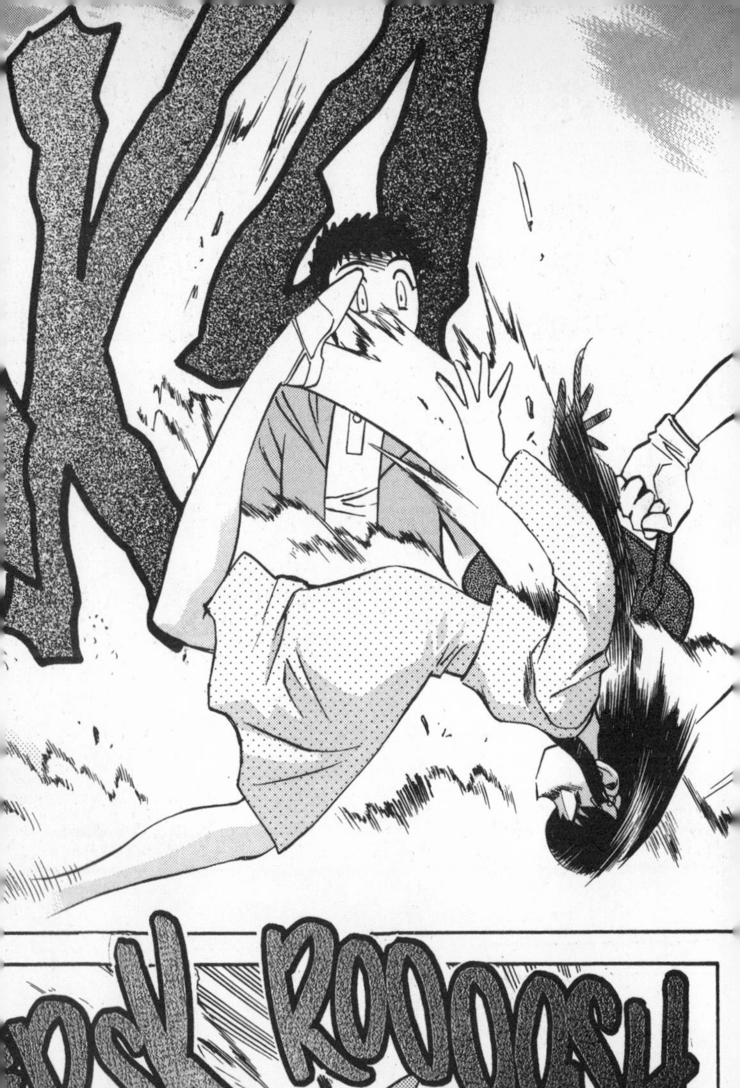

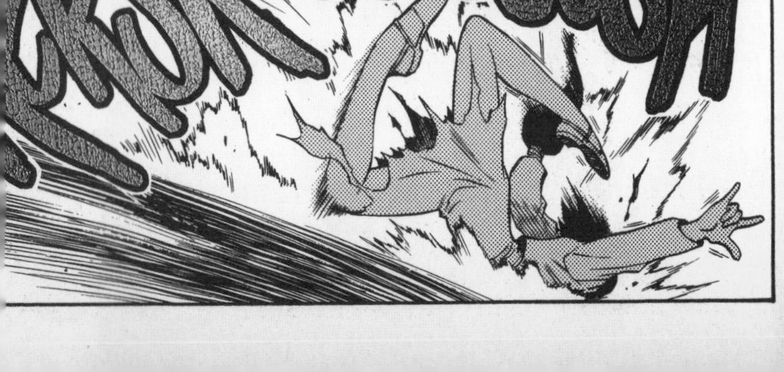
RSK
ROOOOSH

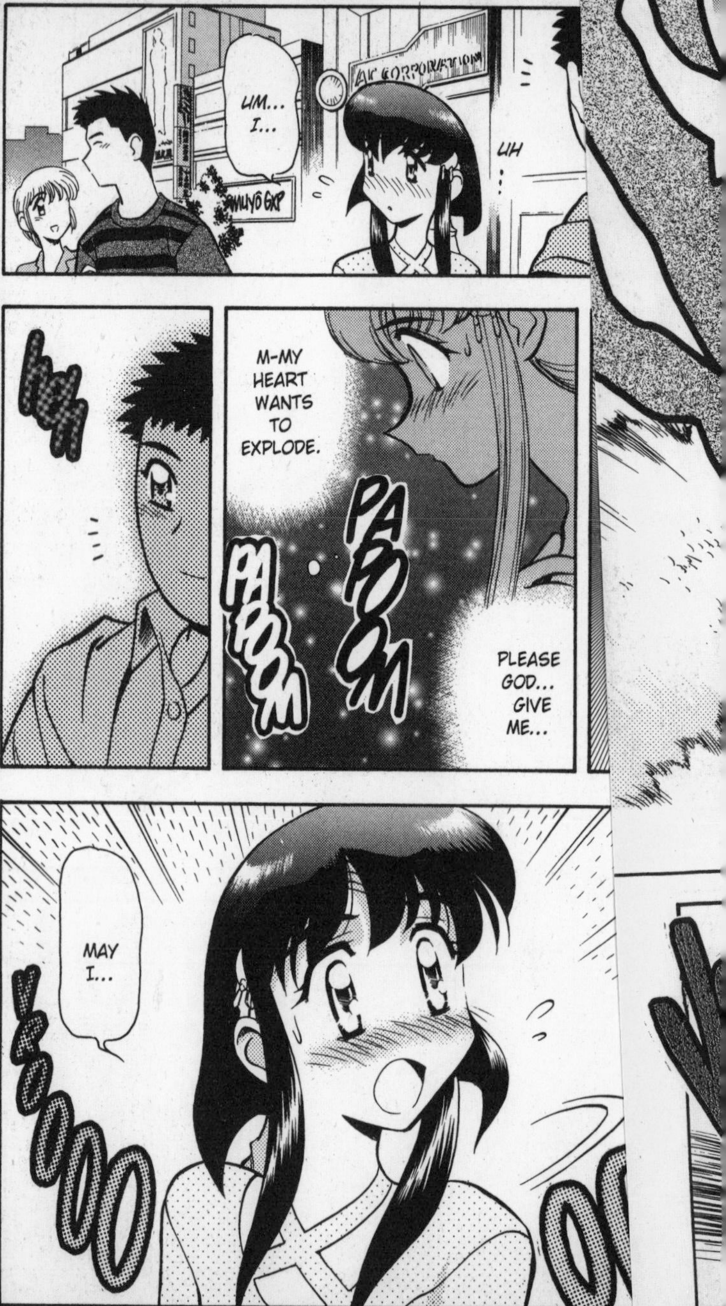
UM... I...
AC CORPORATION
UH...
M-MY HEART WANTS TO EXPLODE.
PADOOM
PADOOM
PLEASE GOD... GIVE ME...
MAY I...

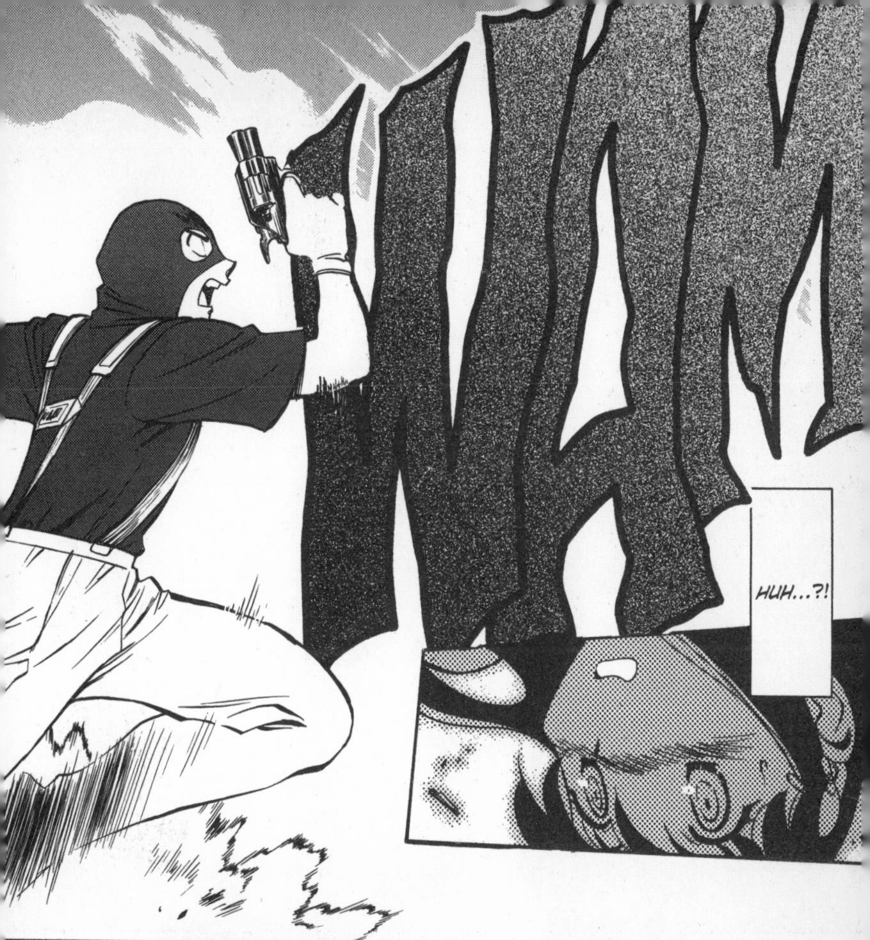
WHAM
HUH...?!

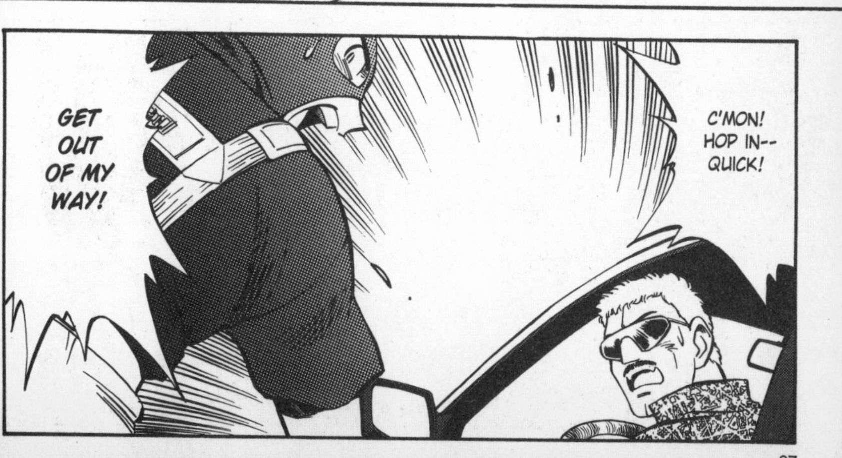
GET OUT OF MY WAY!
C'MON! HOP IN-- QUICK!

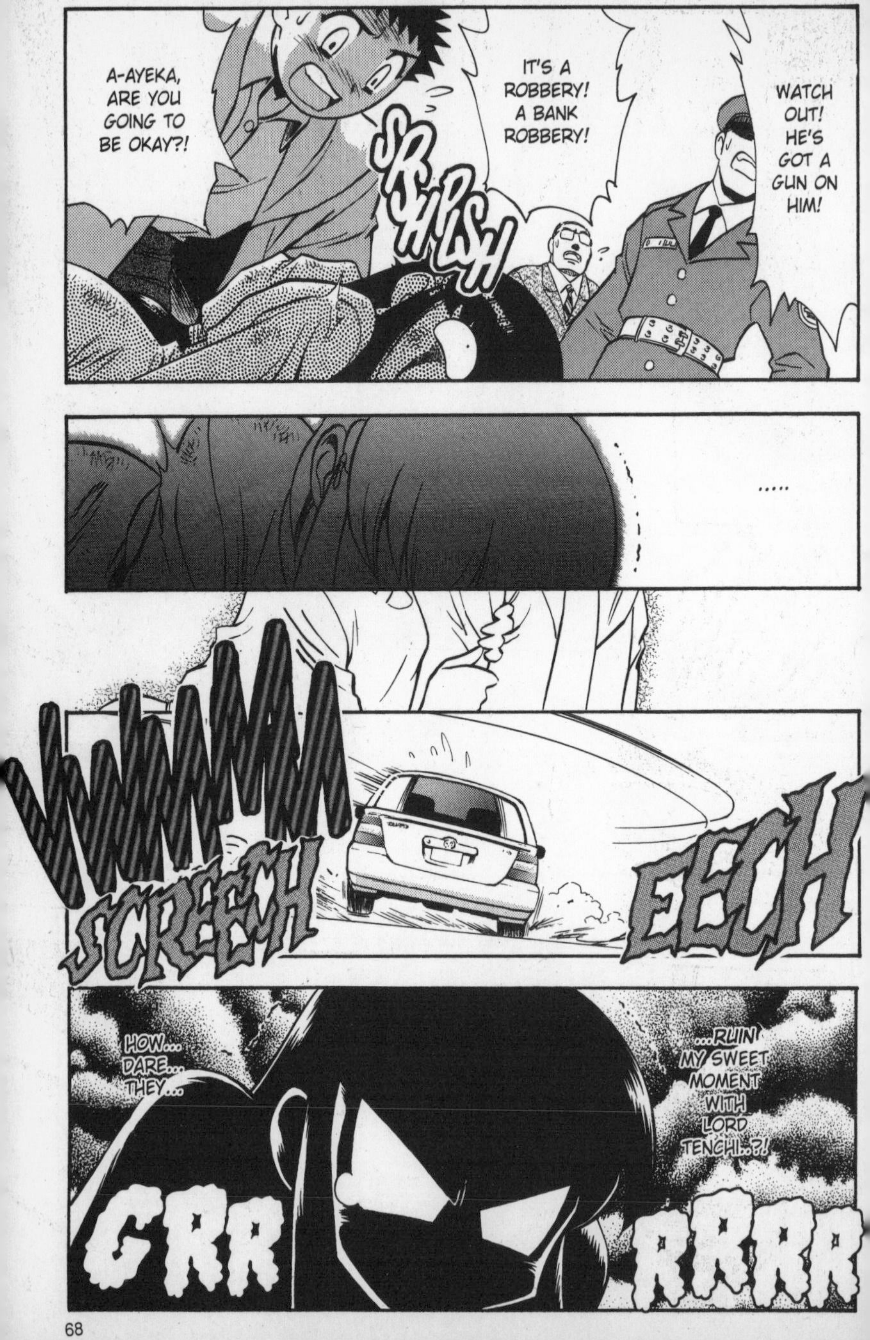
A-AYEKA, ARE YOU GOING TO BE OKAY?!
SPLISH
IT'S A ROBBERY! A BANK ROBBERY!
WATCH OUT! HE'S GOT A GUN ON HIM!
.....
VVVMMM
SCREECH
EECH
HOW... DARE... THEY...
...RUIN MY SWEET MOMENT WITH LORD TENCHI...?!
GRR
RRRR

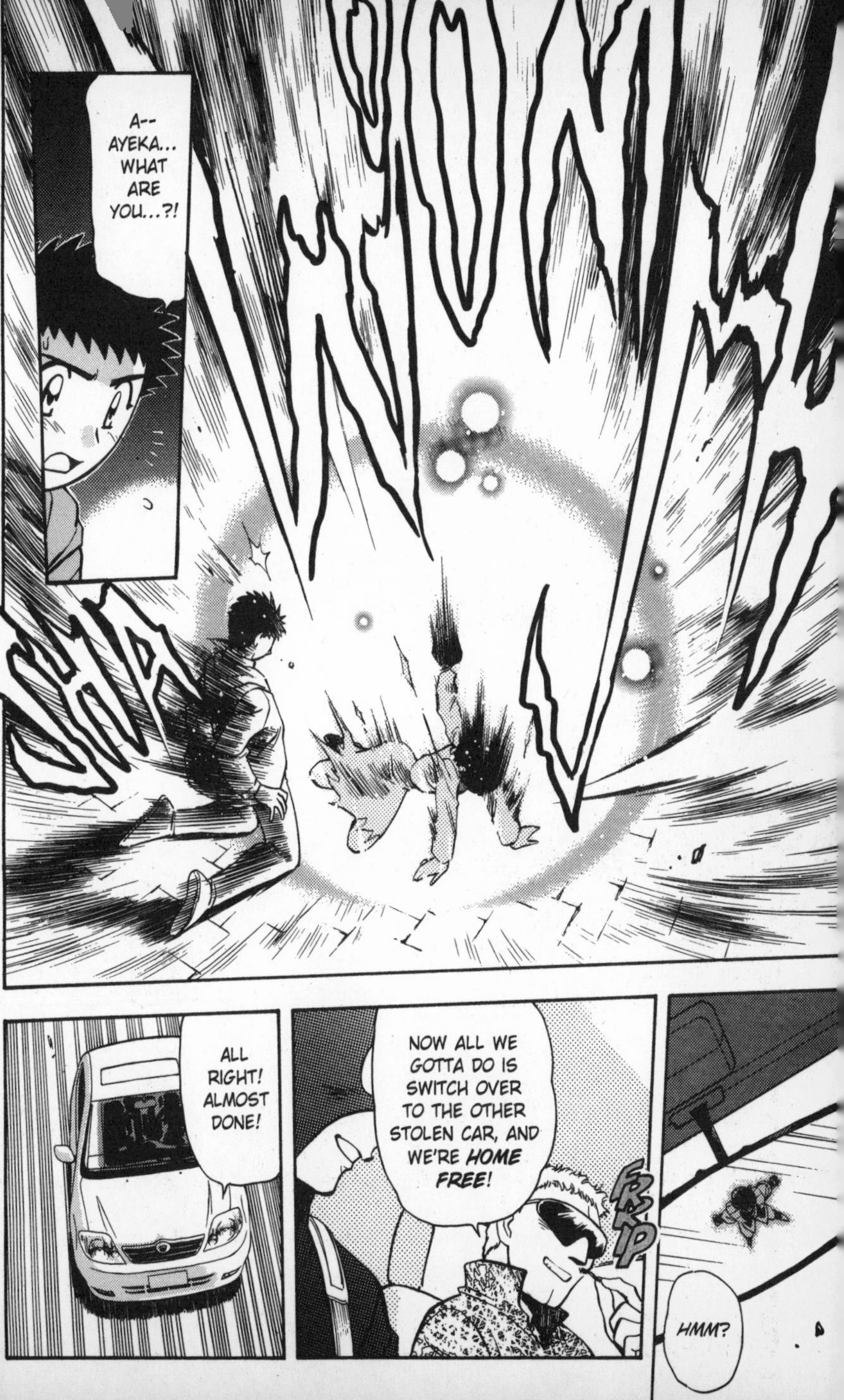
A-- AYEKA... WHAT ARE YOU...?!
ALL RIGHT! ALMOST DONE!
NOW ALL WE GOTTA DO IS SWITCH OVER TO THE OTHER STOLEN CAR, AND WE'RE *HOME FREE*!
HMM?

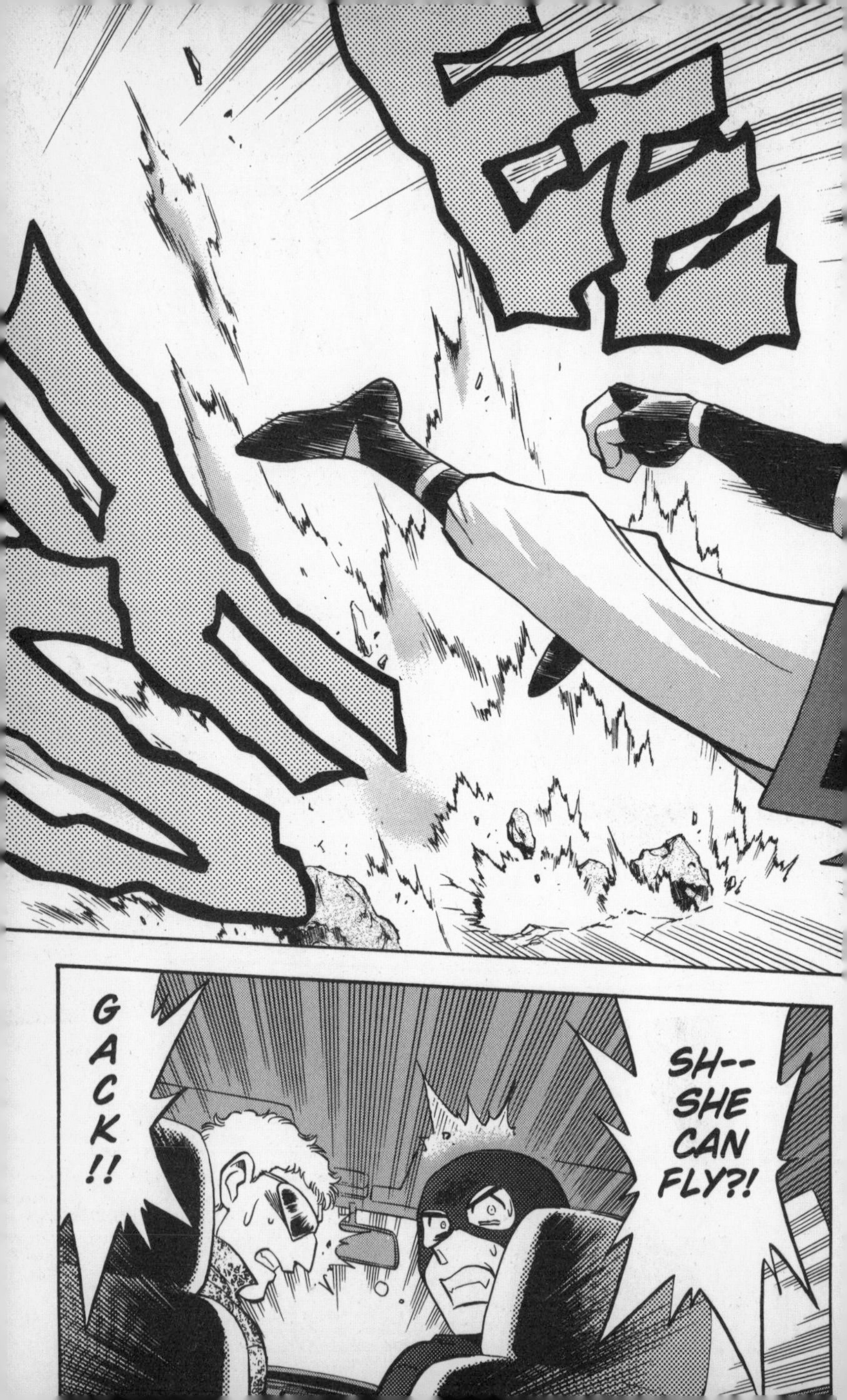
GACK!!
SH-- SHE CAN FLY?!

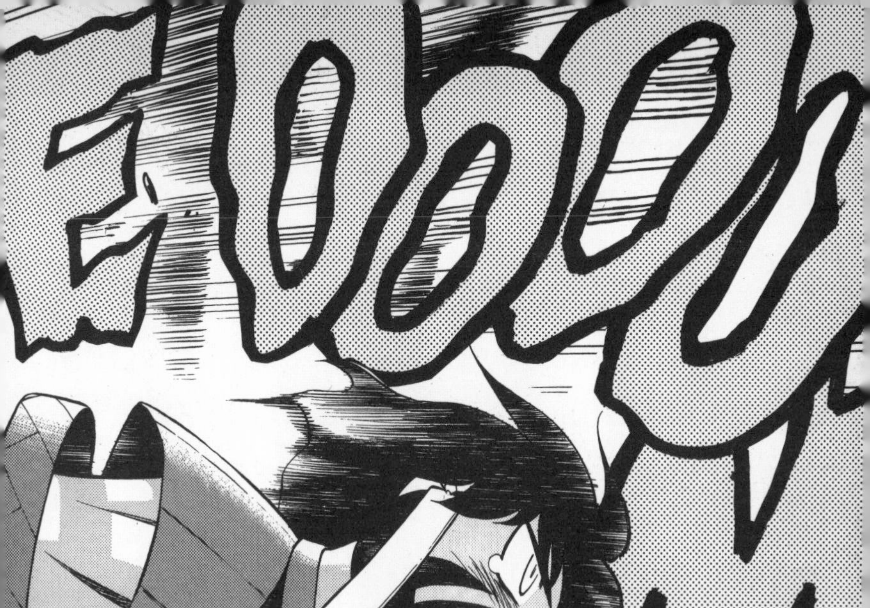

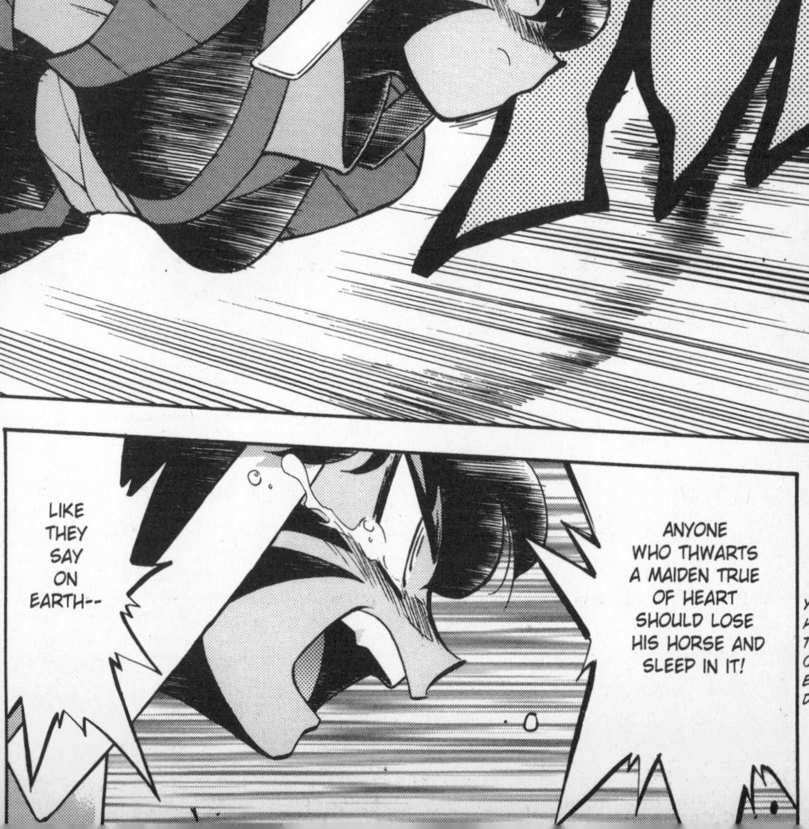
LIKE THEY SAY ON EARTH--
ANYONE WHO THWARTS A MAIDEN TRUE OF HEART SHOULD LOSE HIS HORSE AND SLEEP IN IT!
YEP! HEAR THAT ONE EVERY DAY!

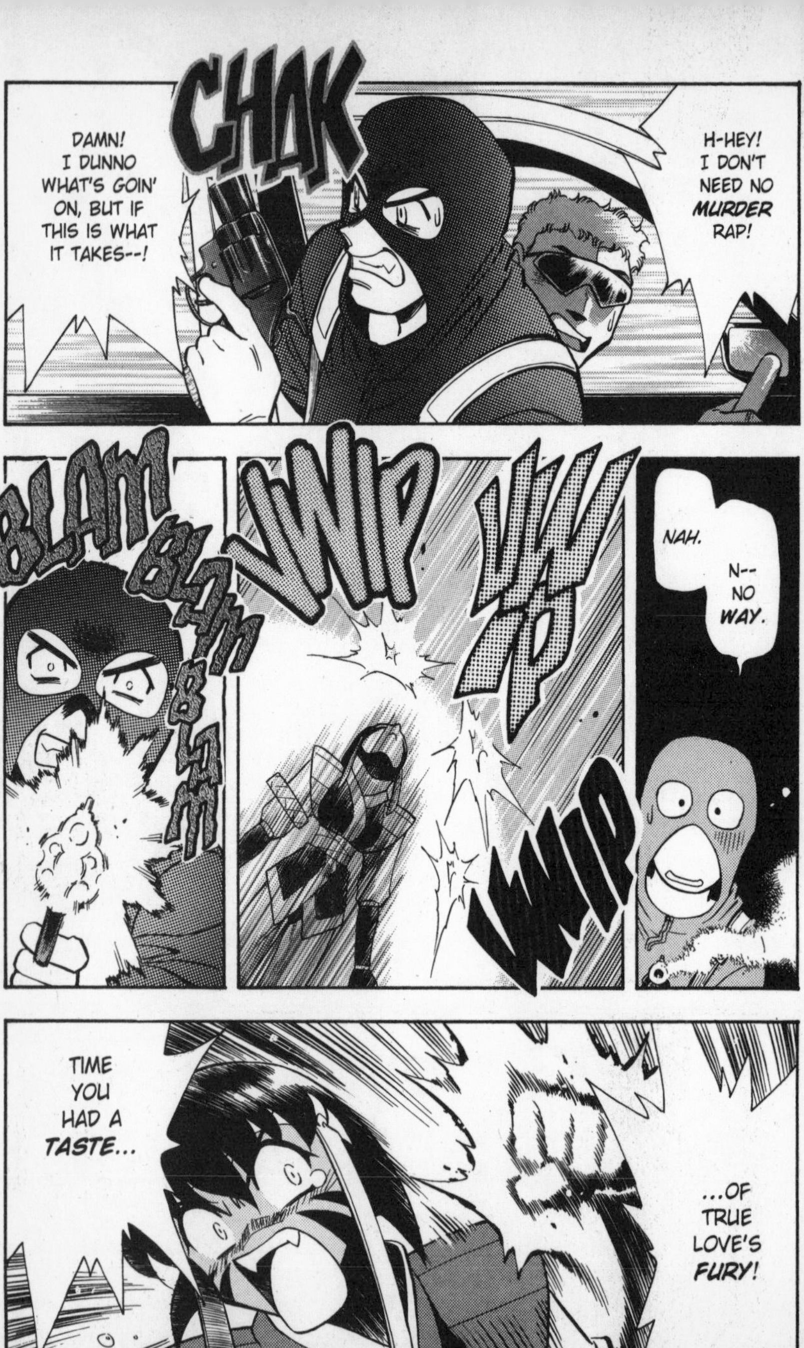
CHAK
DAMN! I DUNNO WHAT'S GOIN' ON, BUT IF THIS IS WHAT IT TAKES--!
H-HEY! I DON'T NEED NO *MURDER* RAP!
BLAM
BLAM
BLAM
WHIP
WHIP
WHIP
NAH.
N-- NO *WAY*.
TIME YOU HAD A *TASTE*...
...OF TRUE LOVE'S *FURY*!

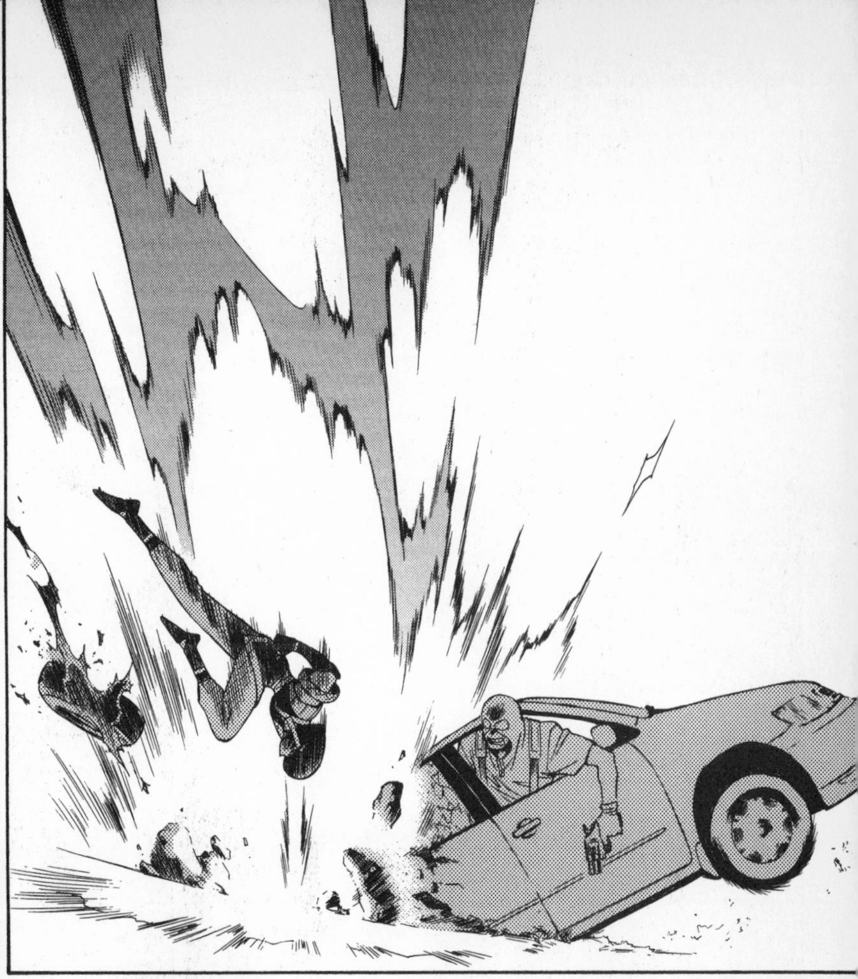
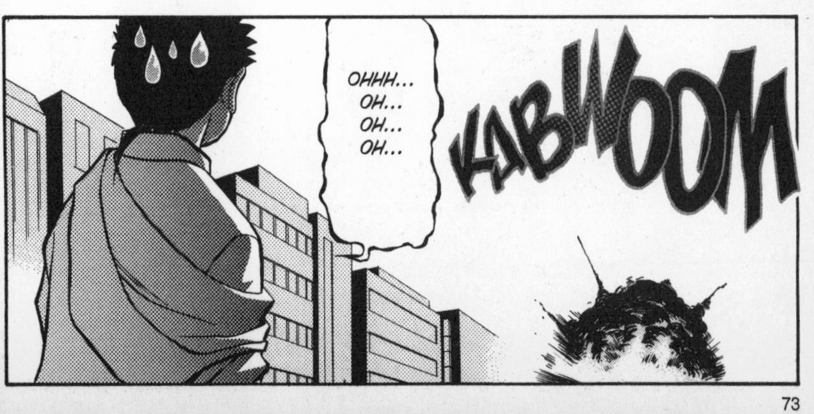
OHHH... OH... OH... OH...
KABWOOM

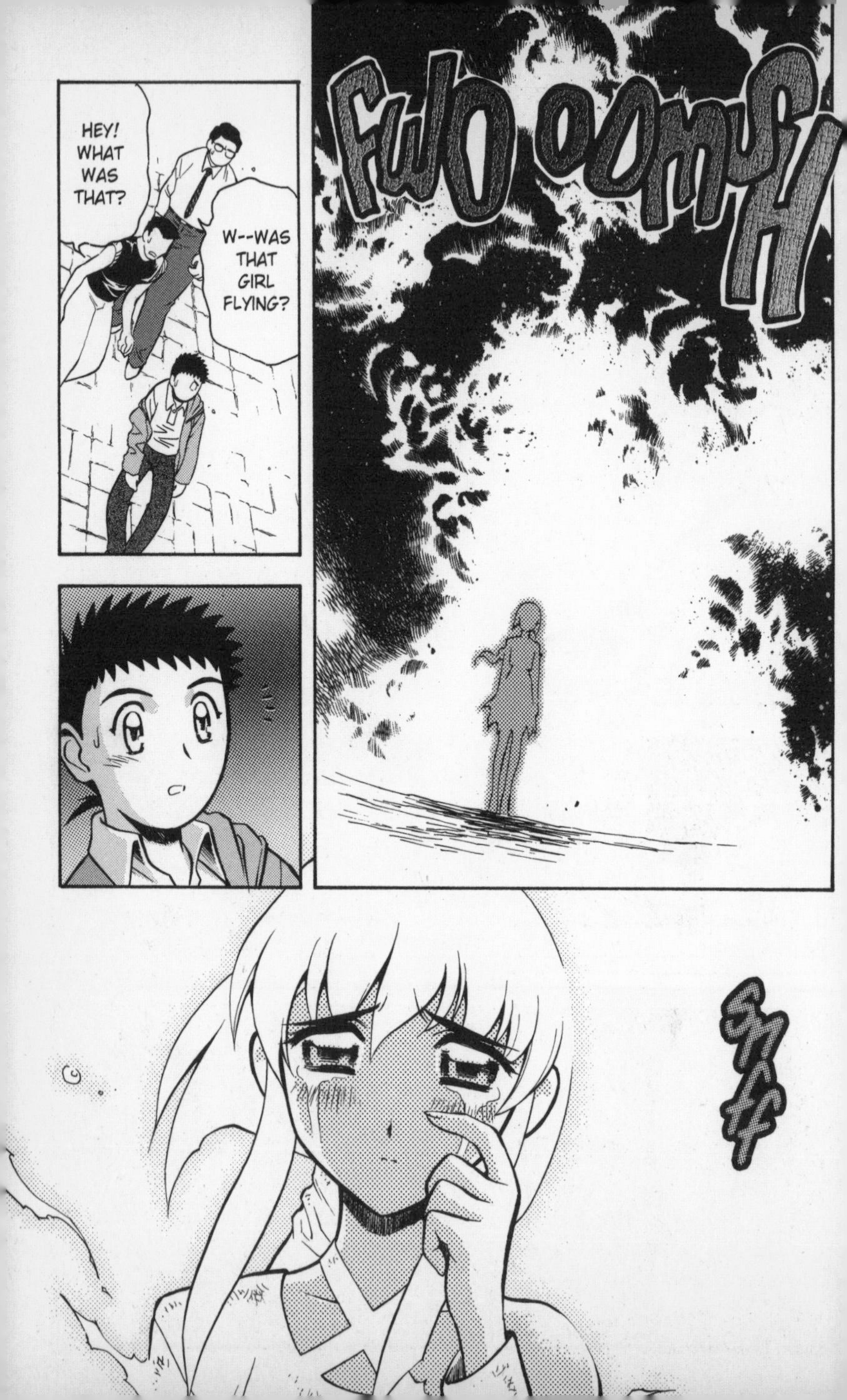
HEY! WHAT WAS THAT?
W--WAS THAT GIRL FLYING?
FWOOOMSH!

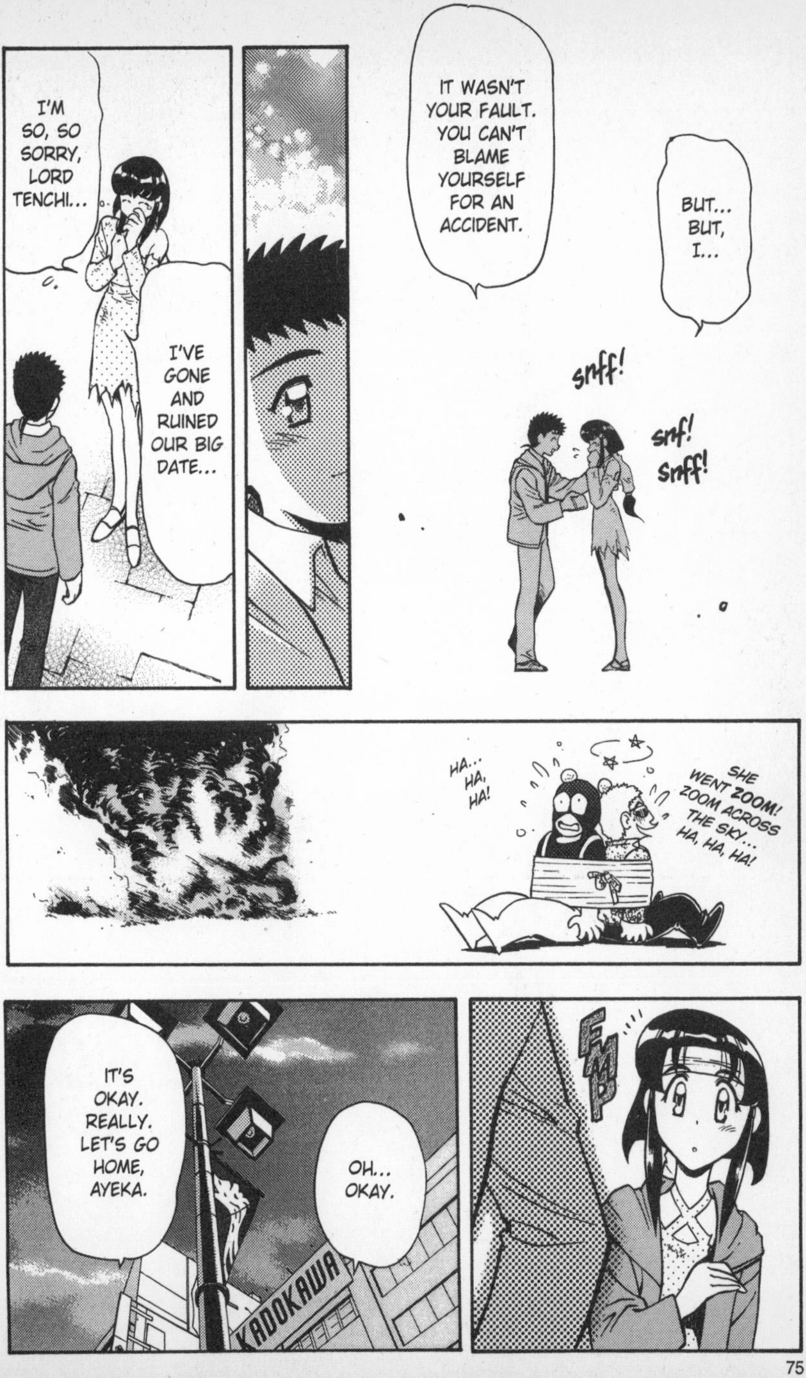
I'M SO, SO SORRY, LORD TENCHI...
I'VE GONE AND RUINED OUR BIG DATE...
IT WASN'T YOUR FAULT. YOU CAN'T BLAME YOURSELF FOR AN ACCIDENT.
BUT... BUT, I...
snff!
snf! Snff!
HA... HA, HA!
SHE WENT ZOOM! ZOOM ACROSS THE SKY... HA, HA, HA!
IT'S OKAY. REALLY. LET'S GO HOME, AYEKA.
OH... OKAY.
KADOKAWA
FMP

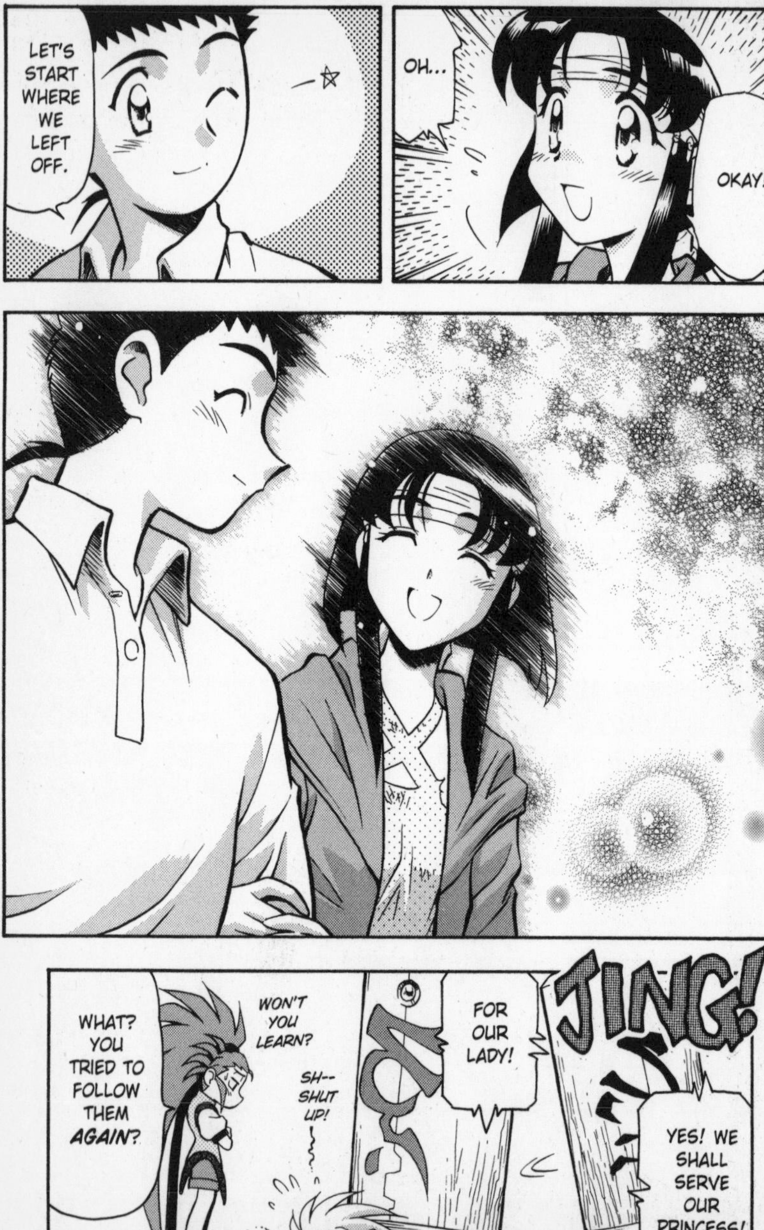
LET'S START WHERE WE LEFT OFF.
OH...
OKAY!
WHAT? YOU TRIED TO FOLLOW THEM *AGAIN*?
WON'T YOU LEARN?
SH-- SHUT UP!
FOR OUR LADY!
JING!
YES! WE SHALL SERVE OUR PRINCESS!

Chapter 4:
A CARROT A DAY

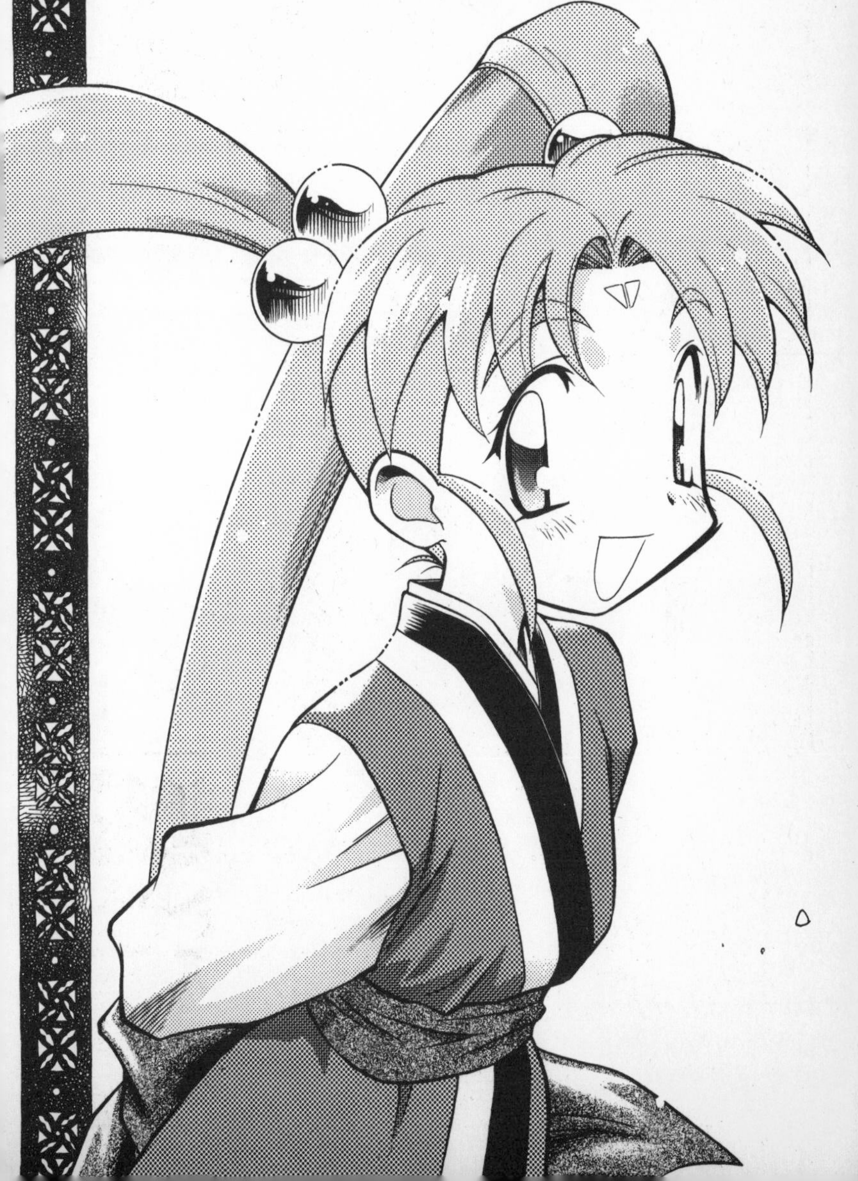

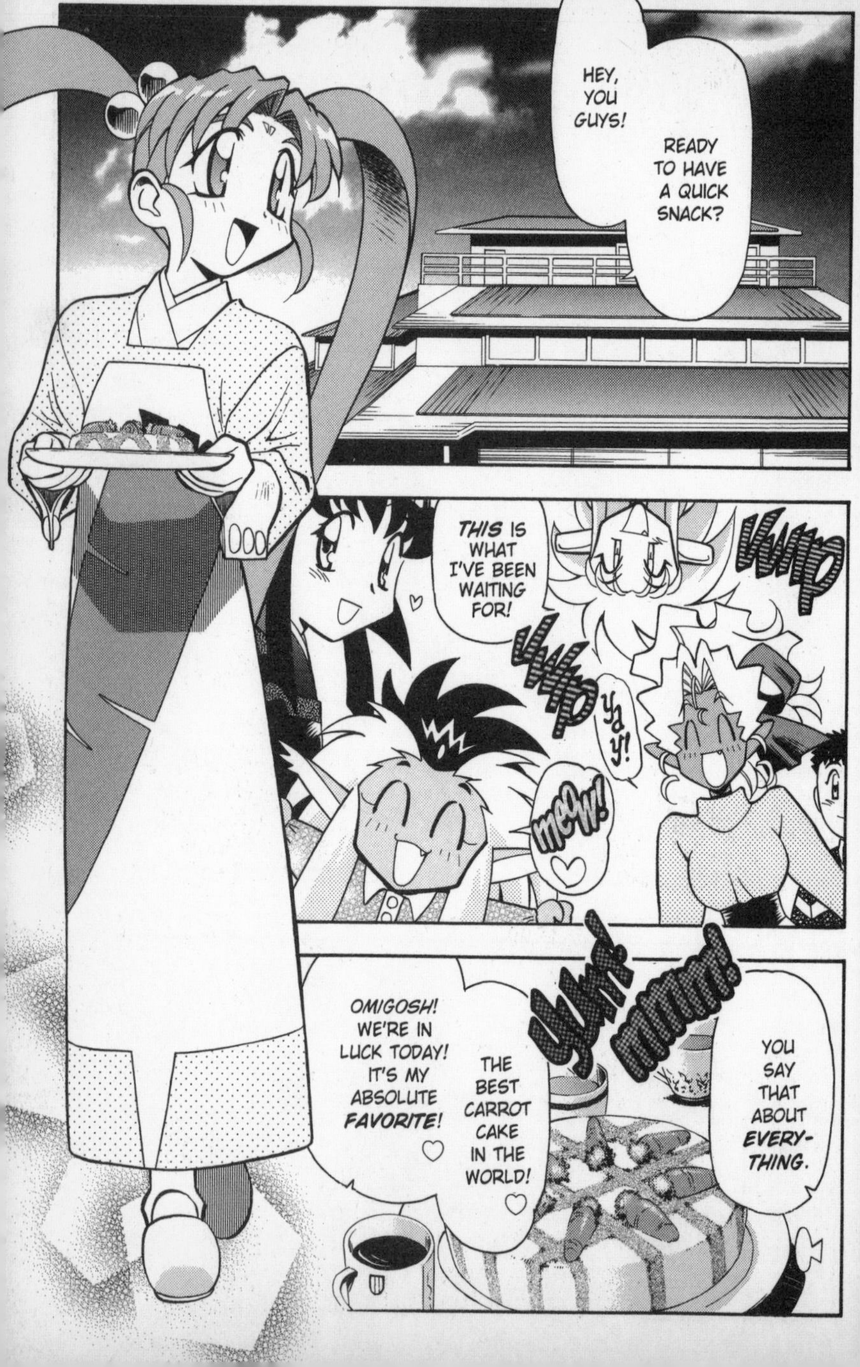
HEY, YOU GUYS!
READY TO HAVE A QUICK SNACK?
THIS IS WHAT I'VE BEEN WAITING FOR! ♡
VUMP
VUMP
yay!
meow! ♡
OMIGOSH! WE'RE IN LUCK TODAY! IT'S MY ABSOLUTE *FAVORITE*! ♡
THE BEST CARROT CAKE IN THE WORLD! ♡
YUM!
MMMM!
YOU SAY THAT ABOUT *EVERY-THING*.

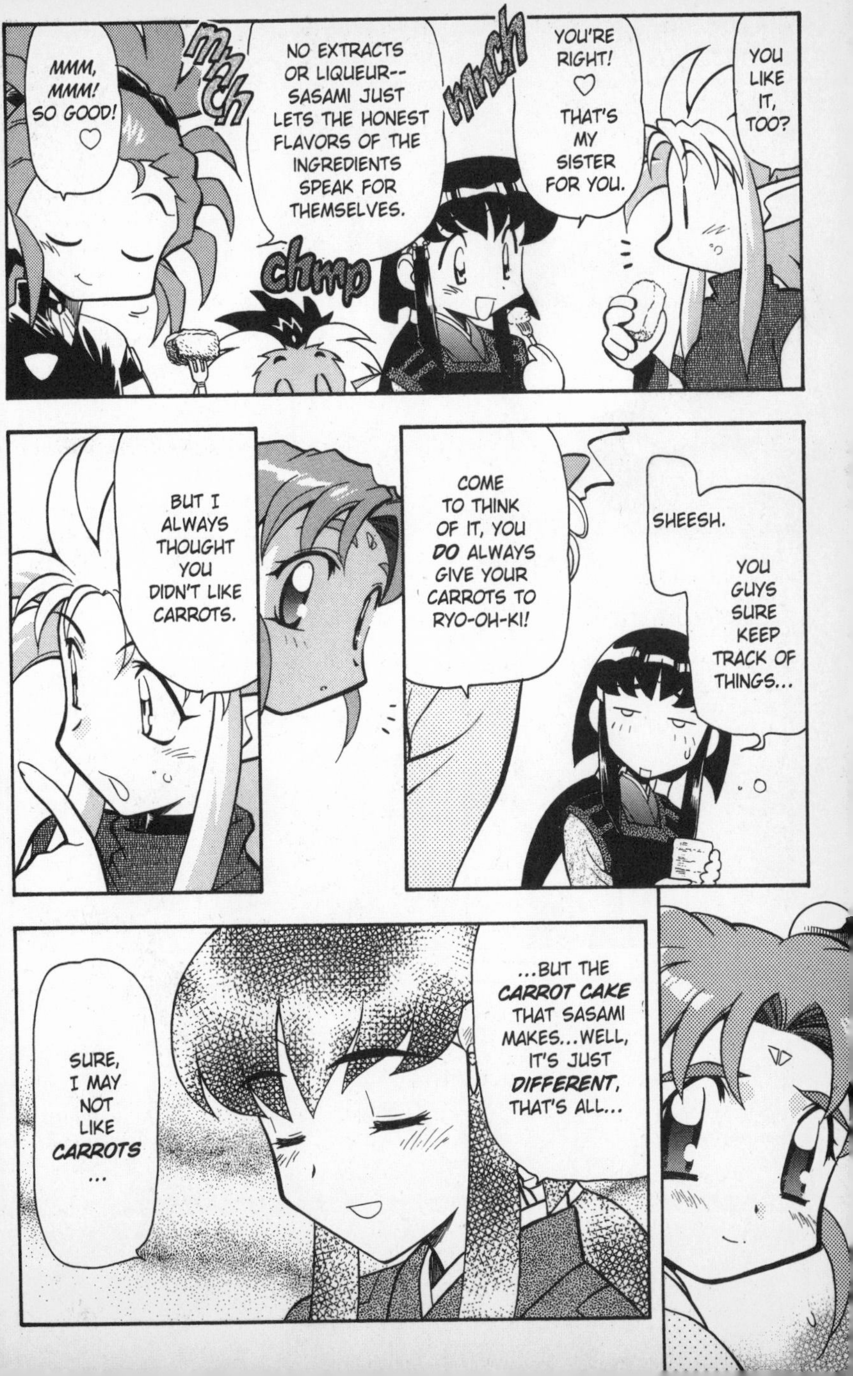
MMM, MMM! SO GOOD! ♡
mnch
NO EXTRACTS OR LIQUEUR-- SASAMI JUST LETS THE HONEST FLAVORS OF THE INGREDIENTS SPEAK FOR THEMSELVES.
chmp
mnch
YOU'RE RIGHT! ♡ THAT'S MY SISTER FOR YOU.
YOU LIKE IT, TOO?
BUT I ALWAYS THOUGHT YOU DIDN'T LIKE CARROTS.
COME TO THINK OF IT, YOU *DO* ALWAYS GIVE YOUR CARROTS TO RYO-OH-KI!
SHEESH.
YOU GUYS SURE KEEP TRACK OF THINGS...
SURE, I MAY NOT LIKE *CARROTS* ...
...BUT THE *CARROT CAKE* THAT SASAMI MAKES...WELL, IT'S JUST *DIFFERENT*, THAT'S ALL...

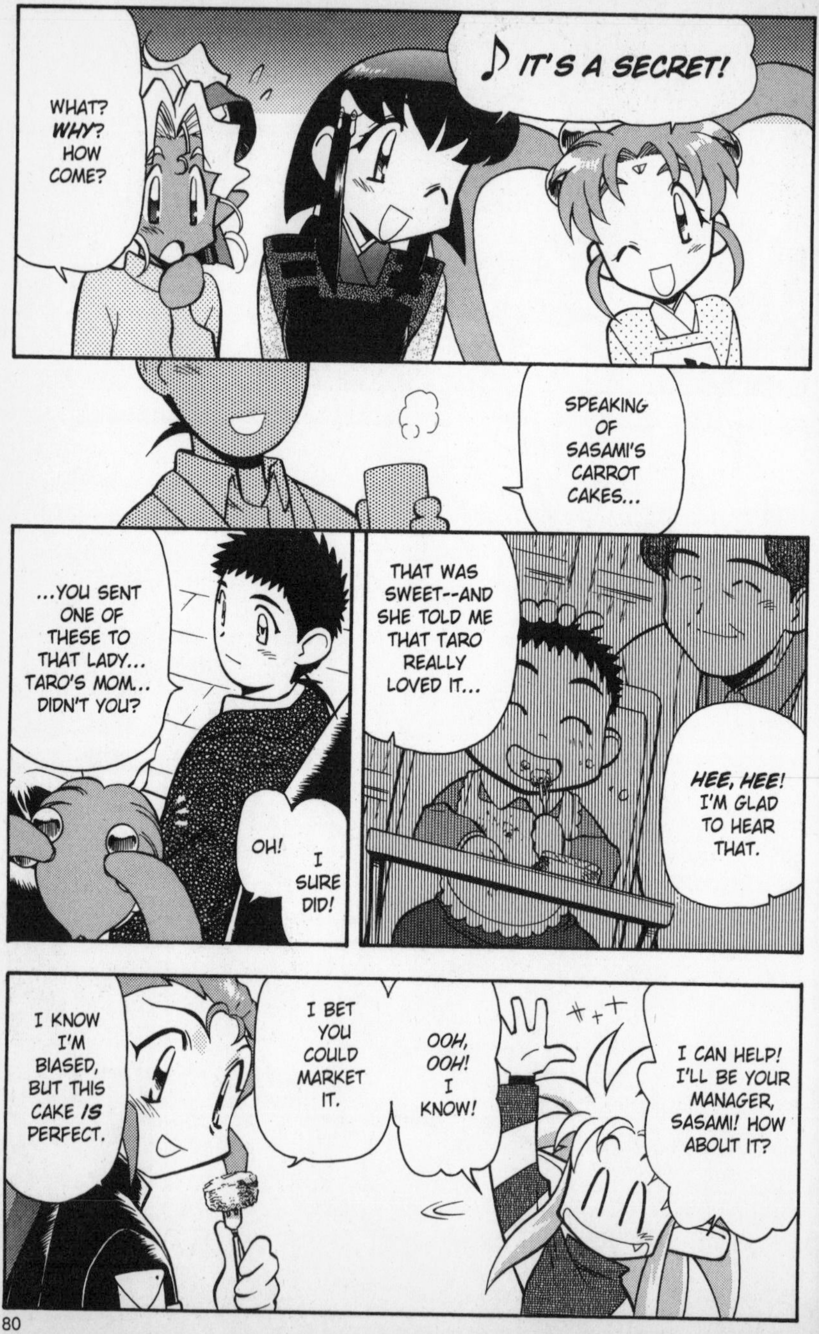

WHAT? WHY? HOW COME?
♪ IT'S A SECRET!
SPEAKING OF SASAMI'S CARROT CAKES...
...YOU SENT ONE OF THESE TO THAT LADY... TARO'S MOM... DIDN'T YOU?
OH!
I SURE DID!
THAT WAS SWEET--AND SHE TOLD ME THAT TARO REALLY LOVED IT...
HEE, HEE! I'M GLAD TO HEAR THAT.
I KNOW I'M BIASED, BUT THIS CAKE IS PERFECT.
I BET YOU COULD MARKET IT.
OOH, OOH! I KNOW!
I CAN HELP! I'LL BE YOUR MANAGER, SASAMI! HOW ABOUT IT?

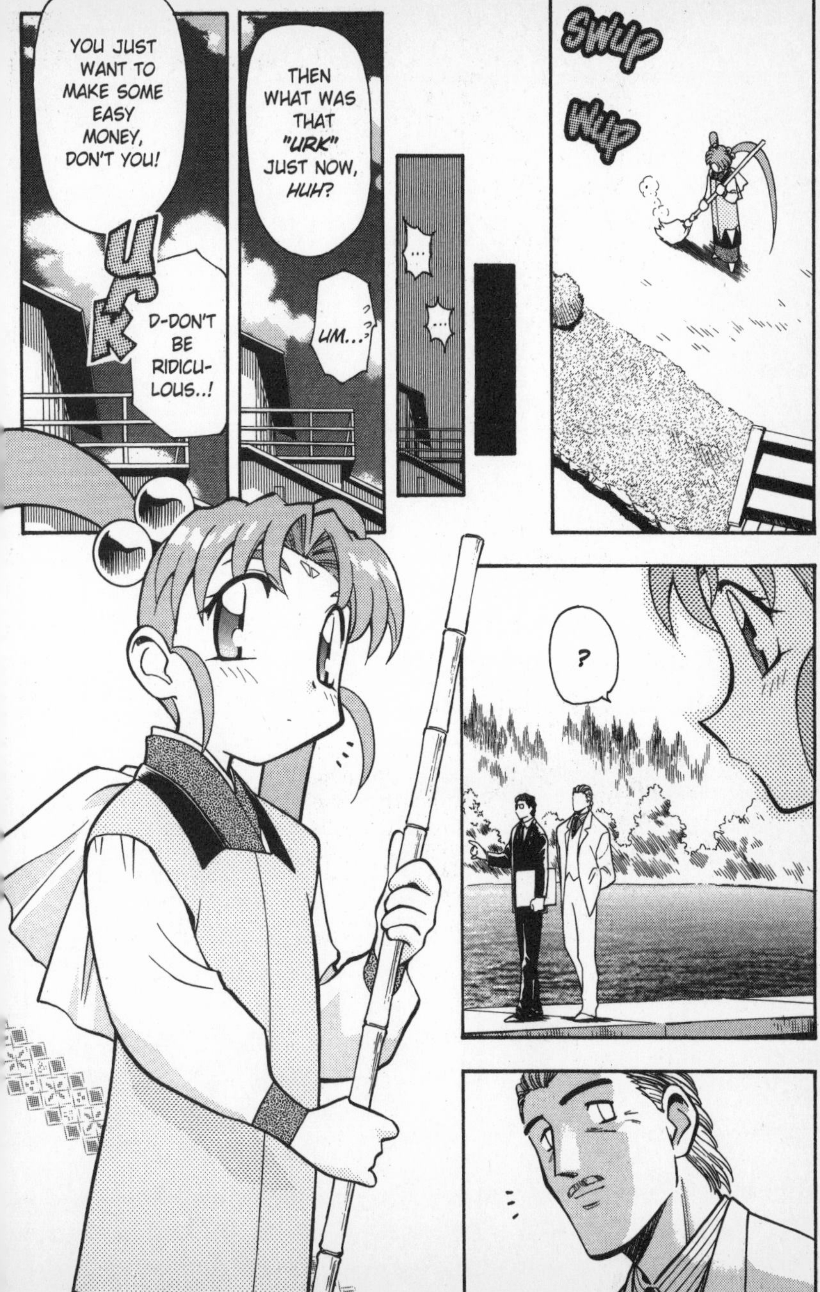
YOU JUST WANT TO MAKE SOME EASY MONEY, DON'T YOU!
URK
D-DON'T BE RIDICULOUS..!
THEN WHAT WAS THAT "URK" JUST NOW, HUH?
UM...?
...
...
SWUP
HUP
?

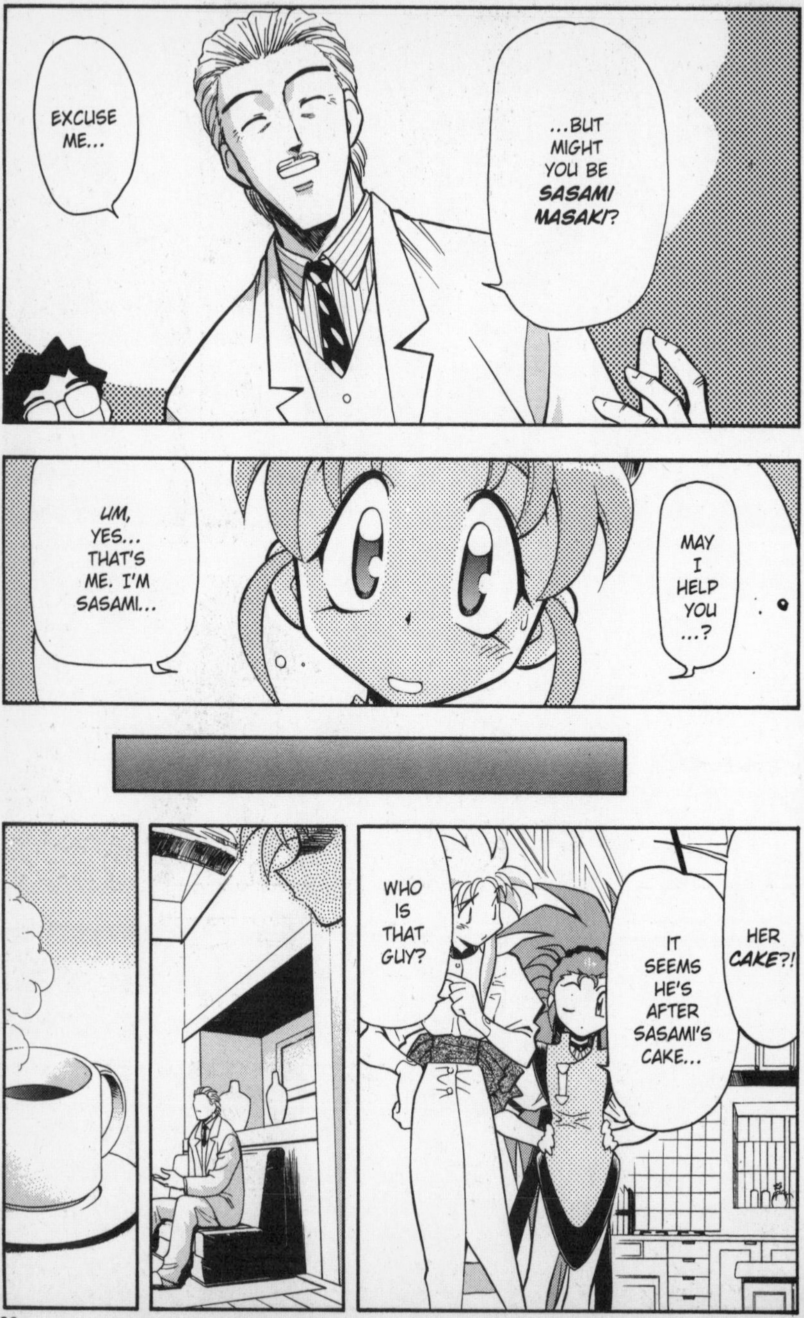
EXCUSE ME...
...BUT MIGHT YOU BE SASAMI MASAKI?
UM, YES... THAT'S ME. I'M SASAMI...
MAY I HELP YOU ...?
WHO IS THAT GUY?
IT SEEMS HE'S AFTER SASAMI'S CAKE...
HER CAKE?!

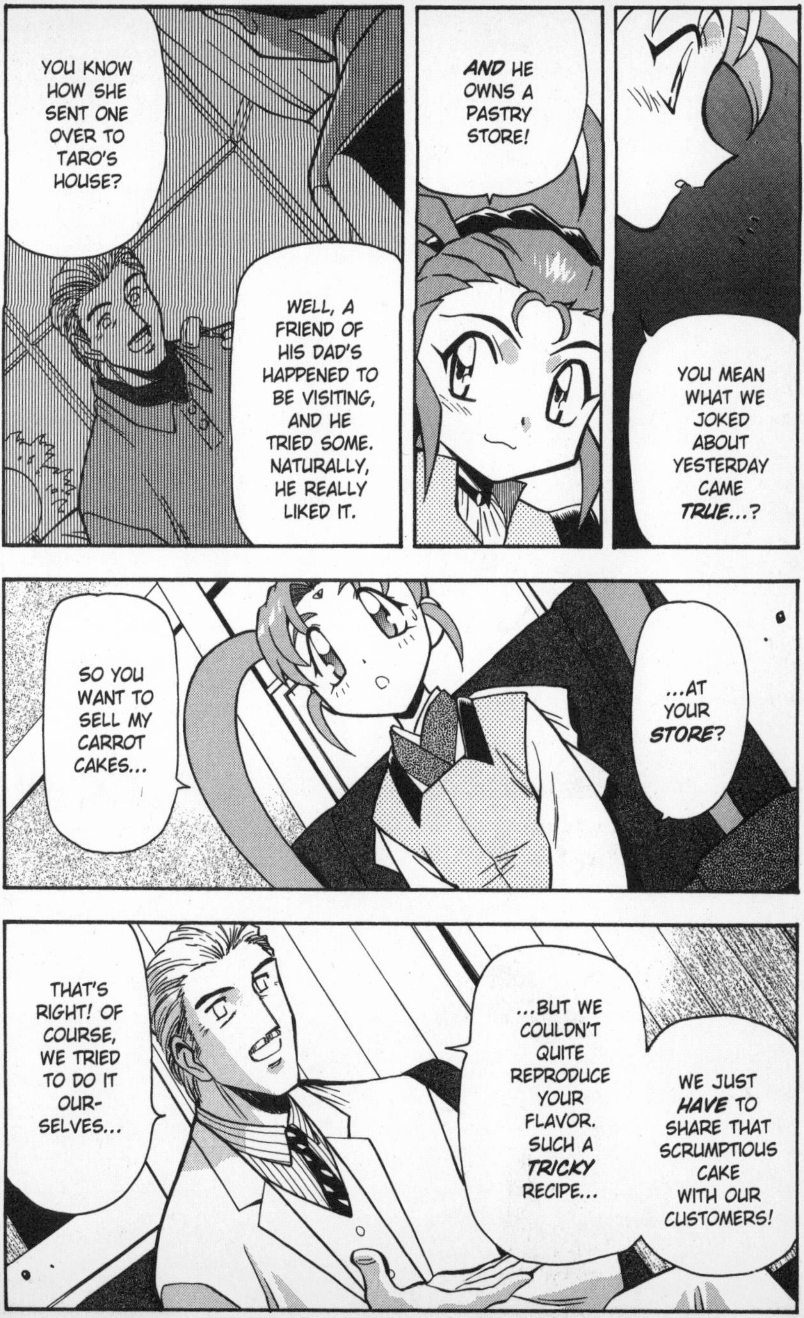
YOU KNOW HOW SHE SENT ONE OVER TO TARO'S HOUSE?
WELL, A FRIEND OF HIS DAD'S HAPPENED TO BE VISITING, AND HE TRIED SOME. NATURALLY, HE REALLY LIKED IT.
AND HE OWNS A PASTRY STORE!
YOU MEAN WHAT WE JOKED ABOUT YESTERDAY CAME *TRUE...*?
SO YOU WANT TO SELL MY CARROT CAKES...
...AT YOUR *STORE*?
THAT'S RIGHT! OF COURSE, WE TRIED TO DO IT OUR-SELVES...
...BUT WE COULDN'T QUITE REPRODUCE YOUR FLAVOR. SUCH A *TRICKY* RECIPE...
WE JUST *HAVE* TO SHARE THAT SCRUMPTIOUS CAKE WITH OUR CUSTOMERS!

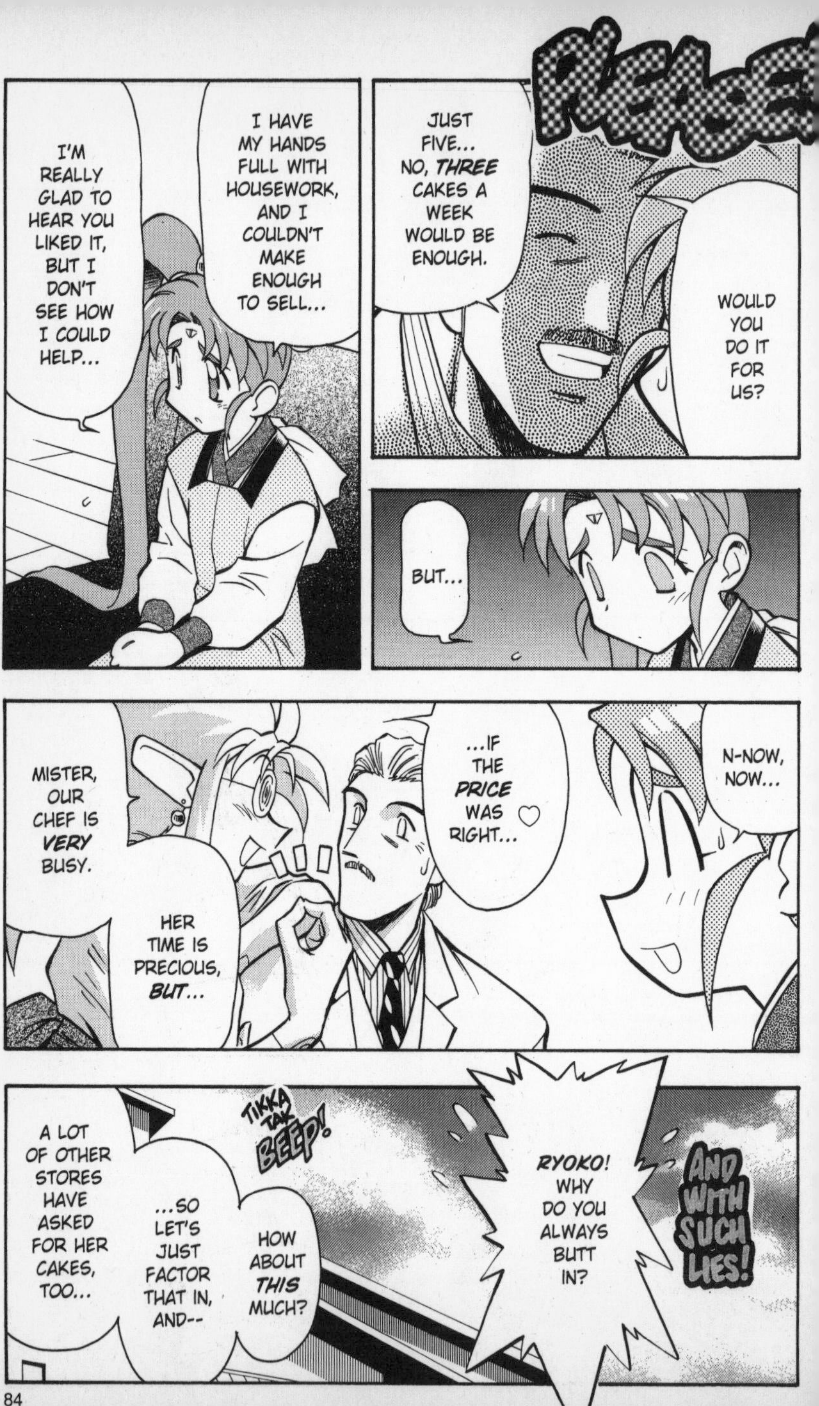
I'M REALLY GLAD TO HEAR YOU LIKED IT, BUT I DON'T SEE HOW I COULD HELP...
I HAVE MY HANDS FULL WITH HOUSEWORK, AND I COULDN'T MAKE ENOUGH TO SELL...
PLEASE!
JUST FIVE... NO, *THREE* CAKES A WEEK WOULD BE ENOUGH.
WOULD YOU DO IT FOR US?
BUT...
MISTER, OUR CHEF IS *VERY* BUSY.
HER TIME IS PRECIOUS, *BUT*...
...IF THE *PRICE* WAS RIGHT... ♡
N-NOW, NOW...
A LOT OF OTHER STORES HAVE ASKED FOR HER CAKES, TOO...
...SO LET'S JUST FACTOR THAT IN, AND--
TIKKA TAK BEEP!
HOW ABOUT *THIS* MUCH?
RYOKO! WHY DO YOU ALWAYS BUTT IN?
AND WITH SUCH LIES!

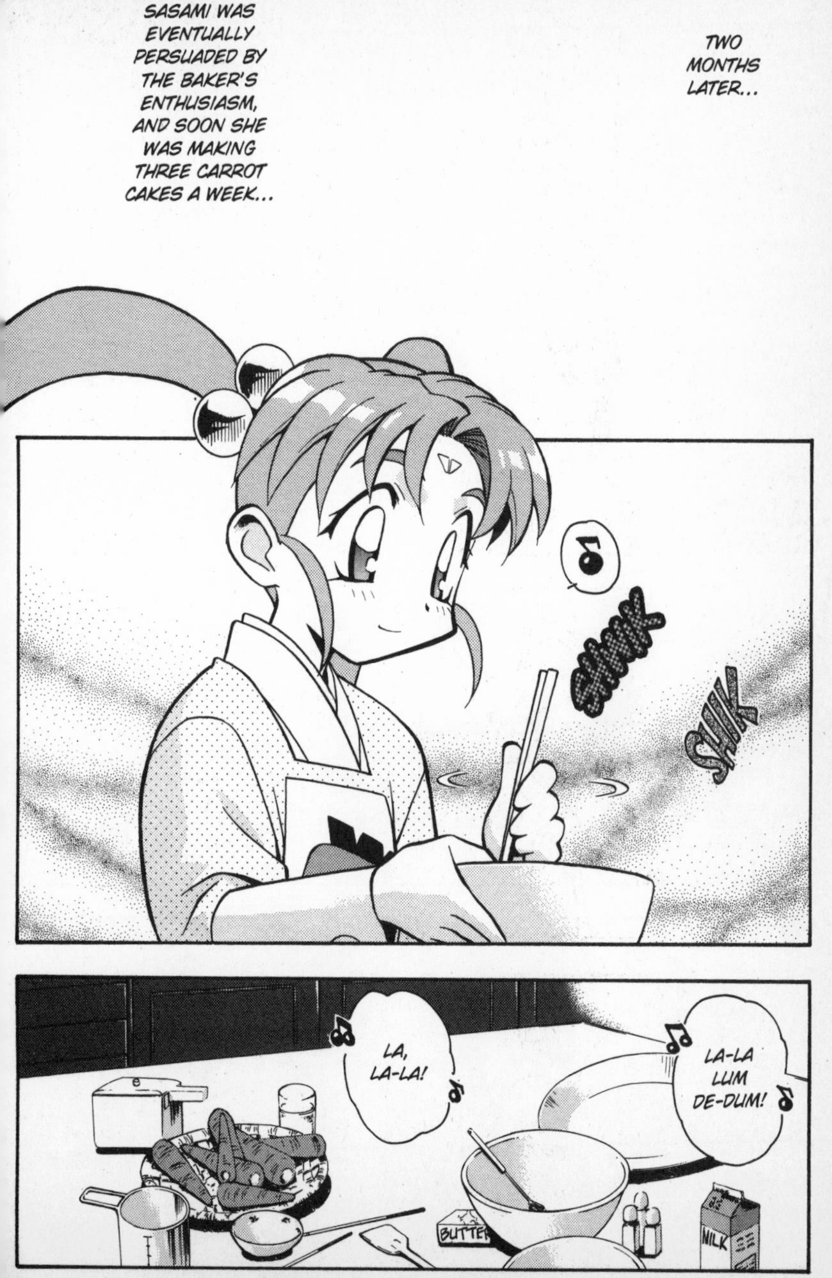
SASAMI WAS EVENTUALLY PERSUADED BY THE BAKER'S ENTHUSIASM, AND SOON SHE WAS MAKING THREE CARROT CAKES A WEEK...
TWO MONTHS LATER...
SHINK
SHIK
LA, LA-LA!
LA-LA LUM DE-DUM!
BUTTER
MILK

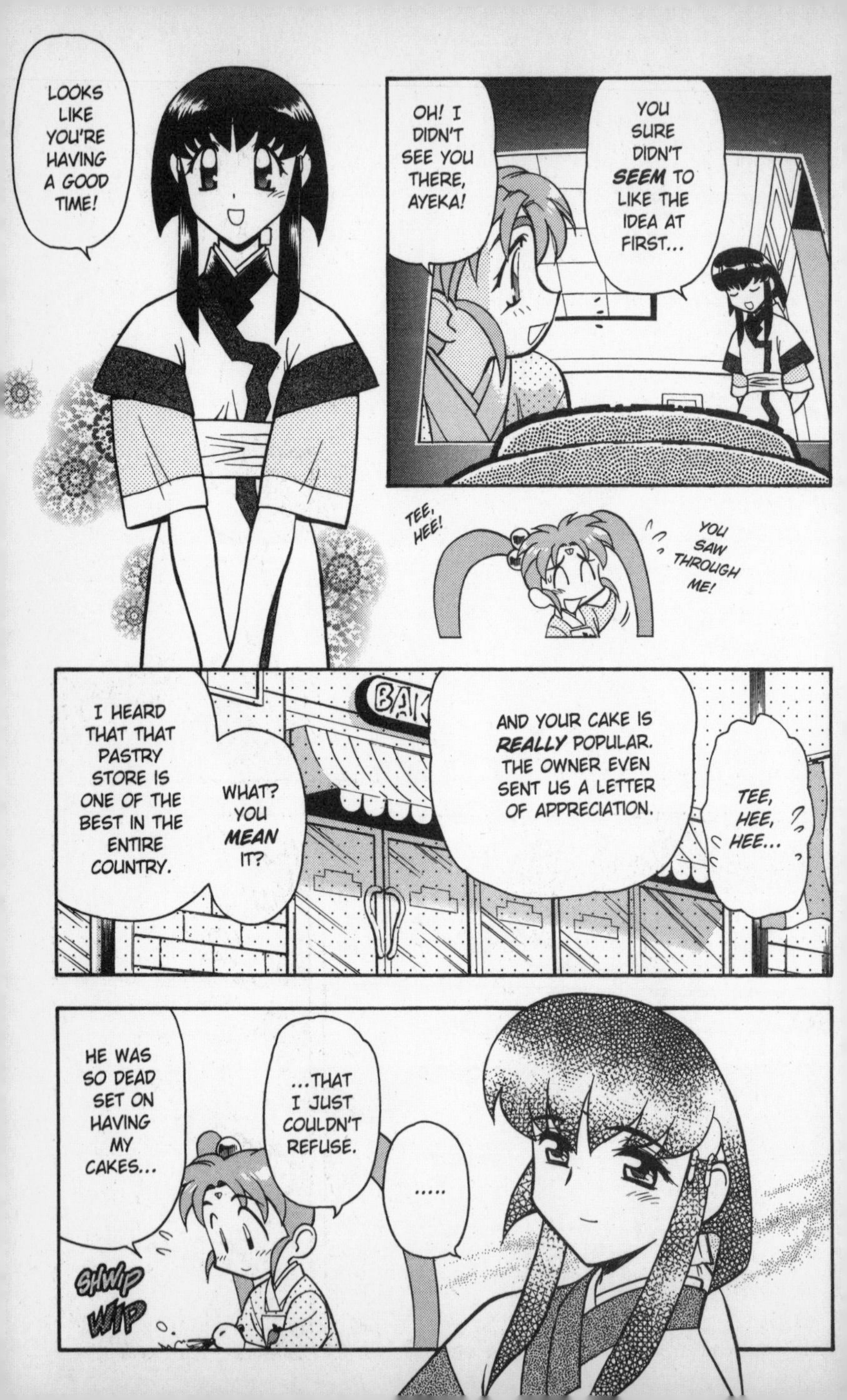
LOOKS LIKE YOU'RE HAVING A GOOD TIME!
OH! I DIDN'T SEE YOU THERE, AYEKA!
YOU SURE DIDN'T SEEM TO LIKE THE IDEA AT FIRST...
TEE, HEE!
YOU SAW THROUGH ME!
I HEARD THAT THAT PASTRY STORE IS ONE OF THE BEST IN THE ENTIRE COUNTRY.
WHAT? YOU MEAN IT?
AND YOUR CAKE IS REALLY POPULAR. THE OWNER EVEN SENT US A LETTER OF APPRECIATION.
TEE, HEE, HEE...
HE WAS SO DEAD SET ON HAVING MY CAKES...
...THAT I JUST COULDN'T REFUSE.
.....
SHWIP WIP

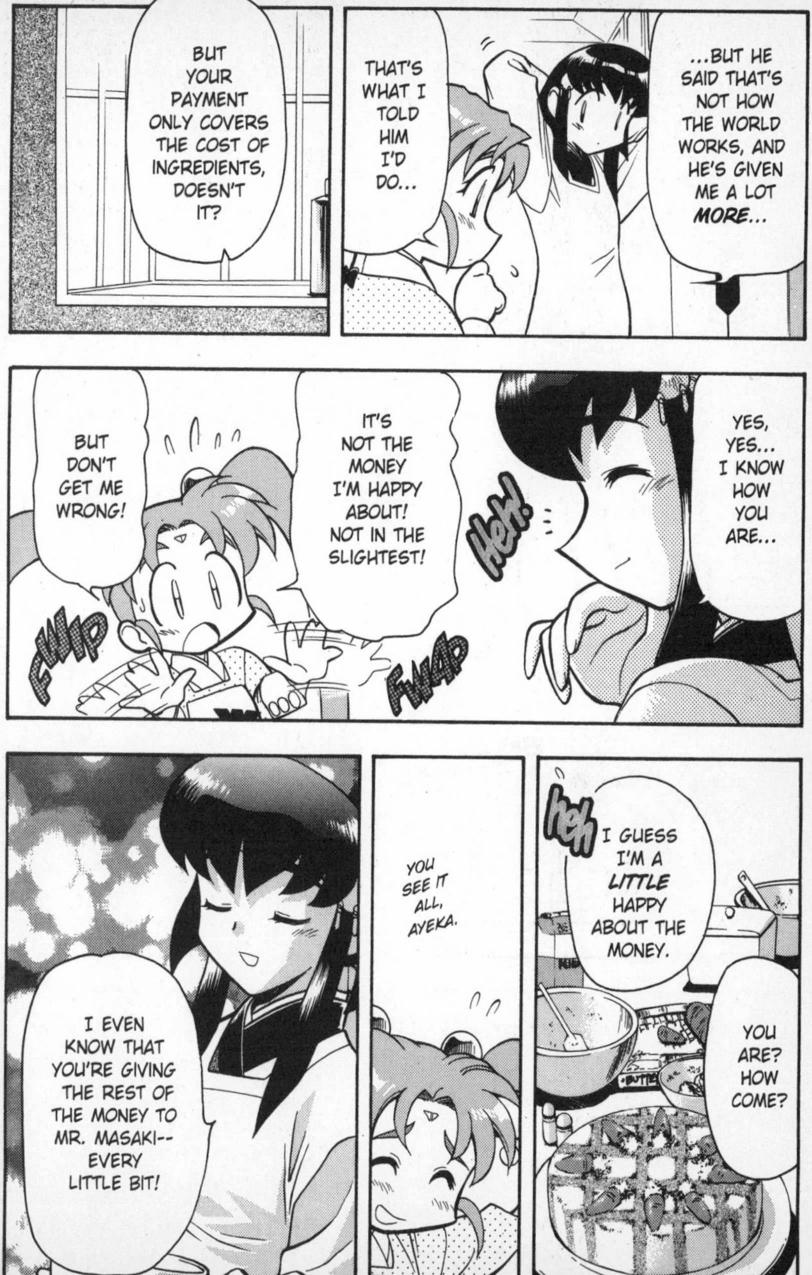
BUT YOUR PAYMENT ONLY COVERS THE COST OF INGREDIENTS, DOESN'T IT?
THAT'S WHAT I TOLD HIM I'D DO...
...BUT HE SAID THAT'S NOT HOW THE WORLD WORKS, AND HE'S GIVEN ME A LOT ***MORE***...
BUT DON'T GET ME WRONG!
IT'S NOT THE MONEY I'M HAPPY ABOUT! NOT IN THE SLIGHTEST!
FWIP
FWAP
Heh!
YES, YES... I KNOW HOW YOU ARE...
I EVEN KNOW THAT YOU'RE GIVING THE REST OF THE MONEY TO MR. MASAKI--EVERY LITTLE BIT!
YOU SEE IT ALL, AYEKA.
heh
I GUESS I'M A ***LITTLE*** HAPPY ABOUT THE MONEY.
YOU ARE? HOW COME?

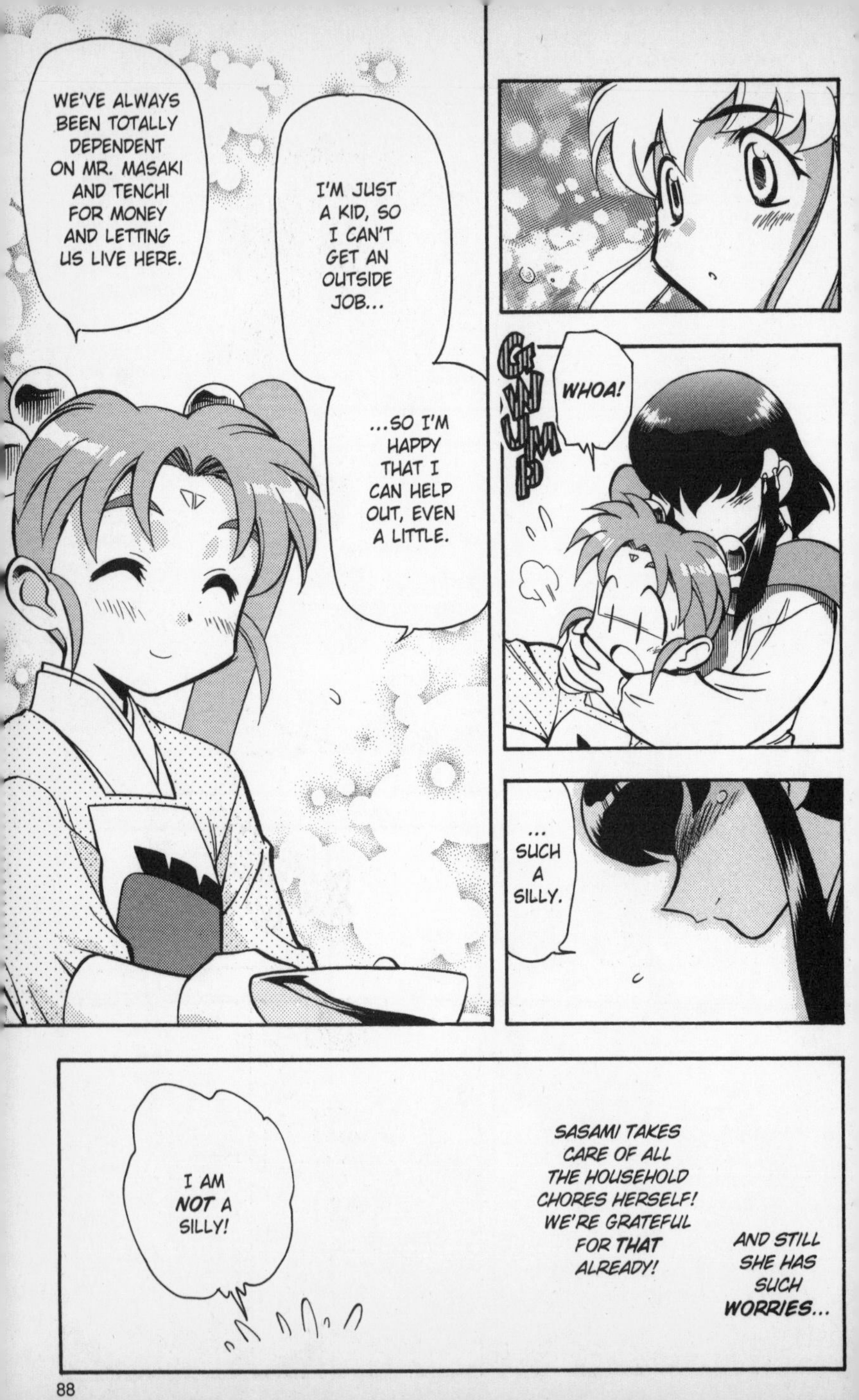
WE'VE ALWAYS BEEN TOTALLY DEPENDENT ON MR. MASAKI AND TENCHI FOR MONEY AND LETTING US LIVE HERE.
I'M JUST A KID, SO I CAN'T GET AN OUTSIDE JOB...
...SO I'M HAPPY THAT I CAN HELP OUT, EVEN A LITTLE.
GNUMP
WHOA!
... SUCH A SILLY.
I AM NOT A SILLY!
SASAMI TAKES CARE OF ALL THE HOUSEHOLD CHORES HERSELF! WE'RE GRATEFUL FOR THAT ALREADY!
AND STILL SHE HAS SUCH WORRIES...

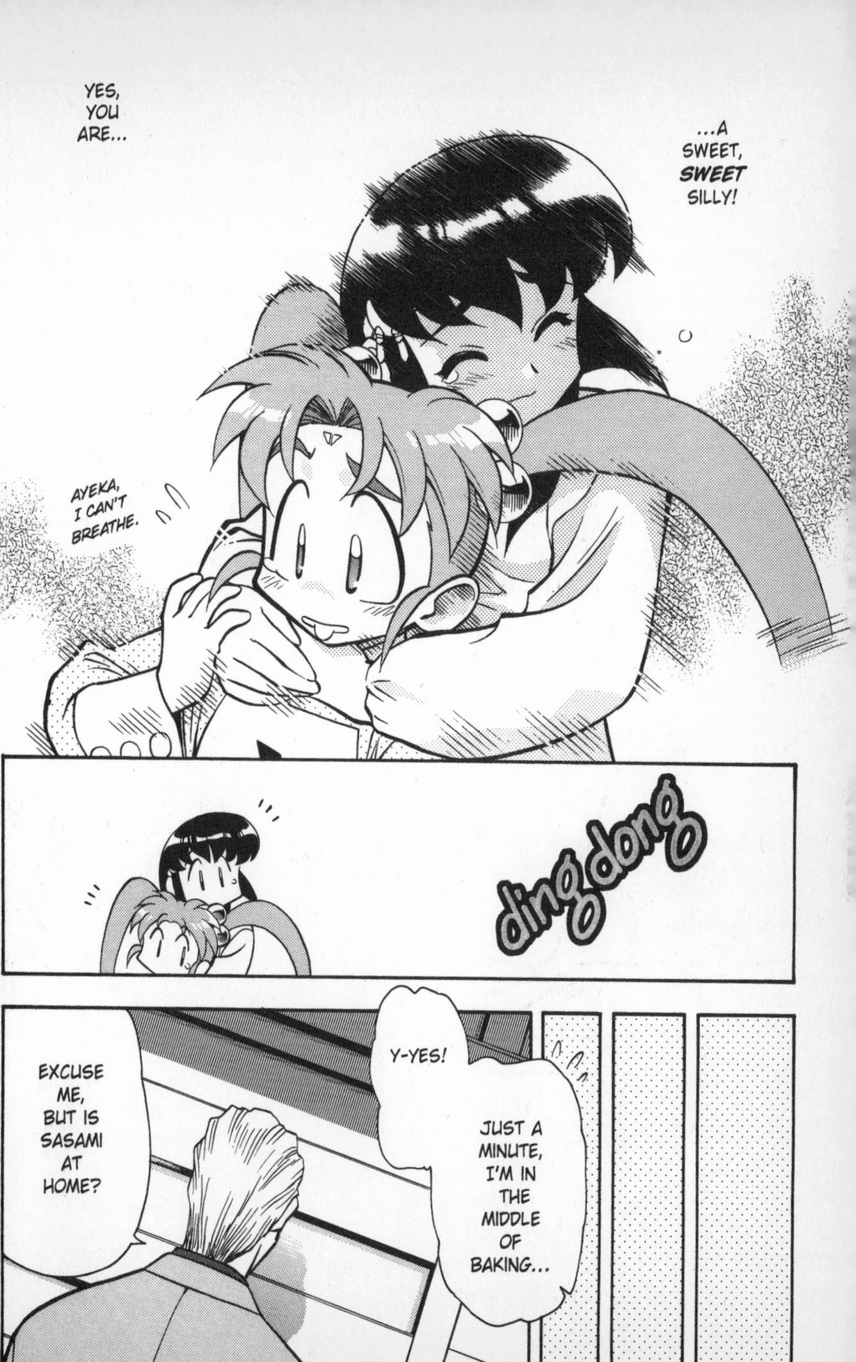
YES, YOU ARE...
...A SWEET, **SWEET** SILLY!
AYEKA, I CAN'T BREATHE.
ding dong
EXCUSE ME, BUT IS SASAMI AT HOME?
Y-YES!
JUST A MINUTE, I'M IN THE MIDDLE OF BAKING...

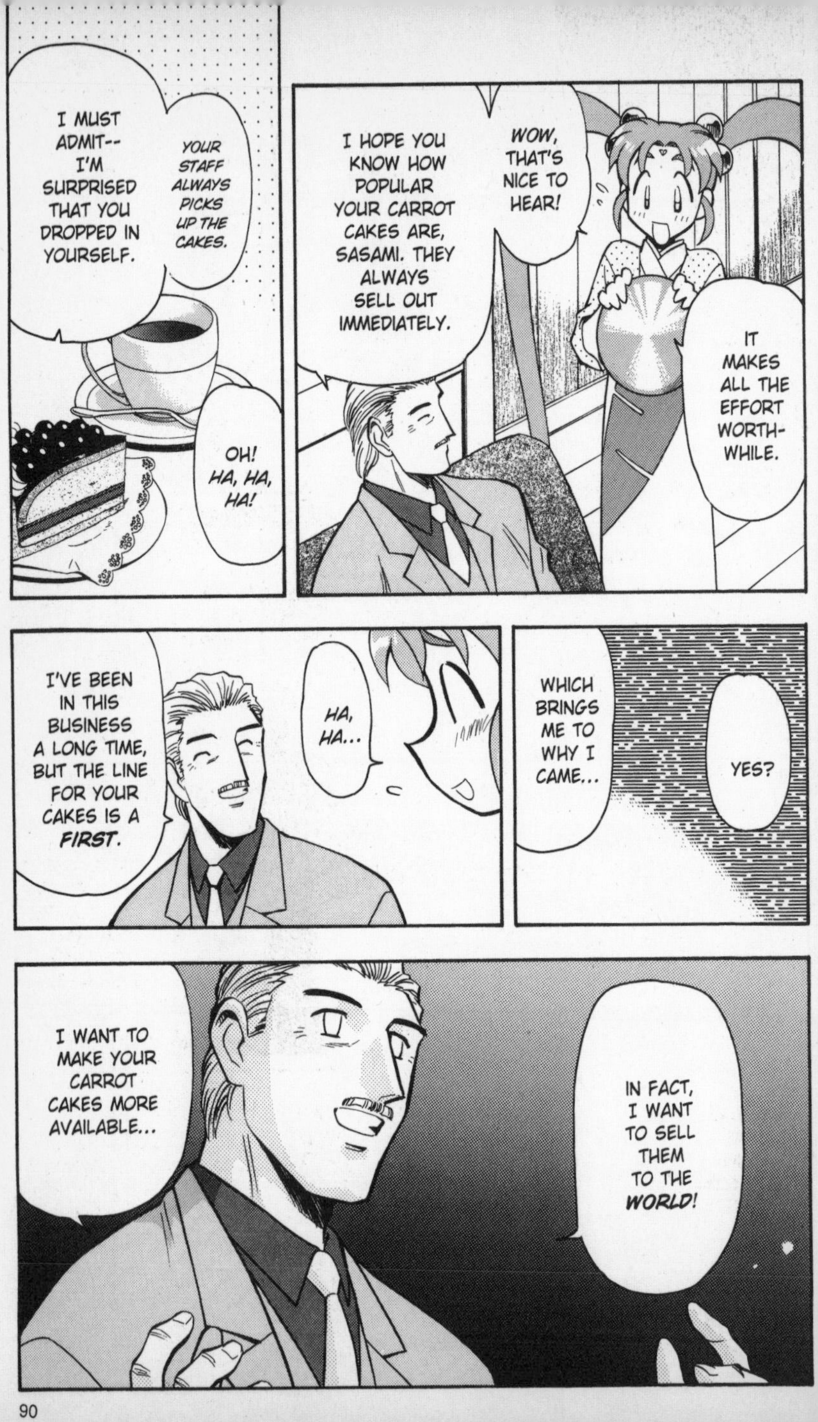
I MUST ADMIT-- I'M SURPRISED THAT YOU DROPPED IN YOURSELF.
YOUR STAFF ALWAYS PICKS UP THE CAKES.
OH! HA, HA, HA!
I HOPE YOU KNOW HOW POPULAR YOUR CARROT CAKES ARE, SASAMI. THEY ALWAYS SELL OUT IMMEDIATELY.
WOW, THAT'S NICE TO HEAR!
IT MAKES ALL THE EFFORT WORTH-WHILE.
I'VE BEEN IN THIS BUSINESS A LONG TIME, BUT THE LINE FOR YOUR CAKES IS A FIRST.
HA, HA...
WHICH BRINGS ME TO WHY I CAME...
YES?
I WANT TO MAKE YOUR CARROT CAKES MORE AVAILABLE...
IN FACT, I WANT TO SELL THEM TO THE WORLD!

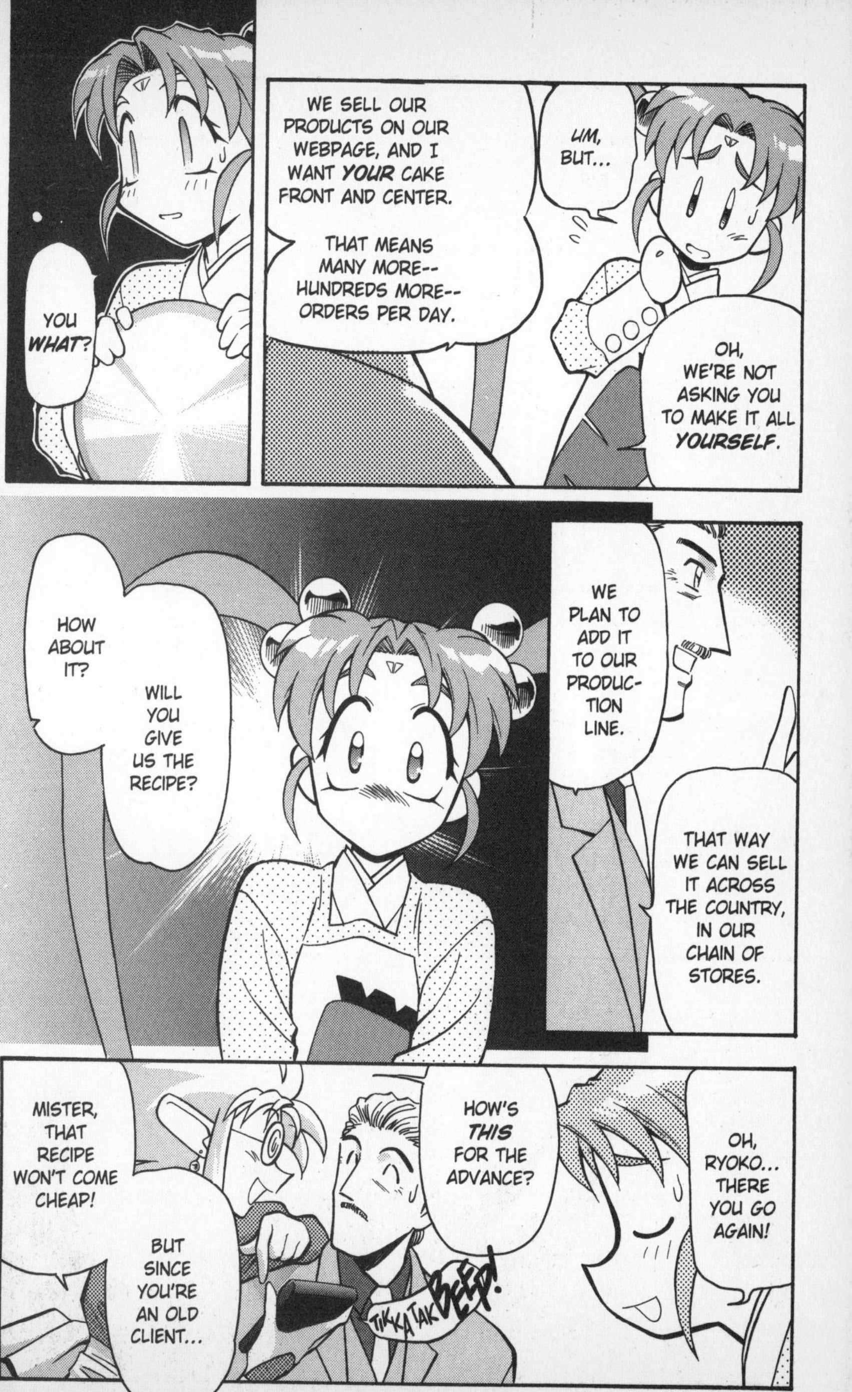
YOU WHAT?
WE SELL OUR PRODUCTS ON OUR WEBPAGE, AND I WANT YOUR CAKE FRONT AND CENTER.
THAT MEANS MANY MORE--HUNDREDS MORE--ORDERS PER DAY.
UM, BUT...
OH, WE'RE NOT ASKING YOU TO MAKE IT ALL YOURSELF.
HOW ABOUT IT?
WILL YOU GIVE US THE RECIPE?
WE PLAN TO ADD IT TO OUR PRODUCTION LINE.
THAT WAY WE CAN SELL IT ACROSS THE COUNTRY, IN OUR CHAIN OF STORES.
MISTER, THAT RECIPE WON'T COME CHEAP!
BUT SINCE YOU'RE AN OLD CLIENT...
TIKKA TAK BEEP!
HOW'S THIS FOR THE ADVANCE?
OH, RYOKO... THERE YOU GO AGAIN!

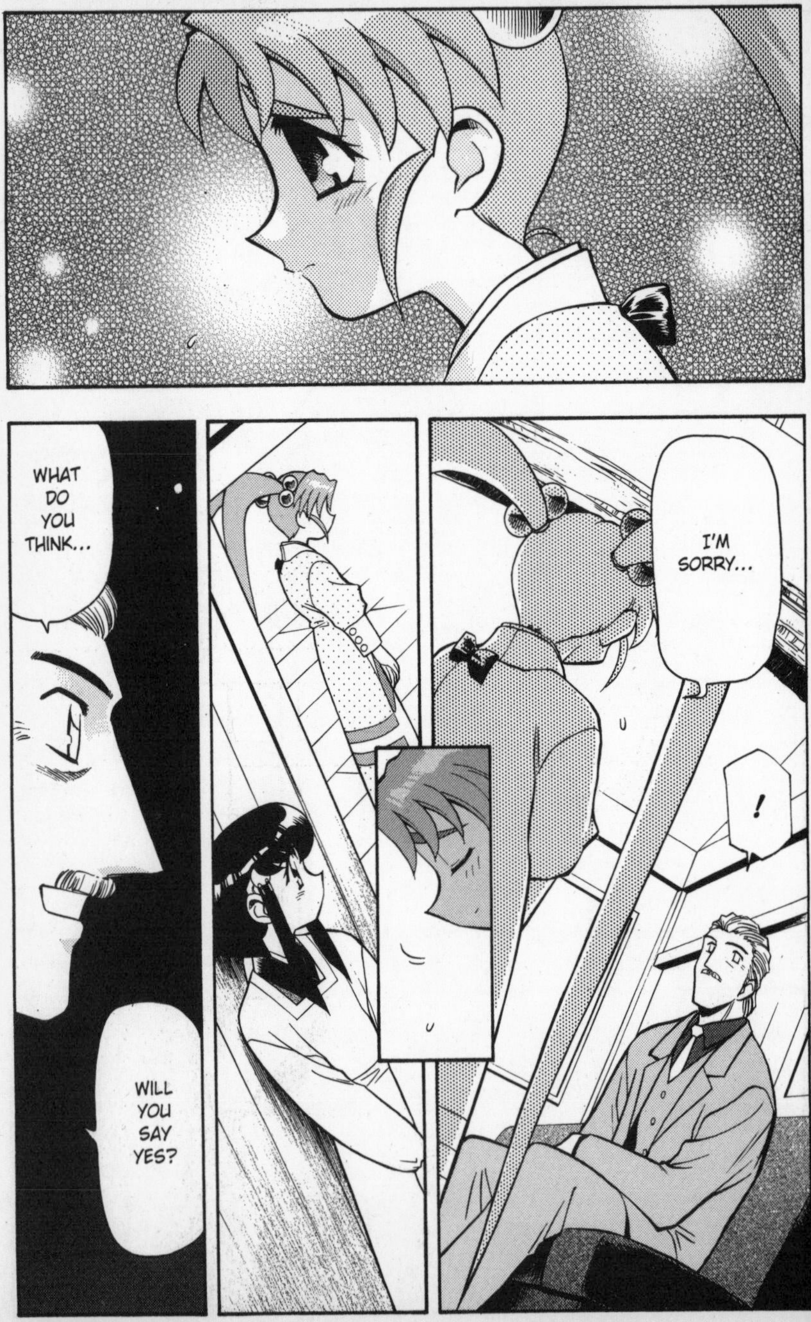
WHAT DO YOU THINK...
WILL YOU SAY YES?
I'M SORRY...
!

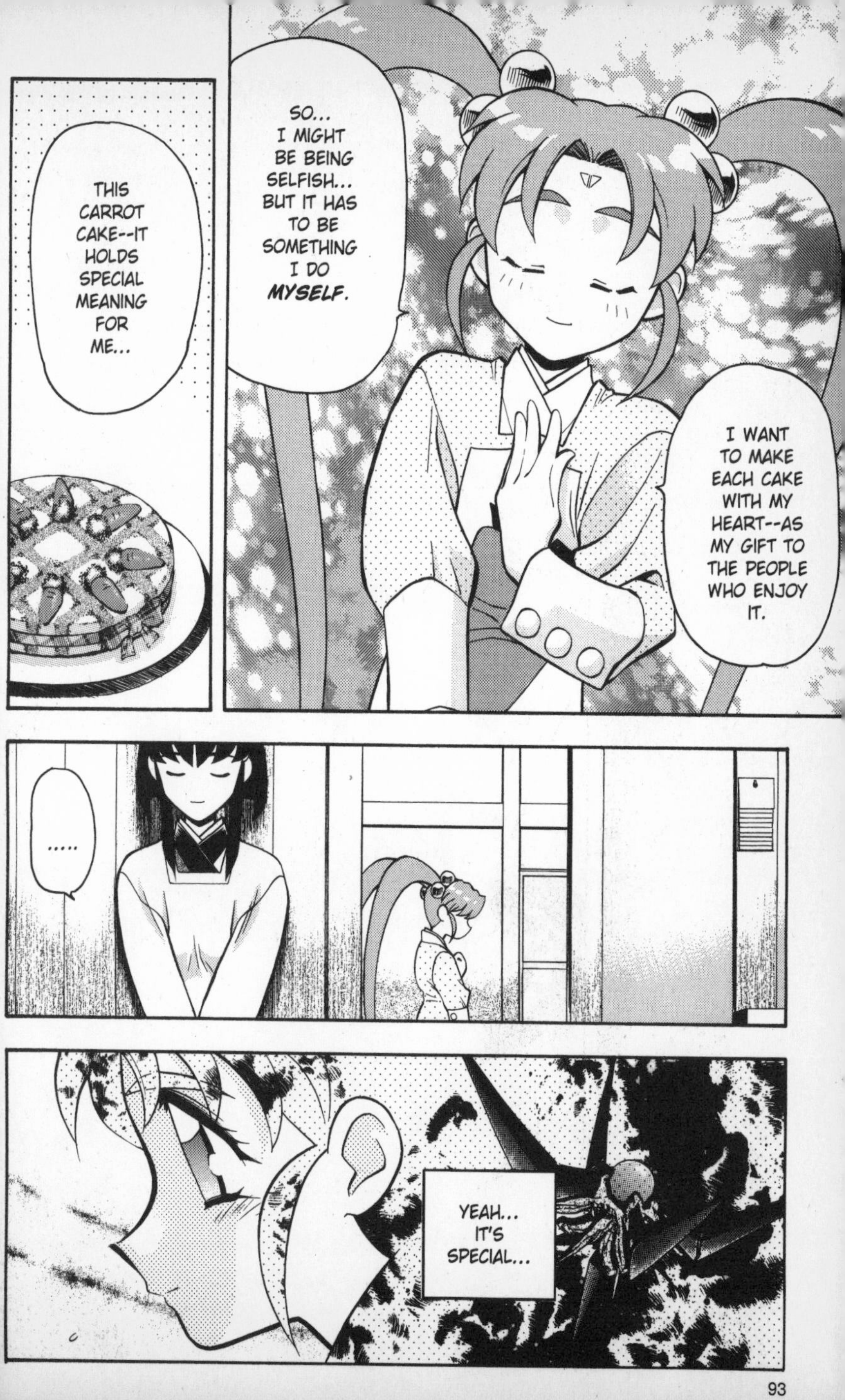
THIS CARROT CAKE--IT HOLDS SPECIAL MEANING FOR ME...
SO... I MIGHT BE BEING SELFISH... BUT IT HAS TO BE SOMETHING I DO *MYSELF*.
I WANT TO MAKE EACH CAKE WITH MY HEART--AS MY GIFT TO THE PEOPLE WHO ENJOY IT.
.....
YEAH... IT'S SPECIAL...

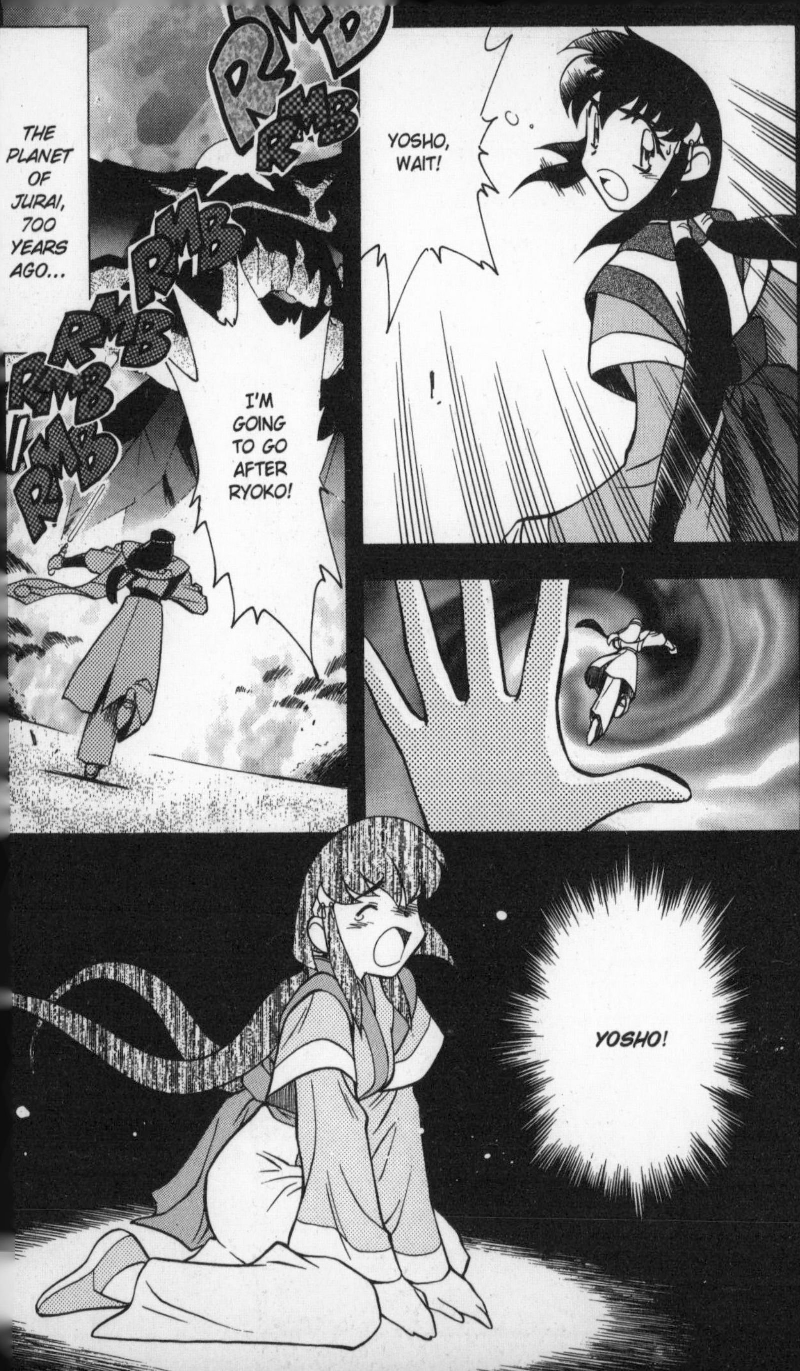
THE PLANET OF JURAI, 700 YEARS AGO...
RMB
RMB
RMB
RMB
RMB
RMB
I'M GOING TO GO AFTER RYOKO!
YOSHO, WAIT!
!
YOSHO!

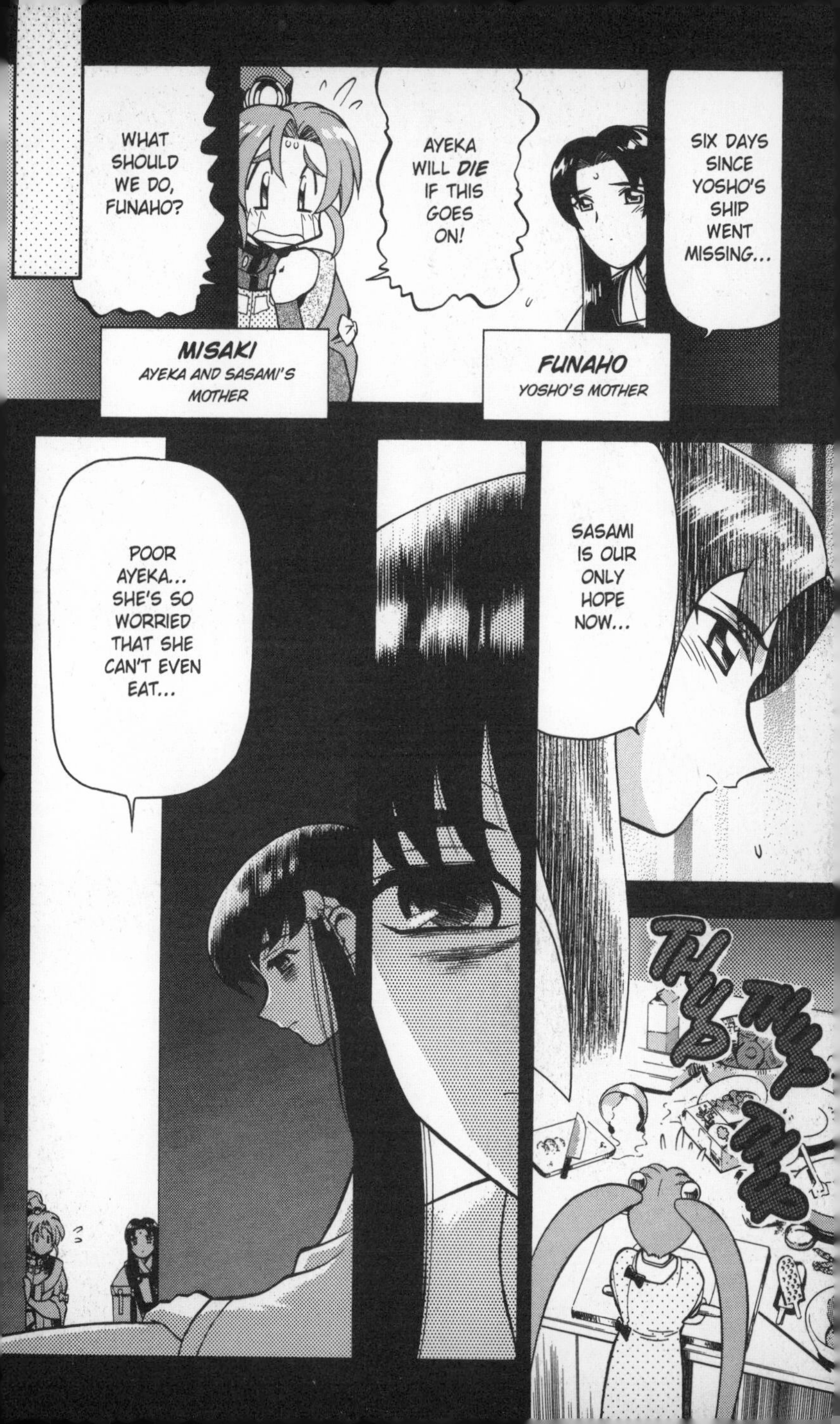
WHAT SHOULD WE DO, FUNAHO?
AYEKA WILL *DIE* IF THIS GOES ON!
MISAKI
AYEKA AND SASAMI'S MOTHER
SIX DAYS SINCE YOSHO'S SHIP WENT MISSING...
FUNAHO
YOSHO'S MOTHER
POOR AYEKA... SHE'S SO WORRIED THAT SHE CAN'T EVEN EAT...
SASAMI IS OUR ONLY HOPE NOW...
THUD
THUD

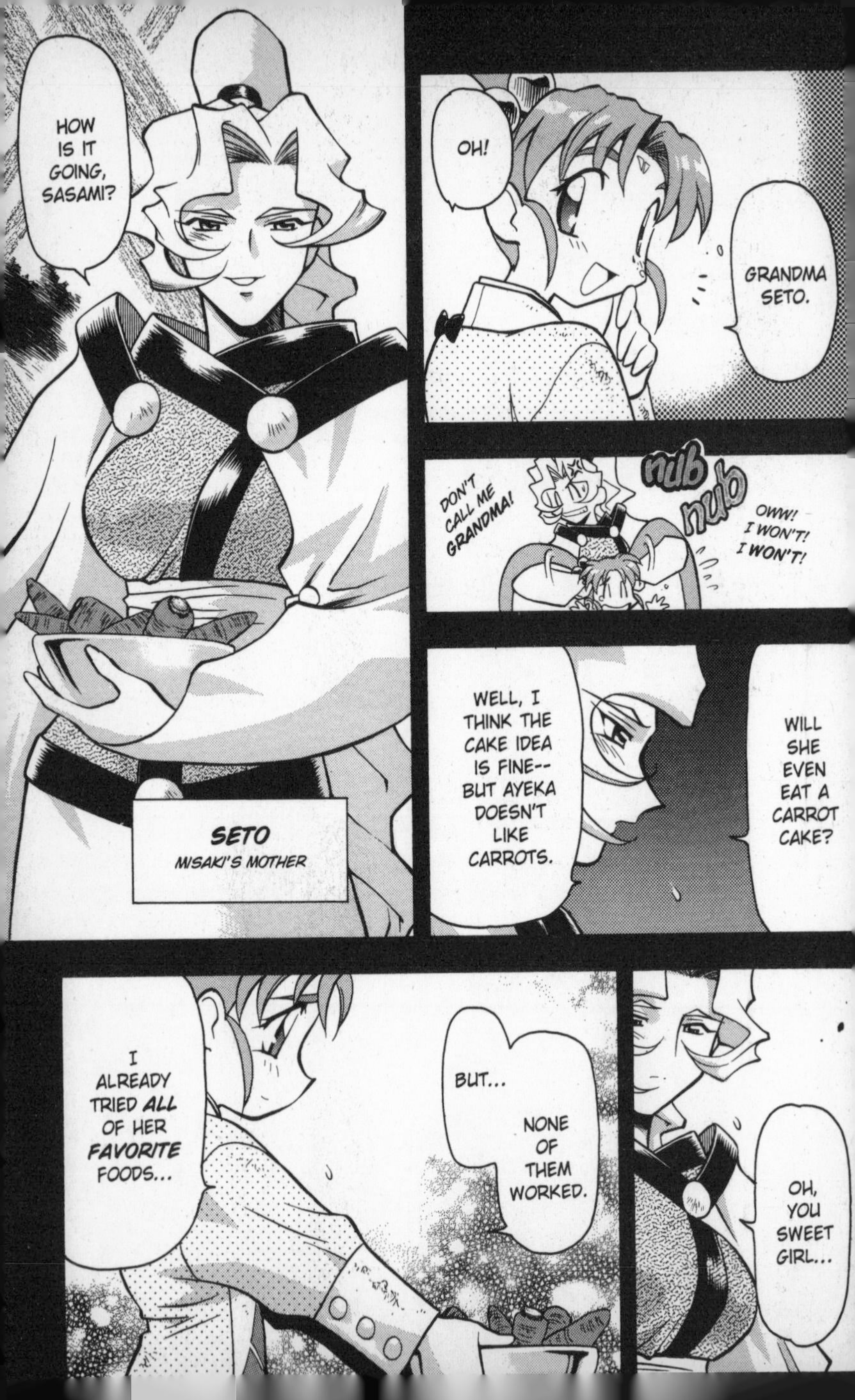
HOW IS IT GOING, SASAMI?
SETO
MISAKI'S MOTHER
OH!
GRANDMA SETO.
DON'T CALL ME GRANDMA!
nub nub
OWW! I WON'T! I WON'T!
WELL, I THINK THE CAKE IDEA IS FINE-- BUT AYEKA DOESN'T LIKE CARROTS.
WILL SHE EVEN EAT A CARROT CAKE?
I ALREADY TRIED ALL OF HER FAVORITE FOODS...
BUT...
NONE OF THEM WORKED.
OH, YOU SWEET GIRL...

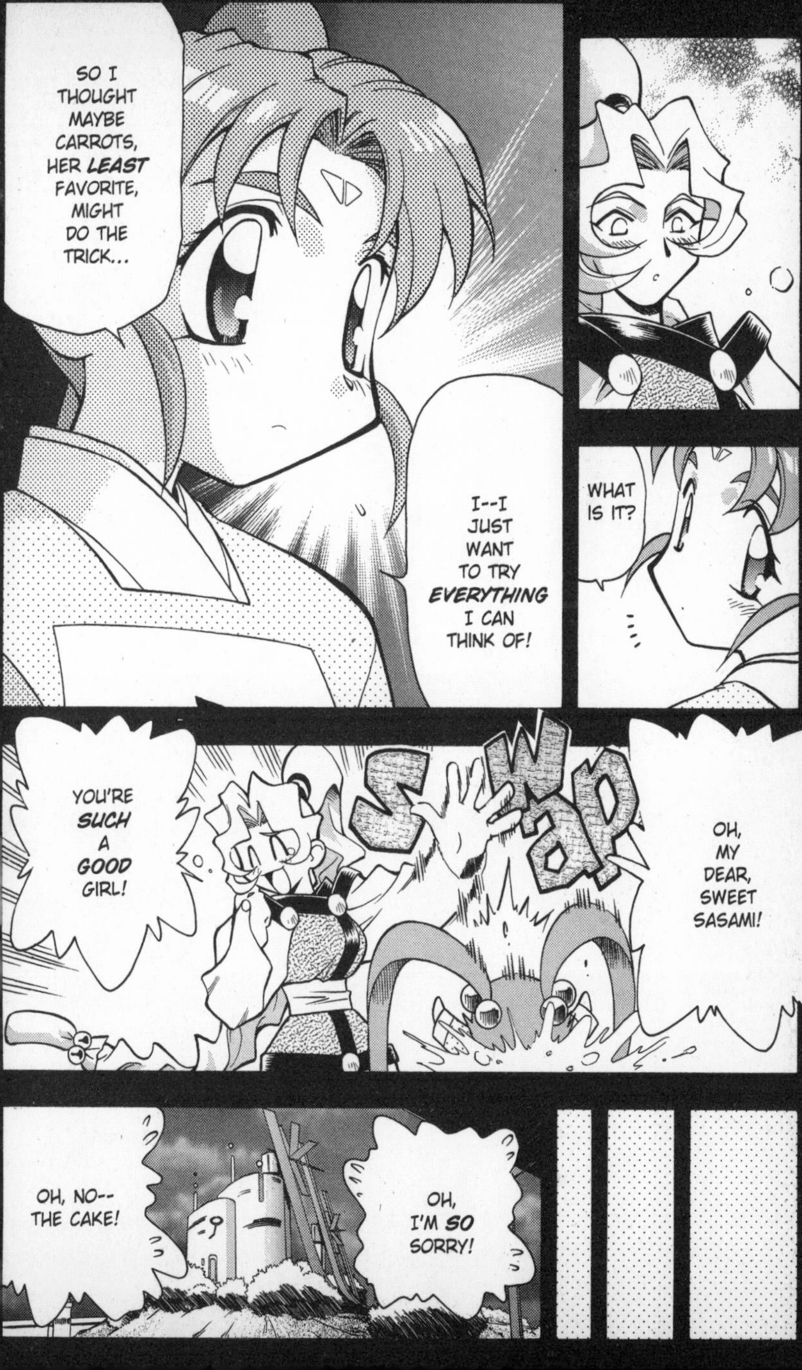
SO I THOUGHT MAYBE CARROTS, HER **LEAST** FAVORITE, MIGHT DO THE TRICK...
I--I JUST WANT TO TRY **EVERYTHING** I CAN THINK OF!
WHAT IS IT?
YOU'RE **SUCH** A **GOOD** GIRL!
SWAP
OH, MY DEAR, SWEET SASAMI!
OH, NO-- THE CAKE!
OH, I'M **SO** SORRY!

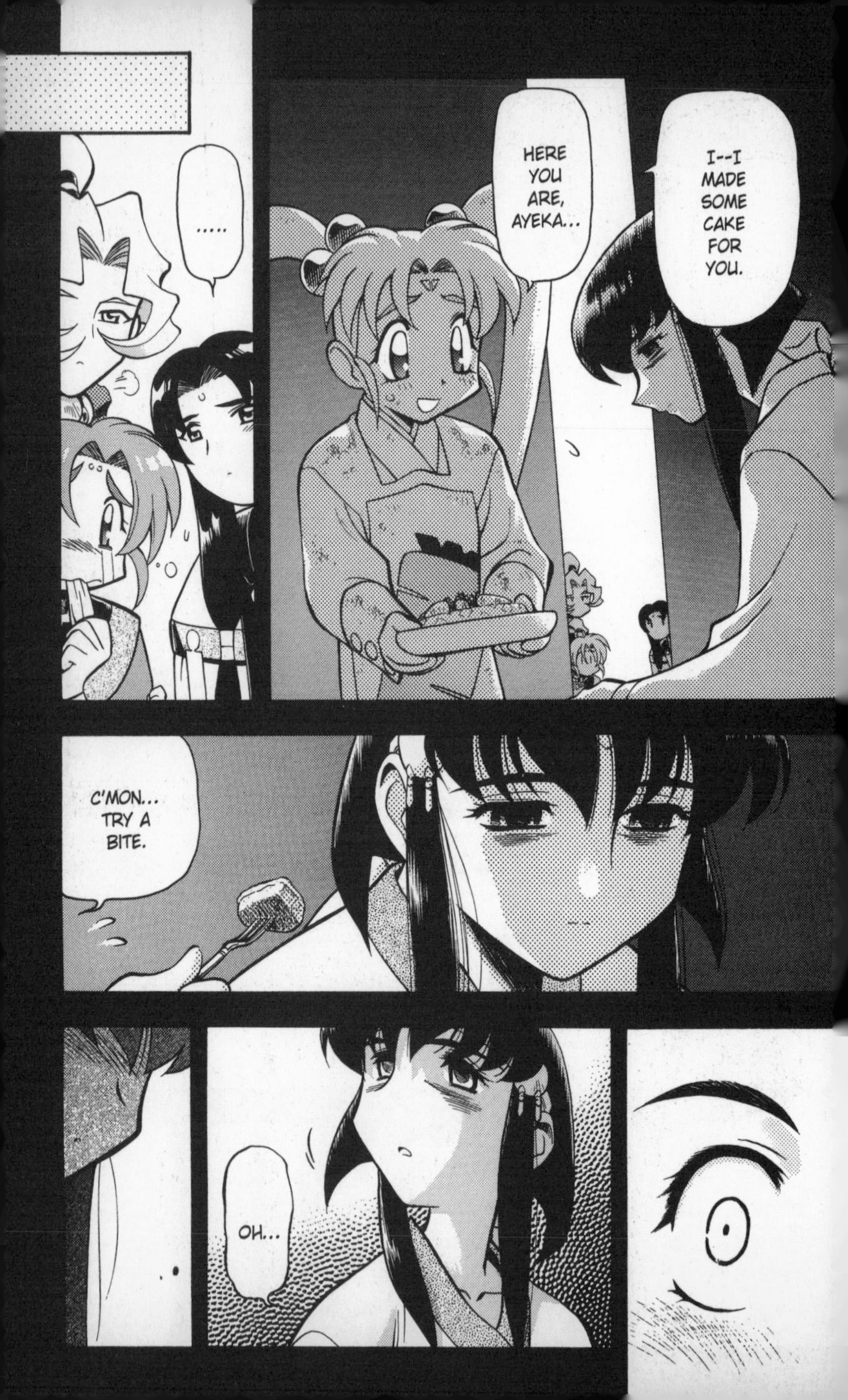
.....
HERE YOU ARE, AYEKA...
I--I MADE SOME CAKE FOR YOU.
C'MON... TRY A BITE.
OH...

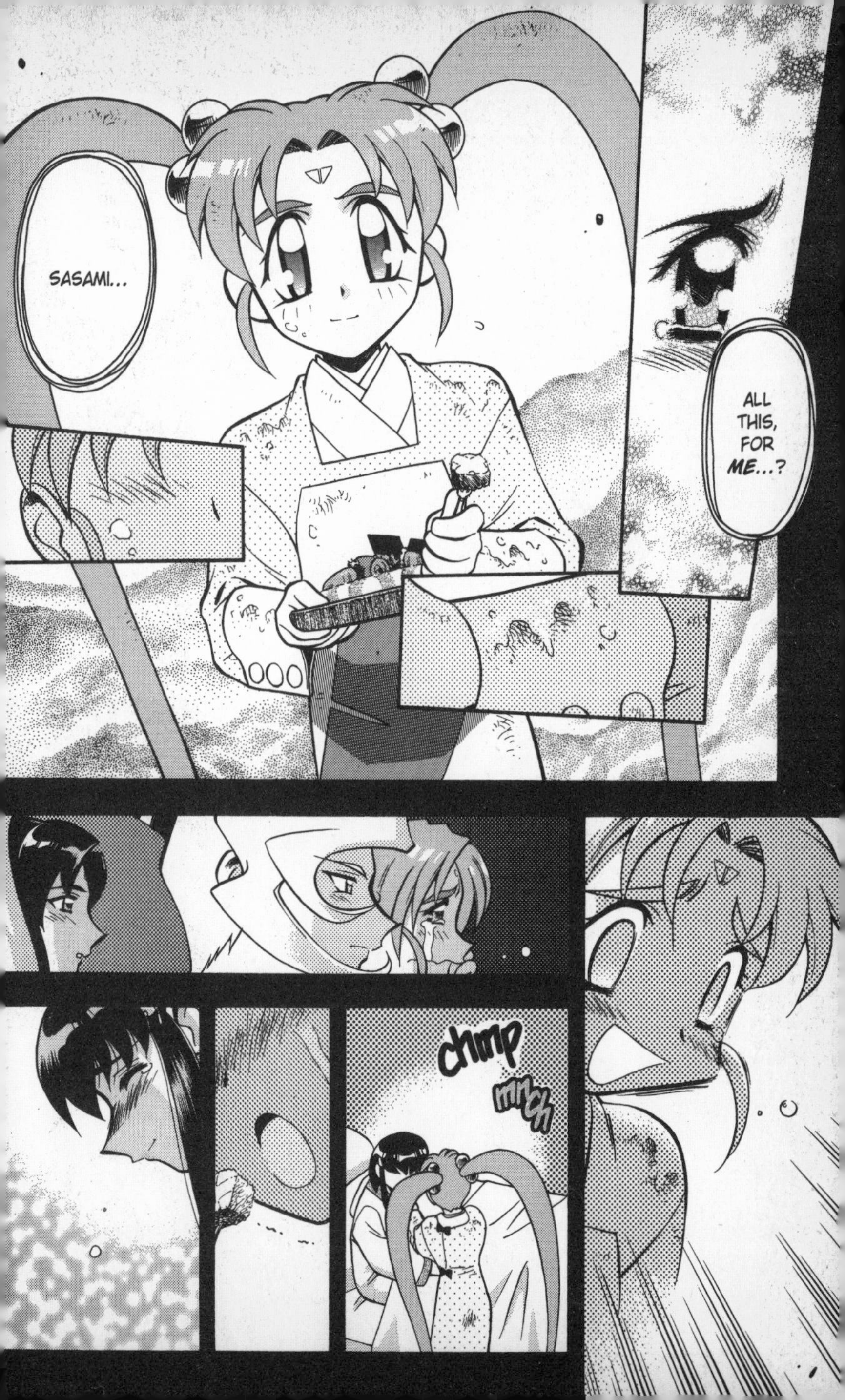
SASAMI...
ALL THIS, FOR ME...?
chimp
mnch

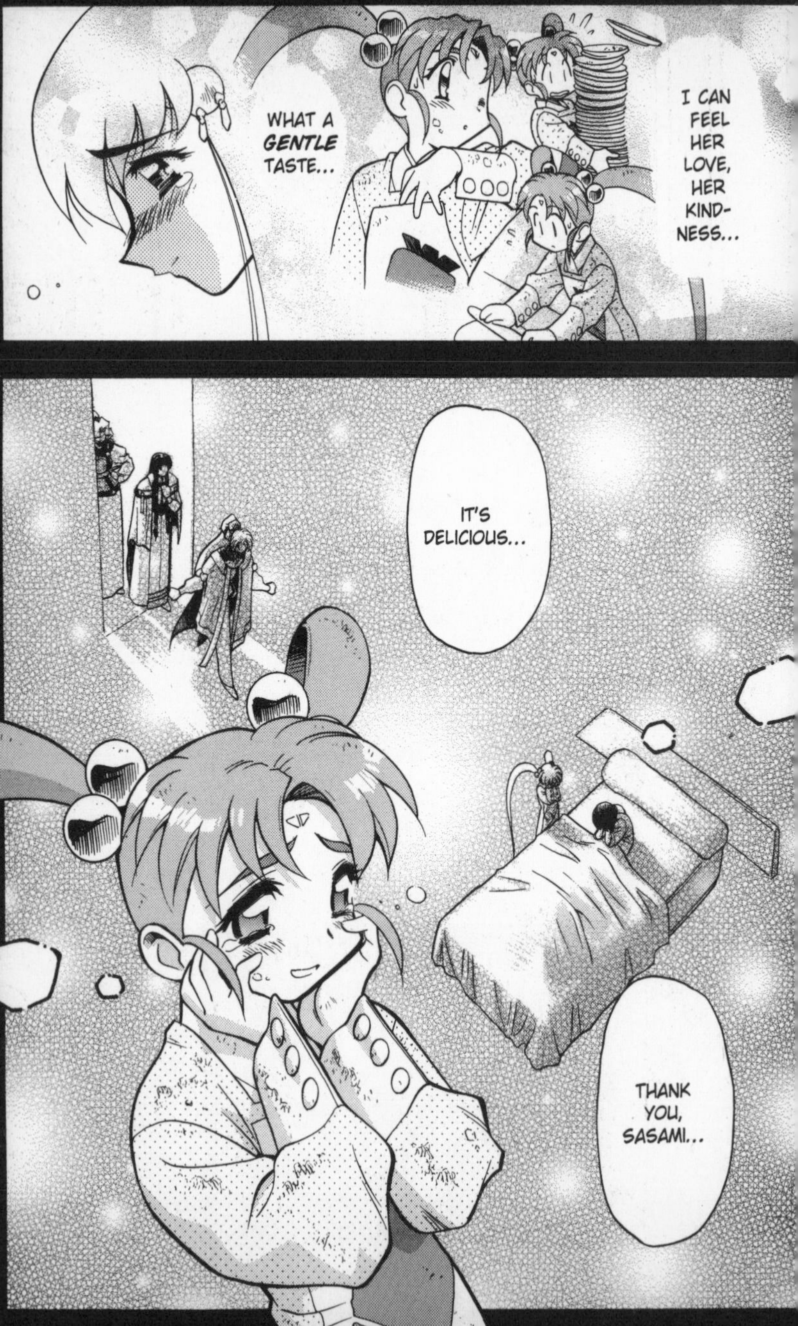
WHAT A *GENTLE* TASTE...
I CAN FEEL HER LOVE, HER KINDNESS...
IT'S DELICIOUS...
THANK YOU, SASAMI...

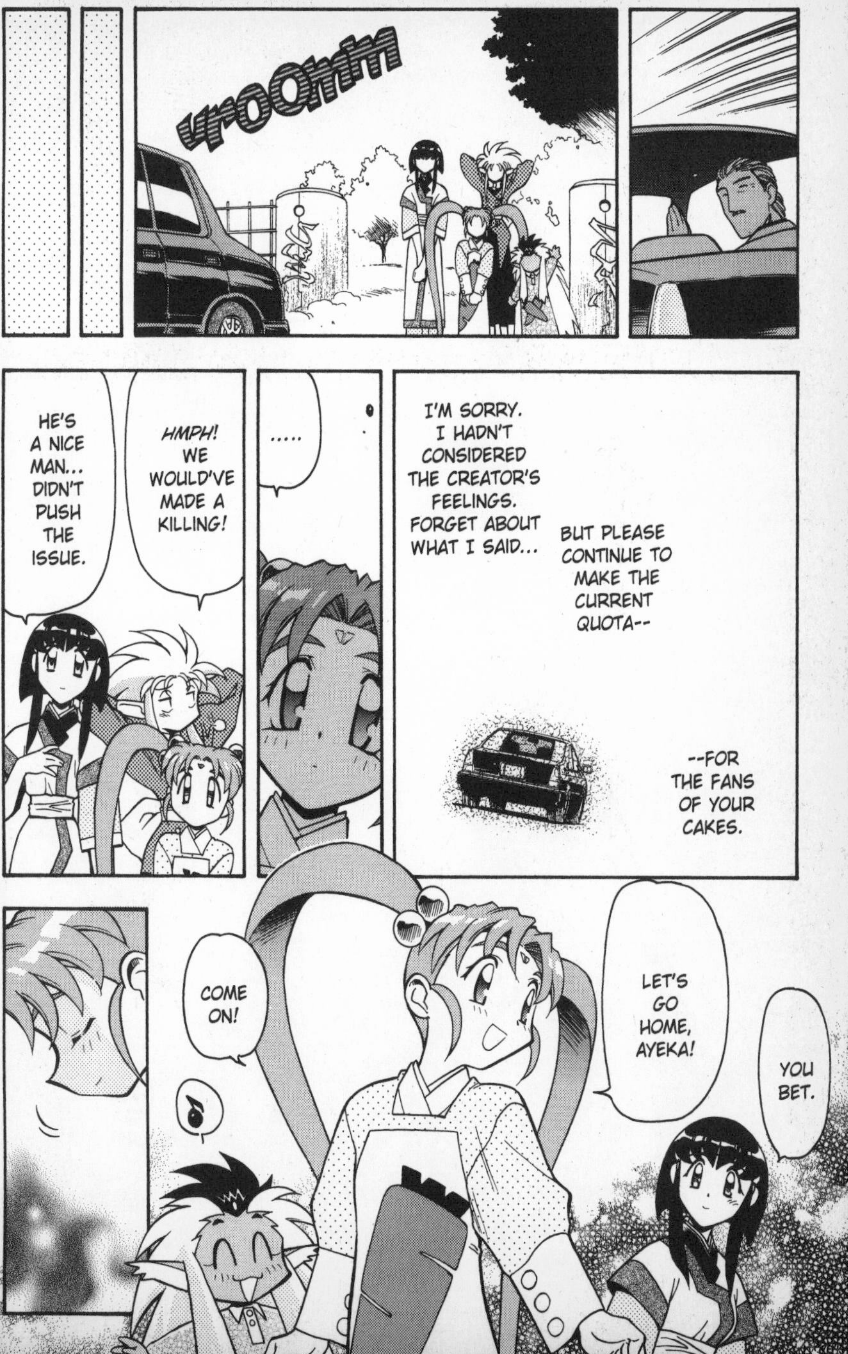
vrooMm
HE'S A NICE MAN... DIDN'T PUSH THE ISSUE.
HMPH! WE WOULD'VE MADE A KILLING!
.....
I'M SORRY. I HADN'T CONSIDERED THE CREATOR'S FEELINGS. FORGET ABOUT WHAT I SAID...
BUT PLEASE CONTINUE TO MAKE THE CURRENT QUOTA--
--FOR THE FANS OF YOUR CAKES.
COME ON!
LET'S GO HOME, AYEKA!
YOU BET.

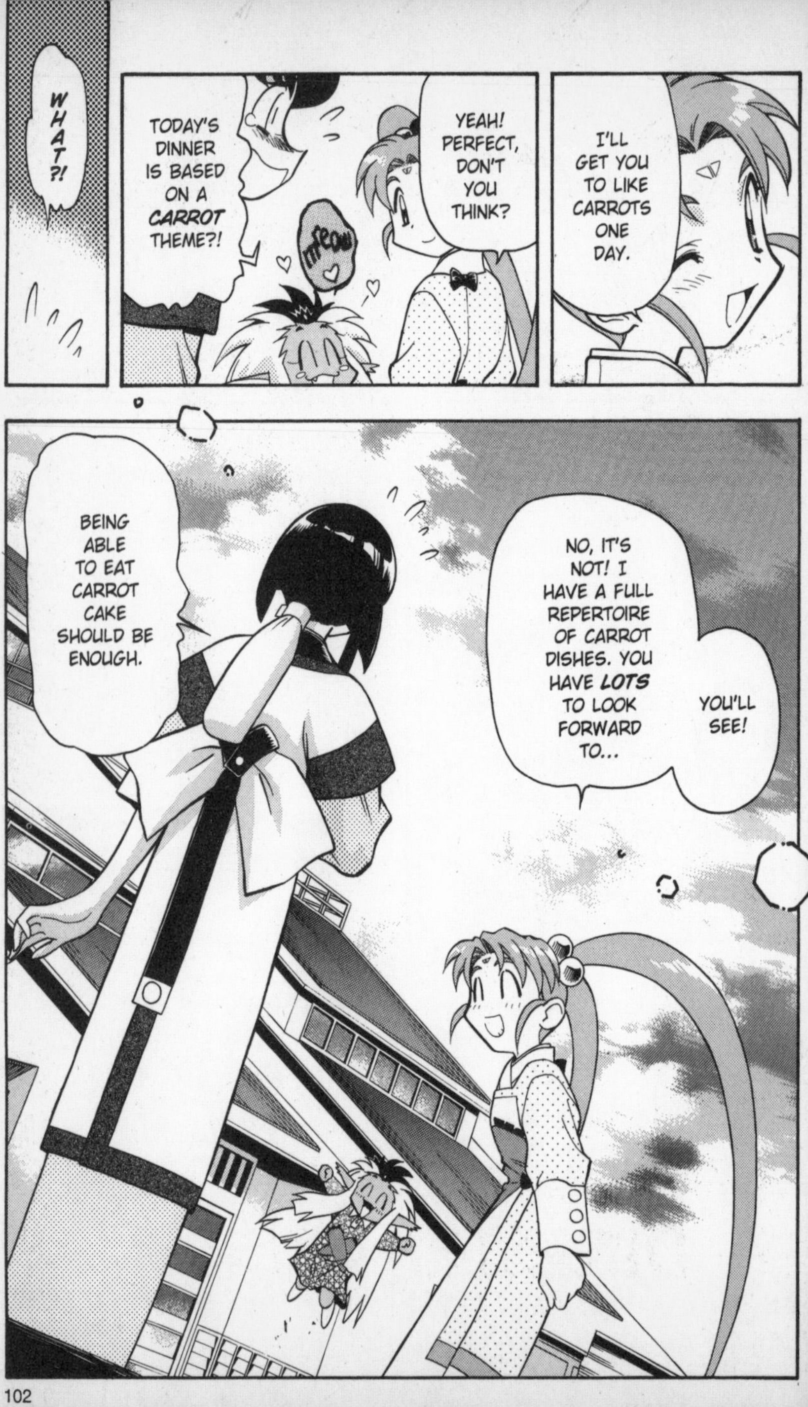
WHAT?!
TODAY'S DINNER IS BASED ON A *CARROT* THEME?!
meow
YEAH! PERFECT, DON'T YOU THINK?
I'LL GET YOU TO LIKE CARROTS ONE DAY.
BEING ABLE TO EAT CARROT CAKE SHOULD BE ENOUGH.
NO, IT'S NOT! I HAVE A FULL REPERTOIRE OF CARROT DISHES. YOU HAVE **LOTS** TO LOOK FORWARD TO...
YOU'LL SEE!

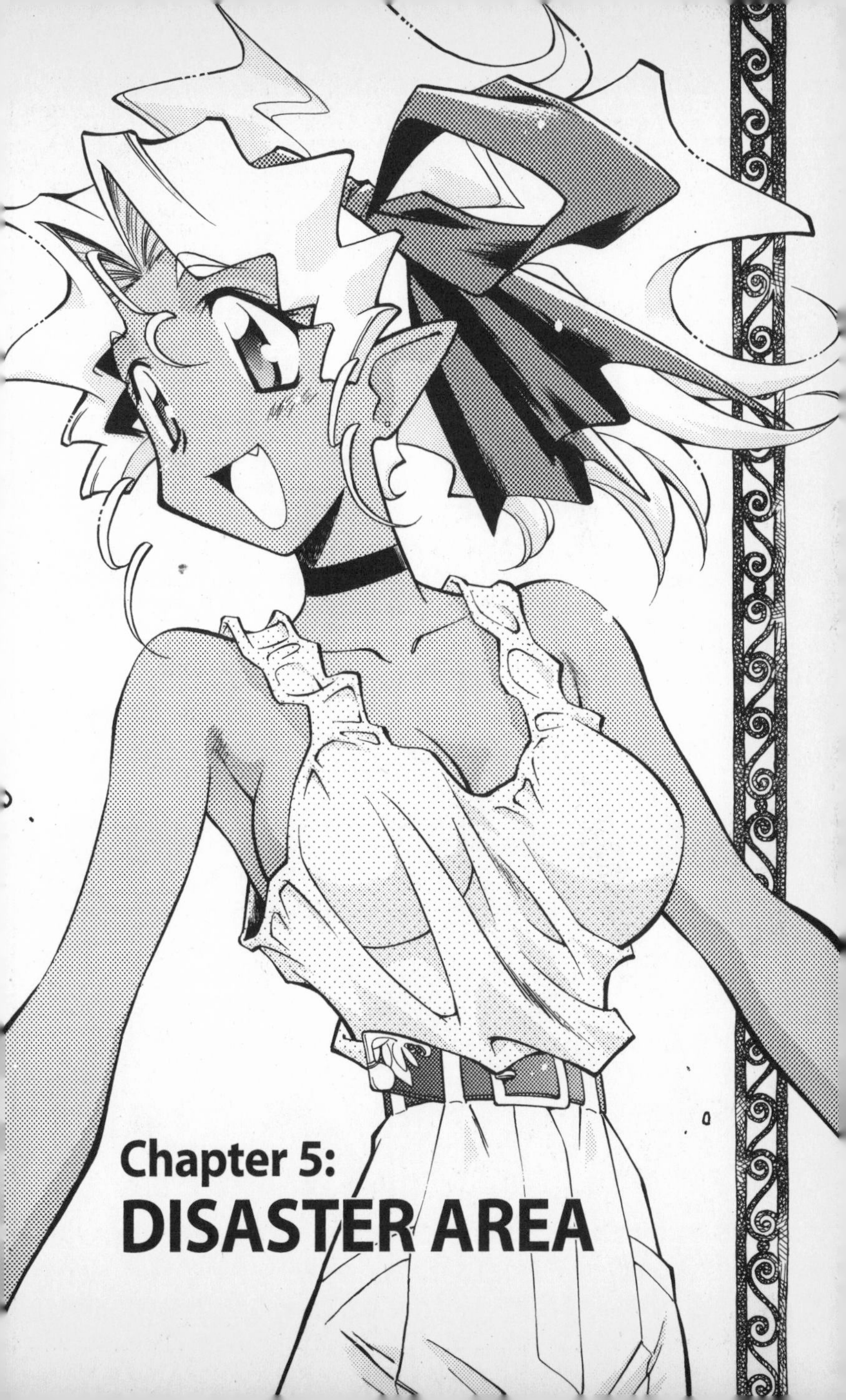

Chapter 5:
DISASTER AREA

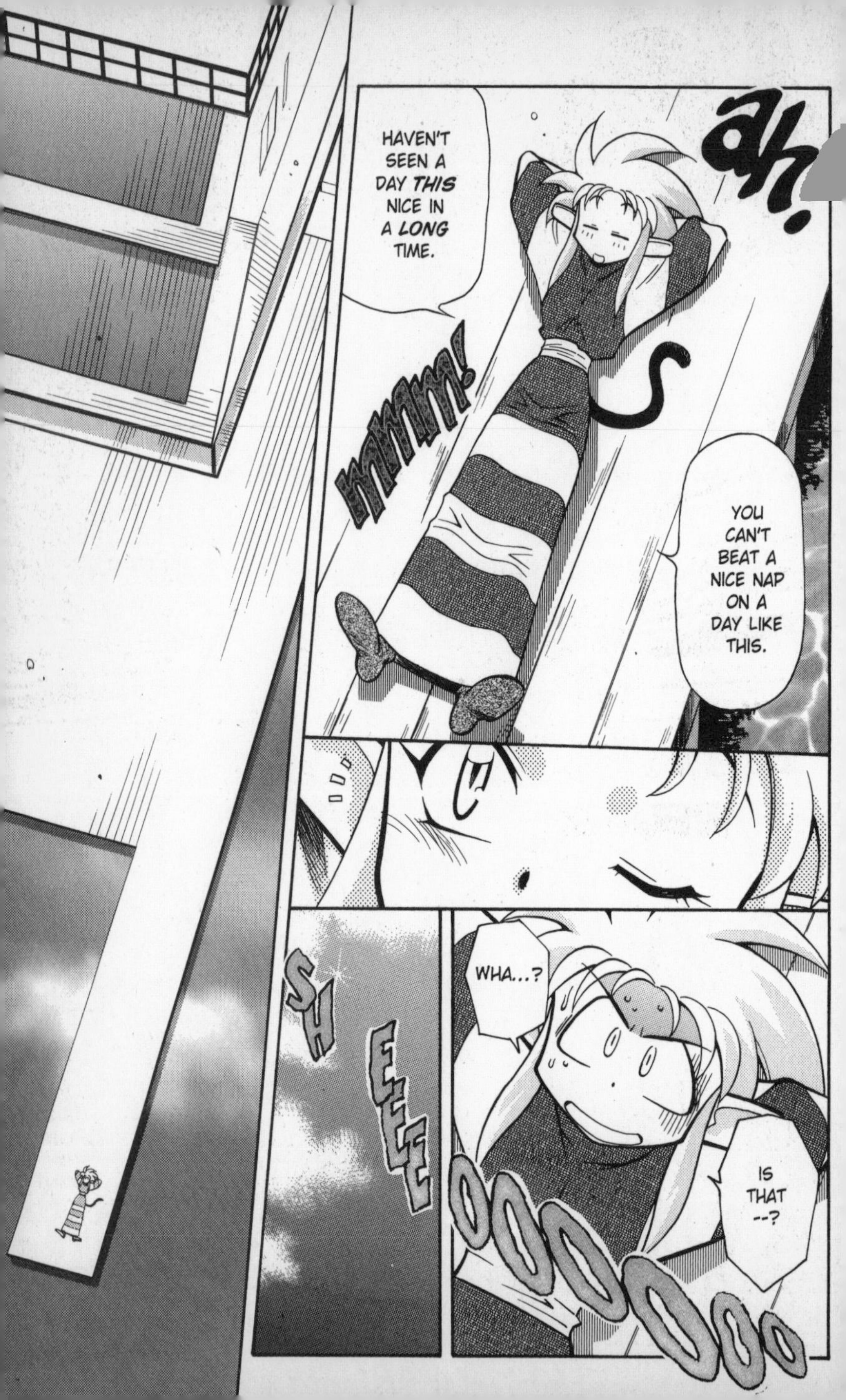
HAVEN'T SEEN A DAY THIS NICE IN A LONG TIME.
ah!
MMMM!
YOU CAN'T BEAT A NICE NAP ON A DAY LIKE THIS.
SHEEE
WHA...?
IS THAT --?
OOOOOOOO

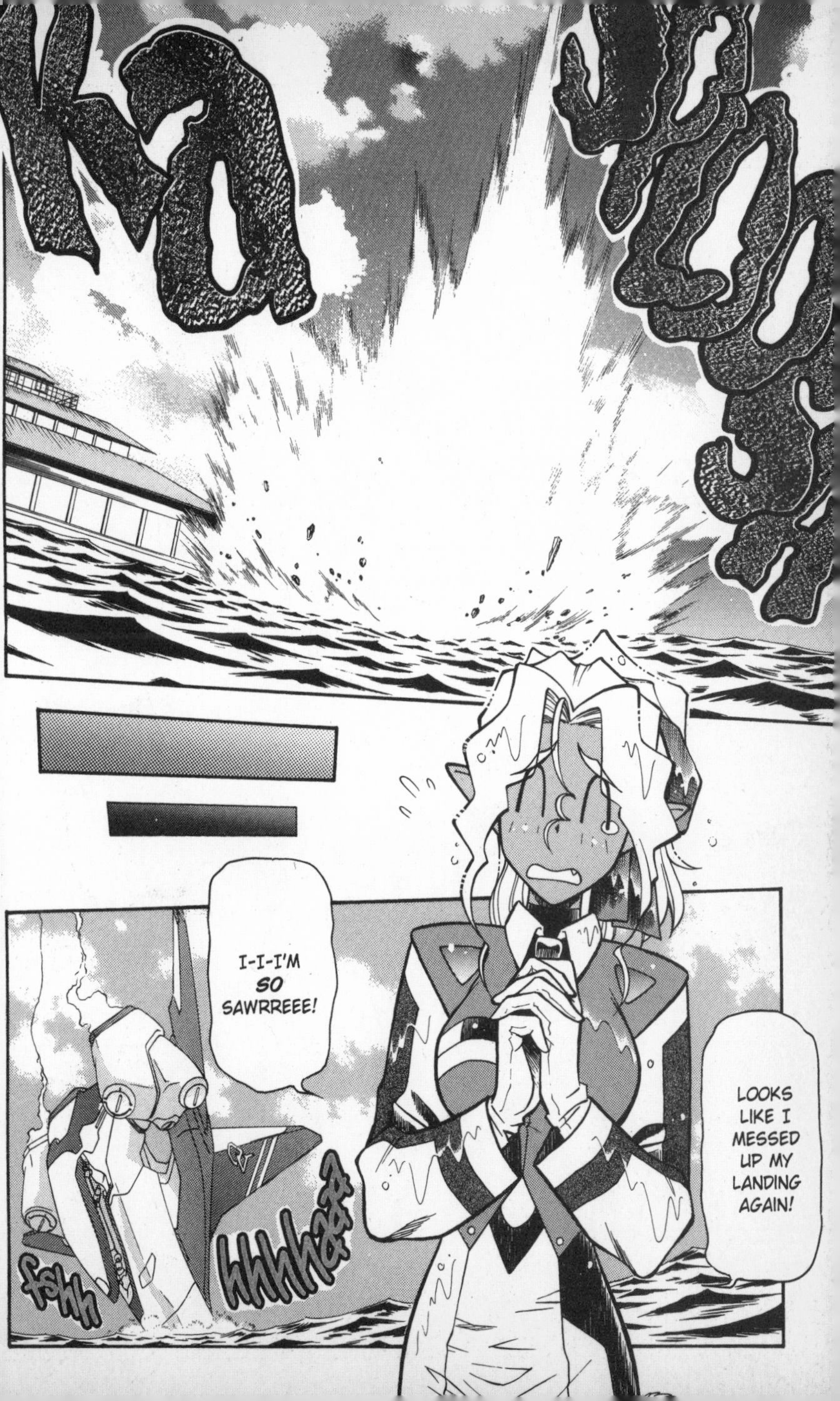
I-I-I'M SO SAWRREEE!
LOOKS LIKE I MESSED UP MY LANDING AGAIN!
fshh

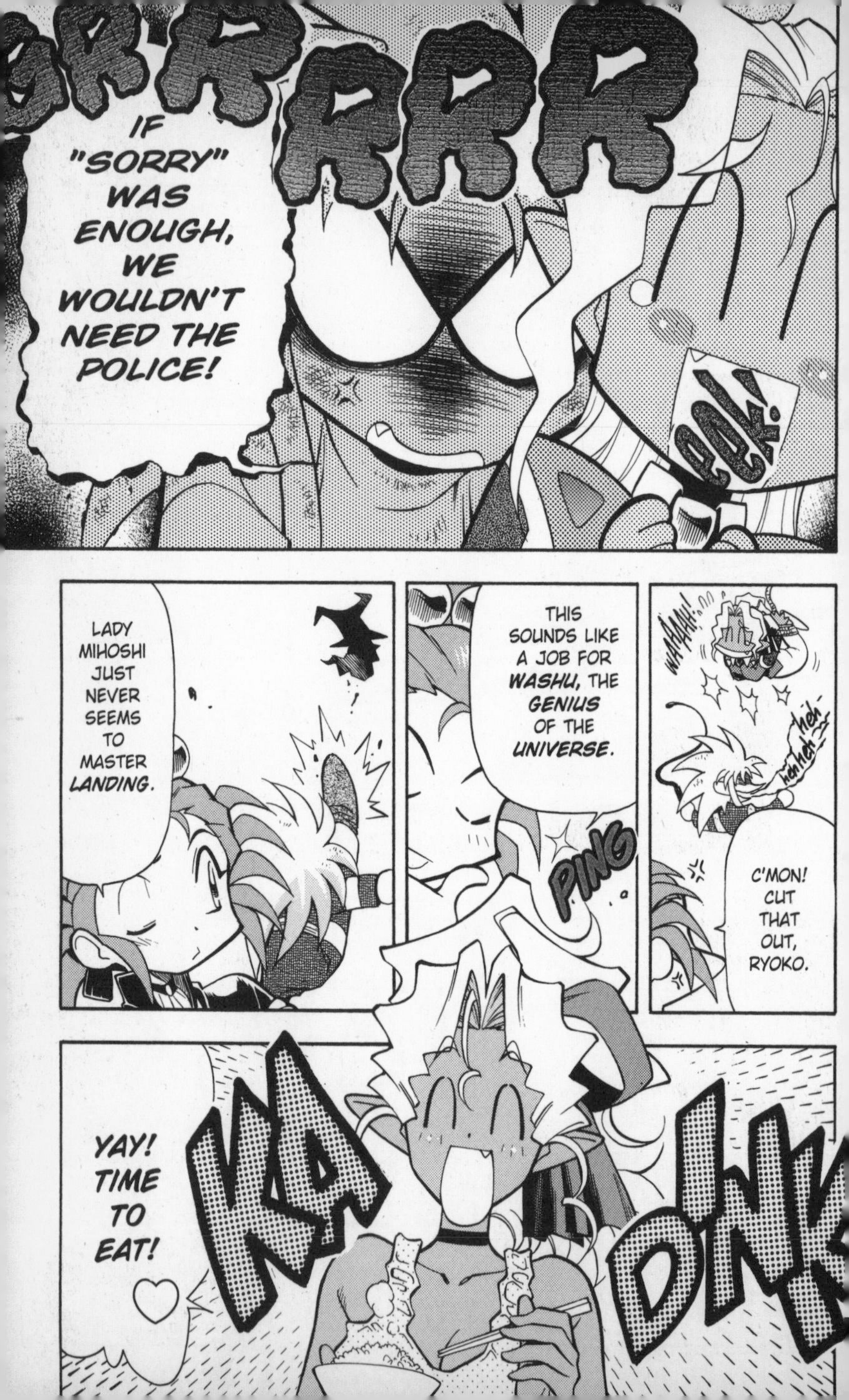
GR'R'RRRR
IF "SORRY" WAS ENOUGH, WE WOULDN'T NEED THE POLICE!
eek!
LADY MIHOSHI JUST NEVER SEEMS TO MASTER LANDING.
THIS SOUNDS LIKE A JOB FOR WASHU, THE GENIUS OF THE UNIVERSE.
PING
WAAAH!
heh heh heh
C'MON! CUT THAT OUT, RYOKO.
YAY! TIME TO EAT!
KA
DINK

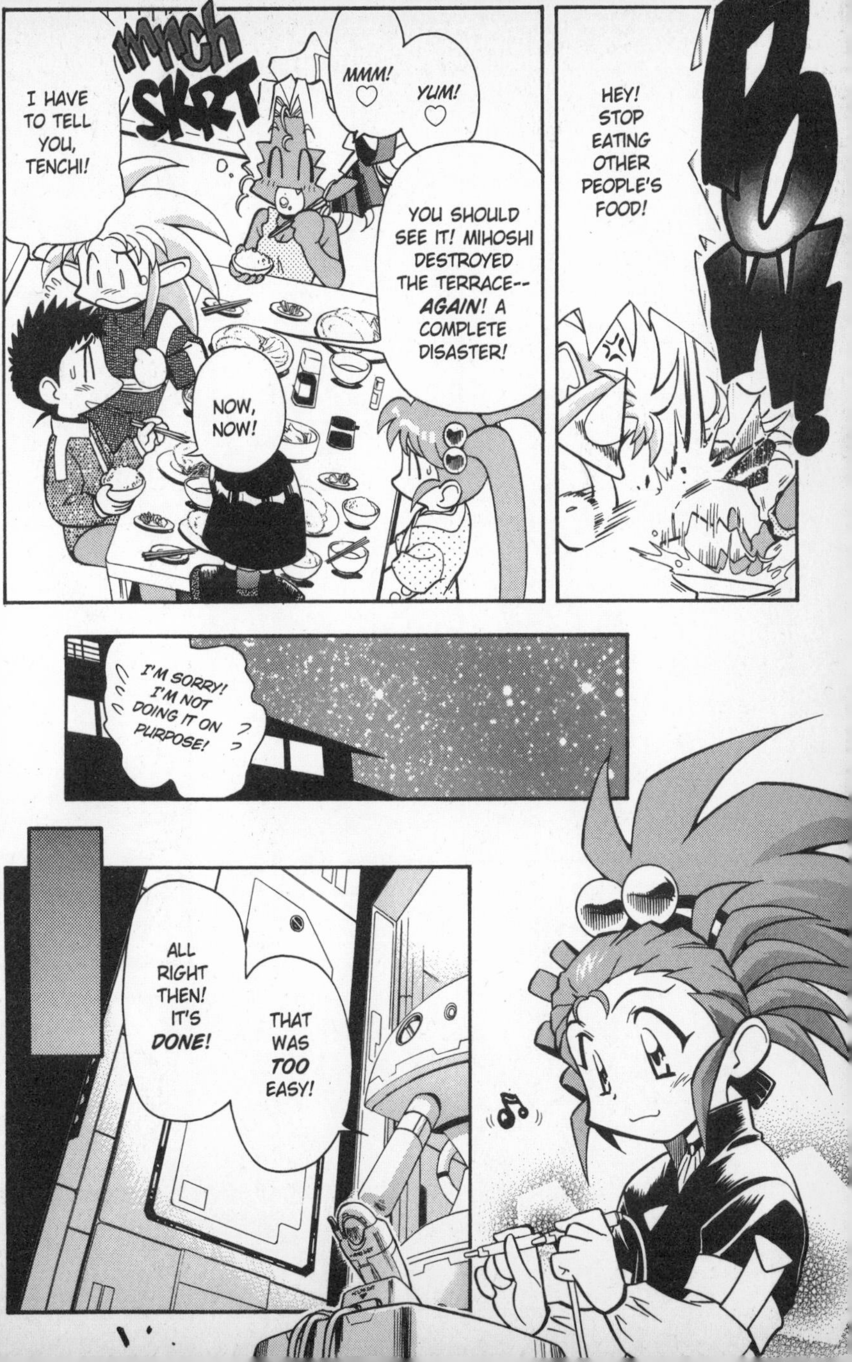
mnch
SKRT
I HAVE TO TELL YOU, TENCHI!
MMM! ♡
YUM! ♡
YOU SHOULD SEE IT! MIHOSHI DESTROYED THE TERRACE-- **AGAIN**! A COMPLETE DISASTER!
NOW, NOW!
HEY! STOP EATING OTHER PEOPLE'S FOOD!
BOW!
I'M SORRY! I'M NOT DOING IT ON PURPOSE!
ALL RIGHT THEN! IT'S **DONE**!
THAT WAS **TOO** EASY!

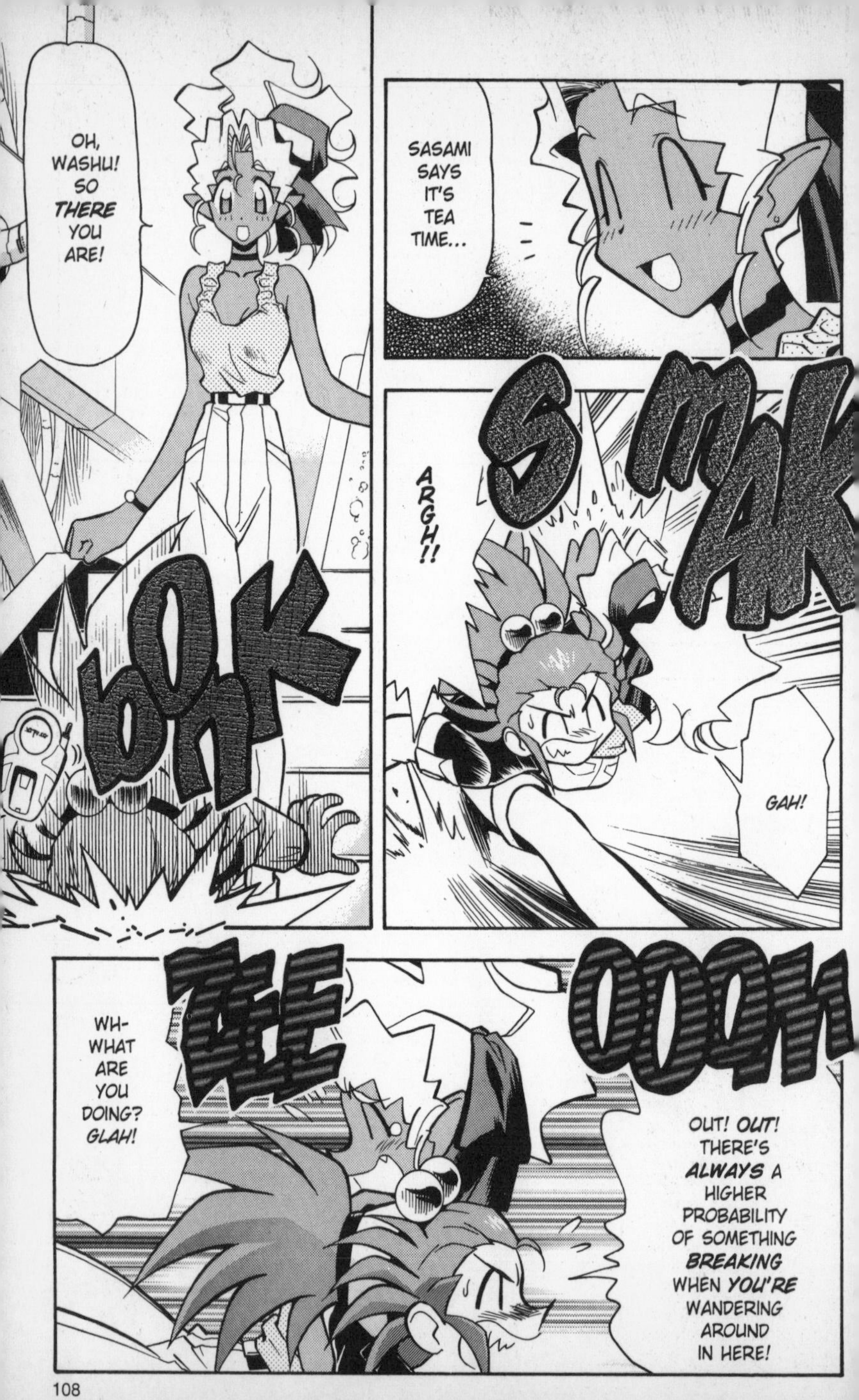
OH, WASHU! SO *THERE* YOU ARE!
BONK
SASAMI SAYS IT'S TEA TIME...
SMAK
ARGH!!
GAH!
ZEE
OOOM
WH- WHAT ARE YOU DOING? *GLAH!*
OUT! *OUT!* THERE'S ***ALWAYS*** A HIGHER PROBABILITY OF SOMETHING ***BREAKING*** WHEN ***YOU'RE*** WANDERING AROUND IN HERE!

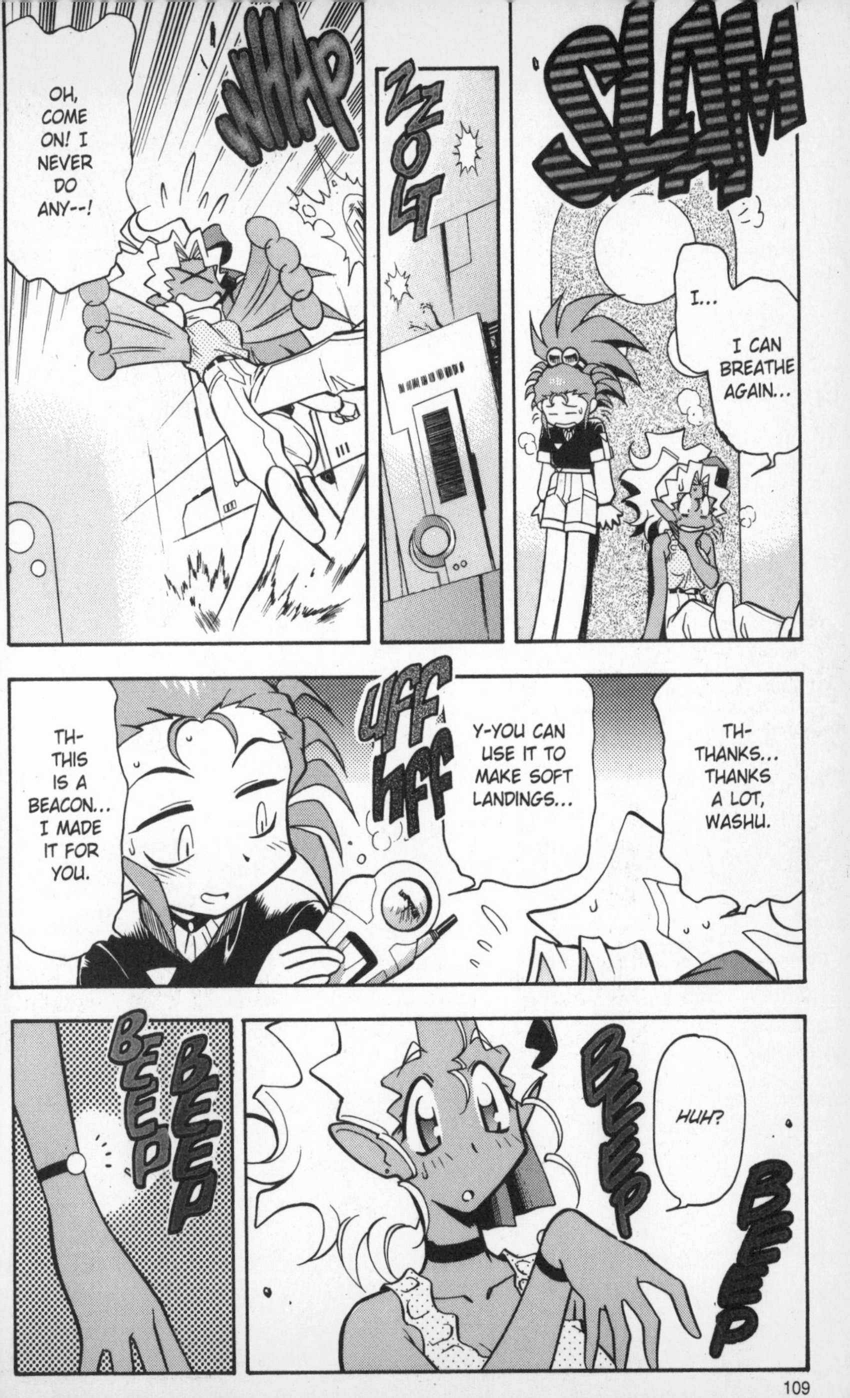
OH, COME ON! I NEVER DO ANY--!
WHAP
ZZOLT
SLAM
I...
I CAN BREATHE AGAIN...
TH- THIS IS A BEACON... I MADE IT FOR YOU.
UFF HFF
Y-YOU CAN USE IT TO MAKE SOFT LANDINGS...
TH- THANKS... THANKS A LOT, WASHU.
BEEP BEEP
BEEP
HUH?
BEEP

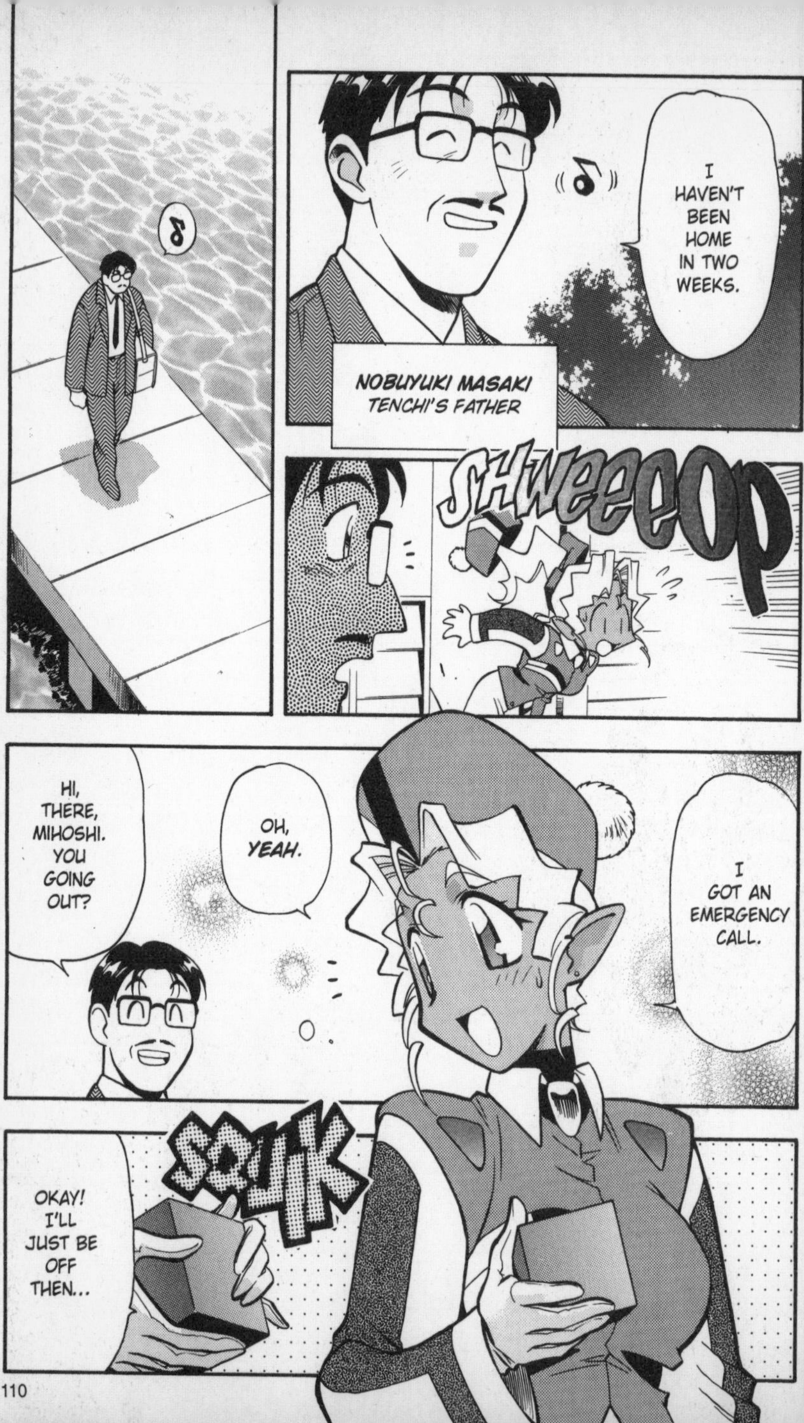
I HAVEN'T BEEN HOME IN TWO WEEKS.
NOBUYUKI MASAKI
TENCHI'S FATHER
SHWEEEOP
HI, THERE, MIHOSHI. YOU GOING OUT?
OH, YEAH.
I GOT AN EMERGENCY CALL.
SQUIK
OKAY! I'LL JUST BE OFF THEN...

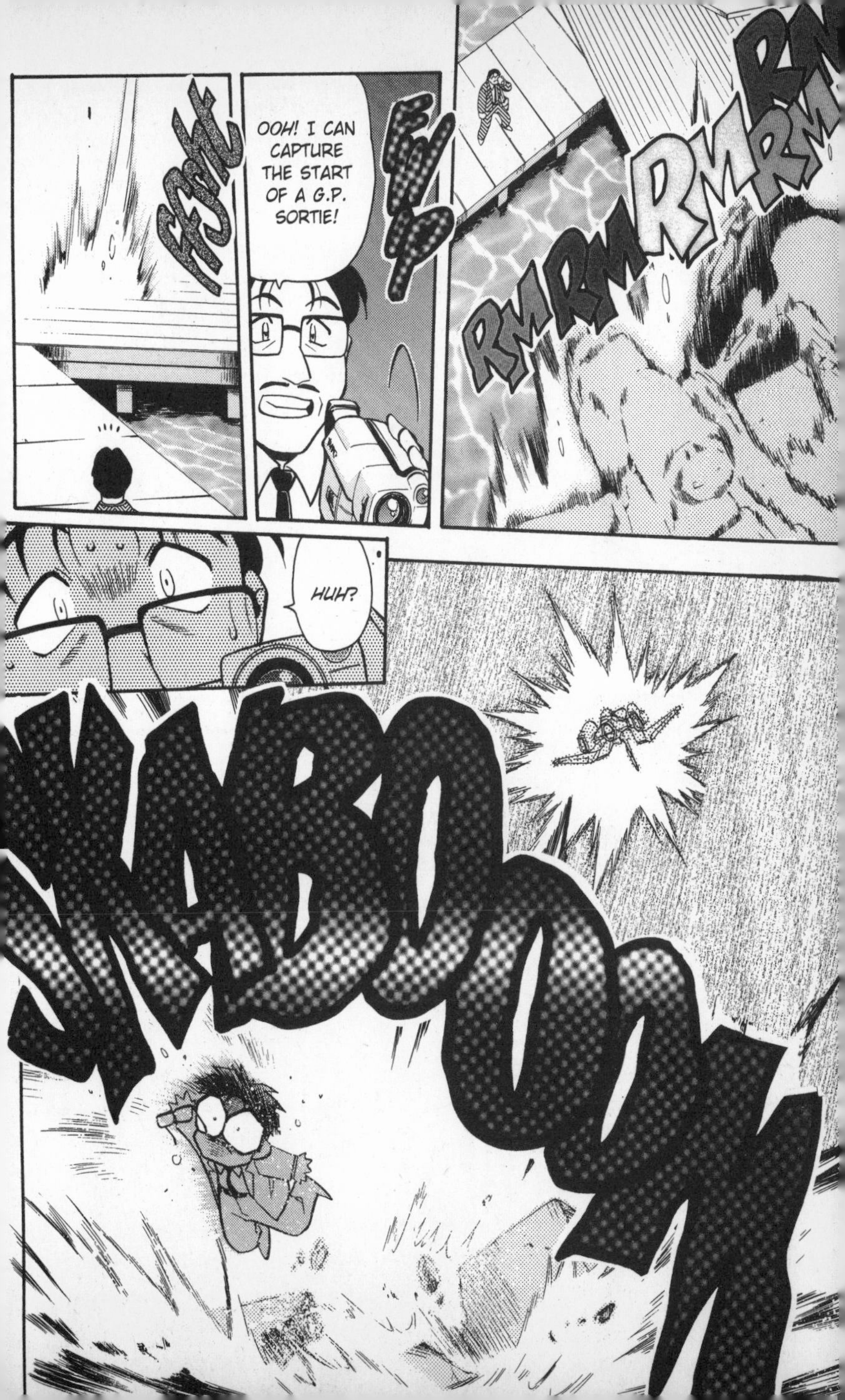
OOH! I CAN CAPTURE THE START OF A G.P. SORTIE!
HUH?

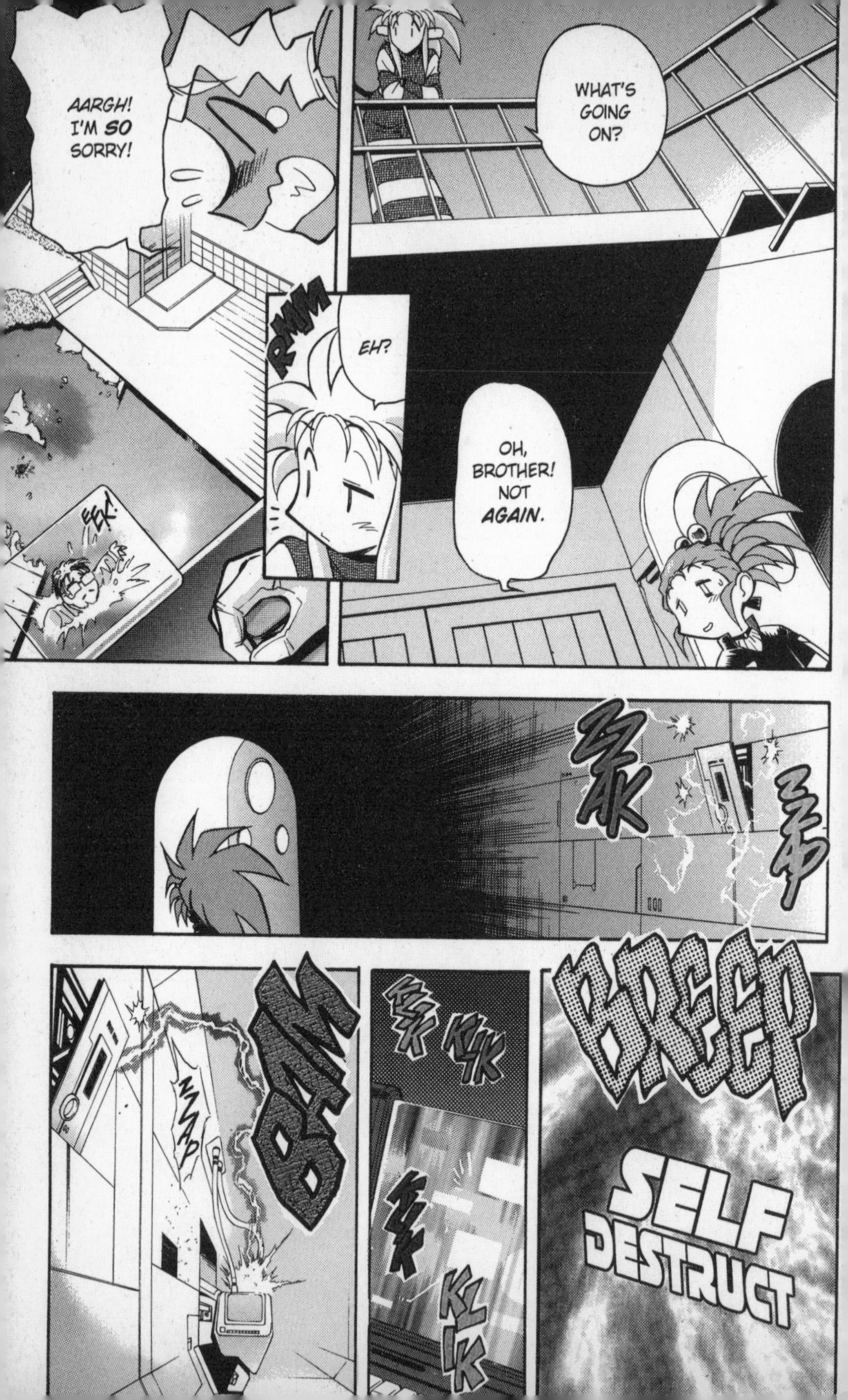
AARGH! I'M SO SORRY!
EEK!
WHAT'S GOING ON?
RMM
EH?
OH, BROTHER! NOT AGAIN.
ZZAK
ZZAP
ZZAP
BAM
KLIK KLIK
KLIK KLIK
BREEP
SELF DESTRUCT

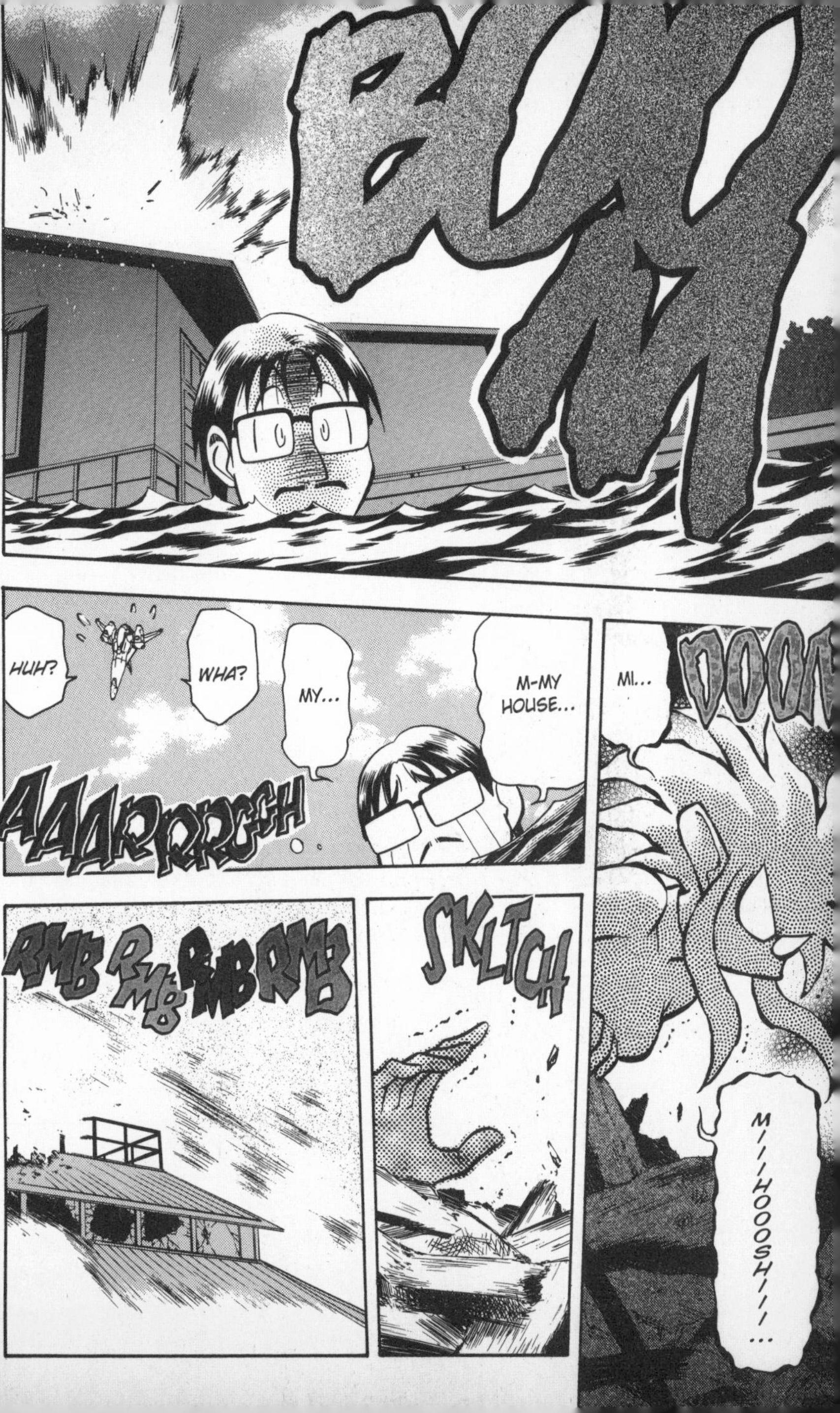
BLAM
HUH?
WHA?
MY...
M-MY HOUSE...
AAARRRRGGH
RMB RMB RMB RMB
SKLTCH
MI...
DOOM
MIIIHOOOSHIII...

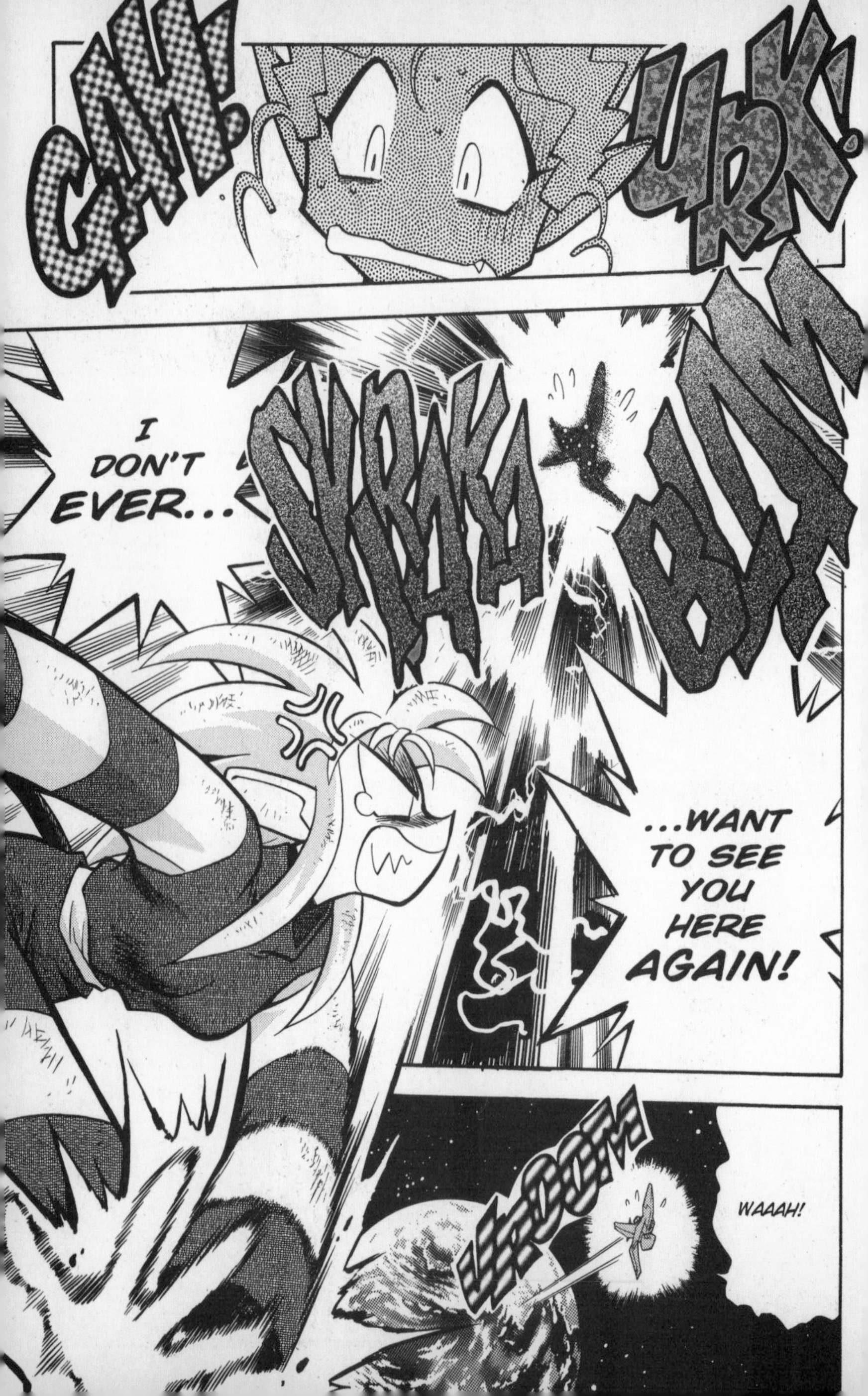
GAH!
URK!
I DON'T EVER...
...WANT TO SEE YOU HERE AGAIN!
WAAAH!

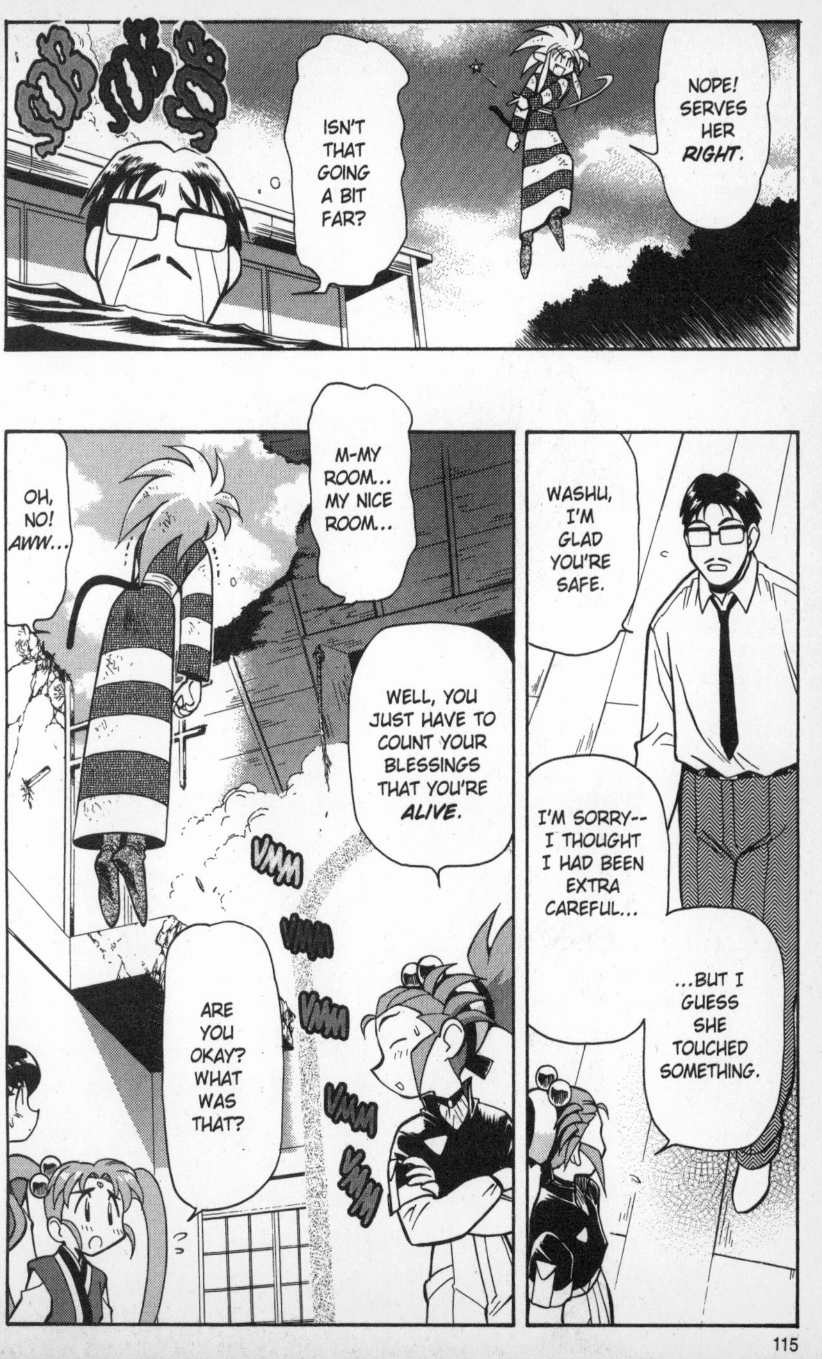
ISN'T THAT GOING A BIT FAR?
NOPE! SERVES HER *RIGHT*.
OH, NO! *AWW...*
M-MY ROOM... MY NICE ROOM...
WELL, YOU JUST HAVE TO COUNT YOUR BLESSINGS THAT YOU'RE *ALIVE*.
VMM
VMM
ARE YOU OKAY? WHAT WAS THAT?
VMM
VMM
VMM
WASHU, I'M GLAD YOU'RE SAFE.
I'M SORRY-- I THOUGHT I HAD BEEN EXTRA CAREFUL...
...BUT I GUESS SHE TOUCHED SOMETHING.

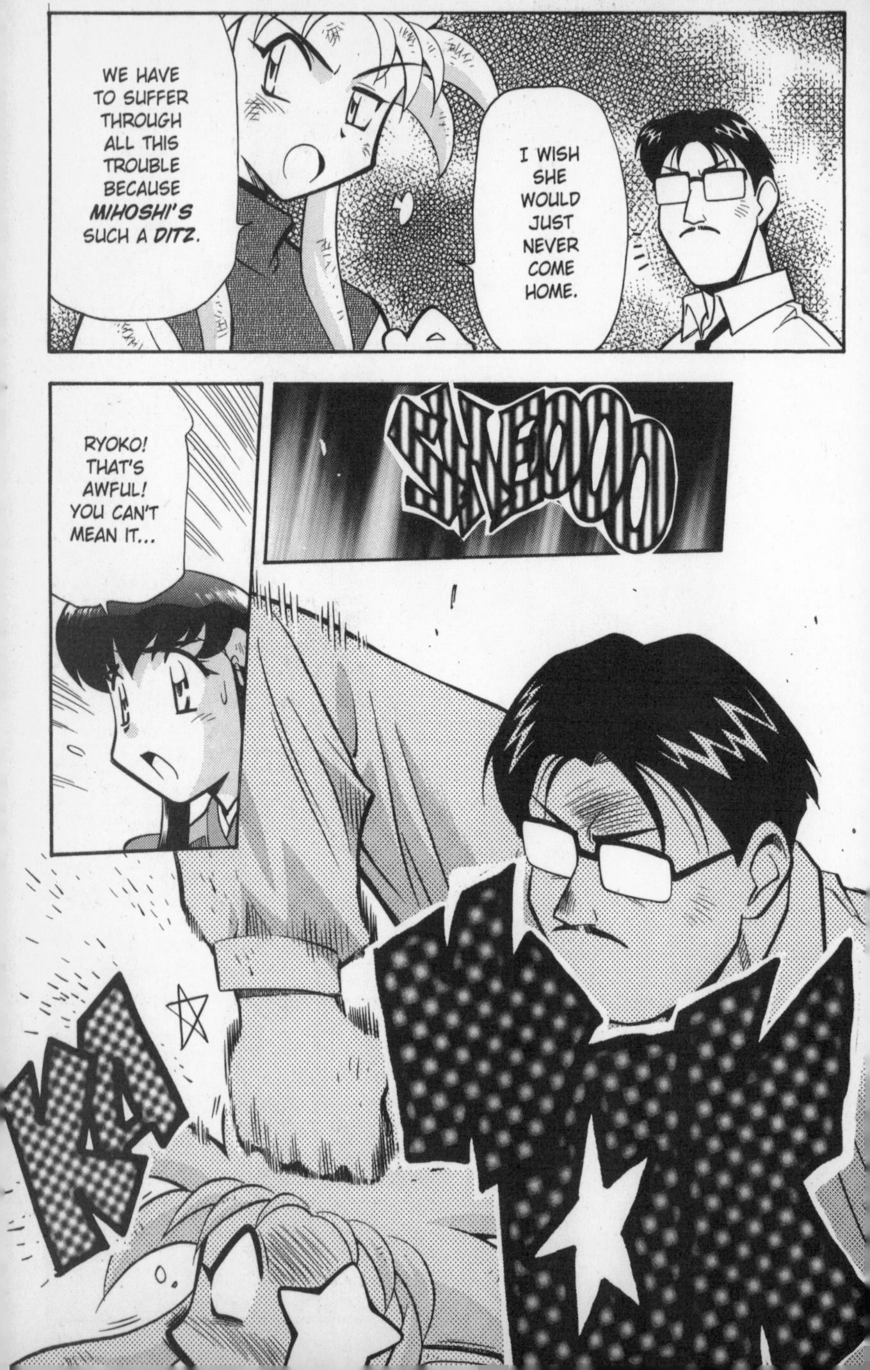
WE HAVE TO SUFFER THROUGH ALL THIS TROUBLE BECAUSE *MIHOSHI'S* SUCH A *DITZ*.
I WISH SHE WOULD JUST NEVER COME HOME.
RYOKO! THAT'S AWFUL! YOU CAN'T MEAN IT...

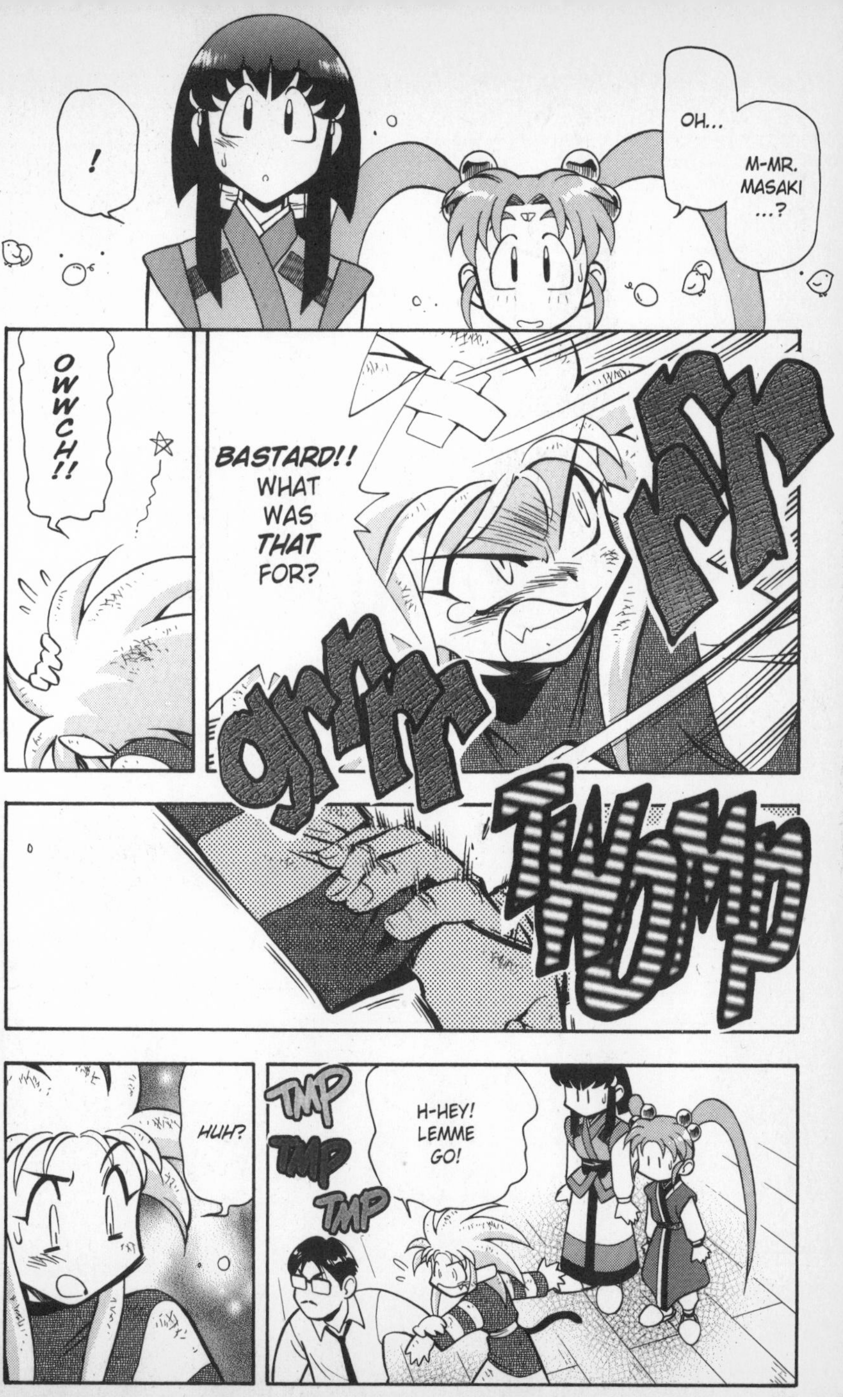
!
OH...
M-MR. MASAKI ...?
OWWCH!!
BASTARD!! WHAT WAS THAT FOR?
GRRR
GRR
THOMP
HUH?
TMP
TMP
TMP
H-HEY! LEMME GO!

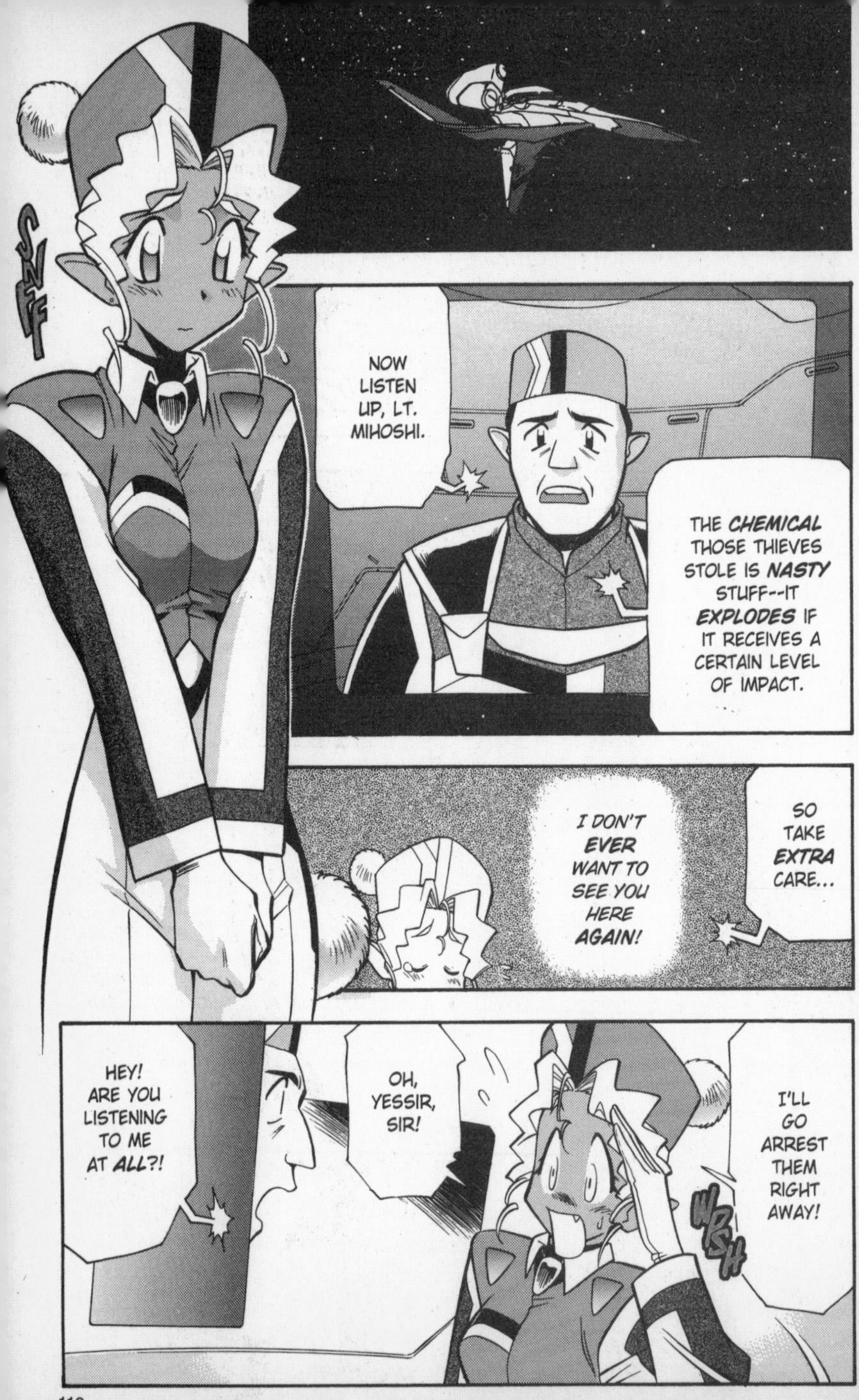
SNFF
NOW LISTEN UP, LT. MIHOSHI.
THE **CHEMICAL** THOSE THIEVES STOLE IS **NASTY** STUFF--IT **EXPLODES** IF IT RECEIVES A CERTAIN LEVEL OF IMPACT.
*I DON'T **EVER** WANT TO SEE YOU HERE **AGAIN**!*
SO TAKE **EXTRA** CARE...
HEY! ARE YOU LISTENING TO ME AT ***ALL***?!
OH, YESSIR, SIR!
I'LL GO ARREST THEM RIGHT AWAY!

OH, HEY!

DAMN! ALL I WANTED WAS FOR HER TO KEEP THEM OUT OF THE SOLAR SYSTEM...

WHY CAN'T SHE *EVER* LISTEN?

ANTACID, CHIEF?

WHERE ARE YOU DRAGGING ME OFF TO?

HEY!

OWW! LEGGO!

I SAID, LET *GO!*

WHAT'S UP? HE'S HARDLY EVER HERE...

NOW YOU *LISTEN,* RYOKO...

...EVEN THOUGH I TOLD HER SHE DIDN'T HAVE TO...

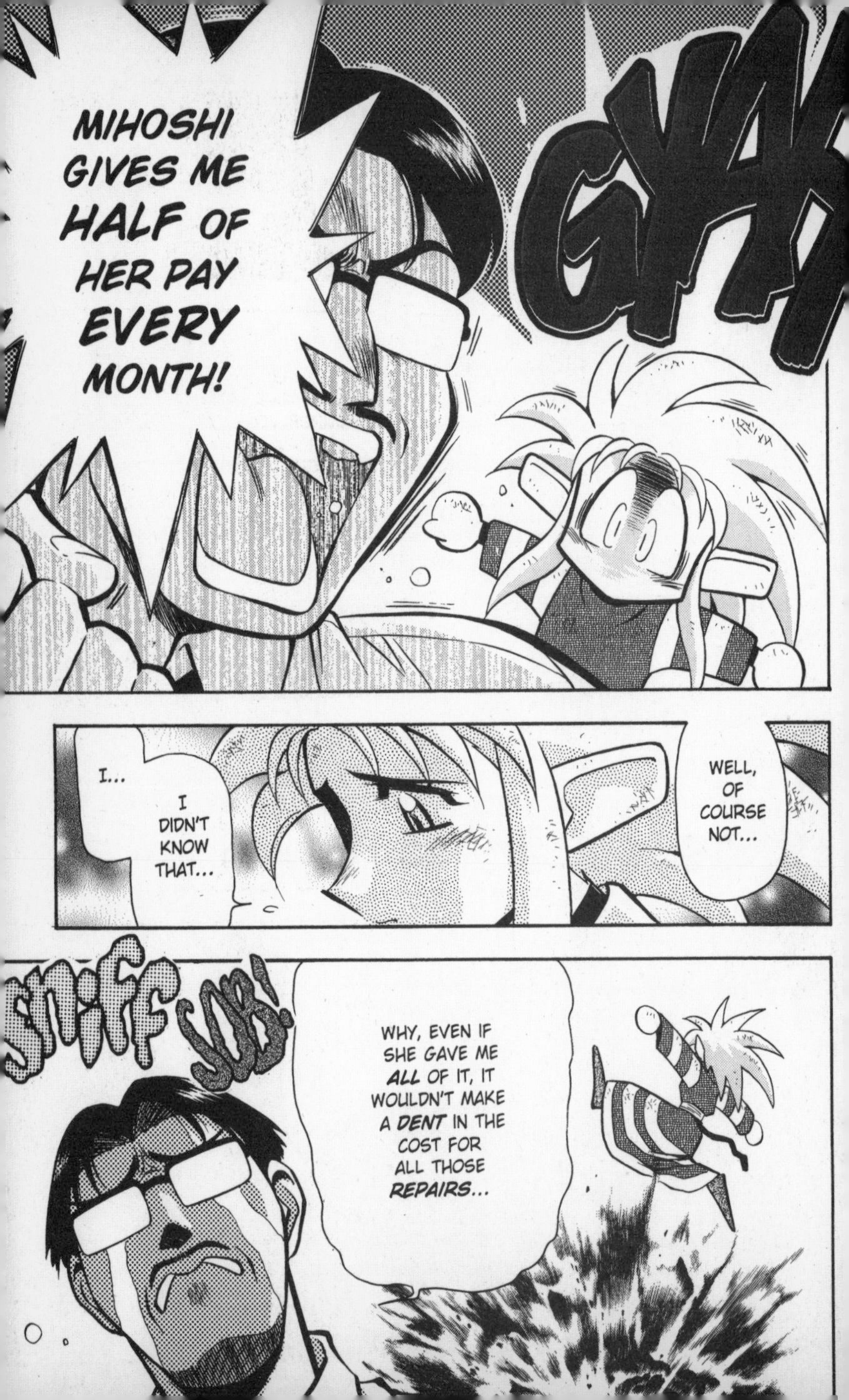
MIHOSHI GIVES ME HALF OF HER PAY EVERY MONTH!
GYAA
I...
I DIDN'T KNOW THAT...
WELL, OF COURSE NOT...
SNIFF SOB!
WHY, EVEN IF SHE GAVE ME ALL OF IT, IT WOULDN'T MAKE A DENT IN THE COST FOR ALL THOSE REPAIRS...

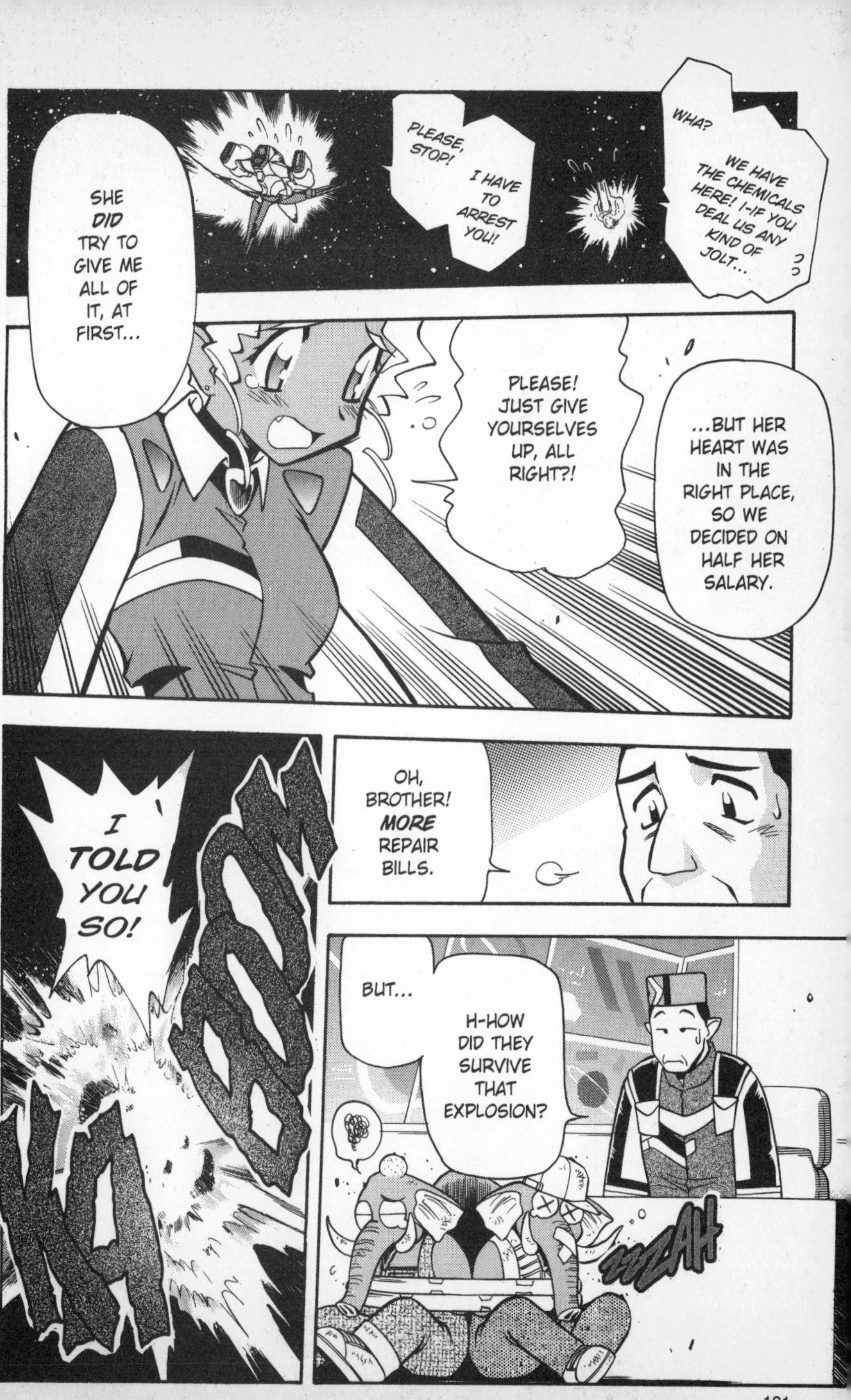
SHE DID TRY TO GIVE ME ALL OF IT, AT FIRST...
PLEASE, STOP!
I HAVE TO ARREST YOU!!
WHA?
WE HAVE THE CHEMICALS HERE! I-IF YOU DEAL US ANY KIND OF JOLT...
PLEASE! JUST GIVE YOURSELVES UP, ALL RIGHT?!
...BUT HER HEART WAS IN THE RIGHT PLACE, SO WE DECIDED ON HALF HER SALARY.
I TOLD YOU SO!
OH, BROTHER! MORE REPAIR BILLS.
BUT...
H-HOW DID THEY SURVIVE THAT EXPLOSION?

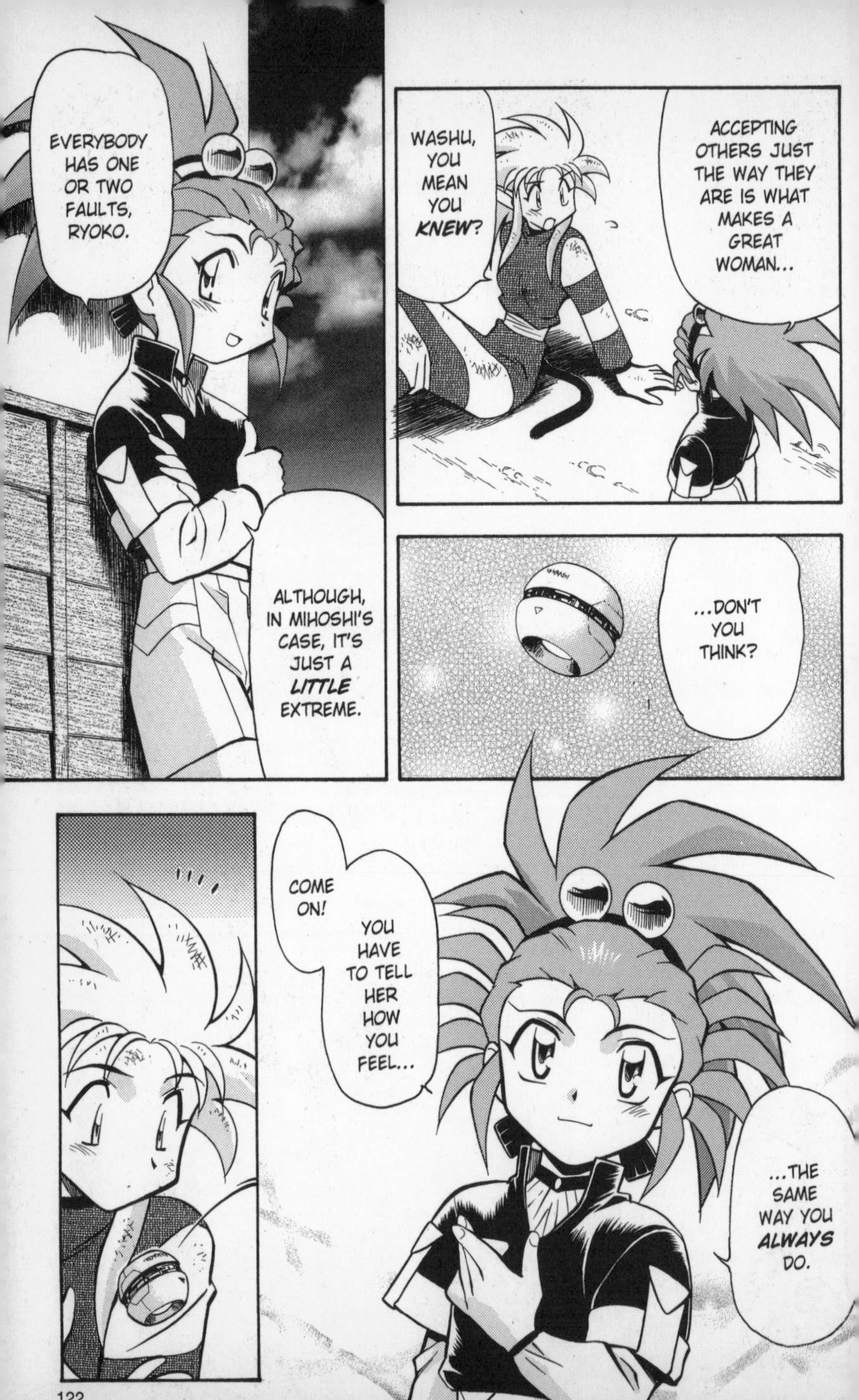
EVERYBODY HAS ONE OR TWO FAULTS, RYOKO.
ALTHOUGH, IN MIHOSHI'S CASE, IT'S JUST A *LITTLE* EXTREME.
WASHU, YOU MEAN YOU *KNEW*?
ACCEPTING OTHERS JUST THE WAY THEY ARE IS WHAT MAKES A GREAT WOMAN...
...DON'T YOU THINK?
COME ON!
YOU HAVE TO TELL HER HOW YOU FEEL...
...THE SAME WAY YOU *ALWAYS* DO.

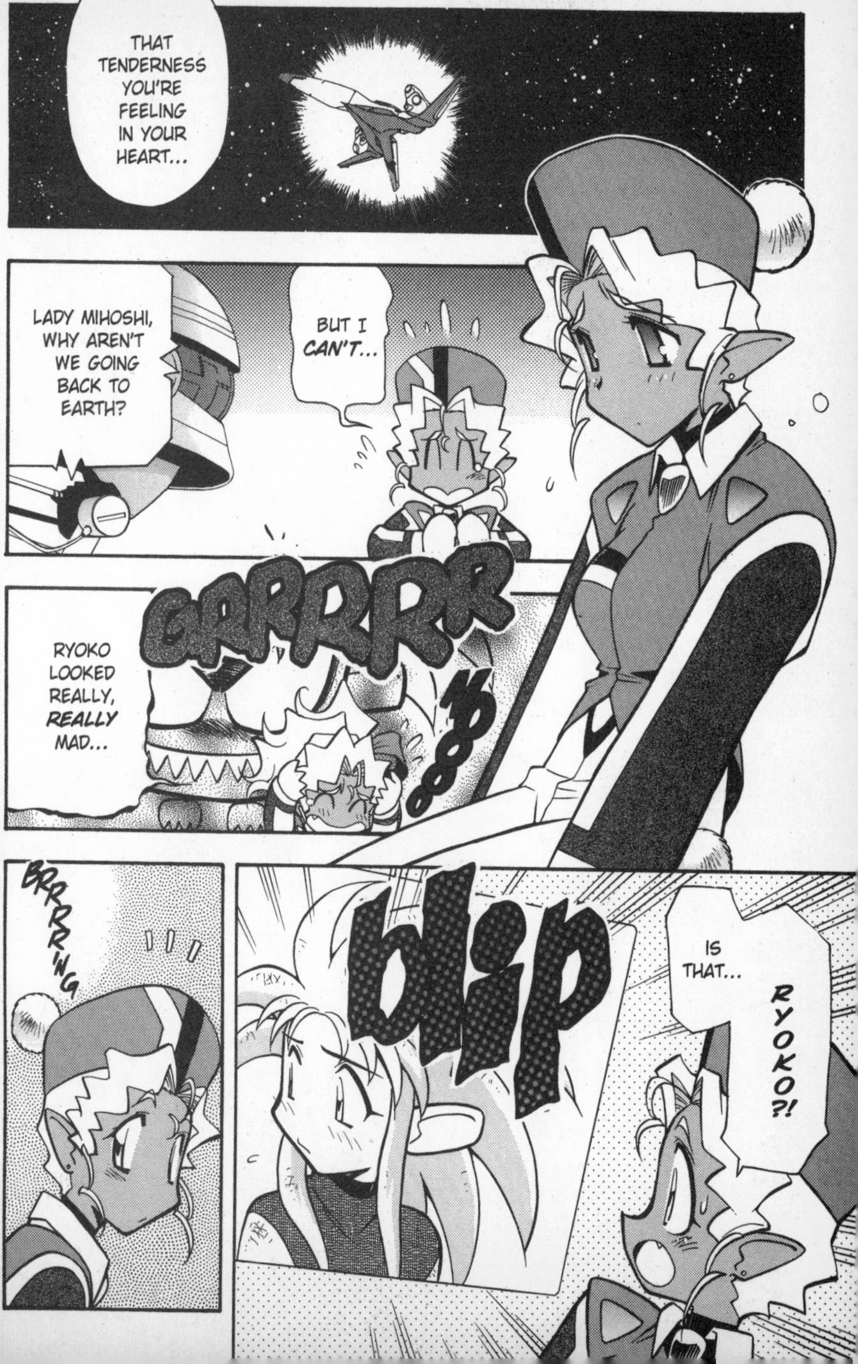
THAT TENDERNESS YOU'RE FEELING IN YOUR HEART...
LADY MIHOSHI, WHY AREN'T WE GOING BACK TO EARTH?
BUT I CAN'T...
GRRRRR
RYOKO LOOKED REALLY, REALLY MAD...
BRRRRING
blip
IS THAT...
RYOKO?!

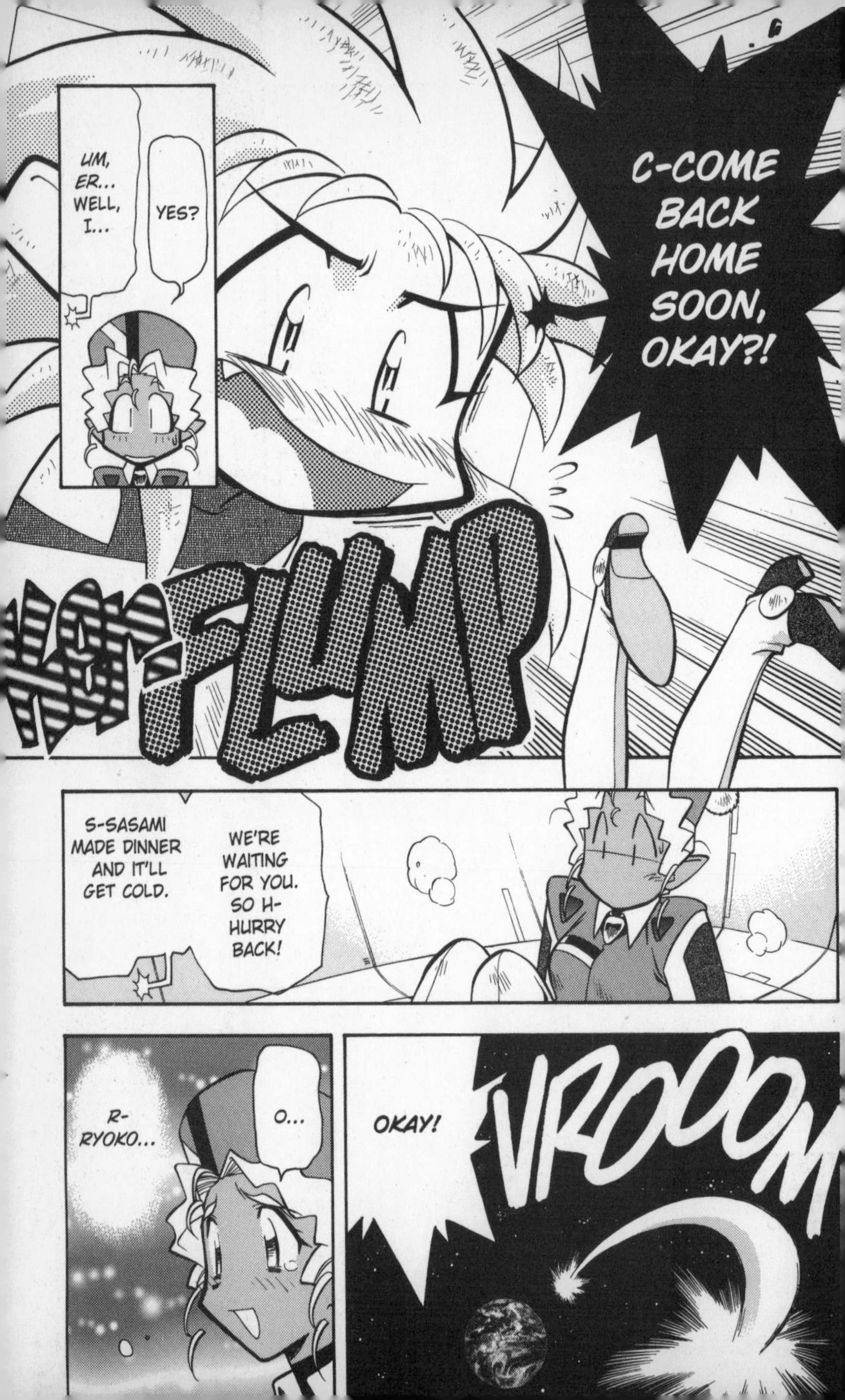
UM, ER... WELL, I...
YES?
C-COME BACK HOME SOON, OKAY?!
FLUMP
S-SASAMI MADE DINNER AND IT'LL GET COLD.
WE'RE WAITING FOR YOU. SO H-HURRY BACK!
R-RYOKO...
O...
OKAY!
VROOOM

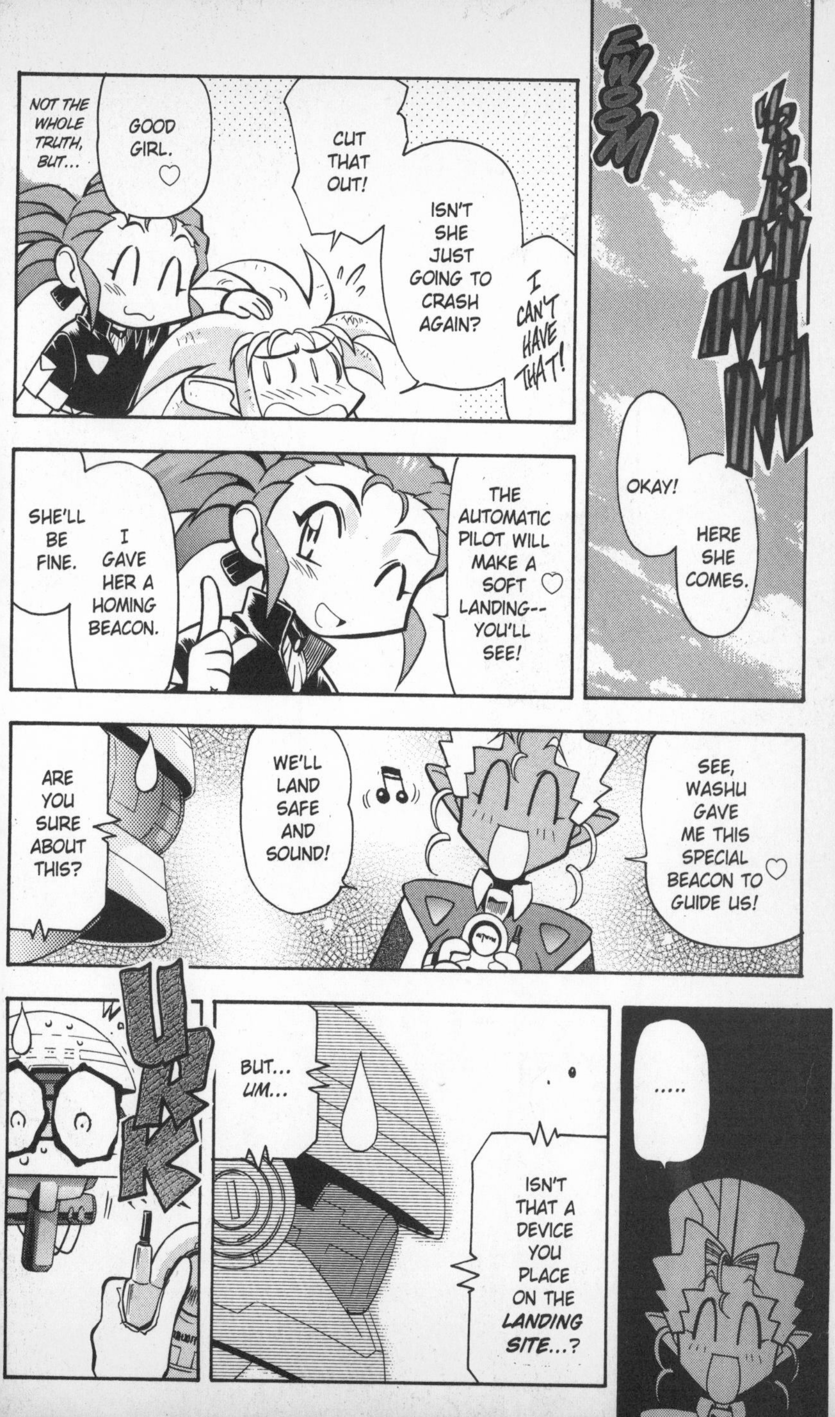
NOT THE WHOLE TRUTH, BUT...
GOOD GIRL. ♡
CUT THAT OUT!
ISN'T SHE JUST GOING TO CRASH AGAIN?
I CAN'T HAVE THAT!
SHE'LL BE FINE.
I GAVE HER A HOMING BEACON.
THE AUTOMATIC PILOT WILL MAKE A SOFT LANDING-- YOU'LL SEE! ♡
FWOOM
OKAY!
HERE SHE COMES.
ARE YOU SURE ABOUT THIS?
WE'LL LAND SAFE AND SOUND!
SEE, WASHU GAVE ME THIS SPECIAL BEACON TO GUIDE US! ♡
UKK
BUT... UM...
ISN'T THAT A DEVICE YOU PLACE ON THE *LANDING SITE*...?
.....

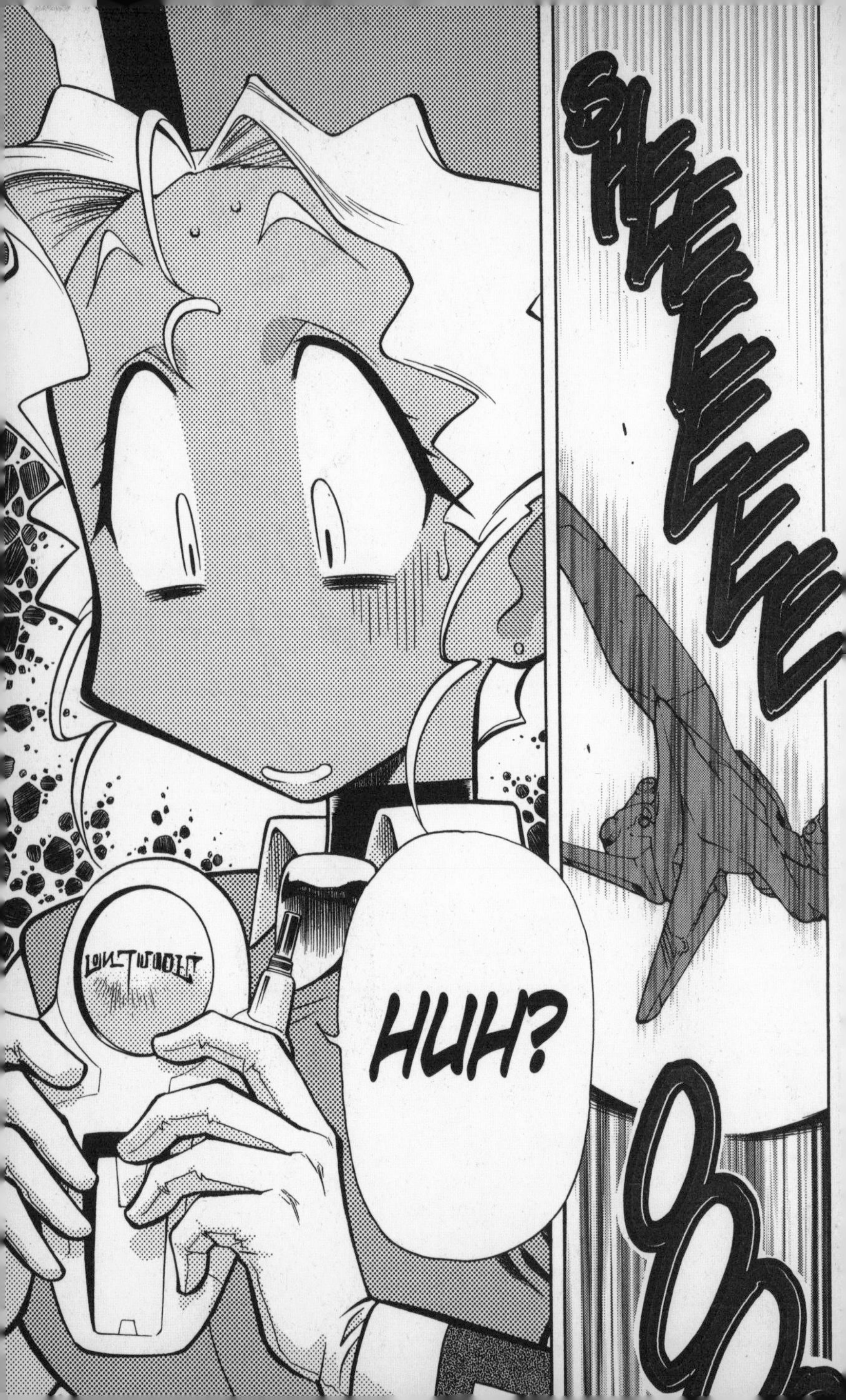
HUH?

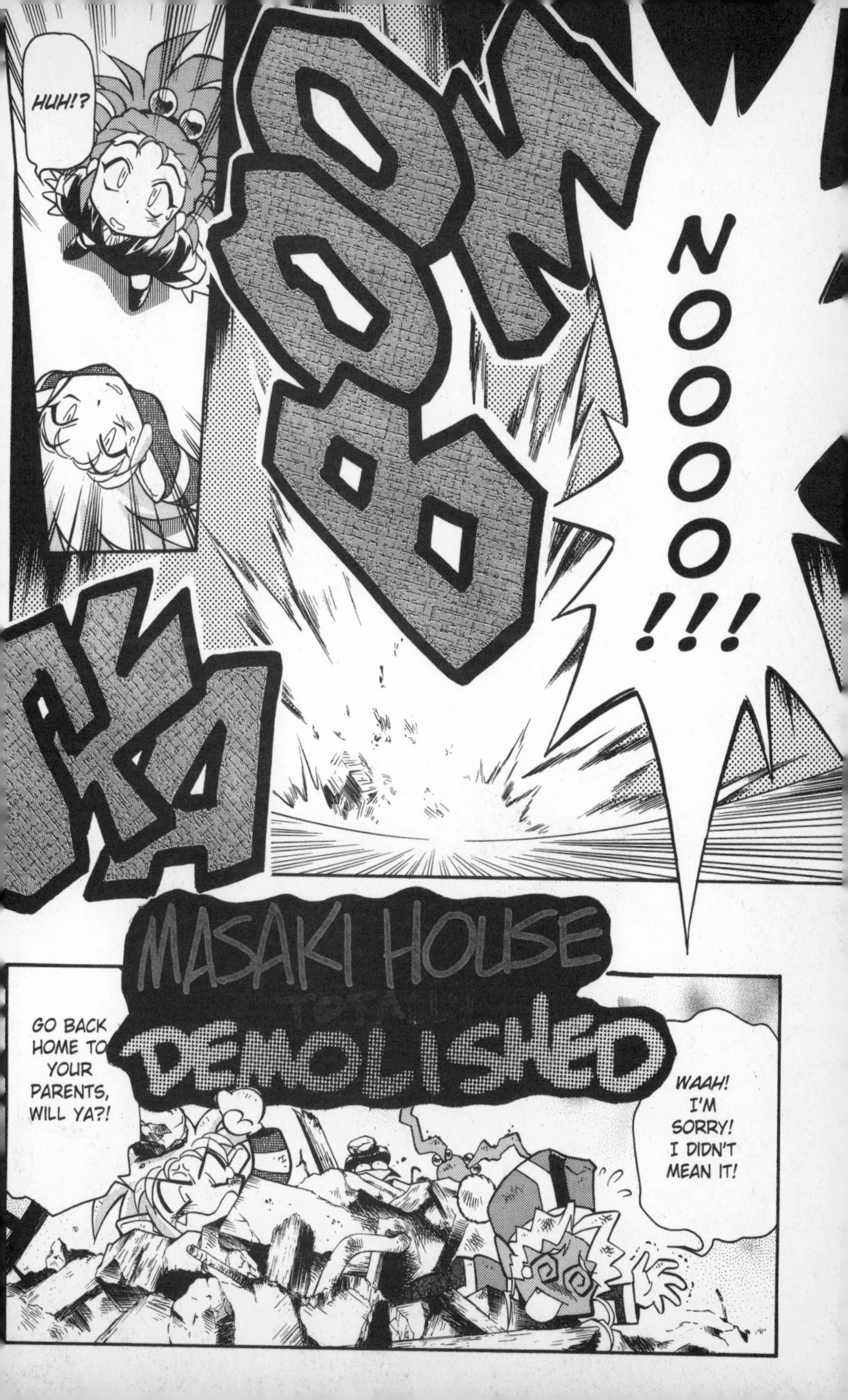
HUH!?
NOOOOO!!!
MASAKI HOUSE TOTALLY DEMOLISHED
GO BACK HOME TO YOUR PARENTS, WILL YA?!
WAAH! I'M SORRY! I DIDN'T MEAN IT!

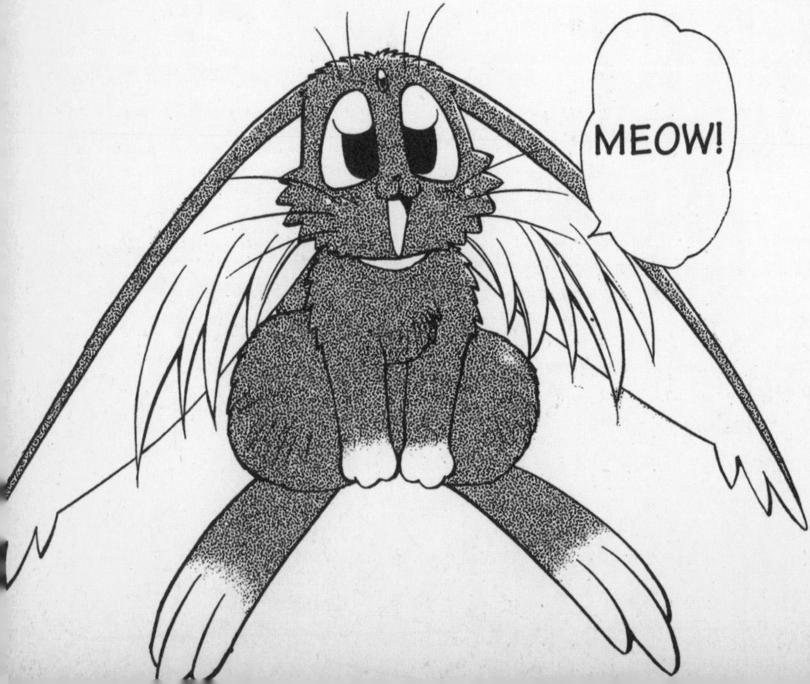
MEOW!

Chapter 6: EXCELLENCE

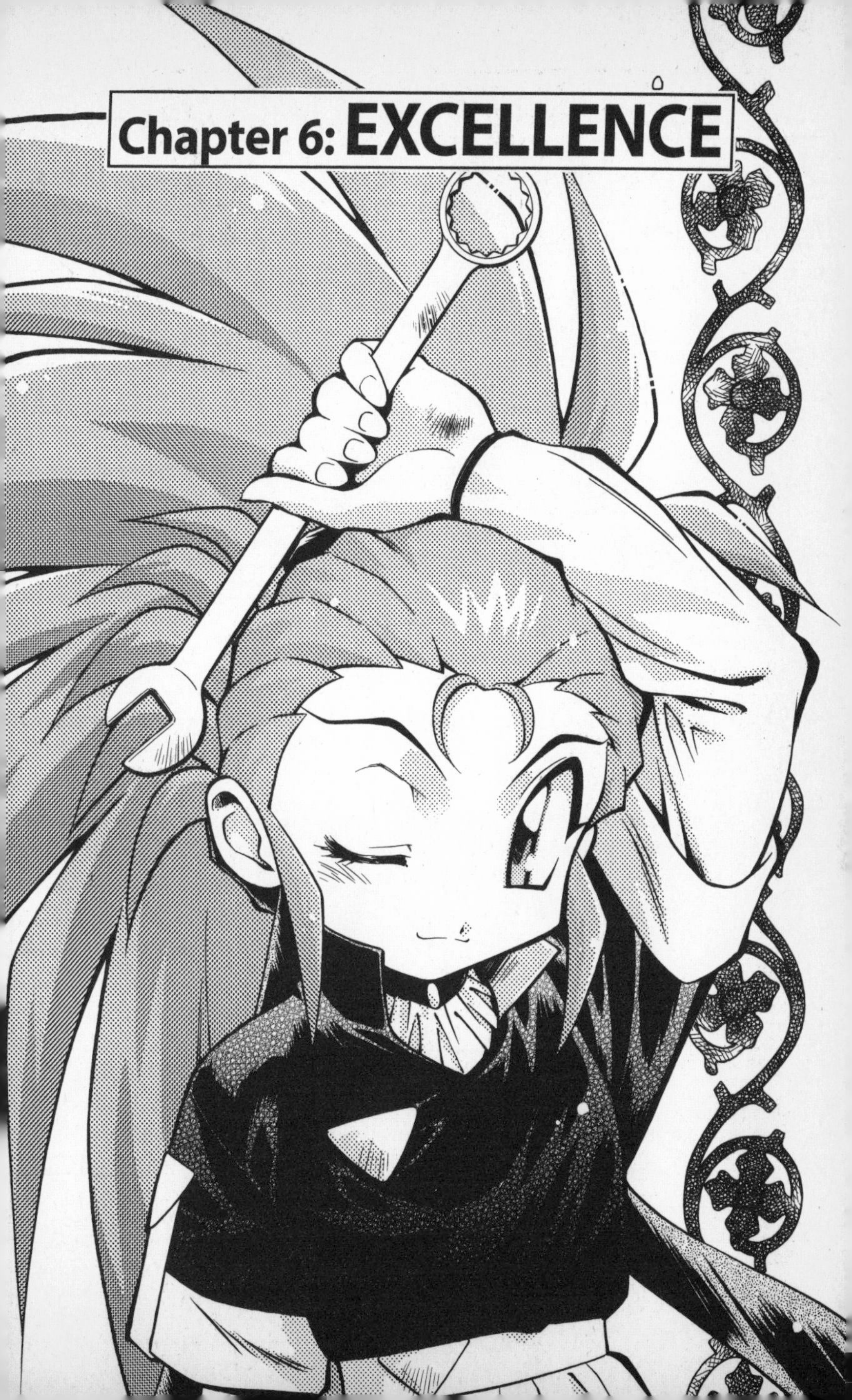

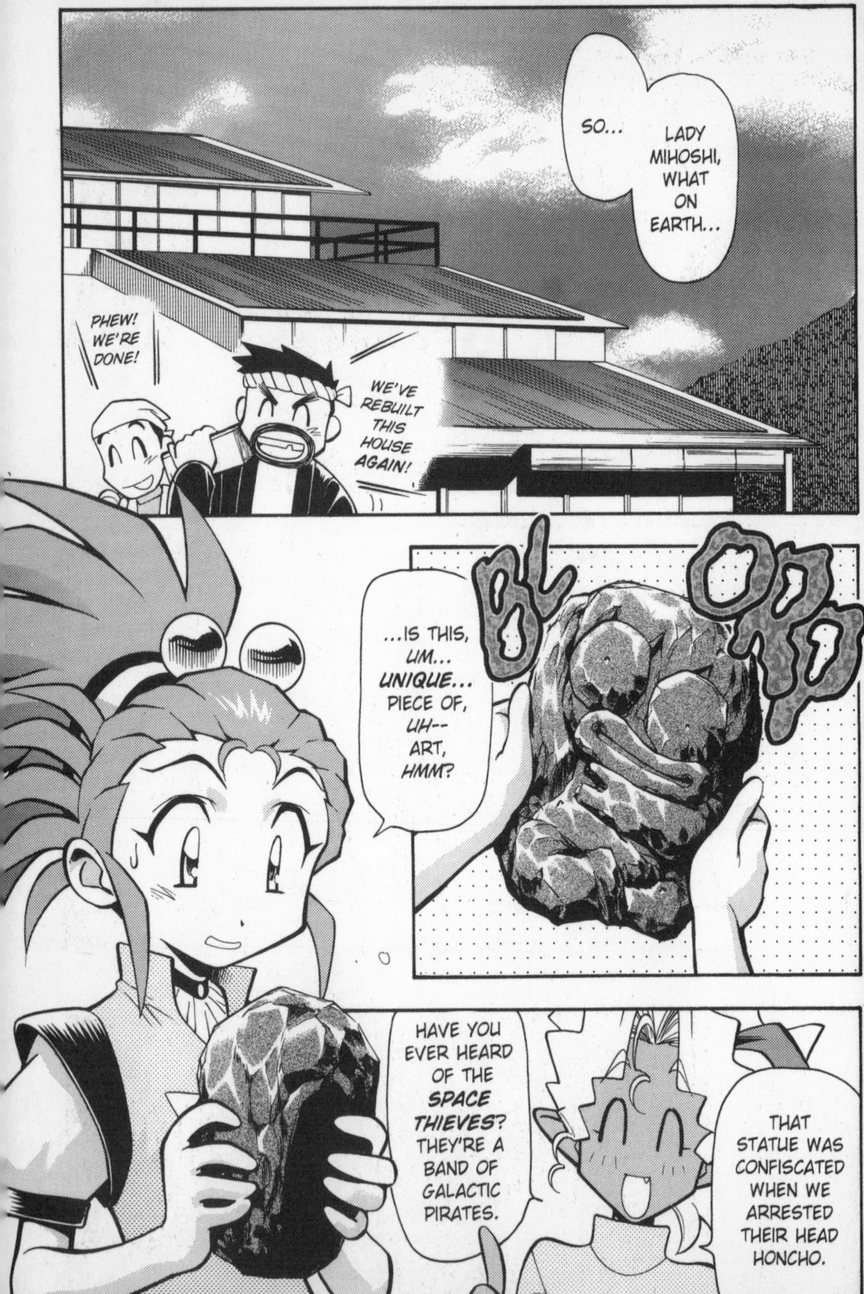
SO... LADY MIHOSHI, WHAT ON EARTH...
PHEW! WE'RE DONE!
WE'VE REBUILT THIS HOUSE AGAIN!
...IS THIS, UM... UNIQUE... PIECE OF, UH-- ART, HMM?
BLORP
HAVE YOU EVER HEARD OF THE SPACE THIEVES? THEY'RE A BAND OF GALACTIC PIRATES.
THAT STATUE WAS CONFISCATED WHEN WE ARRESTED THEIR HEAD HONCHO.

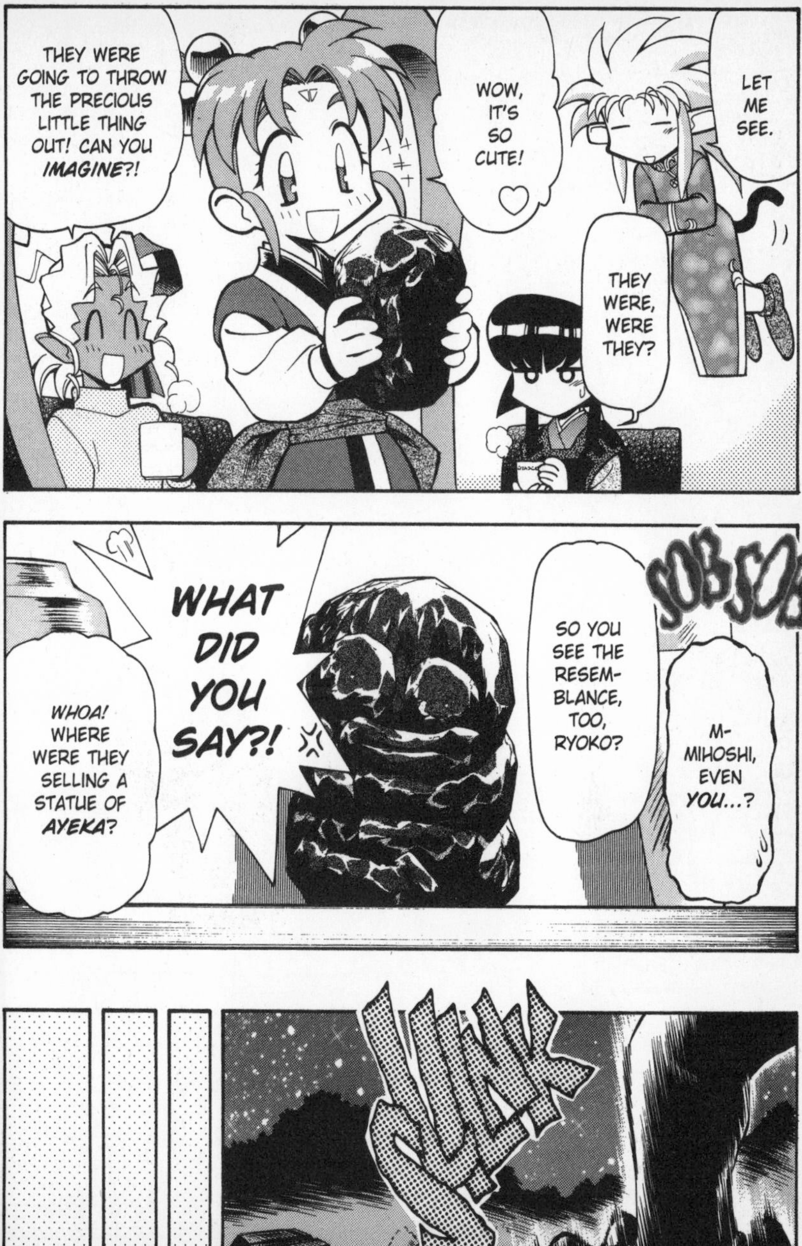
THEY WERE GOING TO THROW THE PRECIOUS LITTLE THING OUT! CAN YOU *IMAGINE*?!
WOW, IT'S SO CUTE! ♥
LET ME SEE.
THEY WERE, WERE THEY?
WHAT DID YOU SAY?!
WHOA! WHERE WERE THEY SELLING A STATUE OF *AYEKA*?
SO YOU SEE THE RESEM-BLANCE, TOO, RYOKO?
SOB SOB
M-MIHOSHI, EVEN *YOU*...?

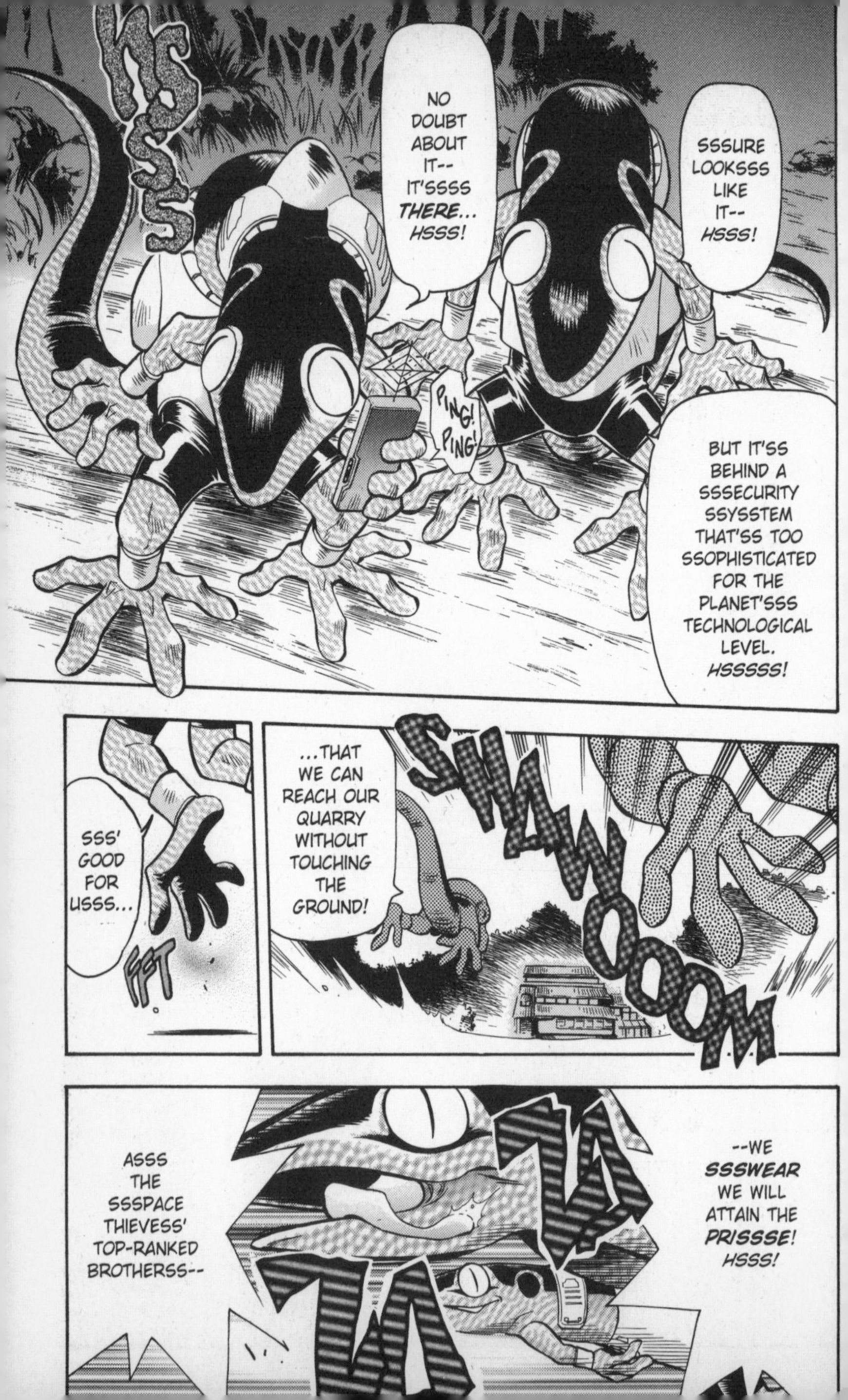
HSSS
NO DOUBT ABOUT IT-- IT'SSSS *THERE...* *HSSS!*
SSSURE LOOKSSS LIKE IT-- *HSSS!*
PING! PING!
BUT IT'SS BEHIND A SSSECURITY SSYSSTEM THAT'SS TOO SSOPHISTICATED FOR THE PLANET'SSS TECHNOLOGICAL LEVEL. *HSSSSS!*
SSS' GOOD FOR USSS...
FFT
...THAT WE CAN REACH OUR QUARRY WITHOUT TOUCHING THE GROUND!
SHWOOOOM
ASSS THE SSSPACE THIEVESS' TOP-RANKED BROTHERSS--
--WE ***SSSWEAR*** WE WILL ATTAIN THE ***PRISSSE!*** *HSSS!*

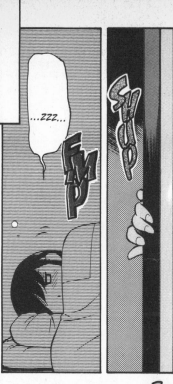

...ZZZ...

FMP

SHUP

URP...

I SHOULD'VE KNOWN BETTER THAN TO DRINK SO MUCH!

THIS IS ALL...

TMP TMP TMP TMP TMP TMP TMP

...RYOKO'S FAULT! MAYBE SOME ASPIRIN, AND B VITAMINS, AND WATER... UNGH...

ha ha ha ha ha ha

DRINK IT DOWN!

IS SOME-ONE IN THERE?

SWSH TSH

133

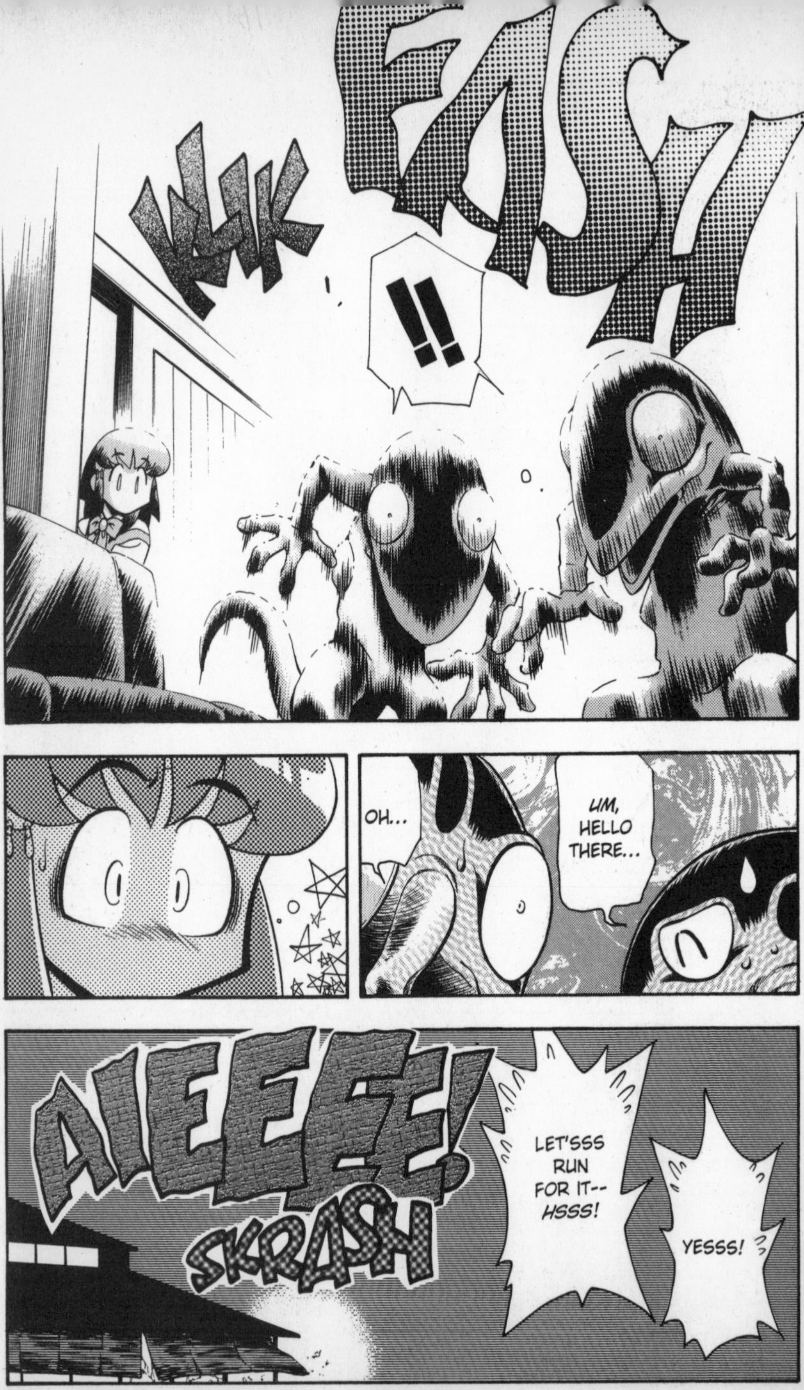
KLIK
FLASH
!!
OH...
UM, HELLO THERE...
AIEEEE!
SKRASH
LET'SSS RUN FOR IT-- HSSS!
YESSS!

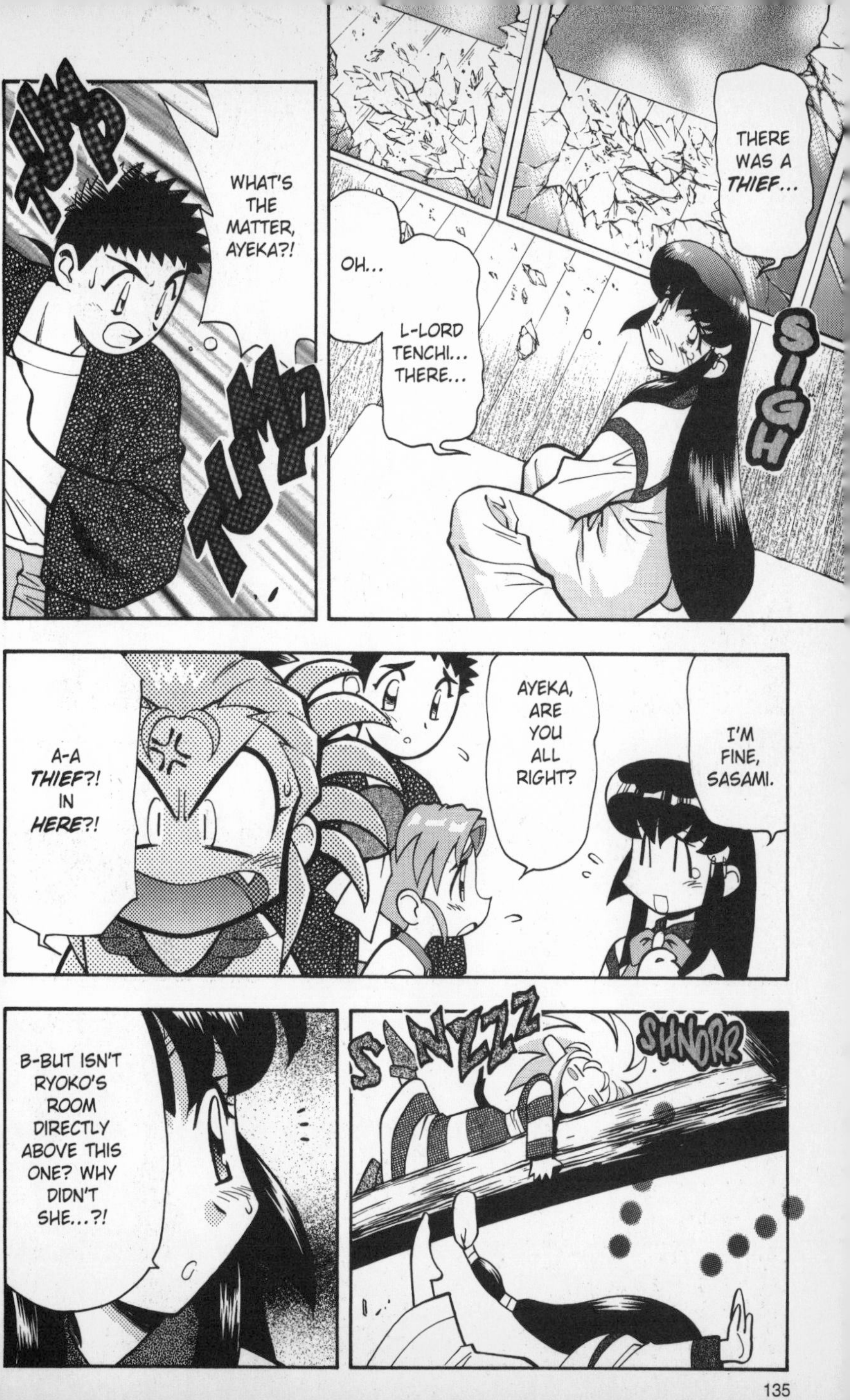
WHAT'S THE MATTER, AYEKA?!
OH...
L-LORD TENCHI... THERE...
THERE WAS A *THIEF*...
SIGH
A-A *THIEF*?! IN *HERE*?!
AYEKA, ARE YOU ALL RIGHT?
I'M FINE, SASAMI.
B-BUT ISN'T RYOKO'S ROOM DIRECTLY ABOVE THIS ONE? WHY DIDN'T SHE...?!
SNZZZ
SHNORR

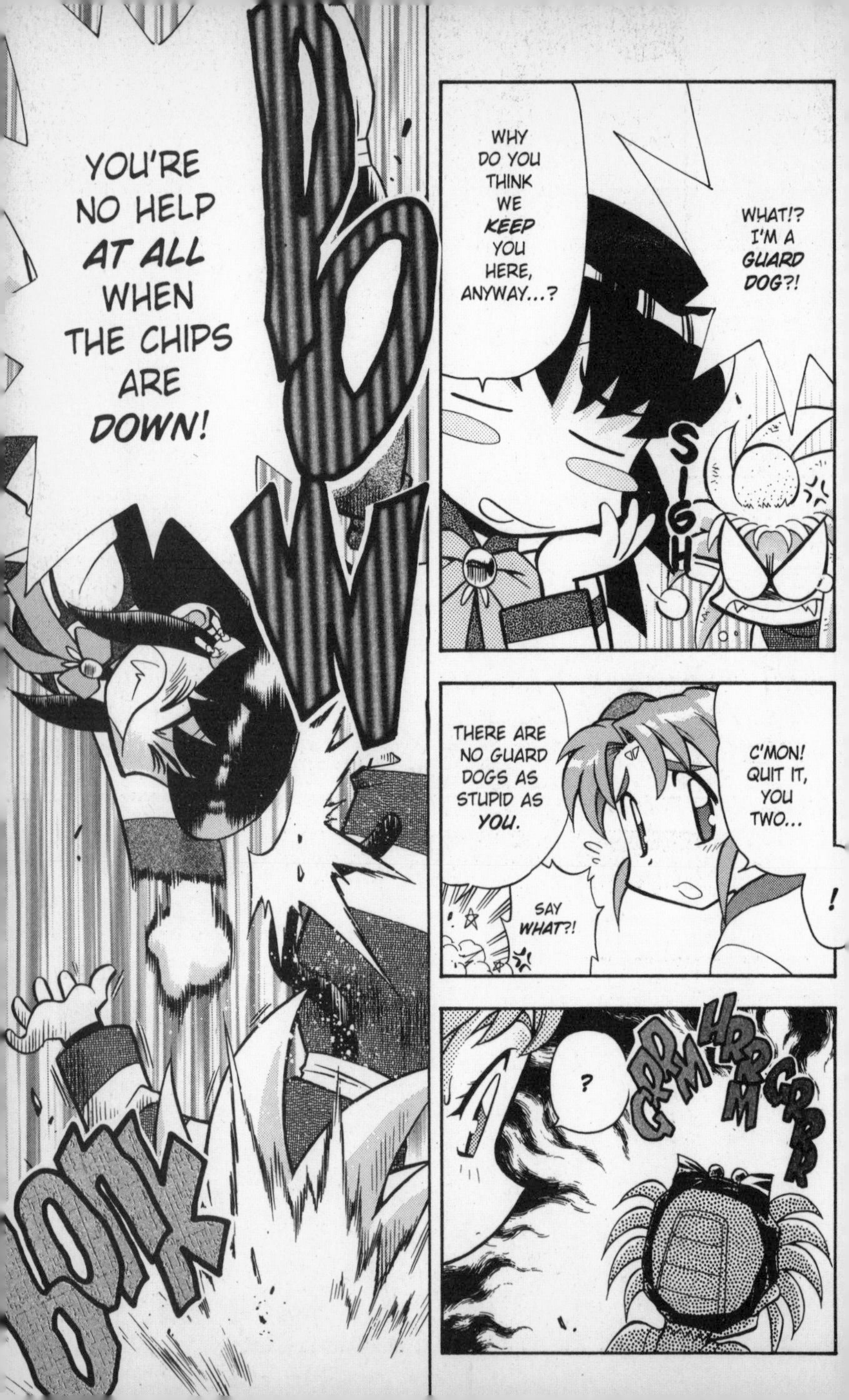
YOU'RE NO HELP AT ALL WHEN THE CHIPS ARE DOWN!
POW
BONK
WHY DO YOU THINK WE KEEP YOU HERE, ANYWAY...?
SIGH
WHAT!? I'M A GUARD DOG?!
THERE ARE NO GUARD DOGS AS STUPID AS YOU.
SAY WHAT?!
C'MON! QUIT IT, YOU TWO...
!
?
GRRM
HRRRM
GRRRR

UH...

ARE YOU OKAY THERE, WASHU?

HOW *DARE* THEY BREAK THROUGH *MY* SECURITY SYSTEM?!

yah ha ha!

I'LL TEACH THEM NOT TO MESS WITH *ME*...!

EEP!

SHE LOOKS SO *SCARY!*

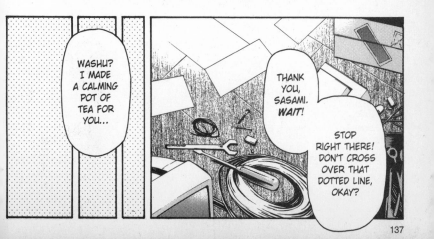

WASHU? I MADE A CALMING POT OF TEA FOR YOU...

THANK YOU, SASAMI. *WAIT!*

STOP RIGHT THERE! DON'T CROSS OVER THAT DOTTED LINE, OKAY?

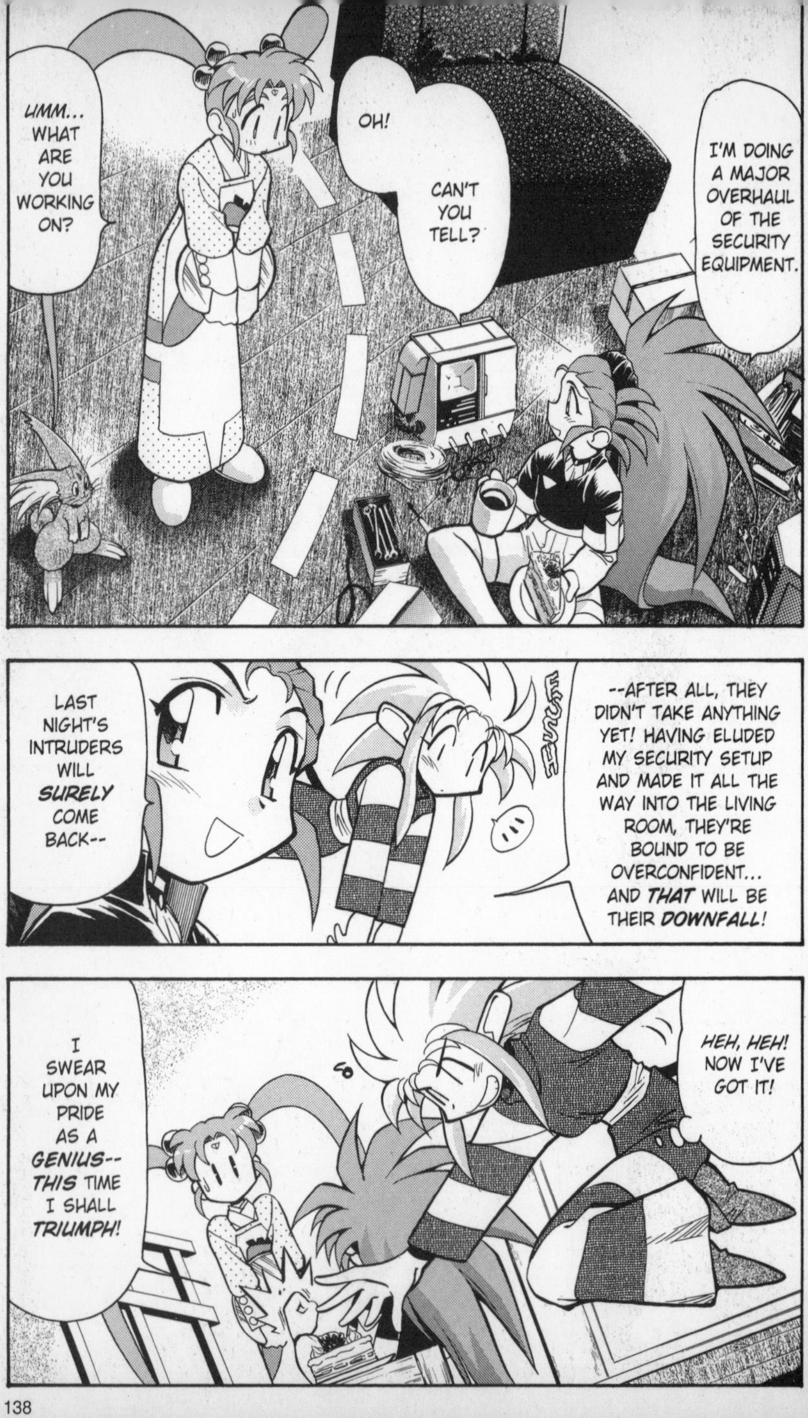
UMM... WHAT ARE YOU WORKING ON?
OH!
CAN'T YOU TELL?
I'M DOING A MAJOR OVERHAUL OF THE SECURITY EQUIPMENT.
LAST NIGHT'S INTRUDERS WILL SURELY COME BACK--
WUSH
--AFTER ALL, THEY DIDN'T TAKE ANYTHING YET! HAVING ELUDED MY SECURITY SETUP AND MADE IT ALL THE WAY INTO THE LIVING ROOM, THEY'RE BOUND TO BE OVERCONFIDENT... AND THAT WILL BE THEIR DOWNFALL!
I SWEAR UPON MY PRIDE AS A GENIUS-- THIS TIME I SHALL TRIUMPH!
HEH, HEH! NOW I'VE GOT IT!

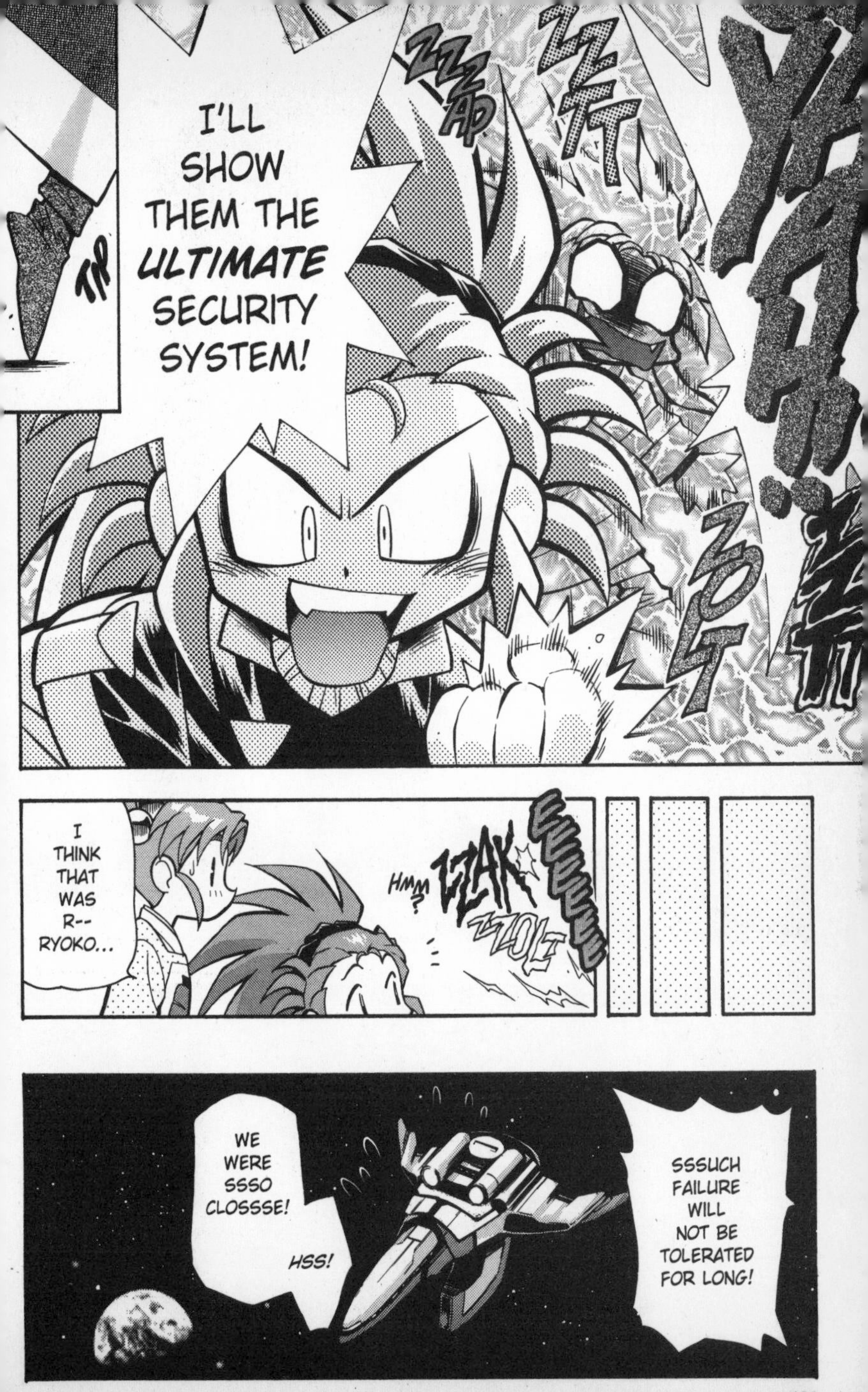
TAP
I'LL SHOW THEM THE ULTIMATE SECURITY SYSTEM!
ZZZAP
ZZZTT
ZOLT
I THINK THAT WAS R-- RYOKO...
HMM?
ZZAK
ZZZOLT
WE WERE SSSO CLOSSSE!
HSS!
SSSUCH FAILURE WILL NOT BE TOLERATED FOR LONG!

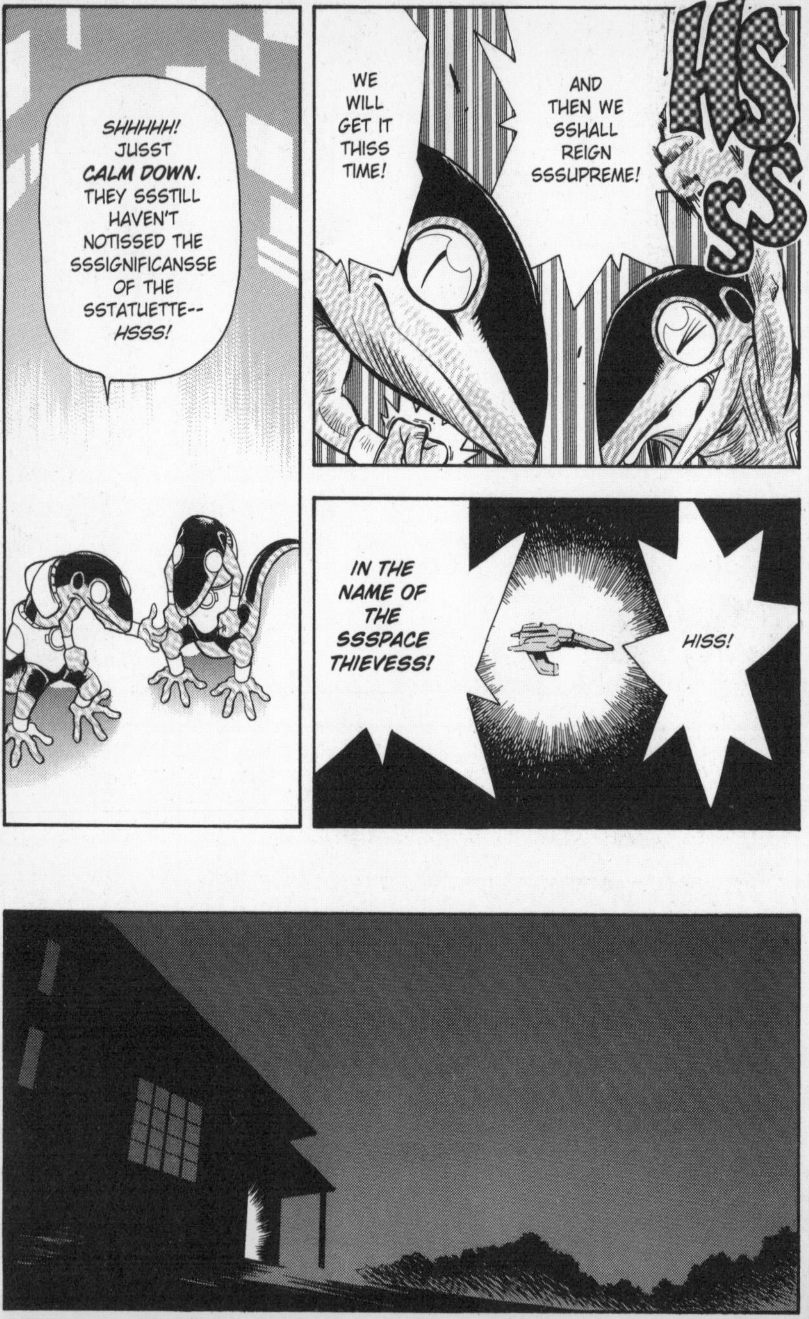
SHHHHH! JUSST CALM DOWN. THEY SSSTILL HAVEN'T NOTISSED THE SSSIGNIFICANSSE OF THE SSTATUETTE-- HSSS!
WE WILL GET IT THISS TIME!
AND THEN WE SSHALL REIGN SSSUPREME!
HSSS
IN THE NAME OF THE SSSPACE THIEVESS!
HISS!

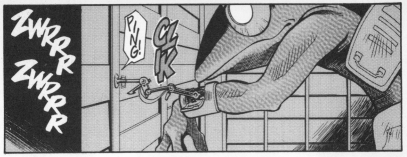

ZWRRR ZWRRR

PING! CLK

DOOR SSENSORSS DISSABLED! HISS!

SHWSH

HEH...A PIESSE OF CAKE!

ZWMM

HMM... IT LOOKSS LIKE...

...THE NUMBER OF INFRARED SSENSORSS HAS GREATLY INCREASSED SSSINCE LASST TIME!

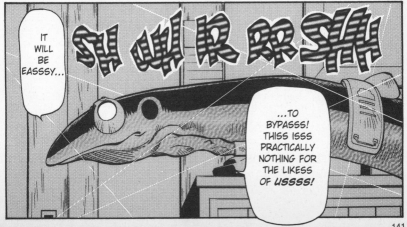

IT WILL BE EASSSY...

SH WM IR RR SHH

...TO BYPASSS! THISS ISSS PRACTICALLY NOTHING FOR THE LIKES OF USSSS!

141

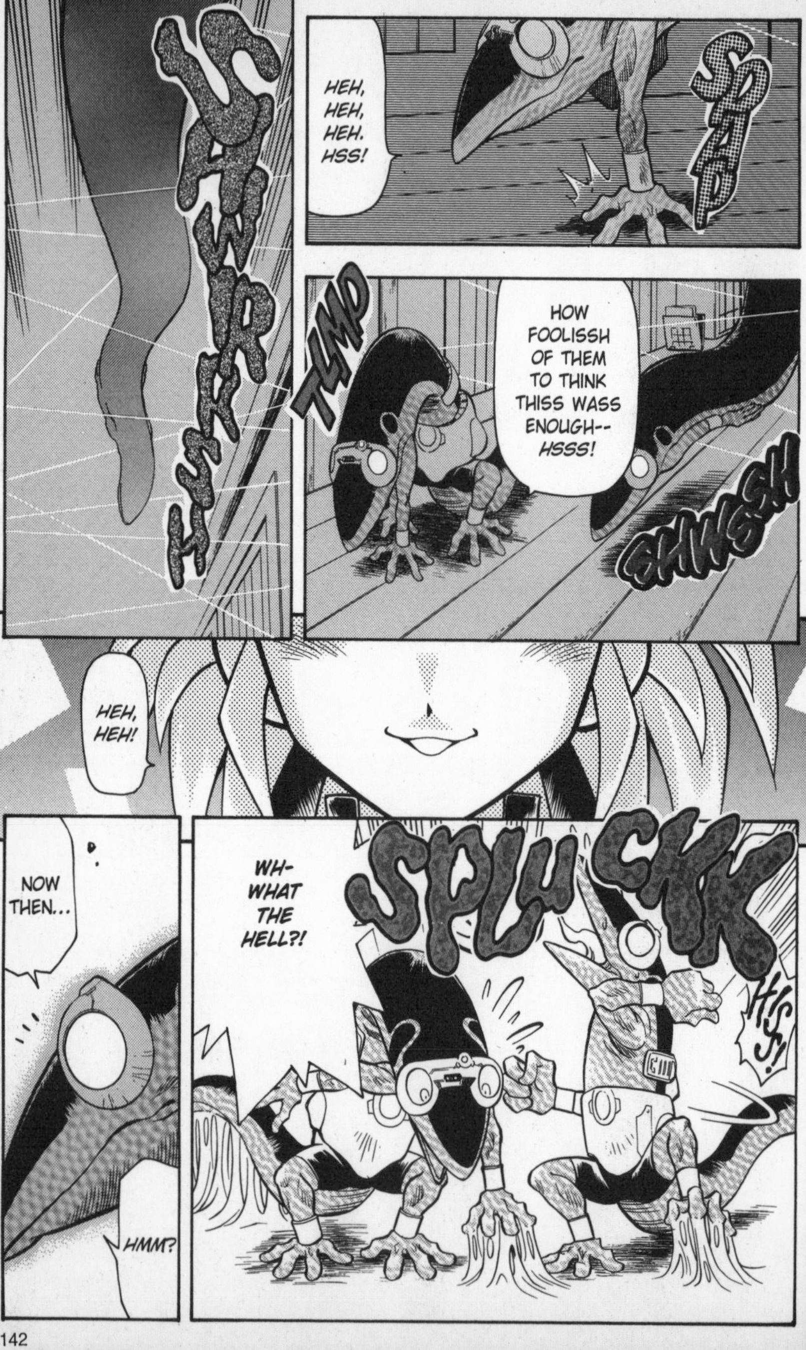
SHWRR
HEH, HEH, HEH. HSS!
SPAD
TUMP
HOW FOOLISSH OF THEM TO THINK THISS WASS ENOUGH-- HSSS!
SHWSSH
HEH, HEH!
NOW THEN...
HMM?
WH- WHAT THE HELL?!
SPLUCHK
HISS!

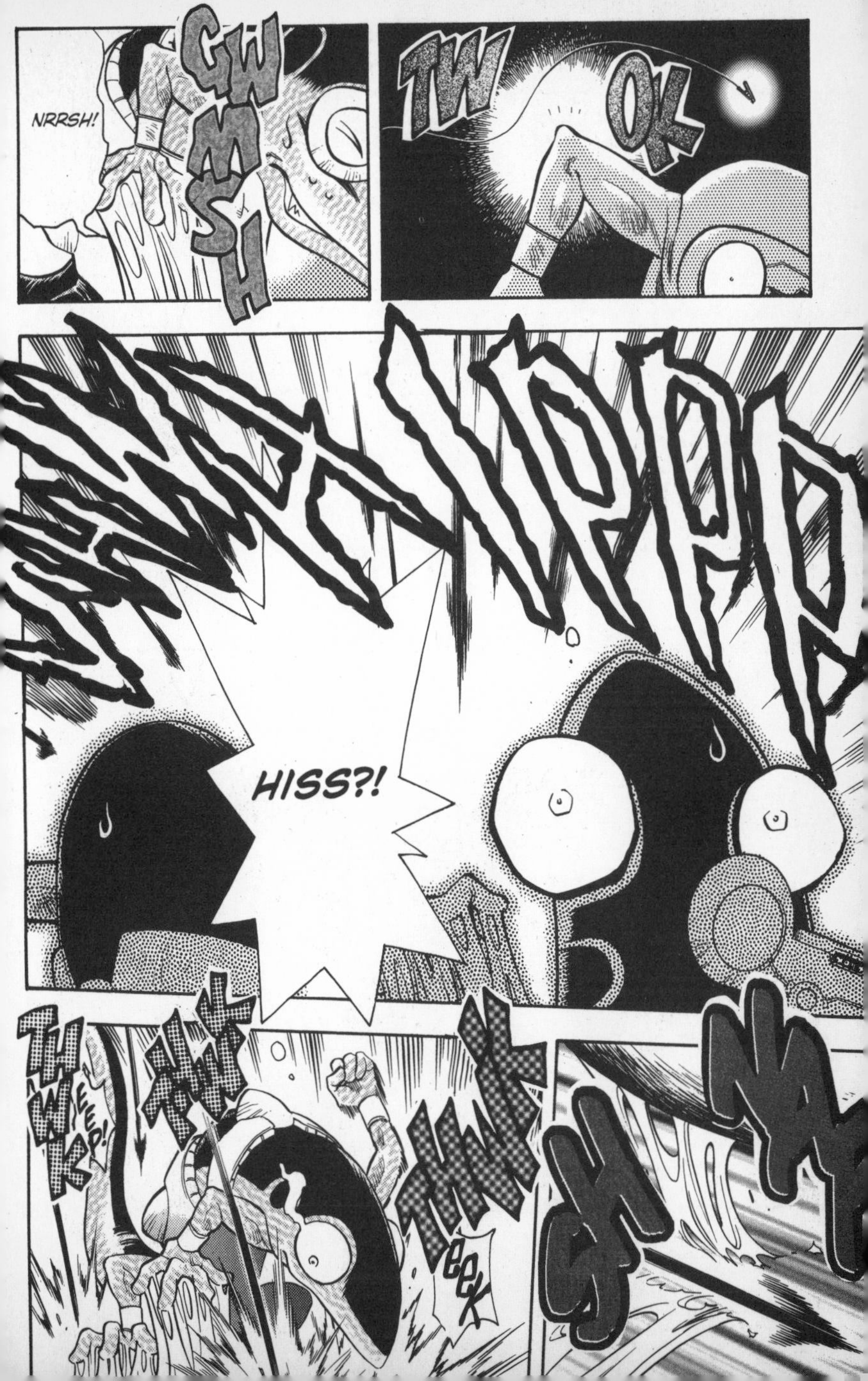
NRRSH!
HISS?!
eeek

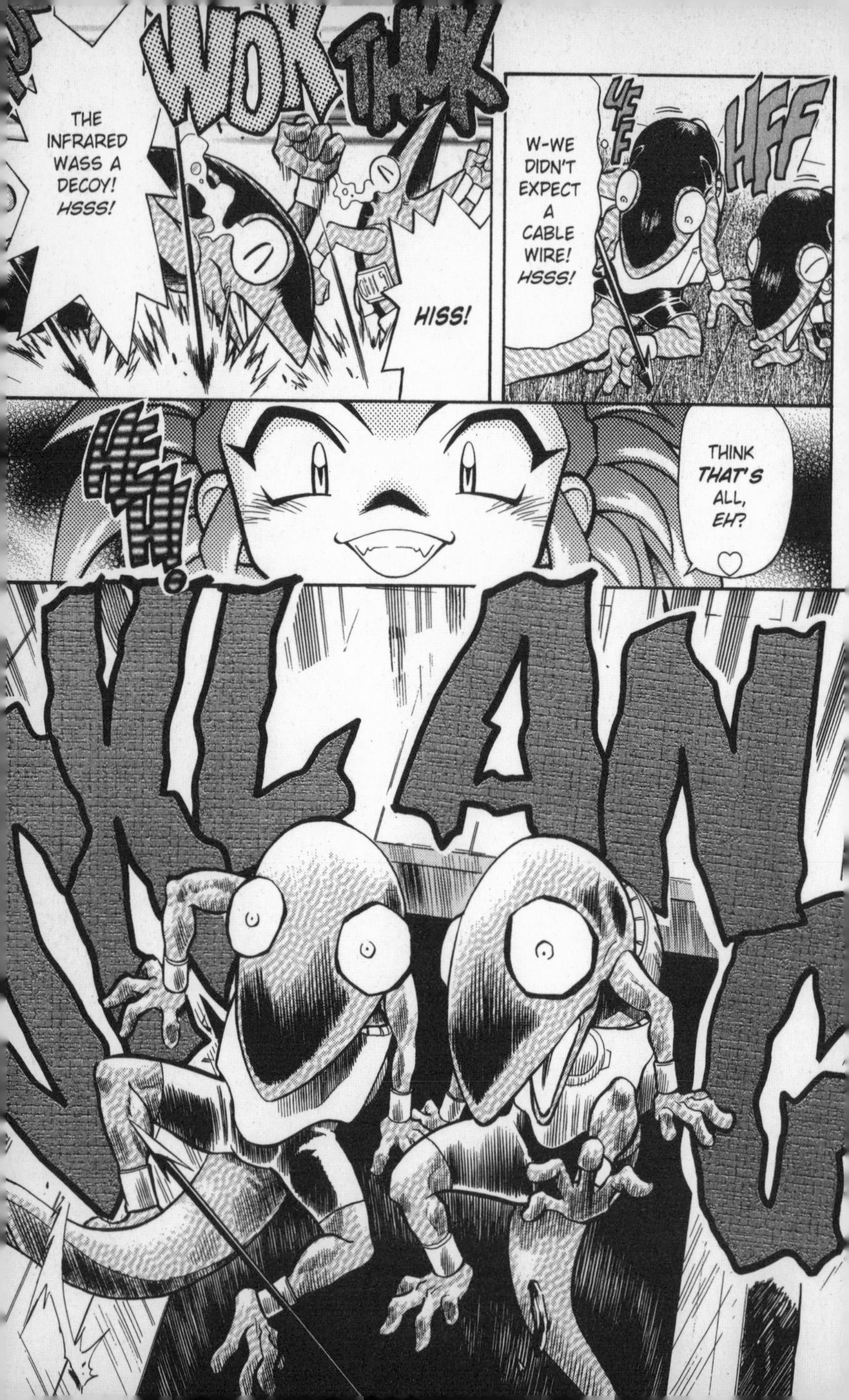
WOK
THOK
THE INFRARED WASS A DECOY! *HSSS!*
HISS!
UFF
HFF
W-WE DIDN'T EXPECT A CABLE WIRE! *HSSS!*
THINK *THAT'S* ALL, *EH?*

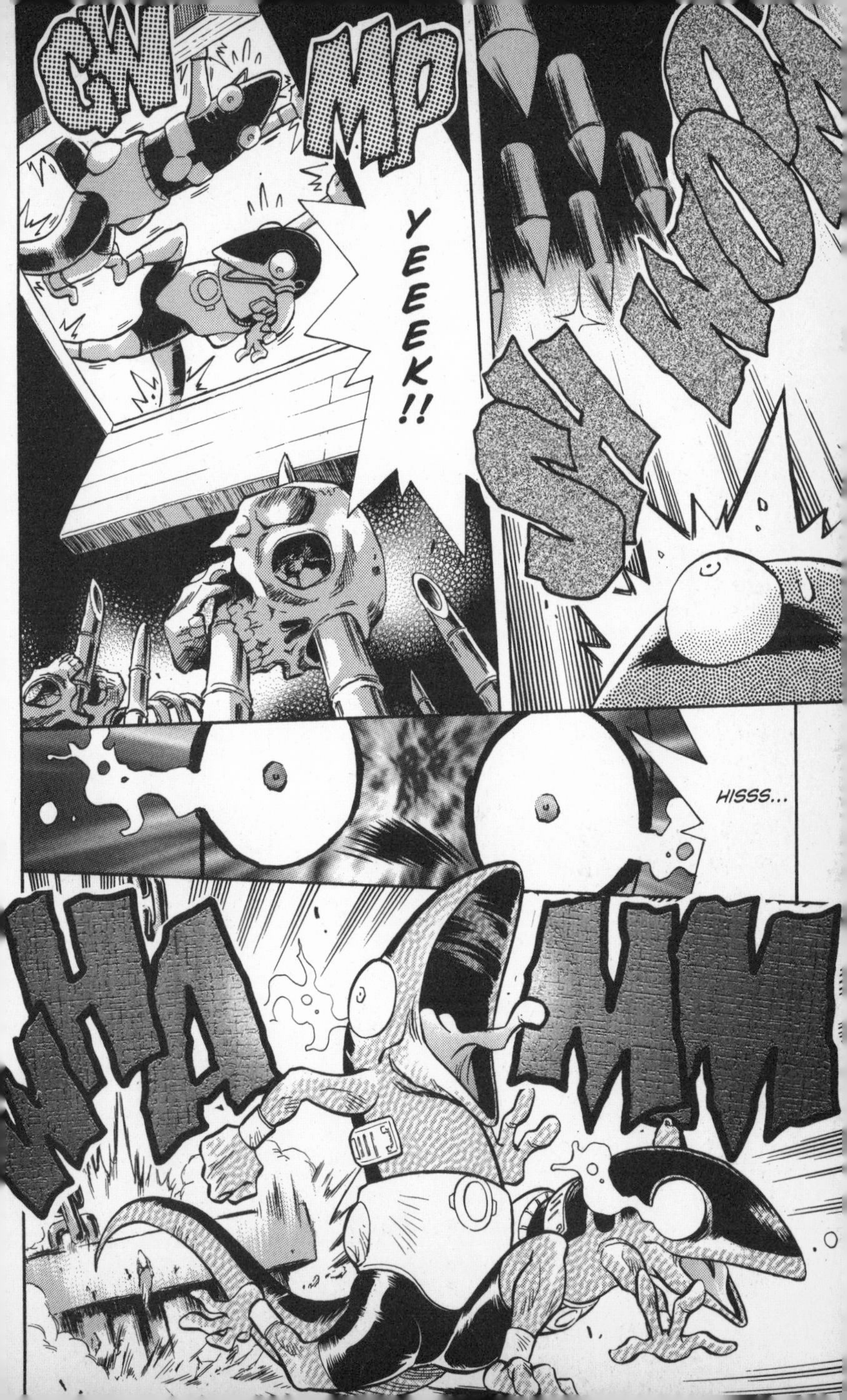

CWUMP
YEEEEK!!
SHOOF
HISSS...
WHAMM

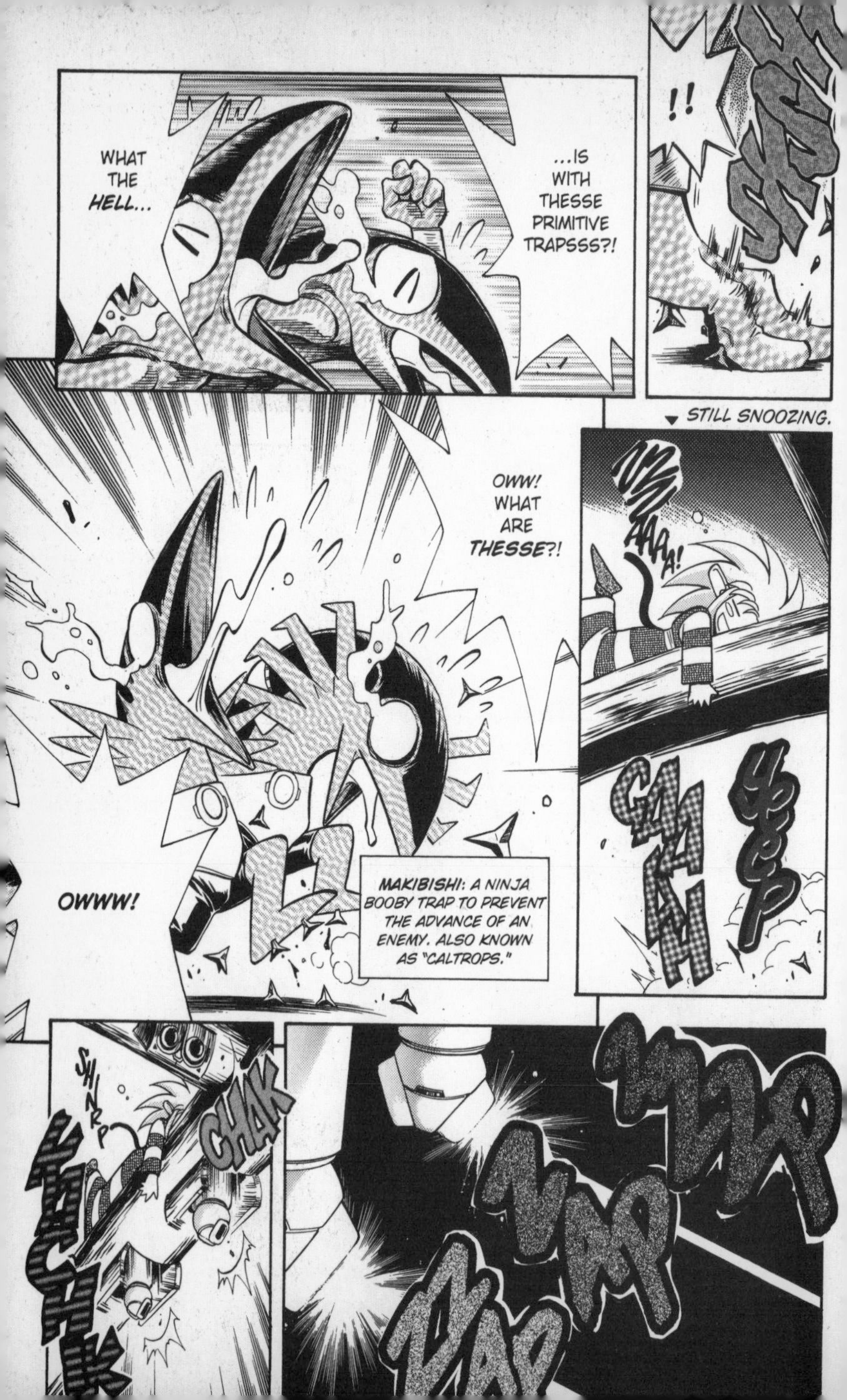
WHAT THE HELL...
...IS WITH THESSE PRIMITIVE TRAPSSS?!
!!
STILL SNOOZING.
OWW! WHAT ARE THESSE?!
OWWW!
MAKIBISHI: A NINJA BOOBY TRAP TO PREVENT THE ADVANCE OF AN ENEMY. ALSO KNOWN AS "CALTROPS."
CHAK

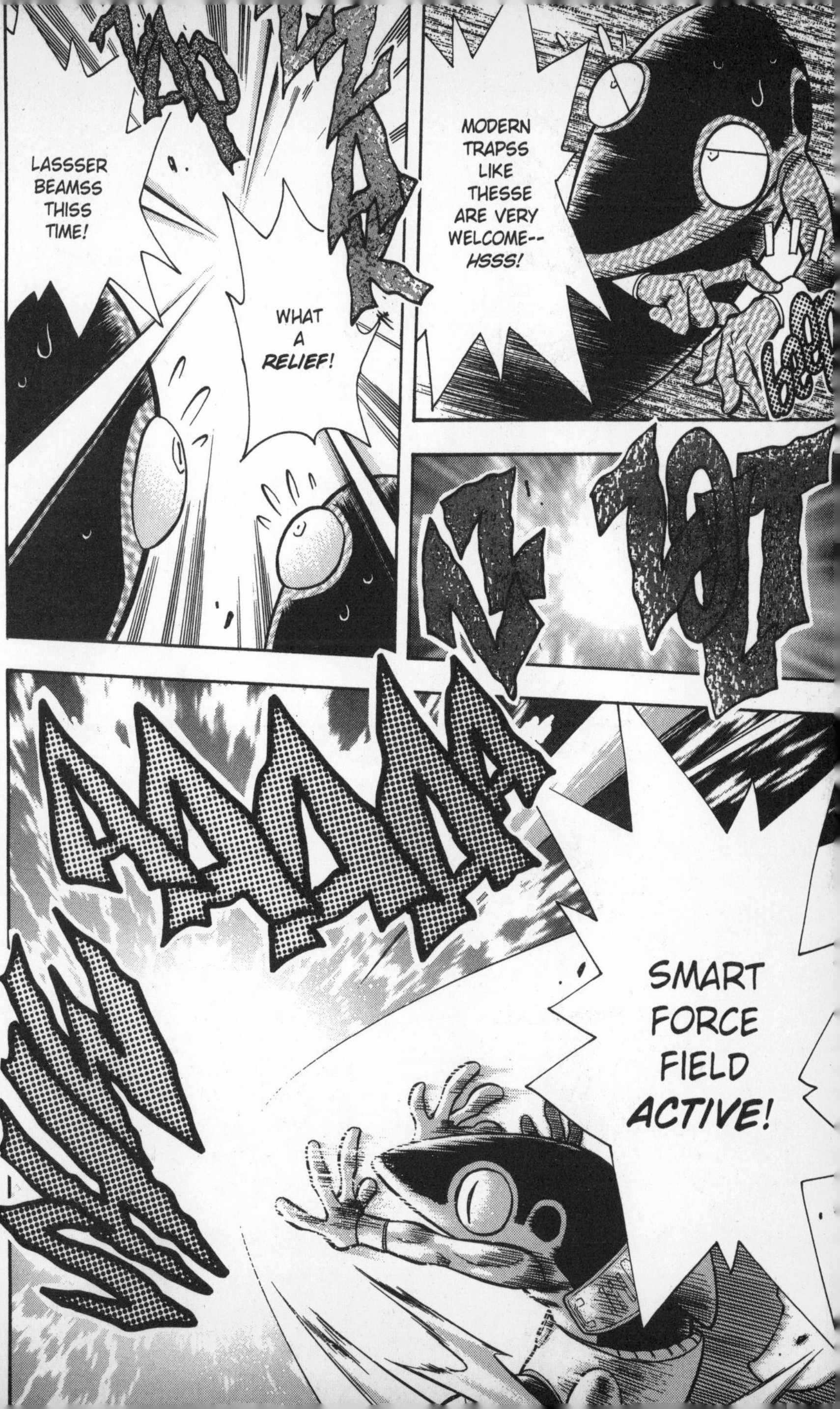
LASSSER BEAMSS THISS TIME!
WHAT A *RELIEF!*
MODERN TRAPSS LIKE THESSE ARE VERY WELCOME-- *HSSS!*
SMART FORCE FIELD *ACTIVE!*

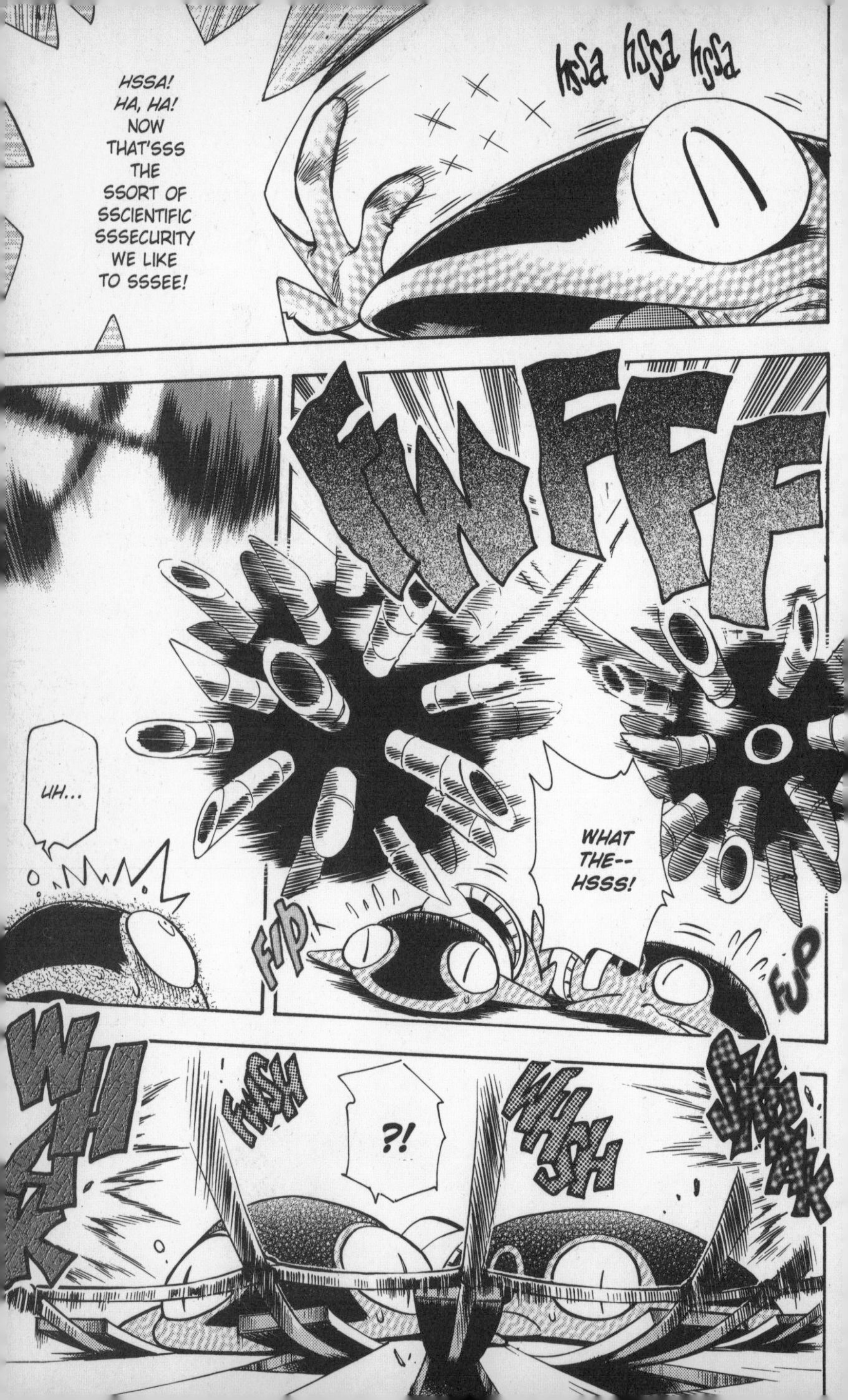
HSSA! HA, HA! NOW THAT'SSS THE SSORT OF SSCIENTIFIC SSSECURITY WE LIKE TO SSSEE!
hssa hssa hssa
UH...
FWFFF
WHAT THE-- HSSS!
FLIP
FLIP
WHAK
FWISH
?!
WHSSH

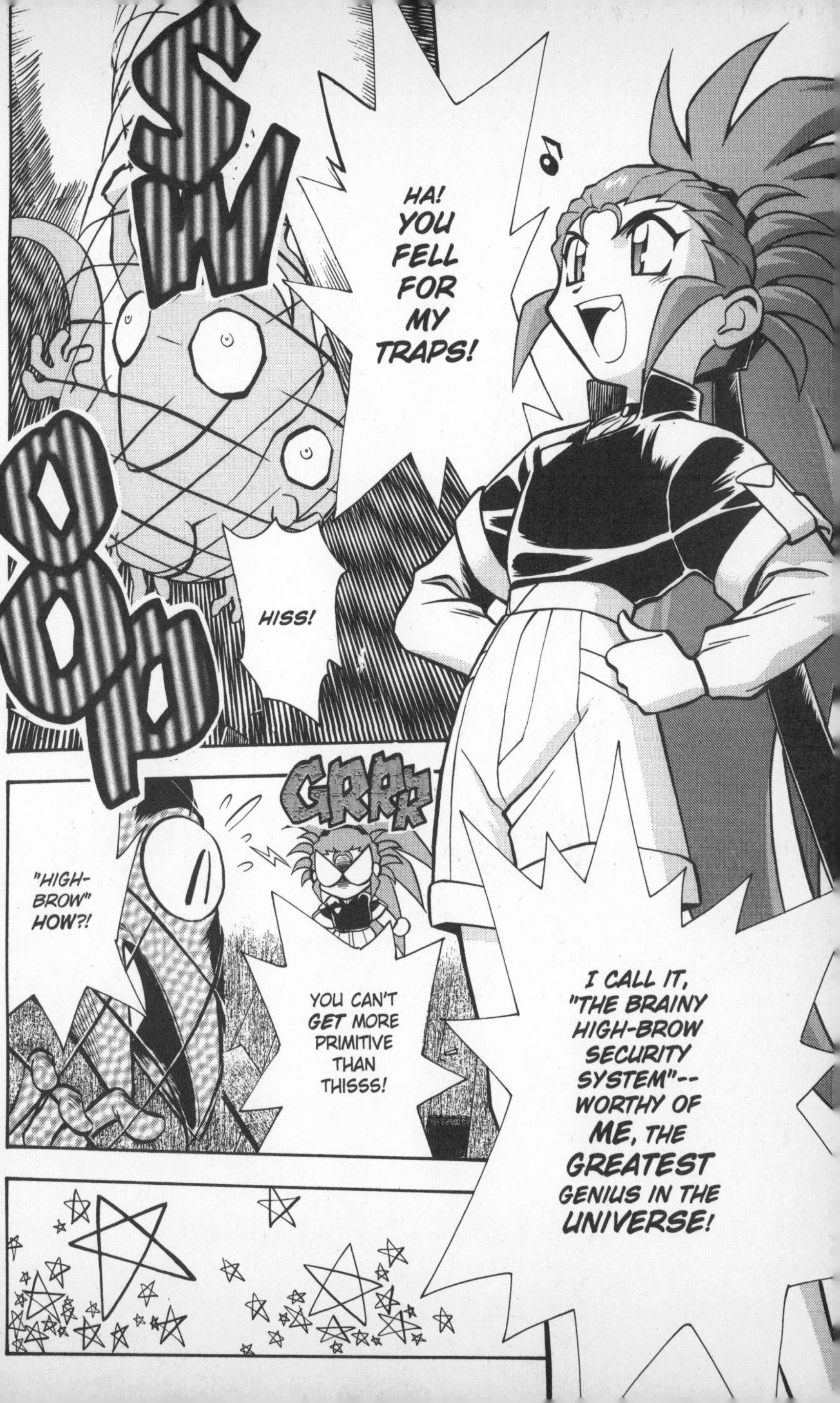
SWOOP
HA! YOU FELL FOR MY TRAPS!
HISS!
"HIGH-BROW" HOW?!
GRRR
YOU CAN'T GET MORE PRIMITIVE THAN THISSS!
I CALL IT, "THE BRAINY HIGH-BROW SECURITY SYSTEM"-- WORTHY OF ME, THE GREATEST GENIUS IN THE UNIVERSE!

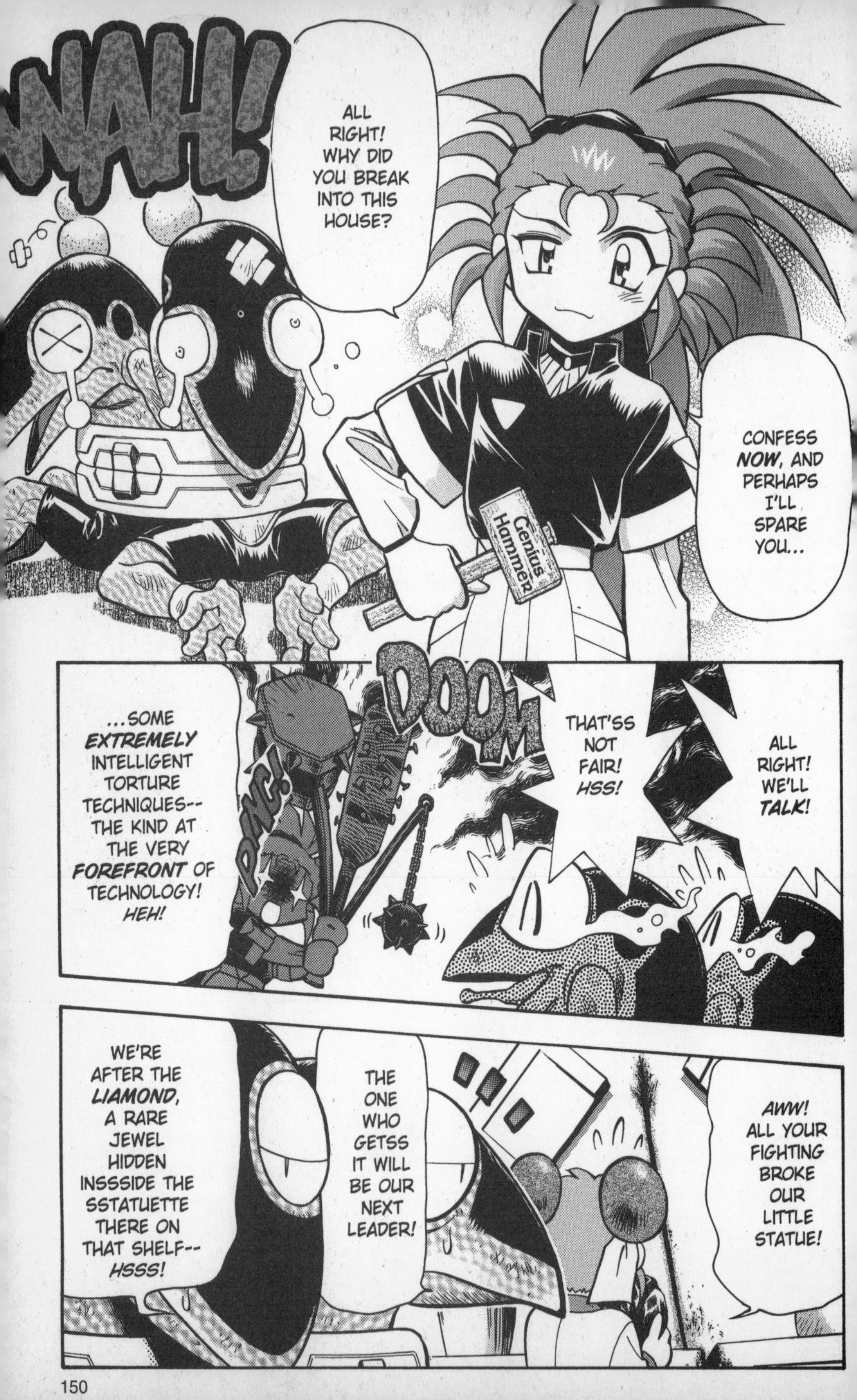
NAH!
ALL RIGHT! WHY DID YOU BREAK INTO THIS HOUSE?
Genius Hammer
CONFESS **NOW**, AND PERHAPS I'LL SPARE YOU...
...SOME **EXTREMELY** INTELLIGENT TORTURE TECHNIQUES-- THE KIND AT THE VERY **FOREFRONT** OF TECHNOLOGY! **HEH!**
DING!
DOOM
THAT'SS NOT FAIR! **HSS!**
ALL RIGHT! WE'LL **TALK!**
WE'RE AFTER THE **LIAMOND**, A RARE JEWEL HIDDEN INSSSIDE THE SSTATUETTE THERE ON THAT SHELF-- **HSSS!**
THE ONE WHO GETSS IT WILL BE OUR NEXT LEADER!
AWW! ALL YOUR FIGHTING BROKE OUR LITTLE STATUE!

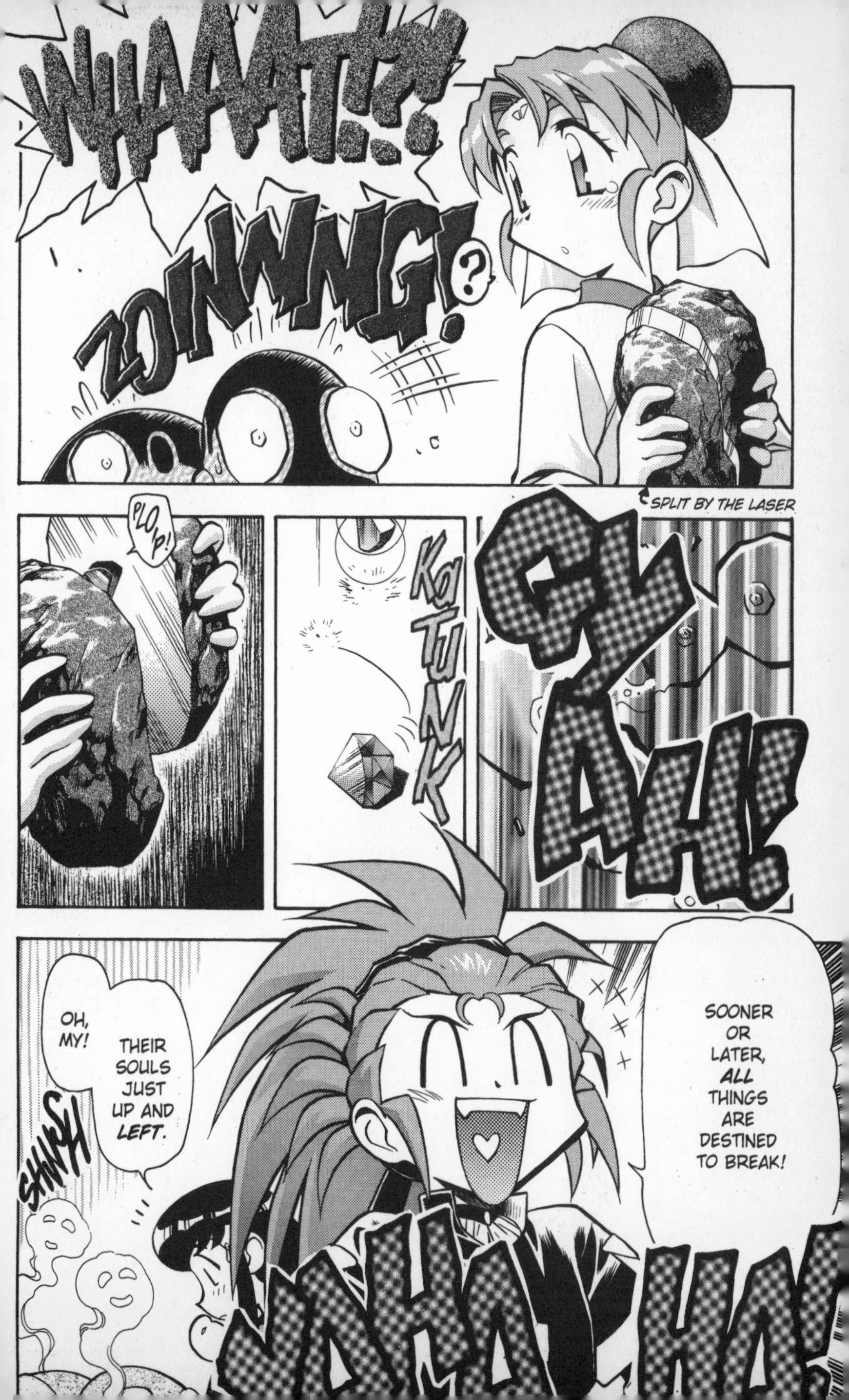
WHAAAT!!?
ZOINNNG!?
SPLIT BY THE LASER
PLOP!
KATUNK
GYAAH!
OH, MY!
THEIR SOULS JUST UP AND LEFT.
SHWSH
SOONER OR LATER, ALL THINGS ARE DESTINED TO BREAK!
WAHA HA!

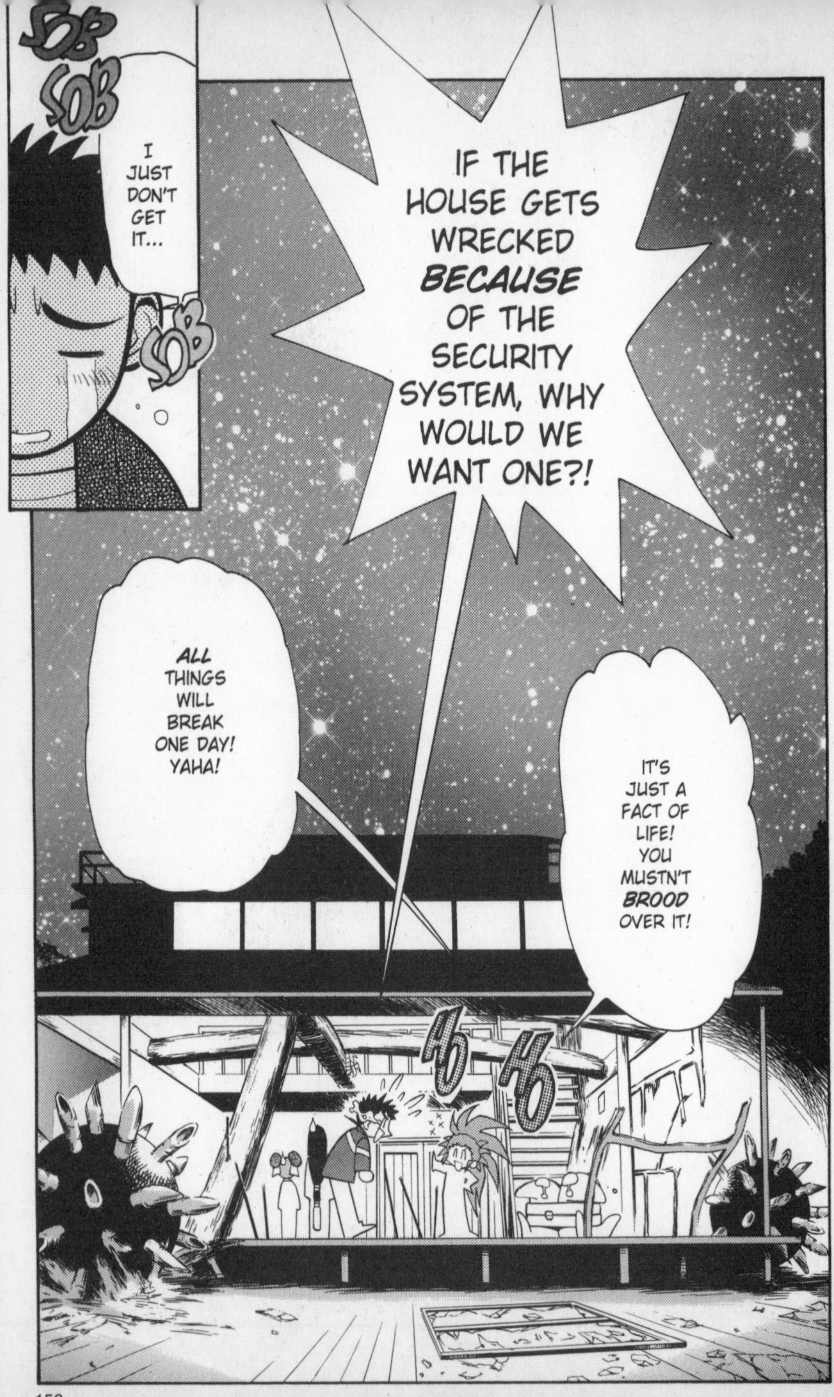
SOB SOB
I JUST DON'T GET IT...
SOB
IF THE HOUSE GETS WRECKED *BECAUSE* OF THE SECURITY SYSTEM, WHY WOULD WE WANT ONE?!
ALL THINGS WILL BREAK ONE DAY! YAHA!
IT'S JUST A FACT OF LIFE! YOU MUSTN'T *BROOD* OVER IT!
HA HA

Chapter 7:
STRENGTH

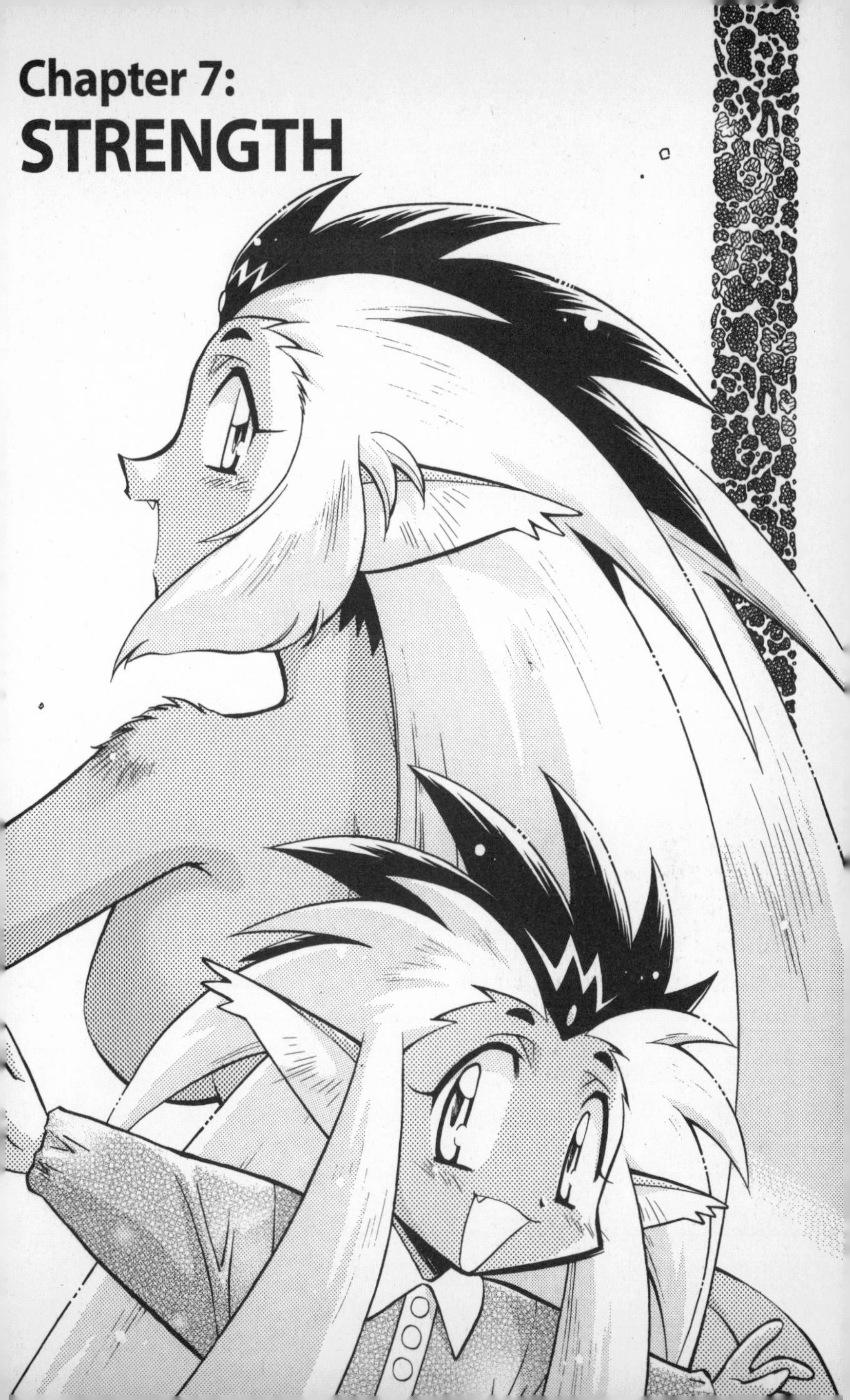

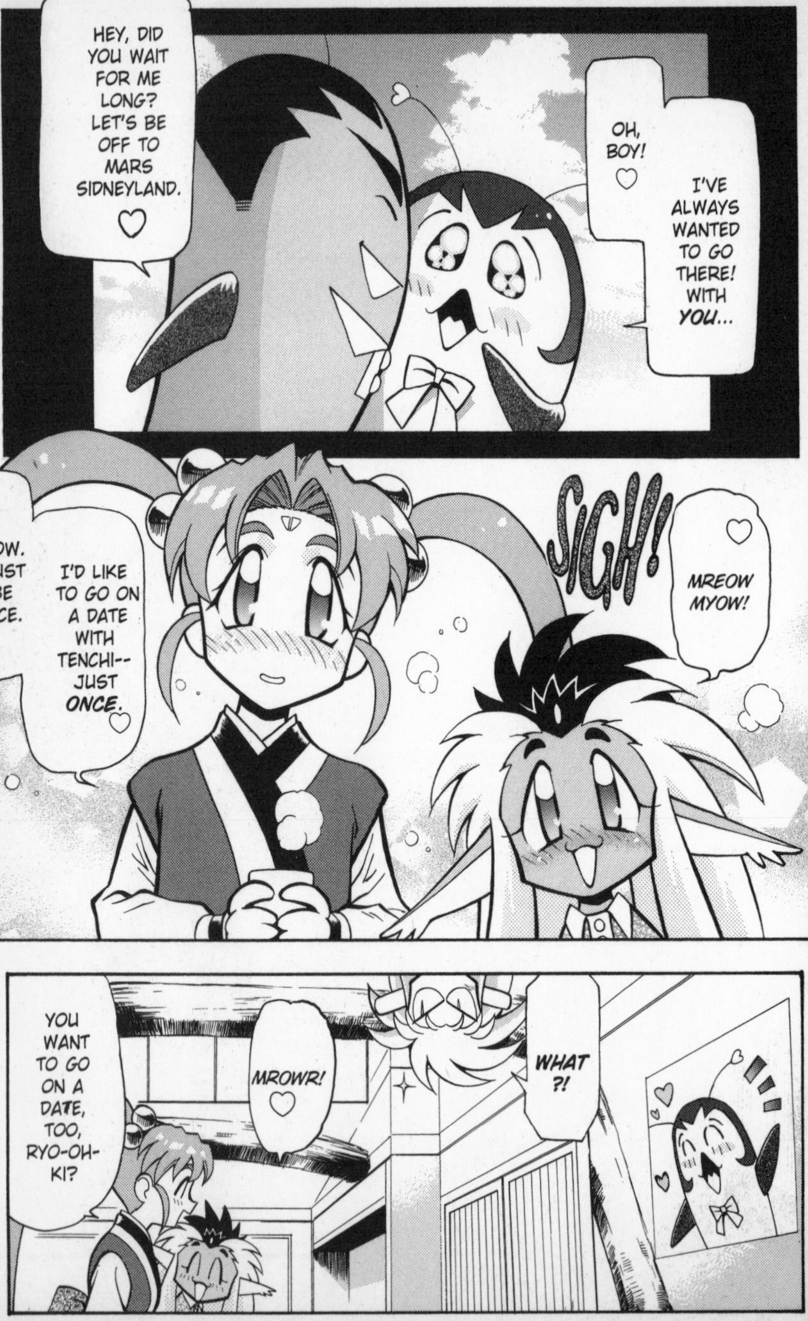
HEY, DID YOU WAIT FOR ME LONG? LET'S BE OFF TO MARS SIDNEYLAND. ♡
OH, BOY! ♡
I'VE ALWAYS WANTED TO GO THERE! WITH *YOU*...
WOW. MUST BE NICE.
I'D LIKE TO GO ON A DATE WITH TENCHI-- JUST **ONCE**. ♡
SIGH!
♡ MREOW MYOW!
YOU WANT TO GO ON A DATE, TOO, RYO-OH-KI?
MROWR! ♡
WHAT?!

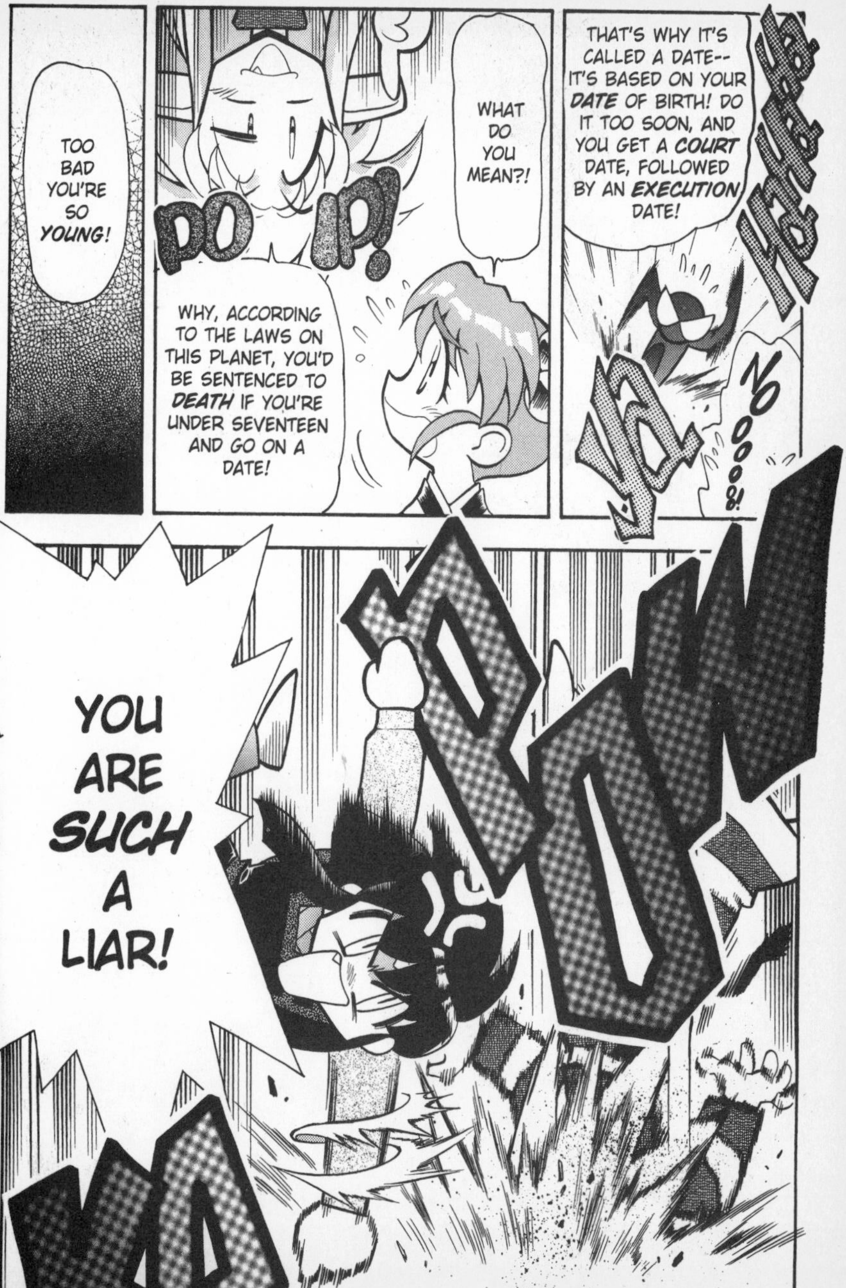
TOO BAD YOU'RE SO *YOUNG*!
WHAT DO YOU MEAN?!
DO IP!
WHY, ACCORDING TO THE LAWS ON THIS PLANET, YOU'D BE SENTENCED TO *DEATH* IF YOU'RE UNDER SEVENTEEN AND GO ON A DATE!
THAT'S WHY IT'S CALLED A DATE-- IT'S BASED ON YOUR *DATE* OF BIRTH! DO IT TOO SOON, AND YOU GET A *COURT* DATE, FOLLOWED BY AN *EXECUTION* DATE!
YOU ARE *SUCH* A LIAR!

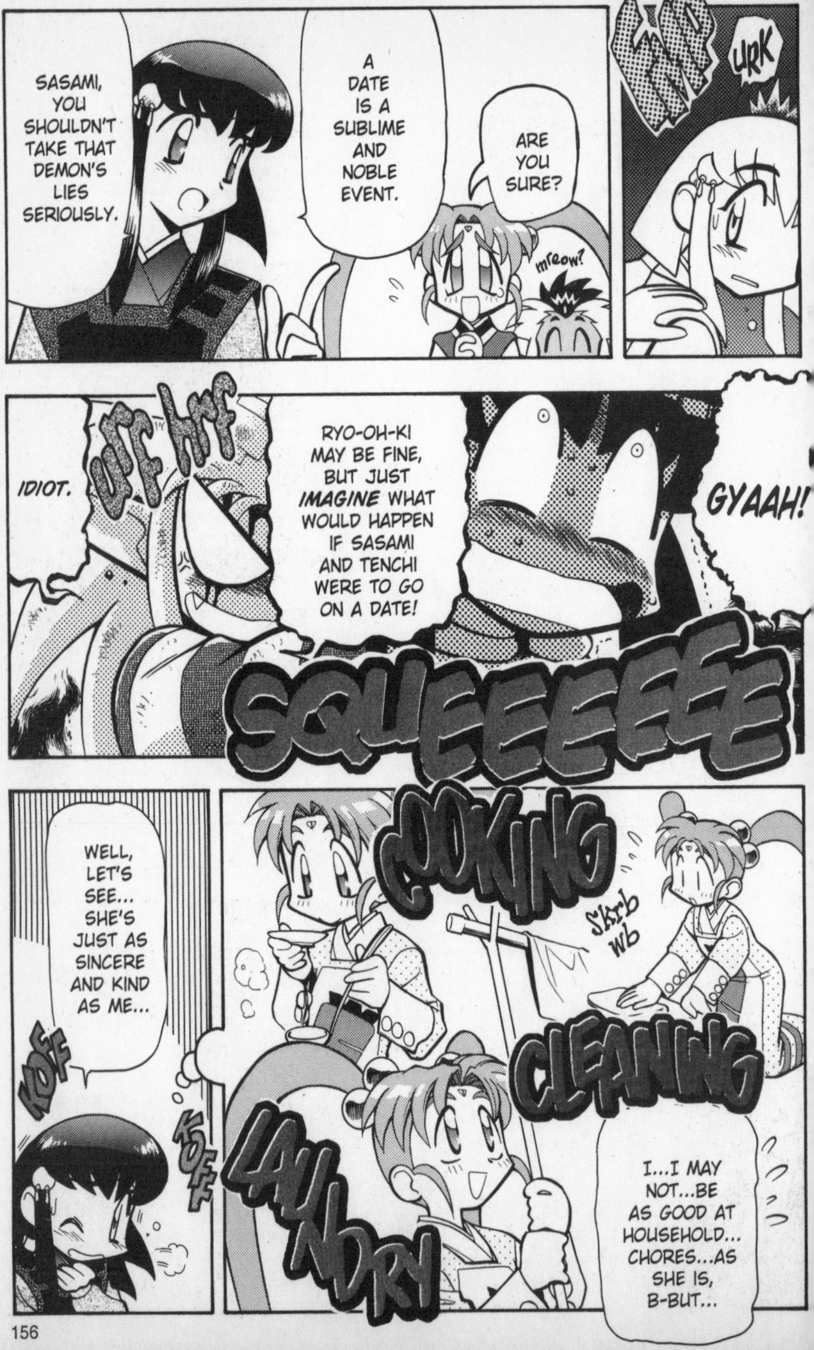
SASAMI, YOU SHOULDN'T TAKE THAT DEMON'S LIES SERIOUSLY.
A DATE IS A SUBLIME AND NOBLE EVENT.
ARE YOU SURE?
mreow?
URK
IDIOT.
urf hrf
RYO-OH-KI MAY BE FINE, BUT JUST *IMAGINE* WHAT WOULD HAPPEN IF SASAMI AND TENCHI WERE TO GO ON A DATE!
GYAAH!
SQUEEEEEE
WELL, LET'S SEE... SHE'S JUST AS SINCERE AND KIND AS ME...
KOFF
KOFF
COOKING
Skrb wb
CLEANING
LAUNDRY
I...I MAY NOT...BE AS GOOD AT HOUSEHOLD... CHORES...AS SHE IS, B-BUT...

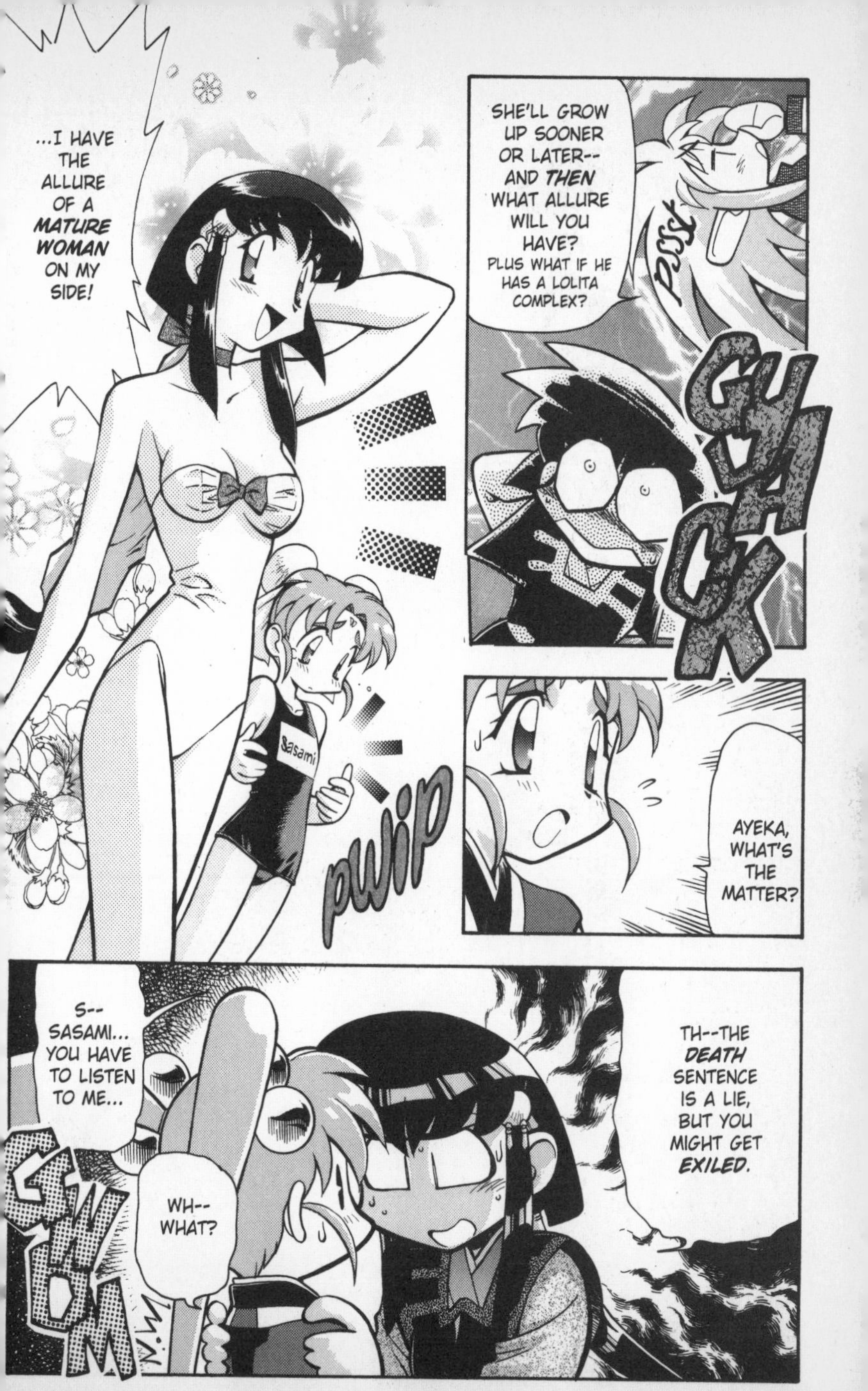
...I HAVE THE ALLURE OF A MATURE WOMAN ON MY SIDE!
Sasami
pwip
SHE'LL GROW UP SOONER OR LATER-- AND THEN WHAT ALLURE WILL YOU HAVE?
PLUS WHAT IF HE HAS A LOLITA COMPLEX?
PSSST
GUHACK
AYEKA, WHAT'S THE MATTER?
S-- SASAMI... YOU HAVE TO LISTEN TO ME...
GWHOM
WH-- WHAT?
TH--THE DEATH SENTENCE IS A LIE, BUT YOU MIGHT GET EXILED.

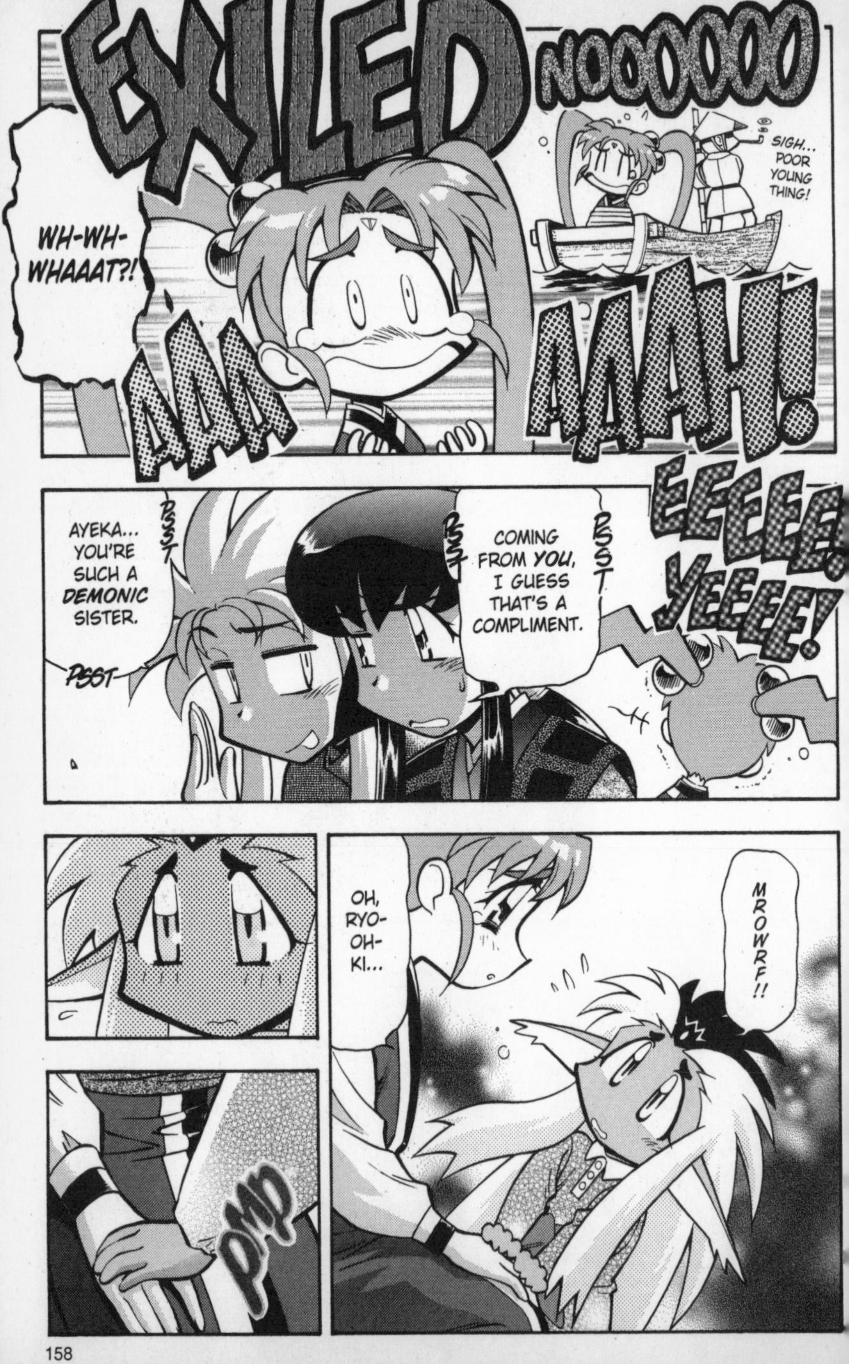
EXILED
NOOOOOO
WH-WH-WHAAAT?!
SIGH... POOR YOUNG THING!
AAAAAAAH!
EEEEE! YEEEE!
AYEKA... YOU'RE SUCH A DEMONIC SISTER.
PSST
PSST
PSST
COMING FROM YOU, I GUESS THAT'S A COMPLIMENT.
PSST
OH, RYO-OH-KI...
MROWRF!!
PMP

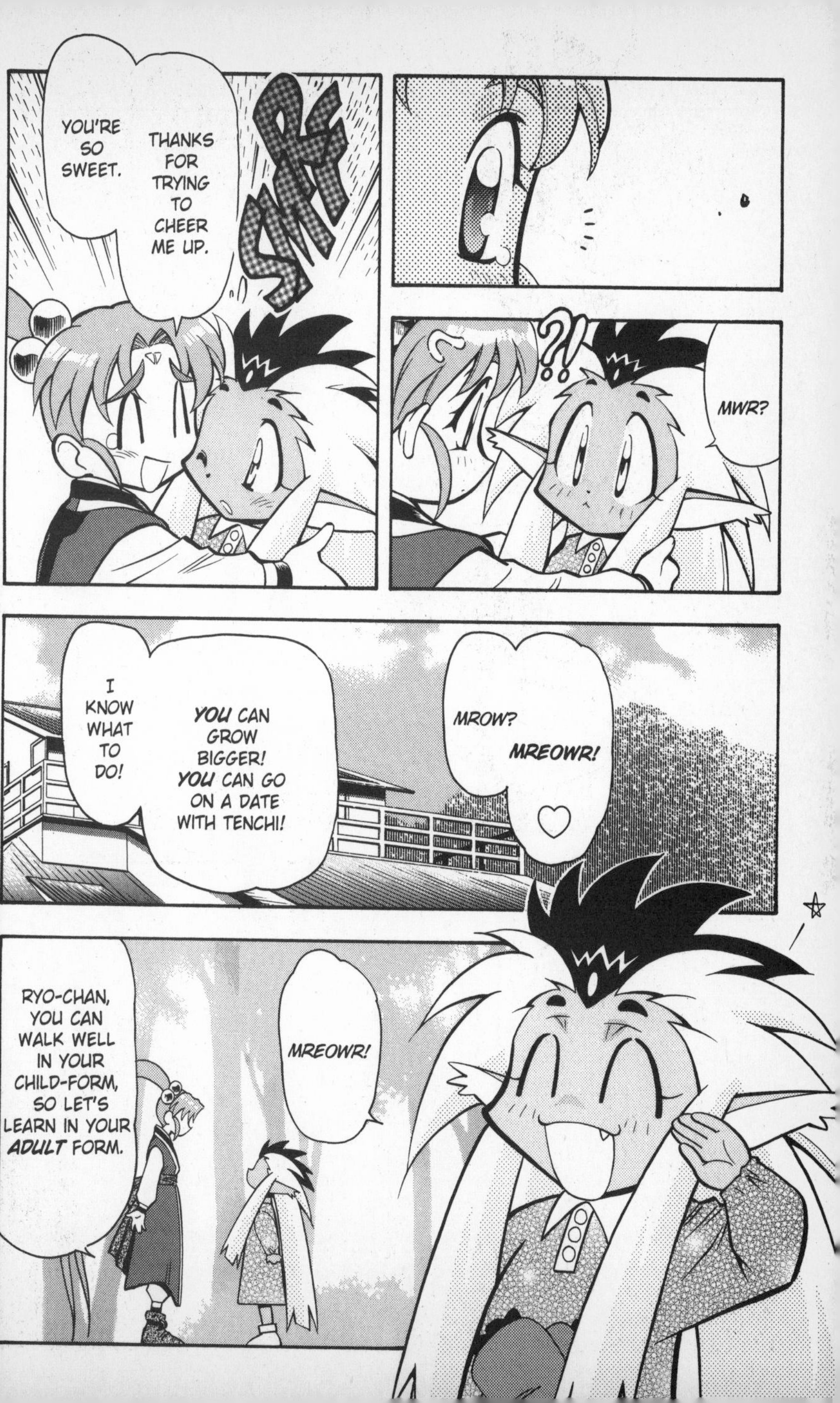

YOU'RE SO SWEET.
THANKS FOR TRYING TO CHEER ME UP.
SMAK
MWR?
I KNOW WHAT TO DO!
YOU CAN GROW BIGGER! YOU CAN GO ON A DATE WITH TENCHI!
MROW?
MREOWR!
RYO-CHAN, YOU CAN WALK WELL IN YOUR CHILD-FORM, SO LET'S LEARN IN YOUR ADULT FORM.
MREOWR!

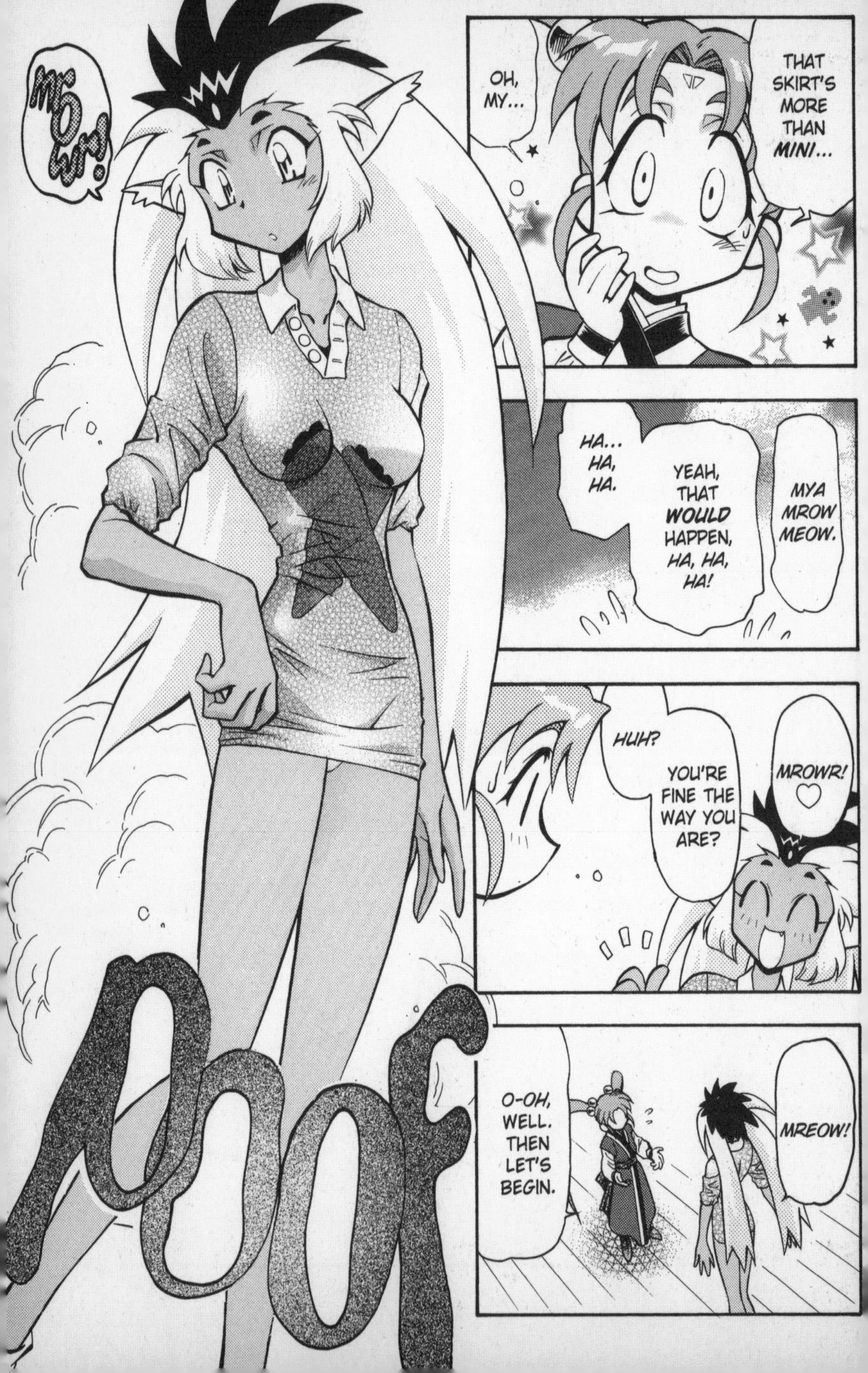
mrowr!
Poof
OH, MY...
THAT SKIRT'S MORE THAN *MINI*...
HA... HA, HA.
YEAH, THAT ***WOULD*** HAPPEN, *HA, HA, HA!*
MYA MROW MEOW.
HUH?
YOU'RE FINE THE WAY YOU ARE?
MROWR! ♡
O-OH, WELL. THEN LET'S BEGIN.
MREOW!

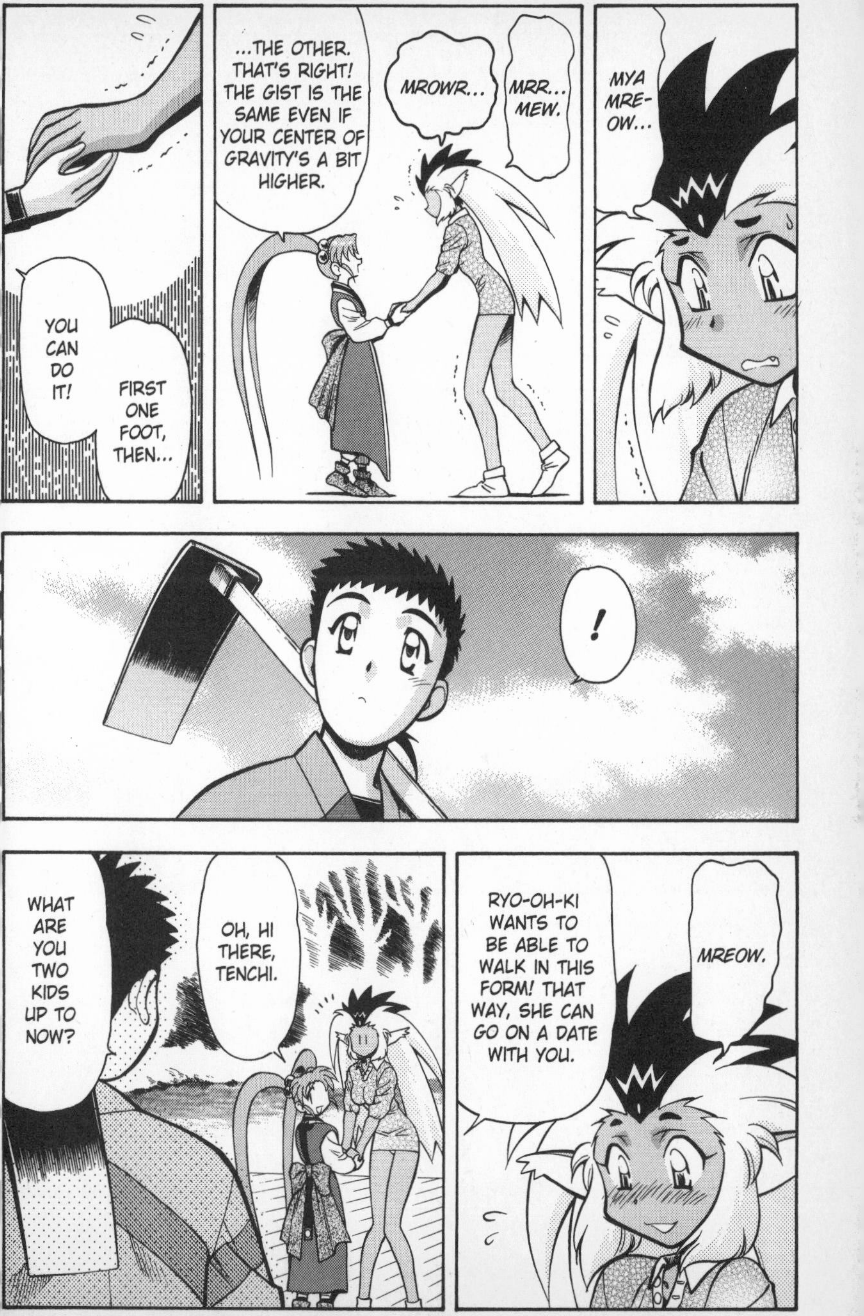
YOU CAN DO IT!
FIRST ONE FOOT, THEN...
...THE OTHER. THAT'S RIGHT! THE GIST IS THE SAME EVEN IF YOUR CENTER OF GRAVITY'S A BIT HIGHER.
MROWR...
MRR... MEW.
MYA MRE-OW...
!
WHAT ARE YOU TWO KIDS UP TO NOW?
OH, HI THERE, TENCHI.
RYO-OH-KI WANTS TO BE ABLE TO WALK IN THIS FORM! THAT WAY, SHE CAN GO ON A DATE WITH YOU.
MREOW.

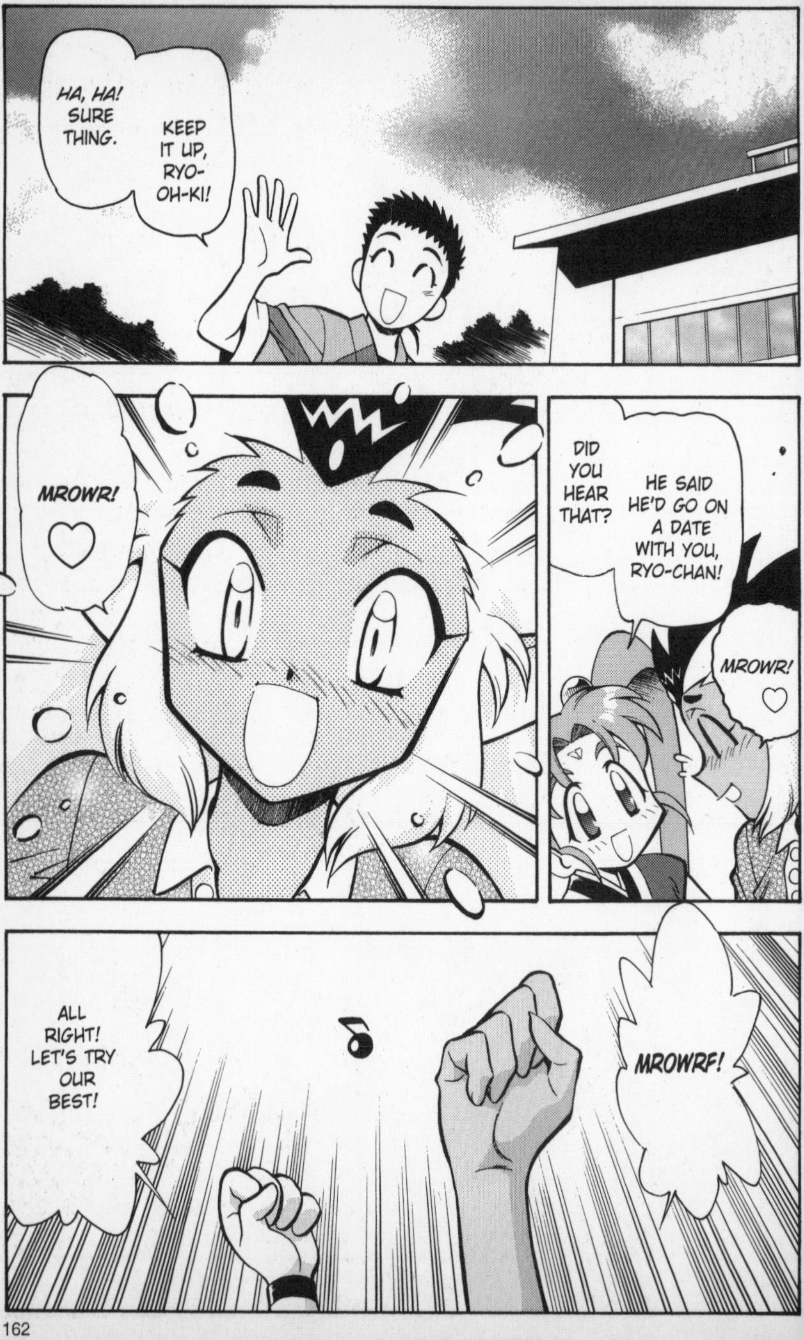
HA, HA! SURE THING.
KEEP IT UP, RYO-OH-KI!
MROWR! ♥
DID YOU HEAR THAT?
HE SAID HE'D GO ON A DATE WITH YOU, RYO-CHAN!
MROWR! ♥
ALL RIGHT! LET'S TRY OUR BEST!
MROWRF!

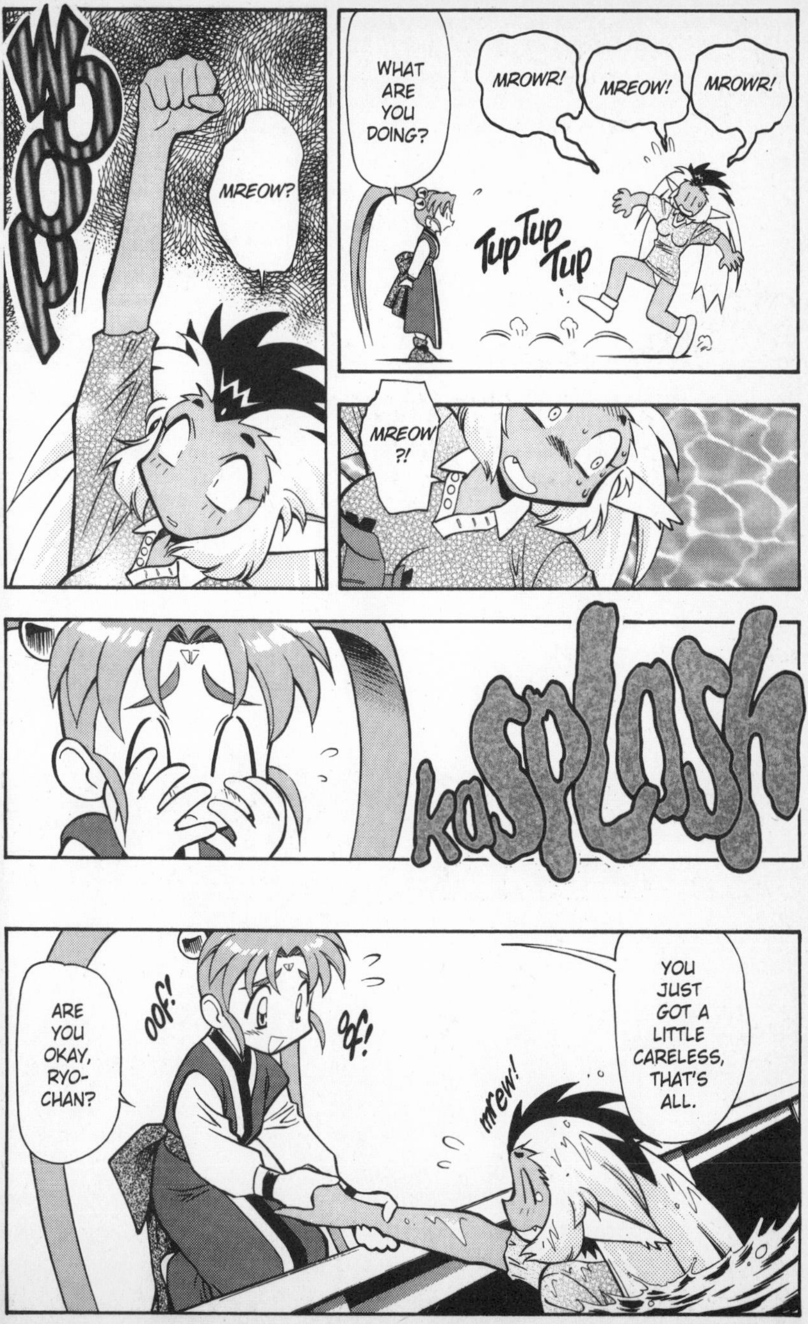
WOOP
MREOW?
WHAT ARE YOU DOING?
MROWR!
MREOW!
MROWR!
TUP TUP TUP
MREOW ?!
KASPLOSH
ARE YOU OKAY, RYO-CHAN?
OOF!
OOF!
MREW!
YOU JUST GOT A LITTLE CARELESS, THAT'S ALL.

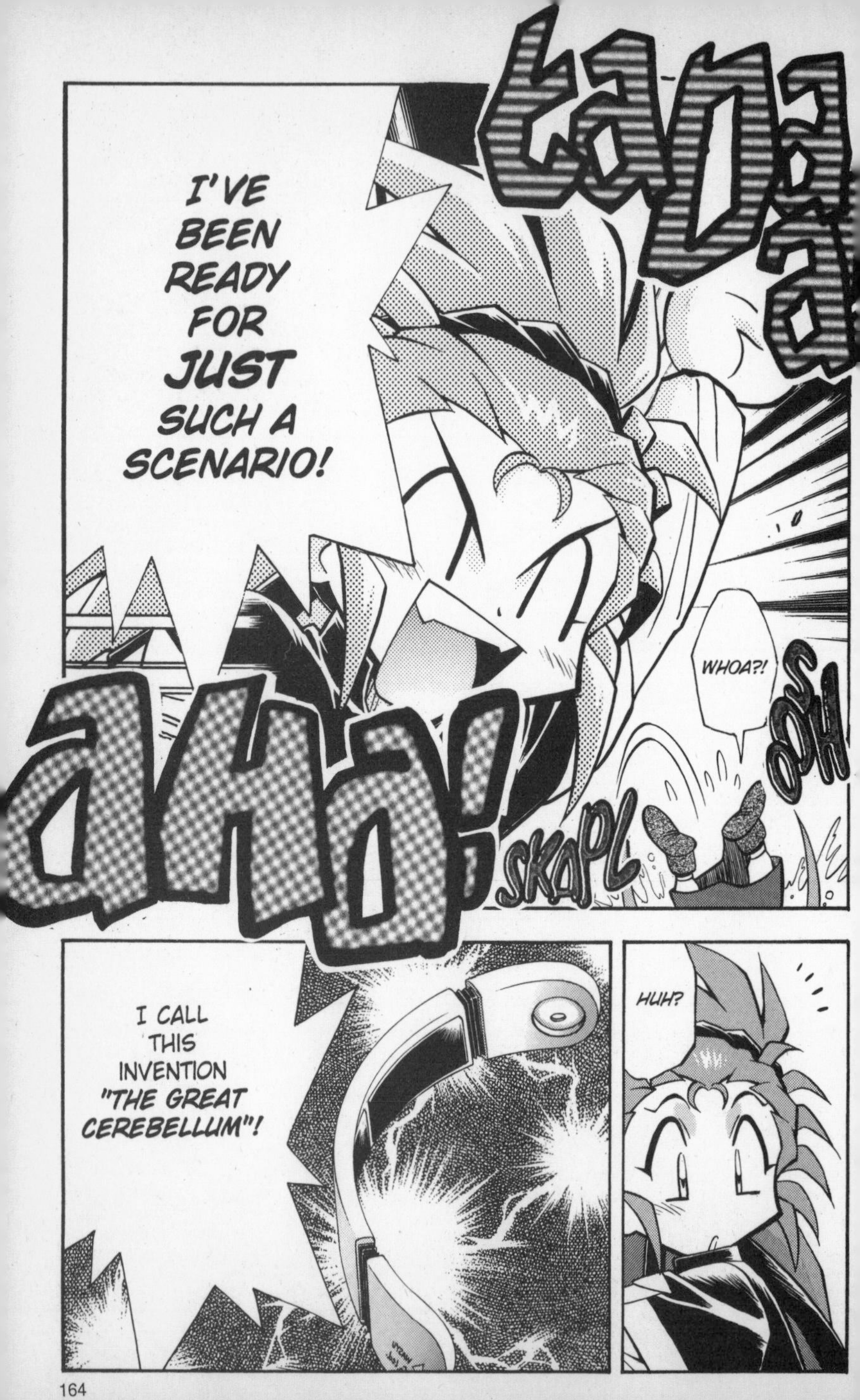
I'VE BEEN READY FOR JUST SUCH A SCENARIO!
aHa!
WHOA?!
SKAPL
I CALL THIS INVENTION "THE GREAT CEREBELLUM"!
HUH?

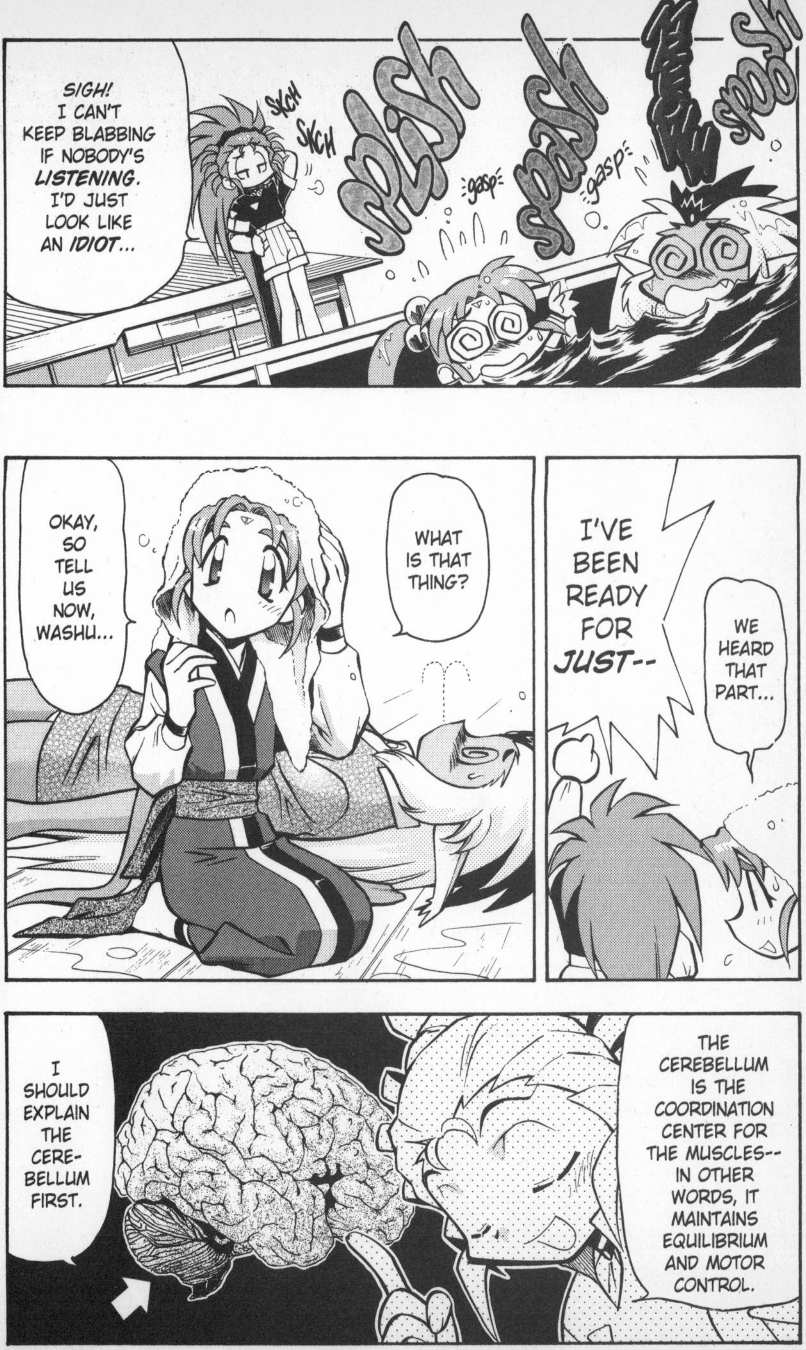
SIGH! I CAN'T KEEP BLABBING IF NOBODY'S LISTENING. I'D JUST LOOK LIKE AN IDIOT...
SKCH
SKCH
splish
gasp
spash
gasp
spoosh
OKAY, SO TELL US NOW, WASHU...
WHAT IS THAT THING?
I'VE BEEN READY FOR JUST--
WE HEARD THAT PART...
I SHOULD EXPLAIN THE CERE-BELLUM FIRST.
THE CEREBELLUM IS THE COORDINATION CENTER FOR THE MUSCLES-- IN OTHER WORDS, IT MAINTAINS EQUILIBRIUM AND MOTOR CONTROL.

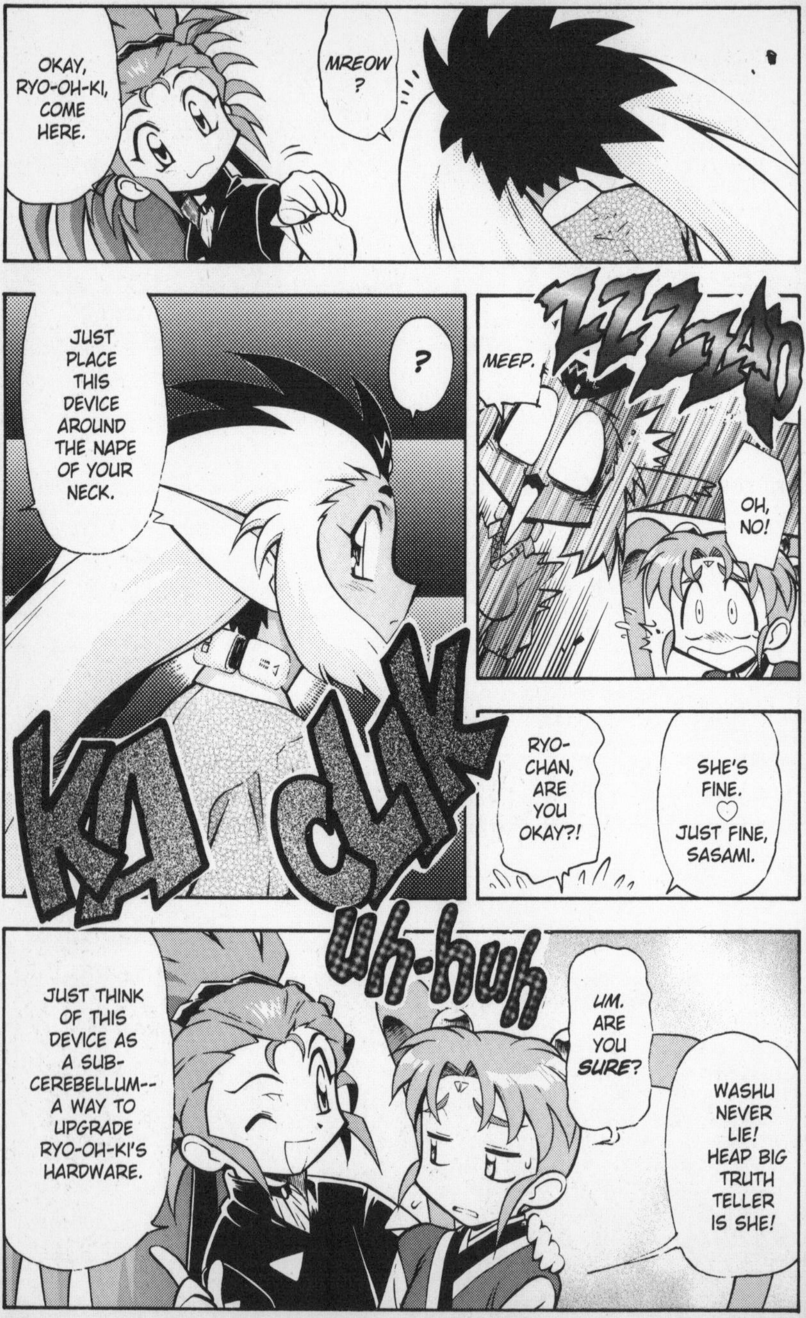
OKAY, RYO-OH-KI, COME HERE.
MREOW ?
JUST PLACE THIS DEVICE AROUND THE NAPE OF YOUR NECK.
?
KA CLIK
MEEP.
ZZZZAP
OH, NO!
RYO-CHAN, ARE YOU OKAY?!
SHE'S FINE. ♡ JUST FINE, SASAMI.
uh-huh
JUST THINK OF THIS DEVICE AS A SUB-CEREBELLUM-- A WAY TO UPGRADE RYO-OH-KI'S HARDWARE.
UM. ARE YOU SURE?
WASHU NEVER LIE! HEAP BIG TRUTH TELLER IS SHE!

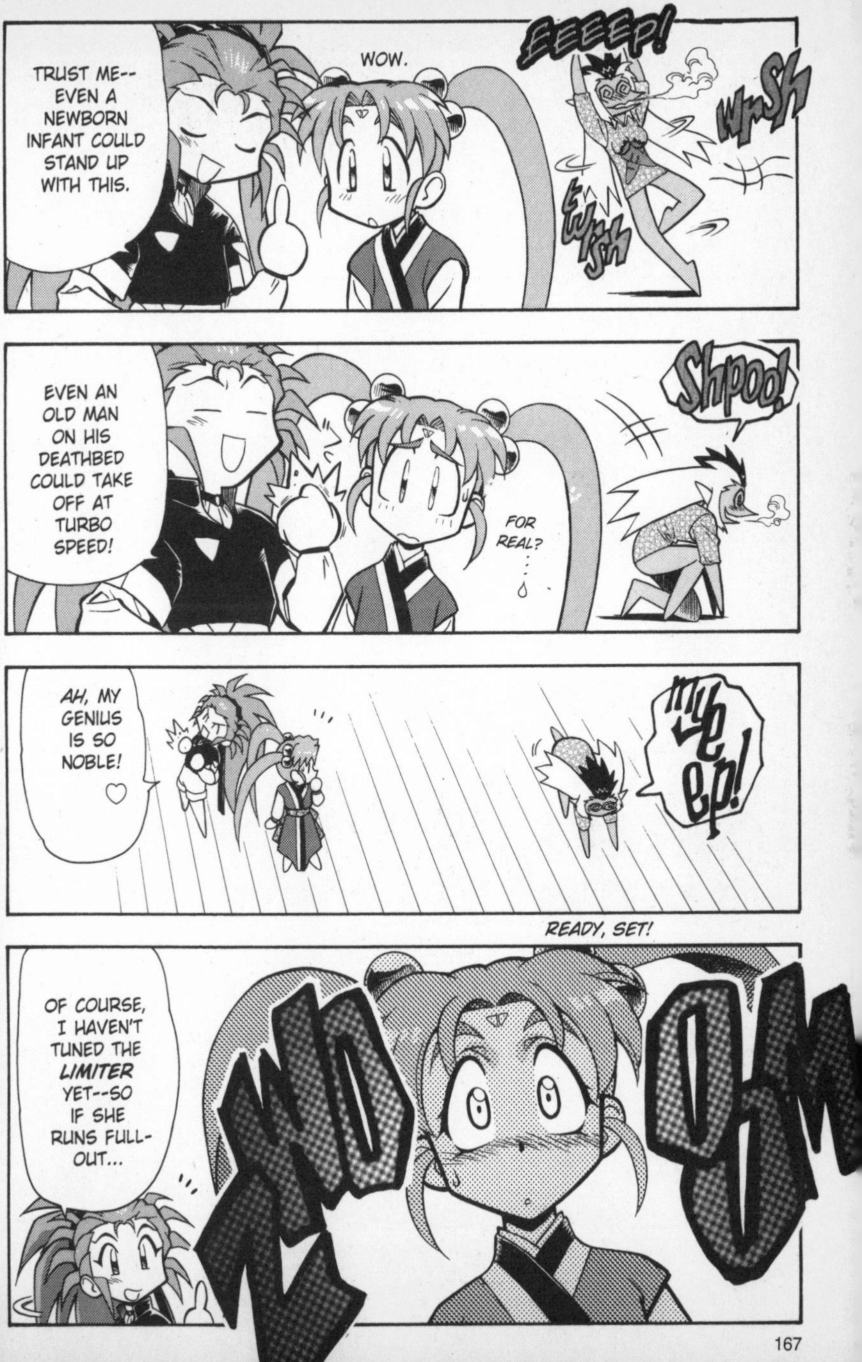

TRUST ME-- EVEN A NEWBORN INFANT COULD STAND UP WITH THIS.
WOW.
EEEEP!
WRSH
TWISH
EVEN AN OLD MAN ON HIS DEATHBED COULD TAKE OFF AT TURBO SPEED!
FOR REAL?
SHPOO!
AH, MY GENIUS IS SO NOBLE! ♡
MWEEP!
READY, SET!
OF COURSE, I HAVEN'T TUNED THE ***LIMITER*** YET--SO IF SHE RUNS FULL-OUT...
WHOOSH

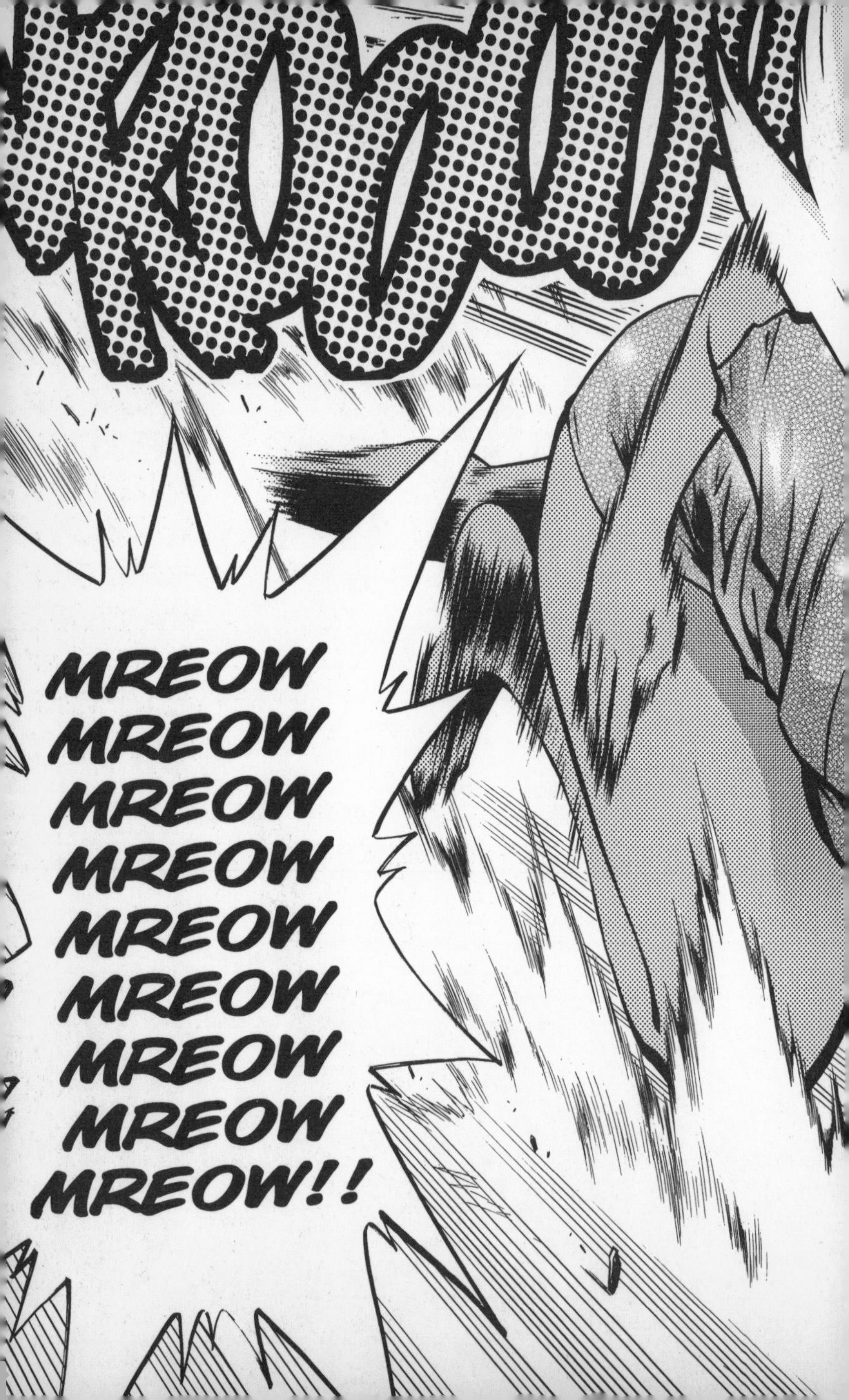
MREOW
MREOW
MREOW
MREOW
MREOW
MREOW
MREOW
MREOW
MREOW!!

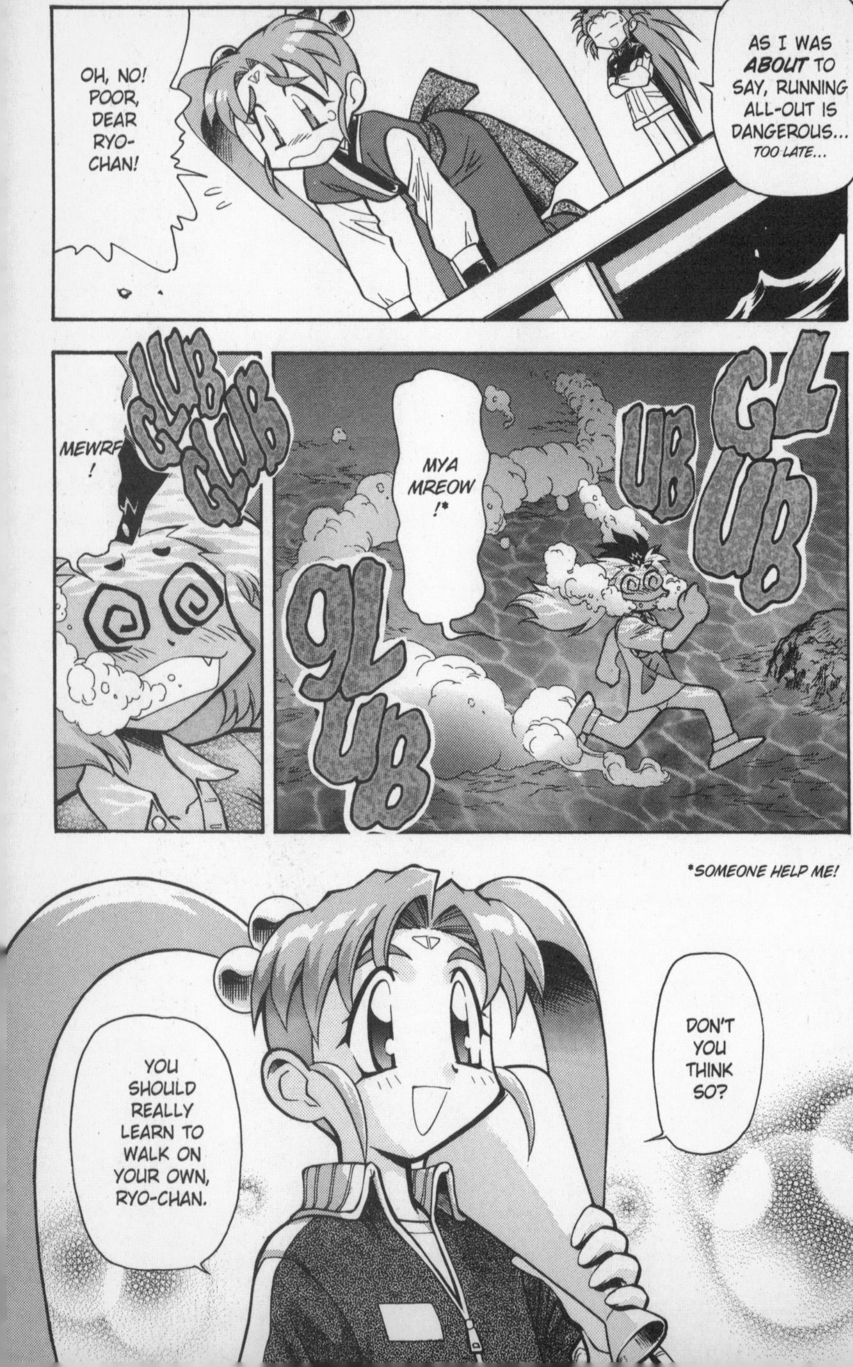
OH, NO! POOR, DEAR RYO-CHAN!
AS I WAS ABOUT TO SAY, RUNNING ALL-OUT IS DANGEROUS... TOO LATE...
MEWRF!
GLUB GLUB
GLUB
MYA MREOW!*
GLUB GLUB
*SOMEONE HELP ME!
YOU SHOULD REALLY LEARN TO WALK ON YOUR OWN, RYO-CHAN.
DON'T YOU THINK SO?

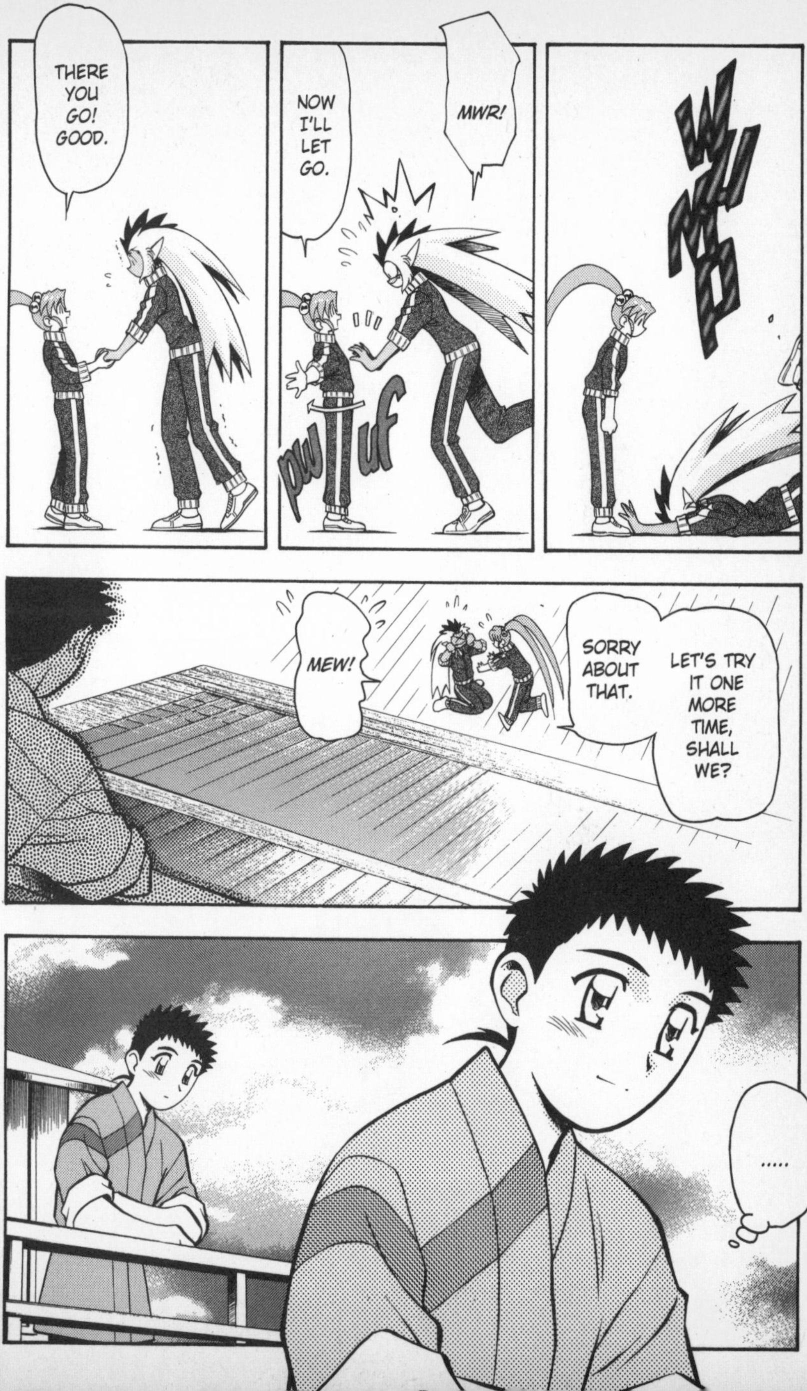
THERE YOU GO! GOOD.
NOW I'LL LET GO.
MWR!
pwuf
WHOOOSH
MEW!
SORRY ABOUT THAT.
LET'S TRY IT ONE MORE TIME, SHALL WE?
.....

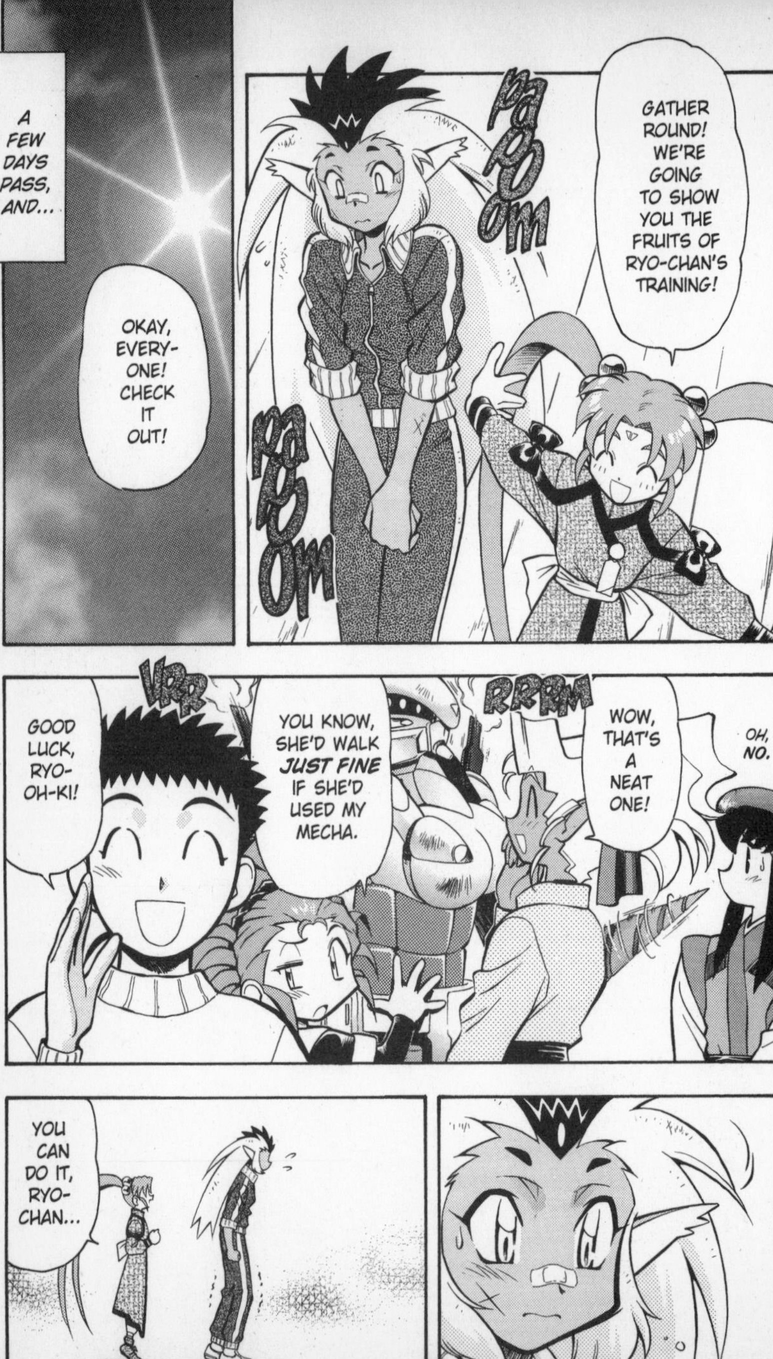
A FEW DAYS PASS, AND...
OKAY, EVERY-ONE! CHECK IT OUT!
PAPOOM
GATHER ROUND! WE'RE GOING TO SHOW YOU THE FRUITS OF RYO-CHAN'S TRAINING!
PAPOOM
GOOD LUCK, RYO-OH-KI!
VRR
YOU KNOW, SHE'D WALK JUST FINE IF SHE'D USED MY MECHA.
RRRM
WOW, THAT'S A NEAT ONE!
OH, NO.
YOU CAN DO IT, RYO-CHAN...

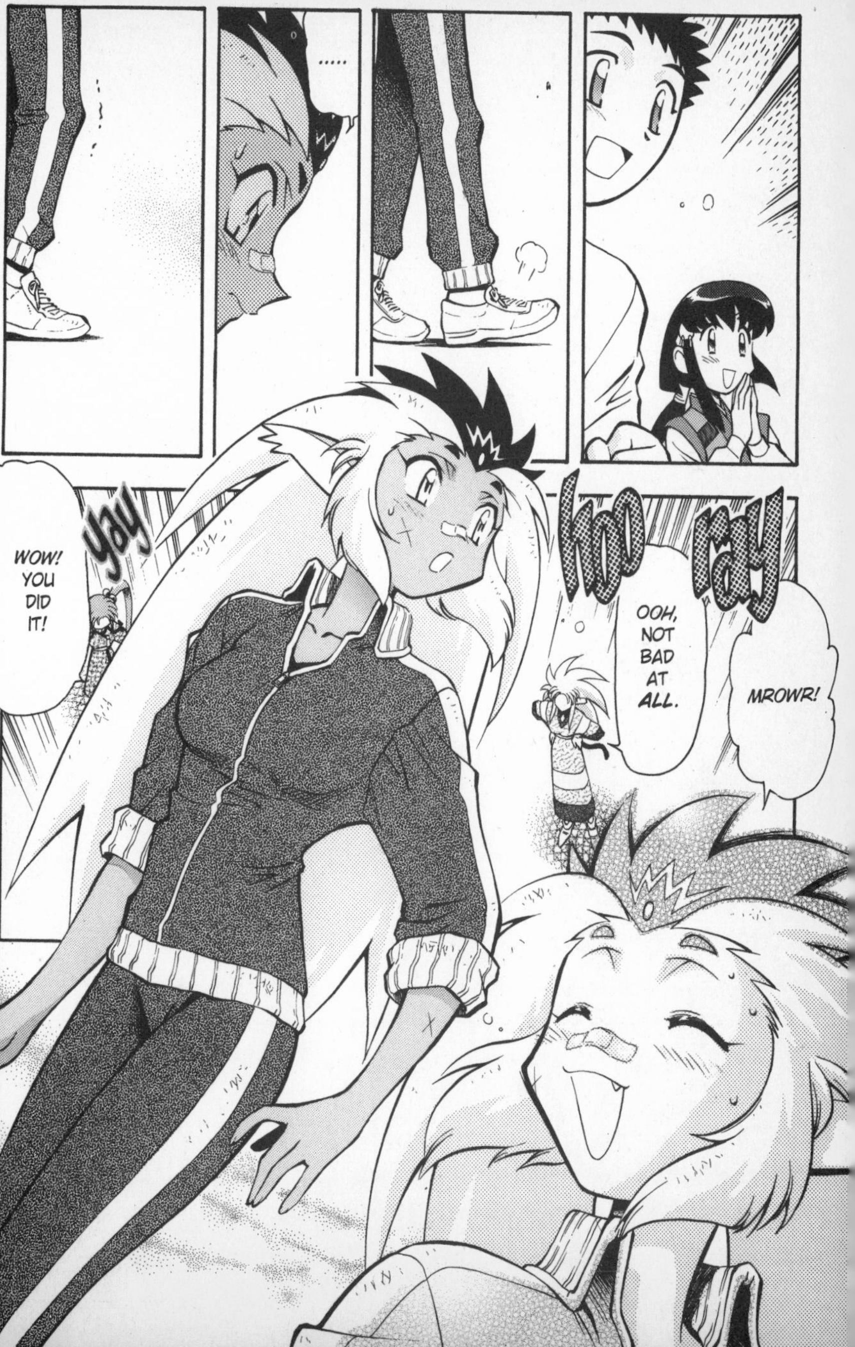
......
WOW! YOU DID IT!
yay
hoo ray
OOH, NOT BAD AT ALL.
MROWR!

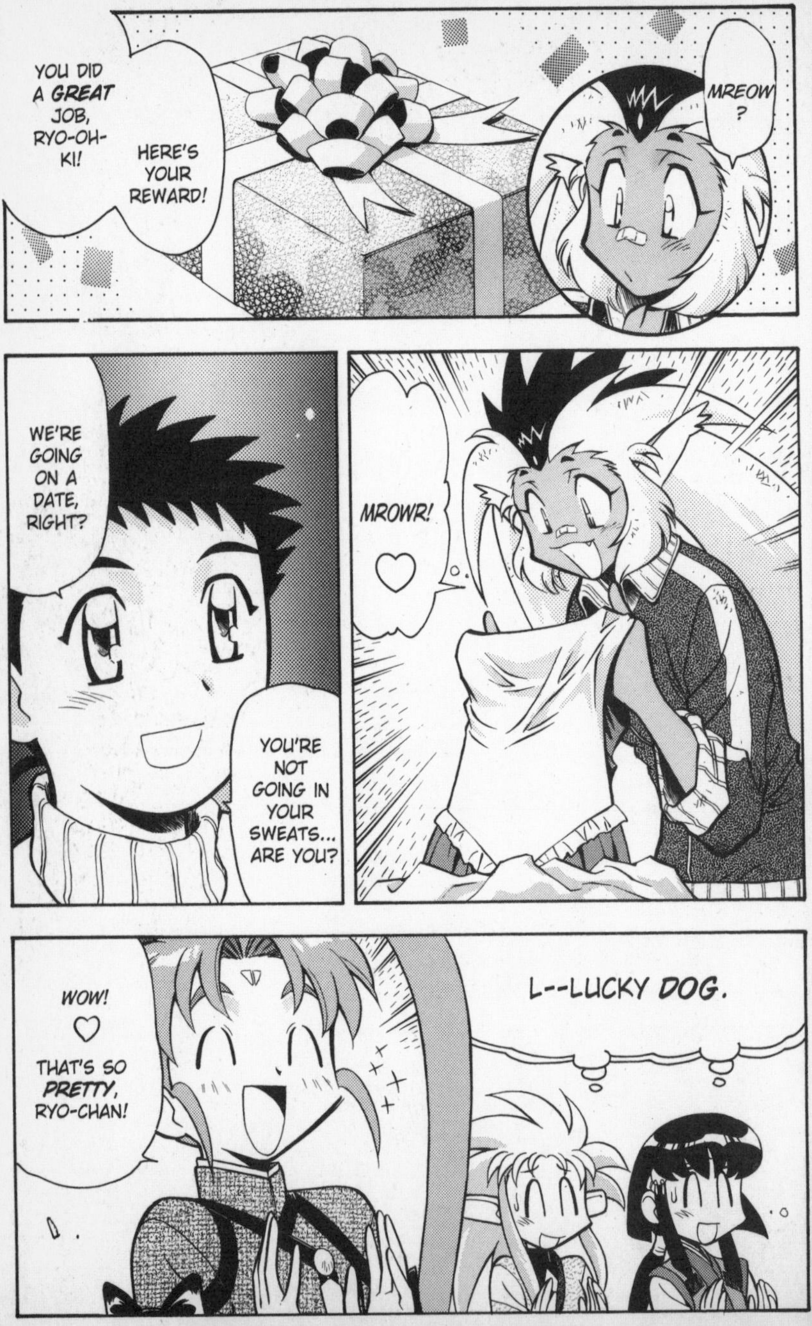
YOU DID A GREAT JOB, RYO-OH-KI!
HERE'S YOUR REWARD!
MREOW?
WE'RE GOING ON A DATE, RIGHT?
YOU'RE NOT GOING IN YOUR SWEATS... ARE YOU?
MROWR! ♡
WOW! ♡ THAT'S SO PRETTY, RYO-CHAN!
L--LUCKY DOG.

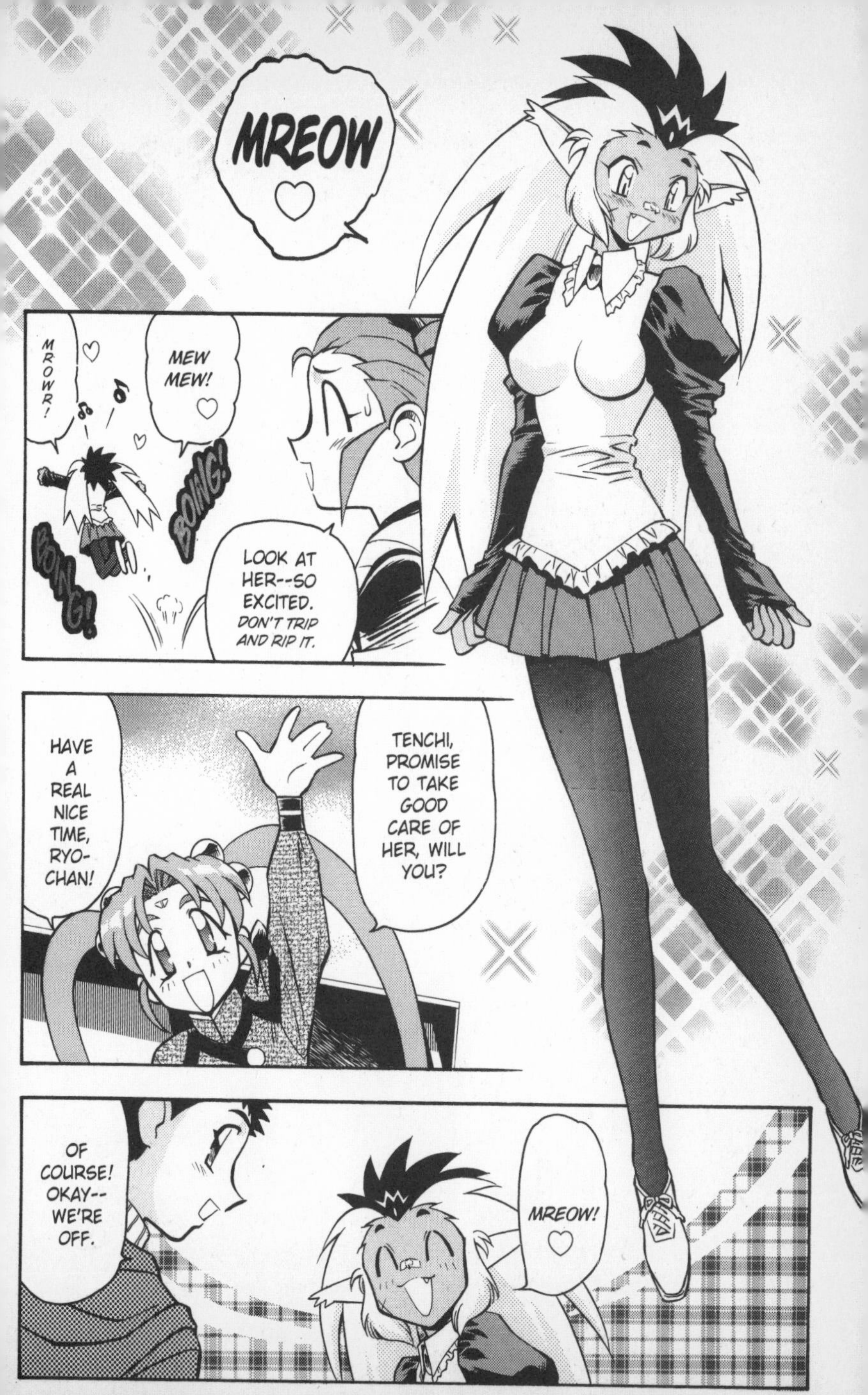
MREOW ♡
MROWR!
MEW MEW! ♡
BOING!
BOING!
LOOK AT HER--SO EXCITED. DON'T TRIP AND RIP IT.
HAVE A REAL NICE TIME, RYO-CHAN!
TENCHI, PROMISE TO TAKE GOOD CARE OF HER, WILL YOU?
OF COURSE! OKAY--WE'RE OFF.
MREOW! ♡

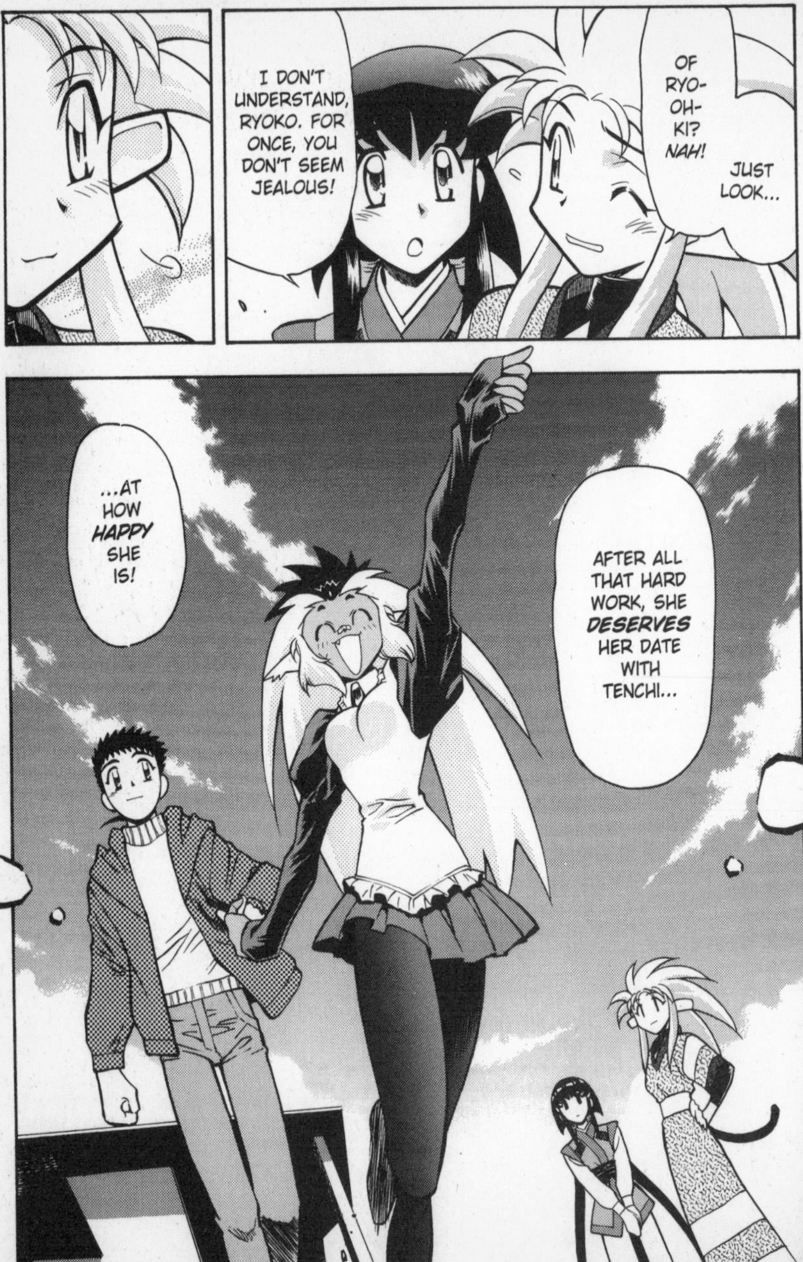
I DON'T UNDERSTAND, RYOKO. FOR ONCE, YOU DON'T SEEM JEALOUS!
OF RYO-OH-KI? NAH!
JUST LOOK...
...AT HOW HAPPY SHE IS!
AFTER ALL THAT HARD WORK, SHE DESERVES HER DATE WITH TENCHI...

THE END... FOR NOW!